The Turn

THE KLUWER INTERNATIONAL SERIES ON INFORMATION RETRIEVAL

Series Editor:
W. Bruce Croft
University of Massachusetts, Amherst

Also in the Series:

INFORMATION RETRIEVAL SYSTEMS: *Theory and Implementation,* by Gerald Kowalski;
ISBN: 0-7923-9926-9

CROSS-LANGUAGE INFORMATION RETRIEVAL, edited by Gregory Grefenstette;
ISBN: 0-7923-8122-X

TEXT RETRIEVAL AND FILTERING: *Analytic Models of Performance,* by Robert M. Losee;
ISBN: 0-7923-8177-7

INFORMATION RETRIEVAL: UNCERTAINTY AND LOGICS: *Advanced Models for the Representation and Retrieval of Information,* by Fabio Crestani, Mounia Lalmas, and Cornelis Joost van Rijsbergen; ISBN: 0-7923-8302-8

DOCUMENT COMPUTING: *Technologies for Managing Electronic Document Collections,*
by Ross Wilkinson, Timothy Arnold-Moore, Michael Fuller, Ron Sacks-Davis, James Thom, and Justin Zobel; ISBN: 0-7923-8357-5

AUTOMATIC INDEXING AND ABSTRACTING OF DOCUMENT TEXTS, by Marie-Francine Moens;
ISBN 0-7923-7793-1

ADVANCES IN INFORMATIONAL RETRIEVAL: *Recent Research from the Center for Intelligent Information Retrieval,* by W. Bruce Croft; ISBN 0-7923-7812-1

INFORMATION RETRIEVAL SYSTEMS: *Theory and Implementation,* **Second Edition,**
by Gerald J. Kowalski and Mark T. Maybury; ISBN: 0-7923-7924-1

PERSPECTIVES ON CONTENT-BASED MULTIMEDIA SYSTEMS, by Jian Kang Wu;
Mohan S. Kankanhalli;Joo-Hwee Lim;Dezhong Hong; ISBN: 0-7923-7944-6

MINING THE WORLD WIDE WEB: *An Information Search Approach,* by George Chang, Marcus J. Healey, James A. M. McHugh, Jason T. L. Wang; ISBN: 0-7923-7349-9

INTEGRATED REGION-BASED IMAGE RETRIEVAL, by James Z. Wang;
ISBN: 0-7923-7350-2

TOPIC DETECTION AND TRACKING: **Event-based Information Organization,** edited by James Allan;
ISBN: 0-7923-7664-1

LANGUAGE MODELING FOR INFORMATION RETRIEVAL, edited by W. Bruce Croft; John Lafferty;
ISBN: 1-4020-1216-0

MACHINE LEARNING AND STATISTICAL MODELING APPROACHES TO IMAGE RETRIEVAL,
by Yixin Chen, Jia Li and James Z. Wang; ISBN: 1-4020-8034-4

INFORMATION RETRIEVAL, *Algorithms and Heuristics,* by David A. Grossman and Ophir Frieder,
2nd ed.; ISBN: 1-4020-3003-7; PB: ISBN: 1-4020-3004-5

CHARTING A NEW COURSE, *Natural Language Proceesing and Information Retrieval,* edited by J. Tait;
ISBN: 1-4020-3343-5

INTELLIGENT DOCUMENT RETRIEVAL, *Exploiting Markup Structure,* by U. Kruschwitz;
ISBN: 1-4020-3767-8

The Turn

Integration of Information Seeking and Retrieval in Context

by

Peter Ingwersen

*Royal School of Library and Information Science,
Copenhagen, Denmark*

and

Kalervo Järvelin

University of Tampere, Finland

 Springer

A C.I.P. Catalogue record for this book is available from the Library of Congress.

ISBN-10 1-4020-3850-X (HB)
ISBN-13 978-1-4020-3850-1 (HB)
ISBN-10 1-4020-3851-8 (e-book)
ISBN-13 978-1-4020-3851-8 (e-book)

Published by Springer,
P.O. Box 17, 3300 AA Dordrecht, The Netherlands.

www.springeronline.com

Printed on acid-free paper

Printed in the Netherlands.

Acknowledgements

We wish to express our gratitude towards our colleagues and students for their encouragements as well as criticism, which we have been pleased to receive during the last five years. This was advantageous in developing our ideas, concepts, models and frameworks presented below.

We wish to acknowledge the support provided by the Nordic Research Academy (NORFA) 1999-2002, during which period Peter Ingwersen was visiting professor at Tampere University, and NORSLIS, the Nordic Research School in Library and Information Science, 2004-05. We also show our gratitude towards our Departments of Information Studies at the University of Tampere and the Royal School of Library and Information Science in Copenhagen for travel support as well as to our international friends, Marco Palmaci in particular, for backing us and making life more fun during the process.

In particular, we wish to thank Pia Borlund and Birger Larsen, Denmark, Jaana Kekäläinen and Pertti Vakkari from Finland, for their continuous and constructive discussions on central matters of concern regarding this book.

We are in particular in depths to our families for their continuing patience and encouragement.

Copenhagen and Tampere, May 2005

Peter Ingwersen & Kalervo Järvelin

Preface

There are many words we would have liked to write into the book title in order to describe the nature of this book. However, all the words did not fit in the title the reader already saw. We therefore chose *The Turn* as the main title to communicate the idea that it is time to look back and to look forward to develop a new integrated view of information seeking and retrieval: the field should turn off its separate narrow paths of research and construct a new avenue. Some of the elements for this avenue are given in the subtitle *Integration of Information Seeking and Retrieval in Context.* These words are intended to persuade a potential reader into the avenue project, preferably through the book. Some of many words that did not all fit into the subtitle are: the cognitive viewpoint; interaction between humans and machines; tasks, contexts and situations; knowledge acquisition, information seeking and use; models, frameworks and theories; research methodology. These are mentioned here because we see them as the foundation of the highway.

The present book takes off from the perspectives, ideas and findings presented in the monograph published thirteen years ago (Ingwersen, 1992). It reflects a further development of the cognitive viewpoint for information seeking and retrieval by providing a contextual holistic perspective. The quite individualistic perspective laid down in the former monograph is hence expanded into a social stance towards information behavior, including generation, searching and use of information. This stance is reflected in the proposed research framework and, in particular, associated with the further development of the conceptions of work and search tasks, information and information acquisition, IR interaction and the polyrepresentation principle. The monograph (1992, p. 123-201) saw IR interaction, the individual searcher's cognitive structures and the interface functionalities as important phenomena for study. The present book ascertains interaction as *the* central research issue in IS&R. The Mediator model with its thirteen basic interface functionalities (1992, p. 203) now represents but one of nine dimensions of our research framework. The monograph predicted a 'cognitive turn' for IR and a contextual IR theory development to take place in the time to come. The present book is/mirrors this turn and novel theoretical perspectives.

It is now the reader's privilege to assess whether or not the highway, as outlined through these words, looks promising enough for continuing beyond this point. Continuing means construction.

Peter Ingwersen and Kalervo Järvelin

Table of Contents

1 Introduction

The Laboratory Model of Information Retrieval (IR) evaluation has its origins in the Cranfield II project (Cleverdon 1967). It is the paradigm of the Computer Science oriented IR research, seeking to develop ever better IR algorithms and systems. In recent years, the TREC conferences (Voorhees and Harman 2000) have been the major forum for research based on the Laboratory Model – Fig. 1.1. An essential component in evaluation based on the Model is a test collection consisting of a document database, a set of fairly well defined topical requests, and a set of (typically binary) relevance assessments identifying the documents that are topically relevant to each request. IR algorithms are evaluated for their ability of finding the relevant documents. The test results are typically expressed in terms of average recall and precision, and recall-precision curves for each algorithm.

The Laboratory Model has recently been challenged by progress in research related to *relevance* and *information seeking* as well as by the growing need for accounting for interaction or human involvement in evaluation. Recent work in analyzing the concept of relevance has resulted in identifying higher order relevances, such as cognitive relevance and situational relevance, in addition to algorithmic and topical relevance (Borlund 2000b; Cosijn and Ingwersen 2000; Saracevic 1996; Schamber et al. 1990). Real human users of IR systems introduce non-binary, subjective and dynamic relevance judgments into IR processes, which affect the processes directly.

Recent theoretical and empirical work in Information Seeking and Retrieval (IS&R for short; Belkin 1993; Byström and Järvelin 1995; Ellis and Haugan 1997; Ingwersen 1996; Kuhlthau 1993a; Schamber 1994; Vakkari 2001a; Wilson 1999) suggests that IR is but one means of information seeking which takes place in a context determined by, e.g., a person's task, its phase, and situation. For larger tasks one may identify multiple stages, strategies, tactics or modes of information access, and dynamic relevance. IR strategies, tactics and relevance assessments are affected by the stages of task performance. Also some user-oriented research in IR, e.g., by Bates (1989; 1990), points out the variety of strategies people might use in information access, topical retrieval being only one.

Because of these empirical findings and theoretical arguments, the traditional Laboratory Model of IR evaluation has been challenged for its (lack of) realism. There are proposals (Borlund 2000a) concerning how IR evaluation should be done validly under these circumstances – realistically and at the same time retaining as much control as possible. There also is empirical work (e.g., Vakkari 2001a) tracing interactive information seeking and IR processes and providing models and methods for the analysis of IS&R. Developers of IR algorithms should therefore consider how the algorithms are to be evaluated – in which frameworks and how guaranteeing validity.

This book reviews the literature in IS&R, discusses the developments of the respective research areas and proposes an extended *cognitive viewpoint* to integrate the results and further work in these areas. We believe that research in IS&R needs new models to formulate its research programs and methodology. Our proposal is based on understanding the situational nature of information and on assuming persons' work tasks or cultural interests, and information needs based on them, as the basis for IS&R.

We begin this chapter by introducing the Laboratory Model of IR evaluation, its criticism and defense as a starting point for exploring broader approaches to research within IS&R (Sects. 1.2 - 1.4). We then follow by discussing some basic principles for designing models for the IS&R research area. Finally, we close the chapter by presenting an overview of the book's contents (Sect. 1.6) and definitions of some central concepts used in the book (Sect. 1.7).

1.1 Motivation and Intention

Research in Information Seeking and Information Retrieval constitute two disparate research areas or camps. Generally, Information Seeking is rooted in Social Science with a background in Library Science whereas much of IR is based on Computer Science approaches. The two camps do not communicate much with each other and it is safe to say, that one camp generally views the other as too narrowly bound with technology whereas the other regards the former as an unusable academic exercise. Ingwersen (1996, p. 13) notes, that "the two predominant research communities do not really explore the ideas, methods and results of each other". We believe that both research areas can be, and should be, extended to capture more of each other and of context. Therefore this book seeks to integrate Information Seeking and Information Retrieval into IS&R.

The goals of a research are may be classified as (a) theoretically understanding the phenomena of the domain of interest, (b) empirically describing and explaining (predicting) phenomena in the domain of interest, and (c) supporting the development of technology – in the broad sense, covering both tools, systems and social practices – in the domain of interest. Much of research in IS&R is applied, driven by a technological interest of developing new tools, systems and/or social practices. However, the applied technological interest is blind if the theoretical and empirical goals are not met.

For example, user studies of the 1970s in Library and Information Science were heavily criticized for blindness for other means of information access people actually use. However, it is still blind to study plain (documentary) information seeking without a work task (or leisure interest) context, a look into information use / generation, and the modern tools supporting this. Likewise, Laboratory IR research has been criticized for its lack of realism. Indeed, it is also blind to develop IR engines for artificial search tasks (topics) without a look into how people seek information and use various tools – without a look into the use context of the engines. Therefore Information Seeking and Information Retrieval research need each other – and an understanding of their context.

To us it seems prohibitive for the development of IR research if the IR community continues to consider the Laboratory Model in isolation of context. The present monograph attempts to provide perspectives from/to context by presenting a research framework that incorporates contextual components, situational factors as well as the traditional search engine and document based approaches. It broadens the scope of IR research towards searcher and task contexts at the same time as demonstrating to information seeking research how to extend its perspective towards both tasks and technology.

A cognitive turn took place in IR in early 1990s. In connection with the OKAPI project and the initiation of the large-scale TREC experiments on IR, Robertson and Hancock-Beaulieu (1992) see the turn to consist of three facets (or revolutions) that are crucial to understand in order to proceed towards a more integrated (holistic) theory of IR: the cognitive; the relevance; and the interactive revolutions. The cognitive and interactive revolutions combined entail the ideas that personal information needs ought to be treated as potentially dynamic, not static, and hence may change over time – probably due to learning and *cognition* in context during IR interaction. Relevance assessments hence also become dynamic and may take place in a variety of dimensions, so that the traditional topicality as a measure of relevance does not stand-alone. It becomes enhanced with the influence of the situational context into situational relevance, i.e., the usefulness of information objects to the user's situation. According to Robertson and Beaulieu the interactive revolution itself points to the fact that (even experimental) IR systems have become increasingly interactive, due to actual application of dynamic relevance feedback and other query modification techniques by searchers over session time. This calls for a new kind of experimental *realism* in evaluative IR research as well as in Information Science in general. The revolutions combined can thus be seen as a real challenge to the various research groupings making up the IR and seeking communities.

The present monograph is based on the cognitive viewpoint developed since the late 1970s (see Chapt. 2 for more details). However, also the cognitive viewpoint has been heavily criticized in the Information Seeking literature as asocial and individualistic – not meeting the standard of modern Social Science understanding of human behavior. In this monograph we seek to take this criticism into account and extend the cognitive viewpoint to cover both technological, human behavioral and cooperative aspects in a coherent way. Ingwersen (1996, p. 13) notes that there exists in the IS&R literature "an inherent and silent agreement that information behavior, seeking and retrieval mainly take place among academics". We aim at integrating research on academic, professional and other (leisure, cultural) information access within the same theoretical approach.

1.2 Laboratory-based Evaluation in IR

The Laboratory Model is depicted in Fig. 1.1. In this view an IR system consists of a database, algorithms, requests, and stored relevance assessments. The system components are represented in the middle and the evaluation components on top, left and bottom in the shaded area. The main thrust of the research has been on document and request representation and the matching methods of these representations. Only recently, in the Interactive Track of TREC (see Over 1997), have users been involved (the right shaded area). Even so, the systems still have been evaluated on the basis of how the users are able to find documents previously deemed relevant in the test collection.

In this view real users and tasks are not seen as necessary. Test requests typically are well-defined topical requests with verbose descriptions that give the algorithms much more data to work with for query construction than typical real life IR situations (e.g., web searching) do. Relevance is taken as topical, but factual features (based on structural data items, like author names and other bibliographic features) could be included. Relevance also is static, between a topical request and a document as seen by an assessor. The assessments are independent of each other (i.e., no learning effects, no inferences across documents) and there are no saturation effects (i.e., in principle the assessors do not get tired of repetition). The assessors do not know, in which order the documents would be retrieved so they cannot do otherwise or properly model user saturation.

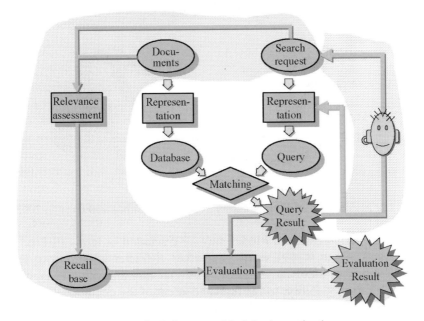

Fig. 1.1. The Laboratory Model schematized

The rationale of evaluating the algorithmic components consists of the goals, scope and justifications of the evaluation approach. The *goal* of research is to develop algorithms to identify and rank a number of topically relevant documents for presentation, given a topical request. Research is based on constructing novel algorithms and on comparing their performance with each other, seeking ways of improving them. On the theoretical side, the goals include the analysis of basic problems of IR (e.g., the vocabulary problem, document and query representation and matching) and the development of theories and methods for attacking them.

The *scope* of experiments is characterized in terms of types of experiments, types of test collections and requests as well as performance measures. The experiments mainly are batch-mode experiments. Each algorithm is evaluated by running a set of test queries, measuring its performance for individual queries and averaging over the query set. Some recent efforts seek to focus on interactive retrieval with a human subject, the TREC interactive track being predominant. The major modern test collections are news document collections. The major performance measures are recall and precision.

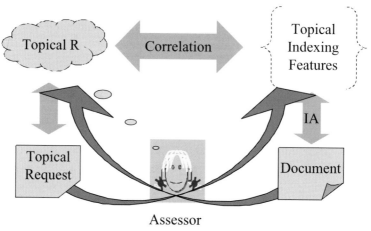

Fig. 1.2. Justification of the Laboratory Model (Kekäläinen and Järvelin 2002a)

The *justifications* of the Model may be discussed in terms of Fig. 1.2. The main strength is that words and other character strings from texts, when distilled as indexing features by an indexing algorithm (IA), correlate, with fair probability, to the topical content of the documents they represent and to the queries which they match (save for problems of homography). When a test user (or algorithm) processes a topical request, it is possible to predict, with fair probability, which indexing features should be considered (save for problems of synonymy, paraphrases). Because the topical request also suggests topical relevance criteria, there is a fair correlation (clearly better than random) between the indexing features of matching documents and a positive relevance judgment. Indexing features correlate to meaning in the topical sense. The more features that can be used as evidence, the better retrieval.

1.3 Some Problems of Laboratory-based Evaluation in IR

We will discuss below some problems of laboratory-based evaluation in IR in the form of 10 objections and responses. The objections are by the critics of the laboratory model and the responses by its defenders. The text is based on an original version by Kekäläinen and Järvelin (2002b).

Objection 1. Lack of users and tasks. There is no real user, task nor situation involved, the Model is essentially based on "objective" assessors. Real IR is a subtask in task-based information seeking, and is thus affected by the latter (Kuhlthau 1993a; Vakkari 2001a; Wilson 1999). To understand and develop IR one should take the task context into account.

Response: True, but users and tasks are not needed for testing the algorithms for the limited task they are intended for: retrieval and ranking of topical documents.

Objection 2. Lack of interaction and dynamic requests. There is no real interaction and dynamics; it is essentially a batch mode evaluation. Real interaction involves user learning, problem redefinition and dynamic relevance. (Borlund 2000a; Vakkari 2001b). Test requests in interactive experiments are too rigid for the test users, and the assessors do not deem all documents that the users consider relevant as relevant, nor do the users accept all documents deemed relevant by the assessors.

Response: True, but real interaction is not needed because all system activities in the interaction may be seen as individual retrieval tasks to be served well as such. Complex dynamic interaction is a sequence of simple topical interactions and thus good one-shot performance by an algorithm should be rewarded in evaluation. Changes in the user's understanding of his information need should affect the consequent request and query.

Objection 3. Lack of tactical variability. The only tactic of interest is a batch mode topical request while people in real life approach information in many different ways, including, e.g., bibliographic and other structured attributes or links (Bates 1989).

Response: True, tactics deserve more attention, but the model is no hindrance.

Objection 4. Lack of uncertainty. The requests are only well-defined topical requests, which do not correctly reflect all kinds of real-life requests; they are too well specified and wordy (Ingwersen and Willett 1995). They do not reflect uncertainty in the users' tasks or situations (Borlund 2000b).

Response: True, typical test requests are too well specified. This should be looked at and can be done within the model. Otherwise, several major IR models developed within Laboratory Model explicitly tackle uncertainty.

Objection 5. Lack of user-oriented relevance. The tests are based on algorithmic and topical relevance, which are unable to take into account the user's situation, tasks, or state of knowledge. There are other layers of relevance, cognitive and situational, which are closer to the user's world. Relevance assessments also are most often binary, and stable – far from real-life. (Cosijn and Ingwersen 2000; Saracevic 1996; Schamber et al. 1990).

Response: True, but user-oriented higher order relevance is not needed for testing the algorithms for the limited task they are intended for. Such relevance is out of scope of the laboratory model unless explicated as request and document features to be processed – the algorithms do not read the users' minds. The heart of IR is matching explicit representations of documents and requests. The machine cannot do better if not designed to do so, which would require explication and operationalization of user-oriented relevance features of documents and requests both theoretically and in practice.

Objection 6. Lack of variety in collections. The test collections, albeit nowadays large, are structurally simple (mainly unstructured text) and topically narrow (mainly news domain). The test documents mostly lack interesting internal structure that some real-life collections have (e.g., field structure, XML, citations). Topically, the test collections cover a narrow domain, news.

Response: True. Test collection variety should be looked at, and the model is no hindrance. There is also recent work in this direction (e.g., TREC Web Track, Hawking et al. 2000, and the INEX campaigns, Fuhr et al. 2002).

Objection 7. Assuming document independence and neglecting overlap. There are unrealistic assumptions regarding document independence (some may be relevant only if juxtaposed) and user saturation (repeated reproduction of very similar "relevant" information results in irrelevance in real-life situations) (Robertson 1977).

Response: True, but the assumptions are a necessity since the relevance assessment stage is not informed about the possible combinations of documents retrieved by a query. No one has been able to formalize the process of arguing across documents, and therefore such a task remains entirely in the user's domain.

Objection 8. Insufficiency of recall and precision. Recall and precision are insufficient as evaluation measures, the former being system-oriented and often irrelevant to the user. They do not handle non-binary relevance (Borlund and Ingwersen 1998; Korfhage 1997). They do not describe users' success in information problem explication.

Response: Recall and precision are major effectiveness measures for the limited retrieval goal. They reflect the kind of relevance that was used in the assessments be it topical or user-oriented. They can handle non-binary relevance assessments, for example, through *generalized recall* and *precision* (Kekäläinen and Järvelin 2002).

Objection 9. Heavy averaging. Many experiments are based on heavy averaging over sets of query results, perhaps never looking at the performance differences at the individual query level (Hull 1996), or individual documents / requests.

Response: Often true, but not a limitation of the model. It may be a limitation of the IR evaluation culture.

Objection 10. Just document retrieval. IR is just document retrieval with little, if any, attention to document/information presentation or use.

Response: True, but document retrieval is a genuine task in information access and deserves attention. Clearly, other stages of information access and use should also be examined as well. There is recent relevant work in Question Answering, e.g., in TREC (Voorhees and Tice 1999), and Information Extraction, e.g., in the Message Understanding Conferences (Gaizauskas and Wilks 1998).

1.4 Extension of the Laboratory-based Evaluation in IR

The laboratory model may be extended toward, for instance, *work tasks* and *higher order relevance* conceptions. However, this requires that features representing persons and their interpretations/perceptions, work tasks, interaction, situations and contexts are somehow incorporated into the model. The incorporation of some of these features into the retrieval algorithms per se may present major challenges. This is briefly discussed below, using task and situation features as an example (Fig. 1.3).

A real user, being thrown into a situation, may well be able to recognize a relevant document once presented (therefore the exclamation mark, Fig. 1.3). However, he may have difficulty in discussing the relevance criteria of the task and situation. Further, he certainly has difficulty in expressing a request and formulating a query to the IR system, at least anything other than topical as long as text is concerned (but save for bibliographic fields etc., if available), because current systems do not provide for anything else. The system designer probably never had any idea of other than explicit topical indexing features, because there is no known pattern of situational indexing features that are explicit in text – the computer does not handle implicit features – and useful to users. Therefore the available indexing features may not correlate to the situational relevance criteria, which the user did not express, save for one thing: topical relevance heavily correlates to situational as suggested by Burgin (1992) and Vakkari (2001b) – however their findings were based on bibliographic metadata. The interpretative situation described by Mark Twain in Sect. 2.3.1 illustrates the problem of lack of features or the presence of inadequate (situational) features in relation to information objects.

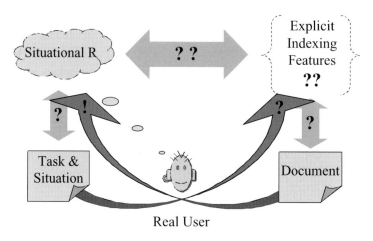

Fig. 1.3. Situational relevance in retrieval (Kekäläinen and Järvelin 2002a)

We therefore conclude that although it is easy to admit the realism of the user-oriented relevance conceptions, for the system designer they currently do not offer much to work with. Neither is there much sense evaluating the algorithms' performance on criteria, which they completely ignore (save for possible correlation of topical and user-oriented relevance). IR systems have been designed on the basis of topical relevance solely. Topical relevance is easy to agree on and it is fairly stable. However, there is no established theoretical connection between situational relevance criteria and explicit document features. This is not to say that such connections cannot exist. One of the aims of this book is to explore, whether user-related features may be incorporated into retrieval systems (either in matching algorithms or interfaces), how they affect user-system interaction, and whether they may be utilized in the interaction.

1.5 Models in the Domain of IS&R

There has been considerable recent interest in producing conceptual models for information seeking and retrieval (IS&R) research. A recent paper by Wilson (1999) reviews models for information behaviour (Wilson 1981), information seeking behaviour (Wilson 1981; 1997; Dervin and Nilan 1986; Ellis et al. 1993, Kuhlthau 1991), and information searching or retrieval (Ingwersen 1996; Belkin et al. 1995a; Spink 1997a). Plain IR Models may be represented as in Fig. 1.1 schematizing the laboratory approach. Belkin and Croft (1987), and Kantor (1994) review IR techniques studied within the laboratory approach. These techniques differ in the way they represent and match documents and search requests. However, they can be mapped to the laboratory model. The following discussion draws on earlier work by Järvelin and Wilson (2003).

Wilson (1999, p. 250) notes concerning the models of information behaviour, among others, that "rarely do such models advance to the stage of specifying relationships among theoretical propositions: rather they are at a pre-theoretical stage, but may suggest relationships that might be fruitful to explore or test." Later (p. 251) he notes that "[t]he limitation of this kind of model, however, is that it does little more than provide a map of the area and draw attention to gaps in research: it provides no suggestion of causative factors in information behaviour and, consequently, it does not directly suggest hypotheses to be tested." Likewise the laboratory model rather is a general map of the terrain than a source of hypotheses to be tested.

It therefore seems that there may be several kinds of conceptual models for IS&R and that, at least for some research purposes, we would benefit from models that suggest relationships that might be fruitful to explore and provide hypotheses to be tested. Therefore it is necessary to discuss the functions of conceptual models in scientific research, with applications in IS&R research in mind. What kind of models are there and in what ways may they help the investigators? What kinds of models are needed for various purposes?

Models or Meta-theories in Research. All research has an underlying model of the phenomena it investigates, be it tacitly assumed or explicit. Such models, called conceptual frameworks (Engelbart 1962), meta-theories (Dervin 1999; Tuominen 2001; Talja, Keso and Pietikäinen 1999), epistemological approaches (Hjørland and Nielsen 2001), paradigms (Kuhn 1970), conceptual models or just models (Wilson 1999), easily become topics of discussion and debate when a research area is in transition. Often two or more models are compared and debated. With an eye on advancing the research area, how should the models be assessed for their possible uses? Therefore we need to discuss the function of conceptual frameworks and principles for judging their merits.

Developing conceptual models means, according to D.C. Engelbart (1962), specifying the following:

- Essential objects or components of the system to be studied.
- The relationships of the objects that are recognized.
- The kinds of changes in the objects or their relationships affect the functioning of the system – and how.
- Promising or fruitful goals and methods of research.

Discussing meta-theories, Tuominen (2001) notes that they consist of sets of interconnected ontological and epistemological assumptions (cf. bullets one and two above). Further, he notes that meta-theories are connected to methodologies guiding data collection and analysis (cf. bullet four). Terminologies of authors may thus vary but the notion exists: there are socially shared *ontological* (what is out there to investigate?), *conceptual* (how to name that?), *factual* (what to take as givens?), epistemological (how can we properly learn about it?), and *methodological* (how can we learn about it?) assumptions in research areas, often competing ones within a single area.

Often meta-theories are implicit, unarticulated, and socially shared: there always is a community reproducing the discourse and sharing the understanding. Tuominen (2001) remarks that criticizing a meta-theory requires distance taking. Dervin (1999) on the other hand notes that meta-theory can be used to release research from implicit assumptions and draw them to daylight for examination. Both support making meta-theories explicit. This monograph seeks to make its meta-theory explicit.

Functions of Conceptual Models. Conceptual models are broader and more fundamental than scientific theories in that they set the preconditions of theory formulation. They, in fact, provide the conceptual and methodological tools for formulating hypotheses and theories. If they are also seen to represent schools for thought, chronological continuity, or principles, beliefs and values of the research community, they become paradigms. The conceptual model of a research area is always constructed – it does not simply lie somewhere there waiting for someone to pick it up.

The literature of Philosophy of Science provides discussions on the functions of scientific theories. We believe that these functions also are suitable functions of conceptual models. Scientific theories are needed (used) for the following functions (Bunge 1967):

(i) Systematisation of knowledge by:
1. Integrating formerly separate parts of knowledge.
2. Generalising and explaining lower abstraction level knowledge (or observations, data) through higher level constructs.

3. Explanation of facts through systems of hypotheses which entail the facts.
4. Expanding knowledge by deducing new propositions based on selected starting points and collected information.
5. Improving the testability of hypotheses through the control context provided by systems of hypotheses.

(ii) Guiding research by:
1. Pointing out fruitful problems.
2. Proposing the collection of data, which nobody would understand to collect without the theory.
3. Proposing totally new lines of research.

(iii) Mapping a chunk of reality by:
1. Representing or modelling the objects (and relationships) of that chunk instead of just summarising the data.
2. Providing a tool for producing new data.

A conceptual model provides a working strategy, a scheme containing general major concepts and their interrelations. It orients research toward specific sets of research questions. A conceptual model cannot be assessed directly empirically, because it forms the basis of formulating empirically testable research questions and hypotheses. It can only be assessed in terms of its instrumental and heuristic value. Typically this happens by assessing the research strategies and programs (and results) it creates. The latter programs consist of interrelated substantial theories and research relevant for evaluating them (Wagner et al. 1992; Vakkari 1998a). If the substantial theories prove to be fertile, the model is so too.

In this monograph we aim at, in particular, *i.1, ii.1, ii.3,* and *iii.1.*

However, waiting for the substantial theories to prove their fertility may take some time. In the meantime, or even before embarking into some line of research, it may be important to argue about the merits of various conceptual models. The following are the types of arguments that can be used to judge the merits of a conceptual model:

(i) General scientific principles:
1. When studying some phenomena, they should be studied under all conditions, including extreme ones. Thus one does not just consider information seeking by academics but also by other professions or by laymen; not just retrieval of newspaper articles but also academic contributions or images.
2. The framework should be bounded in a meaningful way as a system. For understanding information seeking by human actors, the proper system is not some service (e.g., a library) and its clients but rather an

information actor immersed in his / her situation and information environment (e.g., all information access systems).

(ii) When two competing conceptual models are compared the following criteria may be applied to judge their merits:
  1. Simplicity: simpler is better other things being equal.
  2. Accuracy: accuracy and explicitness in concepts is desirable.
  3. Scope: a broader scope is better because it subsumes narrower ones, other things being equal.
  4. Systematic power: the ability to organize concepts, relationships and data in meaningful systematic ways is desirable.
  5. Explanatory power: the ability to explain phenomena reliably and to predict them is desirable.
  6. Validity: the ability to provide valid representations and findings is desirable.
  7. Fruitfulness: the ability of a model to suggest problems for solving and hypotheses for testing is desirable.

In this monograph we aim at, in particular, *i.1, i.2, ii.3-7* by providing a conceptual model for IS&R based on the cognitive viewpoint.

Theoretical development or the construction of new conceptual models in any research area often requires conceptual and terminological development. Conceptual development may mean fulfilling, perhaps in a better way than before, basic requirements for scientific concepts – preciseness, accuracy, simplicity, generality, and suitability for expressing propositions which may be shown true or false. Moreover, good concepts represent essential features (objects, relationships, events) of the research area. More importantly, the concepts should differentiate and classify the phenomena in ways that lead to interesting hypotheses (or research questions). This means that the concepts should relate to each other explicitly and in systematic and fruitful ways. Concepts also need to support research into the phenomena by known research methods (or, somewhat relaxed, by methods that can be developed). They need to be compatible with each other and with research methods (that is, be congruent).

There does not exist a single model of IS&R that would cover all the aspects and phenomena discussed in this monograph. It is questionable whether there can be one single such model. The explicit conceptual models in the literature of IS&R are varied. Below we provide some dimensions for classifying conceptual models. Some of the dimensions are partially overlapping. Some of the sample models cited will be discussed in Chapts. 3 – 5. All kinds of models can be useful – standing at one extreme or in the middle ground does not automatically make a model better (or worse) than others. That depends on the needs of application – the kind of task the model is needed for.

Scope of Models – Broad and Narrow. The scope of some models covers only computational and/or formal aspects of IR (i.e., the Laboratory Model of IR). Other models attempt to cover human aspects in varying scopes, some focusing on information retrieval interaction (e.g., the Mediator Model, Ingwersen 1992), some on information seeking (e.g., Ellis 1989), and some on the (work) context of IS&R (e.g., Paisley 1968). Some models attempt to encompass several domains like the work context and associated information seeking (Byström and Järvelin 1995).

Process Models – Static Models. Some models are explicitly process models or functional models (e.g., Kuhlthau 1991; the Laboratory Model of IR) in that they model the stages of some IS&R process. Other models are static, not explicitly modeling an IS&R process (e.g., Wilson, 1997) as a sequence of stages, although a process may be understood to lie behind the objects represented.

Abstract Models – Concrete Models. Concrete models (e.g., Allen 1969) focus on actual concrete stakeholders in an IS&R process, and their relationships. On the contrary, theoretical or abstract models (e.g., the unit theory by Byström and Järvelin 1995) focus on abstract phenomena, interpretations or structures related to the stakeholders, and the relationships of the former.

Summary Models – Analytical Models. Summary models (e.g., Ingwersen 1996; Paisley 1968; Wilson 1997) seek to summarize the central objects in an IS&R process – not necessarily all concrete – and their gross relationships without classifying and analyzing either. Analytical models (e.g., Byström and Järvelin 1995), often narrower in scope, seek to classify the objects and relationships, and generate testable hypotheses.

General Models – Specific Models. General models claim applicability and validity over a range of empirical domains. For example, the Laboratory Model of IR is meant for any kind of document collection (mass communication, scholarly) in any language (or even any media), for any query representation, etc. Someone might create a specific laboratory model for spoken document retrieval in morphologically complex languages such as Zulu. Likewise, the early information seeking models (Paisley 1968; Allen 1969) were specific models for science and technology whereas some more recent models (e.g., Dervin 1983; Wilson 1997) claim greater generality, i.e., applicability in more general work and leisure contexts.

The challenge of creating an abstract, analytical, general process model for IS&R which covers the whole scope from work tasks through information seeking to information retrieval is a challenge of tall order indeed. The reader will have to wait until, or skip to, Chapts. 6-8 to learn about the present authors' modeling solutions.

1.6 The Structure of the Book

Chapt. 2 presents our Cognitive Framework for Information. We review the development of the epistemological Cognitive Viewpoint and discuss the Cognitive Information Concept for IS&R in relation to processes of information interaction. The focus of the cognitive viewpoint applied to interactive IR has shifted from quite an individualistic and user-driven approach to information transfer during the 80s to a holistic perception in the 90s. All actors participating in IS&R are viewed as contributors in the process via their cognitive states as represented by information objects, database structures, indexing structures and retrieval algorithms, interface designs, human work task perceptions and request representations, etc. Each representation is regarded situated in a context, predominantly of social, cultural or emotional nature. The chapter introduces a principle of complementary social and cognitive influence on the acts of interpretation. A second dimension of the view is the emphasis of the different levels of information processing that humans and computers can perform, also during interaction. This leads to a conditional cognitive information conception with strong elements of intentionality. The cognitive conception is used as a vehicle for understanding human-computer interaction, automatic indexing viewed as the Chinese Room Case (Searle 1984b), and how meaning of messages is lost at sign level and reconstructed during communication and interpretation.

Chapt. 2 also discusses alternative information conceptions. The conditions of the cognitive information conception make a workable framework for understanding the consequences of alternative conceptions. Historically, the information concept was first situated in the technology and system or in the documents stored in systems; over time the conceptions move towards the user, the information seeker's work situation and knowledge state - and towards a social and cultural context. The relationships between information and meaning are discussed. Finally, the chapter views information acquisition as fundamental to IS&R and analyses three cases: To acquire information from (Japanese) signs, unknown to the seeker; to become informed by sensory data in daily-life situations; and information acquisition during scientific discovery.

Chapt. 3 discusses the development of Information Seeking Research from about1960 to about 2000. The sixties were the time when the information seeking research expanded. A major event boosting information seeking research was the 1958 Conference on Scientific Information. In 1977 Wilson and Streatfield moved the research into the working place. The year 1986 brought the landmark review publication in the Annual Review of Information Science and Technology (ARIST) by Dervin and Nilan (1986) which signifies the start of the new user-oriented (or actor-oriented) approach to information seeking. Several user-centered approaches to information seeking developed. Among the major ones were Dervin's Sense-Making Approach, Ellis' (1989; et al. 1993) behavioral model of information seeking strategies, and Kuhlthau's Information Seeking Process Model (1991; 1993a). All these approaches also provided empirical findings. The chapter also looks into conceptual development and research methodologies in information seeking research, as well as the current limitations and open problems exposed by the literature.

Chapt. 4 discusses the development of systems-oriented IR research 1960 – 2000. Several major mathematical retrieval models were developed and the paradigm of laboratory-based evaluation developed. The experiments based on best-match IR methods were carried out originally in small test collections but become extended to large collections. On the practical/industry side, the online IR industry developed systems utilizing Boolean logic that provided global access to large bibliographic and later full-text and web collections. Chapt. 4 begins by a discussion of laboratory-oriented IR models. This is followed by a discussion of issues and findings in the systems-oriented IR research regarding (1) documents, requests, and relevance, (2) indexing, classification and clustering, (3) interfaces and visualization, (4) interaction and query modification, (5) natural language processing, as well as (5) expert systems and interfaces for IR. We focus on research relevant for the cognitive viewpoint. Therefore we bypass much research that is otherwise important to IR. The chapter closes by a discussion of research methods in IR, mainly IR evaluation, and limitations and open problems in contemporary IR research.

Chapt. 5 discusses the development of user-oriented and cognitive IR research 1960 to about 2000. The rise of the online IR industry created user communities. This resulted in the development of the user-oriented IR approach, focusing on intermediaries and later end-users of commercial Boolean IR systems. The Cognitive Approach started in the late 1970's with the aim of understanding human information (retrieval) behavior and bridging the two former approaches. We shall first review some central models of user-oriented and cognitive IR research. Then we discuss issues and findings in (1) cognitive theory building and poly-representation, (2) searchers' cognitive styles, (3) standard online interaction, (4) web IR interaction, (5) searcher-associated best match IR interaction, and (6) relevance. At the end of the section we shall review research methods in user-oriented and cognitive IR before finally considering the limitations and open problems of this research area. The development of expert systems for IR made researchers in both systems and cognitive-oriented approaches to collaborate. These issues are discussed in both Chapts. 4 and 5.

Chapt. 6 proposes our integrated framework for IS&R, based on the cognitive view. We discuss requirements for such models, and its major components: tasks, contexts, situations, and seeking and retrieval processes/tools. We also demonstrate the applicability of the framework from the viewpoint of several partakers of IR processes. Secondly, the complexity of IR processes is discussed. Issues related to information seekers, their situations, work and search tasks, task complexity, knowledge types, and interaction are among others brought forward. The chapter closes with a summary of the characteristics of the proposed framework.

In Chapt. 7 we consider the implications of the proposed cognitive framework in the design and evaluation of IS&R. Discussing 9 broad dimensions: the natural work task and organization dimensions, the perceived work and search task dimensions, the actor dimension, the document dimension, the algorithmic search engine dimension, the algorithmic interface dimension, and the access and interaction dimension, we propose two action lines as needed. On the one hand, IR research needs to be extended to capture more context but without totally sacrificing the laboratory experimentation approach – the controlled experiments. Only by this line of action one may approach real *IR engineering.* On the other hand, current information seeking research needs to be extended both toward the task context *and* the technology. Figuratively, the two action lines induce a space for IS&R research to explore and so far, as we argue: only a small part of that space has been investigated.

Chapt. 8 proposes a research program for further research in IS&R. It analyzes four distinct research set-ups in detail as avenues for extending current research IS&R toward capturing more context.

Chapt. 9 is the conclusion of the book followed by a list of definitions for concepts used, an integrated list of references and an index.

1.7 Some Central Concepts

Below we list some central concepts used throughout the book. Many more concepts are listed in the Definitions section at the end of the book.

1.7.1 The Participants or Components of IS&R

Cognitive Actor. A person responsible for the interpretation or provision of potential information or signs represented as information objects, IT, interface functionalities and during communication. Central actor categories in IS&R are: searchers or seekers; authors; indexers; algorithmic system designers; interface designers; selectors, such as publishers, editors, employers.

Information Objects. Physical (digital) entities in a variety of media that belong to the information space of IR systems, providing potential information. Information objects are used interchangeably with the term documents.

Information Space. Information space is represented by information objects consisting of potential information and commonly structured according to IT settings of information systems.

IR System. An information system which is constituted by interactive processes between its information space, IT setting, interface functionalities and its environment, and capable of searching and finding information of potential value to seeker(s) of information.

Interface. A mechanism located as the go-between two electronic or human components of an information system. In IS&R commonly referred to as the (user) interface between the *IT* and *information space* components of an IR system and the seeking actor(s).

Context. In IS&R *actors* and other components function as context to one another in the interaction processes. There are social, organizational, cultural as well as systemic contexts, which evolve over time.

1.7.2 The Tasks

Daily-life Tasks or Interests. All kinds of work tasks and interests that are not job-related activities or search tasks. Such tasks may be of social and cultural nature, including leisure and entertainment.

Work Task. A job-related task or non-job associated daily-life task or interest to be fulfilled by cognitive actor(s). Work tasks can be natural, real-life tasks or be assigned as simulated work task situations or assigned requests. If perceived and not immediately solvable by actor(s), a work task may lead to state of uncertainty and to search task situations.

Search Task. The task to be carried out by a cognitive seeking actor(s) as a means to obtain information associated with fulfilling a work task. Search tasks are either seeking tasks or retrieval tasks, depending on the involvement of IR systems, and include information need generation, information interaction and search task solving. Search task situations are natural in real-life settings and simulated or assigned (as plain requests) in IR experiments.

1.7.3 The Contents

Information. The concept of information, from a perspective of Information Science, has to satisfy dual requirements: On the one hand information being the result of a transformation of a generator's cognitive structures (by intentionality, model of recipients' states of knowledge, and in the form of signs). On the other hand being something which, when perceived, affects and transforms the recipient's state of knowledge.

Knowledge. An individual's total understanding of itself and the world around it at any given point in time, incorporating thinking and cognition as well as emotional, intuitive properties and (sub)conscious memory (tacit knowledge). In IS&R one may operate with declarative and procedural knowledge as one dimension and, as another dimension, domain knowledge and IS&R knowledge.

1.7.4 The Needs and Relevance

Information Need. Signifies a consciously identified gap in the knowledge available to an actor. Information needs may lead to information seeking and formulation of requests for information.

Request. The formulation of the information need or the underlying states of intentionality, as perceived, and provided at a given point in time by the actual searcher to an IR system or other information sources.

Query. A transformation of a request formulation made by an actor himself/herself, an intermediary or an interface in order to interrogate an IR system's information space, in concordance with the system's indexing and retrieval algorithms.

Relevance. The assessment of the perceived topicality, pertinence, usefulness or utility, etc., of information sources, made by cognitive actor(s) or algorithmic devices, with reference to an information situation at a given point in time. It can change dynamically over time for the same actor. Relevance can be of a low order objective nature or of higher order, i.e., of subjective multidimensional nature.

1.7.5 The Processes

Information Behavior. Human behavior dealing with generation, communication, use and other activities concerned with information, such as, information seeking behavior and interactive IR.

Information Interaction. Signifies the exchange between two or more cognitive actors in contexts of IS&R. In IS&R three kinds of interaction exist: short-term; session-based; and longitudinal IS&R interaction.

Information Retrieval. The processes involved in representation, storage, searching, finding, filtering and presentation of potential information perceived relevant to a requirement of information desired by a human user in context. Information retrieval (IR) is commonly divided into algorithmic IR and interactive IR.

Interactive IR. The interactive communication processes that occur during retrieval of information by involving all major participants in IS&R, i.e., the searcher, the socio-organizational context, the IT setting, interface and information space.

Information Seeking. Human information behavior dealing with searching or seeking information by means of information sources and (interactive) information retrieval systems; also called IS&R behavior.

2 The Cognitive Framework for Information

This chapter outlines the cognitive framework for information transfer and discusses its implications for understanding information conceptions. First, the cognitive epistemological point of view is briefly outlined and discussed in relation to information seeking and information retrieval (IS&R). The section points to that shift in focus of the viewpoint in IR research that occurred during the 1990s. In the subsequent subsections we then present the conditional information concept adhering to the cognitive approach in Information Science and IS&R and discuss its implications for information acquisition.

2.1 The Cognitive View

Information Science is one of several disciplines dealing with aspects of human cognition and cognitive processes through communication and interaction. Others are, for example, Cognitive Psychology, Psycho and Socio-Linguistics, or Science Studies. In line with similar Social Sciences and the Humanities, there exist several epistemological and philosophical ways to approach such activities. To name the most important ones, the processes may be viewed from a standpoint of pragmatism, rationalism, hermeneutics and phenomenology, or approached with a language-philosophical, semiotic, constructivist, sociological or cognitive point of view in mind.

We have based this monograph on the cognitive viewpoint because it demonstrates explicit models for Information Science *and* points to solutions of, foremost, Information Retrieval (IR) problems not solvable otherwise. Further, the view has been used as a conceptual framework for empirical studies leading to novel results and insights in interactive IR, and it seems promising for the integration of IS&R. We regard IS&R processes as processes of cognition.

Although B. C. Brookes made use of its characteristics already in 1975, Mark De Mey coined the cognitive viewpoint for the first time in his epistemological framework presented at the multidisciplinary Workshop on the

Cognitive Viewpoint, in Ghent (1977). There are several reasons for examining this approach in relation to IS&R.

First, it may serve as a *holistic* framework for theory building and research work in IS&R. Other IS&R approaches, based on, for instance, pragmatism or rationalism, may indeed provide models (Salton 1968a; 1989). But these are quite limited in scope due to their lack of context and their focus on selected system components of information transfer and knowledge communication. So far hermeneutics as well as language-philosophy have been applied to the meta-theoretical levels of information (Winograd and Flores 1986) and Information Science (Brier 1996) or limited to issues of knowledge representation (Blair 1990). So-called social-realistic domain analytic approaches concentrate on frameworks for knowledge organization and representation and attempt to approach certain phenomena of retrieval and seeking processes, like the information need development (Hjørland and Albrechtsen 1995; Hjørland 1997).

Secondly, the view leads to a profound understanding of the concept of information for Information Science, further discussed in succeeding sections. This understanding helps to model and interpret other conceptions, central to IS&R, for instance, the concepts of work tasks, evaluation, relevance, and information acquisition and use.

Third, thus far the cognitive view underlies a substantial portion of several authors' theoretical and empirical contributions to R&D in Information Science and interactive IR in particular. The view has matured into a state where a workable research methodology is under rapid development and validation internationally. B. C. Brookes (1977; 1980) was the first to refer explicitly to the viewpoint. N. Belkin also applied the view to the conception of information (1978), later reviewing its impact on work in IR (1990). Influenced by the results of the mentioned Workshop, Ingwersen explored the viewpoint in several contributions to IR, for instance in 1982 and 1984. In 1992 (p. 15-48) and 1995 he provided a detailed discussion of its scope, perspectives and relations to other epistemological approaches which, in 1996, led to a first formulation of a cognitive theory for Information Retrieval. This development in 1990-96 and beyond was substantially influenced by empirical findings concerned with the nature of the work task situation and its role in Information Seeking and IR (Järvelin 1986; Byström and Järvelin 1995). Often, these contributions isolate the cognitive approach in IR from behaviorist and cognitivistic traditions by associating it with socio-hermeneutic and communication theoretical perspectives of Information Science. In particular during the 1990s the application of the cognitive approach to IR and, to a certain extent, to information seeking studies has gained momentum. The Chapts. 6 and 7 outline the future prospects of an IS&R research methodology founded in the cognitive view.

2.1.1 The Central Dimensions of the Cognitive View

De Mey formulates the central point of the cognitive view to be:

> "that any processing of information, whether perceptual or symbolic, is mediated by a system of categories or concepts which, for the information processing device, are a model of his [its] world." (De Mey 1977, p. xvi-xvii; 1980, p. 48)

– whether the device is a human being or a machine. In relation to Information Science, seeking and retrieval it is important to note *five central and interrelated dimensions* of the cognitive view:

1. Information processing takes place in senders *and* recipients of messages;
2. Processing takes place *at different levels*;
3. During communication of information any actor is *influenced* by its past and present experiences (*time*) and its social, organizational and cultural environment;
4. Individual actors *influence* the environment or domain;
5. Information is *situational* and *contextual*.

First, it is equally valid to the view whether the processing device acts as a sender or recipient of signs, signals or data, for example, during communication processes. This implies that the view not only treats the human actor as the recipient *but also* as generator of signs to and from machines and knowledge resources, see Fig. 2.1, Sect. 2.2.

The cognitive viewpoint is consequently not limited to user-centered approaches to information. Essentially, it is *human*-oriented and encompasses all information processing devices generated by man as well as information processes intended by man. The former refers, for instance, to computers or other forms of technology; the latter signifies acts of generation, transfer, and perception of information, for instance, by technological means. Hence, the viewpoint involves humanistic aspects with respect to contents of messages, technological insights of tools for processing, and social scientific dimensions due to the information activities taking place in a social contextual space.

Secondly, information processing takes place *at different levels* depending on whether the device is a machine or a human actor. The cognitive viewpoint, as well as its application in relation to the information concept for Information Science, attempts to provide *conditions* as to how and when to talk about 'information processing' and 'information' vs. data processing, signals or signs. The issue is a matter of the *interpretative capability* of the device or actor.

In association with the viewpoint, De Mey established a valuable evolutionary view consisting of four stages through which thinking on information processing has developed (1977, p. xvii; 1980, p. 49):

1. A *monadic stage* during which information units are handled separately and independently of each other as if they were simple self-contained entities.
2. A *structural stage* where the information is seen as a more complex entity consisting of several information units arranged in some specific way.
3. A *contextual stage* where in addition to an analysis of its structural organization of the information-bearing units, there is required information on context to disambiguate the meaning of the message.
4. A *cognitive or epistemic stage* in which information is seen as supplementary or complementary to a conceptual system that represents the information-processing system's knowledge of its world.

The stages 1-3 correspond to of the morpho-lexical, the syntactic, and the semantic levels of language understanding, that is, the *linguistic surface levels* of data processing. The fourth stage corresponds to the pragmatic processing level in linguistics. At this level the individual actor processes *information*. Thus, information becomes a construct deriving from two potential sources: the actor's own world model in context (by thinking and interpretation) or/and a perceived message in context. The less the context that is available to the actor, the more freedom exists for interpretation. This phenomenon of *semantic openness* may obviously not only entail uncertainty as to the meaning of a message (its sense) but may also influence the informative potential or value of the message to an actor - whether sender or recipient.

All four processing stages are open to human actors. Machines are *always limited* or reduced to data processing at the tri-partite linguistic surface levels, since machines are algorithmically predictive, and consequently not self-contained (Ingwersen 1992; 1996) nor auto-poietic (Winograd and Flores 1986). The result is that *context* plays a central role in information processing, for instance, to disambiguate messages. Context may derive from a variety of knowledge sources open to the individual actor, including itself as a source. This is significant in IS&R processes where several source types commonly are involved.

Third, the current cognitive state of *any* individual actor is *under influence* of its past and its social and cultural context. According to the view the individual 'cognitive model', also named 'state of knowledge', consists of knowledge structures or, as we prefer, *cognitive structures* defined to include emotional state that are based on individually interpreted situations and perceived social/collective experiences, education, etc. (Ingwersen 1982, p. 168). The dimension of *time* hence plays an important role for such processes of interpretation and cognition. For a detailed analysis of context types in IS&R, see Sect. 6.2.2.

The viewpoint's epistemological and paradigmatic nature is further discussed by De Mey (1982), in which he outlines the pioneering work in Cognitive Science by J. Piaget since 1929 on the development of cognitive structures. Then, in 1984, De Mey stresses that there might be "[a] greater variety of such structures than expected by Piaget, and they might be more connected to domains of knowledge than to psychological development or age [of the individual]" (1984, p. 108).

Evidently, the individual actor can personify the information seeker or user; but it should be stressed that it may indeed also represent *any* other *actor* taking part in interactive IS&R processes, each one within its own knowledge domain. Such actors are, for instance: retrieval engine designers; database producers; algorithm developers; authors; indexers; thesaurus and classification system generators; work task responsibles; managers; etc. We will argue that for each actor the other actors, over time, consequently may function as its environment. Some actors, like authors or indexers, produce conceptual structures during information processing. Other actors are responsible for system structures or algorithms – and may be remote in time. Some are present during information activities, like a searcher. In most other cases the actors are only indirectly visible, but *represented* by the results of their information processing activities, like information objects, including references or outlinks on the Web (authors), or journal and database structure and contents (editors and producers). Thus, the different actors probably interpret a particular situation in ways somewhat different from one another, due to time gaps and the specific cognitive state and context associated with each actor. The types of actors, cognitive variation and manifestations of information activities that actually take part in the process are associated with the media applied, the domain, and the processing (writing) style in question.

Fourth, on the other hand one may emphasize that *collective cognitive structures* may very well be generated and modified over time (Ingwersen 1982, p. 169). Such structures are the result of *social interaction* between individual actors entailing shared understanding of concepts as well as perceptions of work tasks, situations and relevance. Such social constructs may hence be quite temporary, like conference program committees, or they may constitute longer-term professional bodies, scientific knowledge domains, schools or paradigms (Kuhn 1972). The dynamic influence of individual and collective cognitive structures on work task situations and their further perception and cognition by the individual actors are all important factors for understanding IS&R.

The *mutual* connections and influences between the individual actor and the social or organizational domains, knowledge and behavior, culture, goals and purpose (intentionality) as well as individual and collective preferences and emotions, expectations and experiences, are thus reflected in this cognitive view of Information Science, Information Seeking and IR.

Fifth, due to its contextual nature, the time dimension, and under influence of social interaction between individual actors, information as well as IS&R thus becomes *situational*. This central dimension of the conception of the cognitive view adheres to the Russian socio-linguist Luria and his empirical work in the 1920s on human classification of objects (1976).

Luria demonstrated how educational background as well as day-to-day work routines and situations trigger the way humans classify objects and describe their relationships into *situational* and *categorical* (generic and part-whole) classes and relations. Such classificatory behavior has impact on the perception by the individual actors of, for instance, work and search task situations, interests, topics, relevance assessments or knowledge organization in the information space as well as in the social/organizational environment.

2.1.2 From an Individualistic Cognitive View...

A consequence of the cognitive view and the above dimensions is a *variety of individual differences* in the cognitive structures, the situational perception and interpretation of the world by actors. From the 1970s and to the end of the 1980s IR research based on a cognitive approach saw the task of IR as to *bring into accord* this variety of cognitive structures from all the different participating actors. In reality, however, investigations and modeling focused typically on the searcher and his/her behavior, problem and search situation as well as the end user-intermediary (or interface) interaction (Ingwersen 2001b). This is probably the reason behind the notion of cognitive user-oriented information retrieval research by Ellis (1992). Essentially, the research foci constituted the rationale behind the Monstrat Model (Belkin et al. 1983) and a fair number of later attempts to knowledge-based (intelligent) IR solutions in the late 1980s that did not meet the expectations (Brooks 1987). This notion of bringing into accord cognitively different structures immediately ought to have ensured the creation of a workable holistic approach to IR in which – for instance – document structures could be incorporated. With the exception of Brookes (1980), this was unfortunately not the case during the first period.

This emphasis on the individual searcher (user and/or intermediary) behavior during interaction with IR systems in reality excluded the simultaneous investigation into the cognitive structures embedded into such systems, the information space and the contextual environment. In particular, non-Boolean best-mach IR systems were *not* incorporated into the cognitive or user-centered research settings – with the exception of the THOMAS system (Oddy 1977a; 1977b).

2.1.3 ... to the Holistic Cognitive View

The shift at the start of the 1990s took place due to several circumstances in IR research (Ingwersen 2001b, p.11-13). User modeling and knowledge-based retrieval as well as interface design, including studies of human-computer interaction for IR, did not seem to improve IR performance when viewed isolated from the information space and the context of the searcher. Situational relevance (Schamber, Eisenberg and Nilan 1990) re-entered the discussion and opened up a Pandora's Box of relevance within the various IS&R research communities during the 1990s. Slightly later Robertson and Hancock-Beaulieu analyzed the research situation, in particular associated with experimental IR, and called for the well-known three revolutions challenging the field: the relevance revolution; the cognitive revolution; and the interactive revolution.

At the same time Ingwersen (1992) discussed the state of IR theory from an *interactive* perspective and attempted to advance a holistic cognitive view on IR research. In this view, originating from de Mey (1980; 1982), cognition takes place in contextual interaction. The emphasis is placed on his four evolutionary stages of information processing outlined above. According to the view IR implies a continuous process of *interpretation* and *cognition* in context by all participating actors on both the systems (and document) side and on the side of the human actor during IS&R interactions. However, exactly the four processing stages define in a broad sense the cognitive limitations and characteristics involved at both sides in an asymmetrical way.

The work task (or daily-life task or interest) situation is seen as the central element of the context. It triggers the cognitive space of the human actor into a perceived work task, a problematic situation, and probably an information need perception. The new approach implies that several *different manifestations* of the same situation may be available from the human actor at a given point in time. Simultaneously, in information space the documents similarly demonstrate cognitive variety of representations.

From 1990, information seeking is increasingly seen as contextual to interactive IR, as summarized by Wilson (1999) and, as early as 1980, indirectly modeled in a cognitive theoretical framework.

The turn into a holistic cognitive view implies a shift *from* believing in the possibility of bringing the variety of cognitive and functionally different structures in IR in harmony, *to* the acceptance that such structures are inherently different, and should be exploited as such. It is the asymmetric cognitive nature of the man-machine relationships that creates the obstacles for information transfer.

According to the holistic cognitive view of the dynamics of IR interaction, the man-machine situation should be designed to *support* the user during the interactive process of IR. Man-machine interaction in IR is thus a question of making the total system, including the interface, to support the searcher who then feeds back useful data so that the system may better support the searcher: Support that supports support that supports. Ultimately, information retrieval in its real sense only takes place in the mind of the information seeker, that is, (acquiring) information is seen as the process of transforming a current cognitive state into a new state, as cognition, leading to knowledge.

2.1.4 The Role of Context in Individual Cognition

The final issue is whether the context or environment is *the* determining factor for individual cognition or whether it is the individual perception of that context situated in interaction that determines the outcome? The issue is interesting because the cognitive viewpoint is epistemologically based on the conception of social interaction between individual cognitive structures in context. In our view each actor in interactive IR and information seeking interacts with other actors at various levels under influence of social contexts and work task or interest situations over time. This influence is not regarded as determining for the individual cognition processes: The perception, interpretation and cognition of the individual actor is *determined* by its/his/her prevailing cognitive structures - and *influenced* but *not* directed or dictated by the environment or domain. Hence, it is the individual perception of the situation in context that prevails. Similarly, the individual actor influences the social/organizational environment. By means of his/her perception of that context – and via social interaction – each actor may contribute to its modification over time. If we did regard the context as being the determining factor for individual cognition then there could be no advance or change in that context – only predetermined aggregation of knowledge. In our view the individual actor possesses relative autonomy and may therefore – influenced by the environment – contribute to the change of a scientific domain, of professional work strategies and management, or indeed a paradigm. This combined bottom-up and top-down view of cognition is named the *principle of complementary social and cognitive influence.*

This principle is useful in several ways in IS&R studies. When applying and intersecting a variety of representations of information objects, some of which are derived from the context, like inlinks and citations given to web pages and scientific authors, articles, or journals, the principle may be used to make a balanced overlap of retrieved documents in the cognitive sense. The complementarity ensures that the contextual representative structures (e.g., citations) are treated like, for instance, author-derived cognitive representations, such as, text words.

In relevance assessments the principle also shows where we may observe socio-cognitive relevance judgments, e.g., made through social interaction by groups of individual editors in journals or by program committee members in conferences – in many cases influenced by the prevailing scientific paradigm (Cosijn and Ingwersen 2000).

The performance of professional or scientific thesauri in specific environments seems increased when the terms used in the semantic structure are of complementary social and cognitive nature, i.e., they consist of a mixture of academic domain concepts and local and work-associated term relations (Nielsen 2000).

By means of increased dynamics in the use of ICT individual web users increasingly perform remote social interaction that influences their individual or group information and seeking behavior. Individual data creation increases. This leads to a growing demand for filtering and refinement of information from the environment.

2.2 The Cognitive Information Concept in IS&R

With reference to the cognitive viewpoint *information* is one of the most central phenomena of interest to information seeking and retrieval and information science in general. Understanding this phenomenon is an imperative for enhancing our conception of other central phenomena, such as, information need formation and development, relevance, or knowledge representation, acquisition and use.

Prerequisites for such a concept for Information Science are that it is must be related to knowledge, be definable and operational, i.e., non-situation specific, and it must offer a means for the prediction of effects of information. The latter implies that we are able to compare information, whether it is generated or received. Hence, we are not looking for a definition of information but for an *understanding and use* of such a concept, which may serve Information Science and does not contradict other information-related disciplines. However, at the same time it needs to be specific enough to contribute to the analysis of IS&R phenomena.

The viewpoint also clearly demonstrates that communication processes play a fundamental role, involving sender, message, channel, recipient, *and* a degree of shared context. The special case for Information Science, and in particular IS&R, lies in the notion of *desired information* and that messages take the form of *intentional signs*. A relevant information concept should consequently be associated with all components in the communication process and involve intentionality (Searle 1984a).

Three central dimensions of the cognitive view come into play, namely the first, second, and third dimension outlined above, Sect. 2.1.1. Essentially, they state that both the reception *and* the generation of information are acts of information processing made in *context* - but often at *different* linguistic levels.

The way this processing is carried out is dependent on the cognitive (world) model of the actor – whether human or machine. However, since its formulation in 1977 (De Mey 1977, p. xvi-xvii; 1980, p. 48) up to the mid 1990s, the cognitive viewpoint has basically been (mis)interpreted as an approach in which the human searcher constantly acts as the recipient of something (data, signs, potential information) generated by a 'system' incorporating knowledge sources. It is as if the system does not operate as a recipient. For instance, Brookes' well-known Equation model (1980), has commonly been understood in this limited way. Similarly, by placing his notion of anomalous state of knowledge (ASK) firmly under the recipient component in his communication model (1978, p. 81), Belkin opens up for a distinct focus on searchers as recipients. Also Ingwersen becomes seduced by that interpretation in his earlier contributions founded in the cognitive view (1982; 1984). However, as shown previously the viewpoint actually suggests that the machine or a system may indeed *also* act as a recipient applying its own world model, yet apparently at a different level of communication. This interchange of positions established by Ingwersen (1992; 1996) makes the viewpoint a much more forceful theoretical foundation for IR interaction, information seeking and HCI in general. The view explains and predicts the processing activity in all actors. Thus, following the cognitive view the concept of information, from the perspective of information science, has to satisfy *two conditions* simultaneously (Ingwersen 1992, p. 33):

On the one hand information being something which is the
  result of a transformation of a generator's knowledge structures
  (by intentionality, model of recipients' states of knowledge, and in the
  form of signs)
and on the other hand being something which,
  when perceived, affects and transforms the recipient's state of knowledge.

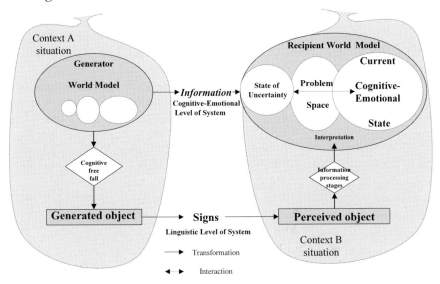

Fig. 2.1. The cognitive communication system for Information Science, information seeking and IR. Revision of Ingwersen (1992, p.33; 1996, p.6), from Belkin (1978).

Evidently, any transformation of state of knowledge involves an effect on the state. It is important to stress, however, that an effect on state of knowledge, and an ensuing reaction, does not necessarily require any transformation of a knowledge state. When a computer starts printing due to a perceived and understood print command, it is simply an effect, not a change of state of knowledge. The command remains a sign – not information.

This conditional information concept is originally an extension of Belkin's (1978) and Brookes' (1980) information conceptions. It is associated with Wersig's concept from 1973. A further analysis forms part of Sect. 2.3.

In order to understand this information conception we may consequently analyze the properties of the cognitive models involved on *both sides* of the communication channel as described below and illustrated in Fig. 2.1.

2.2.1 Properties of Cognitive Models

Fig. 2.1 depicts one instance of communication at two levels from generator to recipient, each in their own context with situation-specific circumstances influencing the state of knowledge or cognitive model. The contexts are open-ended, implying that factors from contexts further out into the environment may influence the current one and the given situations (A and B). At generation time, the situation A in context A triggers the generator's state of knowledge to produce a message at the cognitive-emotional level – the left-hand side. The message takes the form of signs at the linguistic surface level of the communication system. Regardless whether the signs are stored for later communication, for instance in an information system, or immediately communicated, its meaning (sense) and context is lost - named the *cognitive free fall*. The generator has lost control of the message. At the right-hand side the intentional recipient perceives the signs at a linguistic surface level, in his/her/its context B. Only through the stages of information processing, De Mey (1977; 1980), and supported by the cognitive model of the recipient, may the message effect the current cognitive state of that recipient. In order to turn into information the signs transform the cognitive state by means of an actor's interpretation processes. The information perceived may be different from that intended by the generator.

The transformation will be influenced by the open-ended situation in context B. Signs may indeed have effect on the recipient, but information may not be conceived. The cognitive-emotional state in context (B) may contain doubt, perceive a problem about the processing and/or interpretation of the signs, and reach a state of uncertainty. In itself this state could be said to hold information (on uncertainty or doubt), but then this generated information is of generic nature, e.g. "to me the signs seem to be of Asian origin – but I do not understand them". Fig. 2.1 is extended from Ingwersen (1992) by including different contexts and situations and by viewing the act of communication at a given point in time, that is, at the instance of reception of signs.

In *human information processing* the cognitive model is the individual cognitive space which controls the perception and further processing of external input, for instance, during communication and IS&R. The space consists of dynamic and interchangeable cognitive and emotional structures. This individual cognitive space is determined by the individual perceptions and experiences gained over time in a social and historical context. In relation to IS&R the cognitive model affects the personal interpretation of seeking, domains and work tasks over time. The acquired knowledge consists of IS&R knowledge *and* domain knowledge – the two knowledge types fundamental to all IS&R activities (Ingwersen 1992)[1]. The current cognitive state represents the perception and interpretation of the current domains and work tasks or interests, i.e., of the actual context and situation (A or B).

In *automatic (symbolic) information processing* the cognitive model may be dynamic but *not* self-contained. It consists of the human cognitive structures embedded in the system prior to processing. Its individual cognitive structures, e.g., in the form of algorithms or textual strings, may interact with one another and with structures generated by humans external to the system – when ordered and capable of doing so. However, the processing will only take place at a *linguistic sign level* of communication - never at a cognitive level, see Fig. 2.1 and De Mey's stages 1-3 of information processing, Sect. 2.1.1.

2.2.2 Automatic Indexing: The Chinese Room Case

In automatic information processing no emotional structures are involved and the problem space as well as the state of uncertainty are reduced to calculated probabilities – if at all present. This is in concordance with Searle's Chinese Room case (1984b).

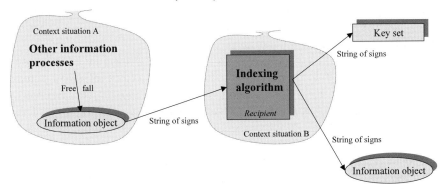

Fig. 2.2. The Chinese Room case (Searle 1984b), transformed into an automatic indexing scenario

---

[1] In Ingwersen (1992) domain knowledge was frequently also named 'conceptual knowledge'.

For example, an indexing algorithm (acting as recipient) operating on a stored information object, Fig. 2.2, does only act horizontally at sign level (Fig. 2.1), most often at lexical or syntactic linguistic levels, rarely at a semantic level, and never at a pragmatic cognitive level. The first condition for information is satisfied: the information object (signs) is created by information processes by means of intent and in the form of signs. But due to the purpose behind the algorithmic functionality induced by its designer in *his* original context (B), i.e., foreseeing the indexing situations to occur (situation B), the second condition is not completed since the algorithm cannot be changed or it cannot alter its structure which, since its creation, remains at the sign level[2]: The object may be open to an automatic indexing process by the algorithm (perception) which constructs a number of keys and maintains the object as a string of signs (effect). The states of the algorithm and object are not changed[3]; but a new set of structures at sign level (the keys) is produced according to the functionality of the algorithm and adhering to (a new) condition one.

This case, common in IS&R, can be transformed into the extreme. The indexing algorithm may include an encryption functionality that definitively alters the structures of the object, later to be deciphered by a recipient actor - if possible by means of some keys. Similar to the Chinese Room case neither the algorithm nor the person in the Chinese Room (a black box) have the ability to understand the meaning of the original object or the new object in the form of sign strings. Additionally, the indexing mechanism may indeed construct wrong keys due to lack of contexts.

Only to human generators or recipients of communicated signs the perception may *also* take place at a *cognitive/emotional level*, transforming the current cognitive states into new states, conceivably providing information transformed into cognition and knowledge.

2.2.3 The Cognitive Free Fall – and Reconstruction

The most important dimension of the cognitive view is that during *any act* of human or computerized communication the viewpoint regards *all* communicated messages as *signs* transferred at a linguistic surface level. The signs may be transformed into information at a cognitive level only via

---

[2] One might argue that not even the first condition is fulfilled if the object was not intended for indexing in the first place.

[3] Even if an indexing algorithm indeed may change its functionality owing to other algorithmic rules overriding the former, e.g., by passing a frequency threshold as in recommender systems, this still takes place at linguistic surface levels. No change of state of *knowledge* occurs.

perception and interpretation by the individual recipient's current cognitive state *in context*. The interpretation or association then transforms the cognitive state into a new state and the second condition is fulfilled.

Consequently, this view implies an immediate *cognitive 'free fall'* of a message into the lowest levels of linguistic nature, Figs. 2.1 and 2.2, left-hand side. The consequence is that *any intentionality, meaning,* implicit *context, and* potential *informativeness* underlying the generated and communicated message are *immediately lost.* They have to be rebuilt and recovered, i.e., interpreted and constructed, by the recipient by means of those presuppositions in context, which make him/it participate in the communication act. Computers (or books for that matter) hold predefined and fixed presuppositions, whilst those of humans are individually unpredictable, sometimes irrational, formed as they are by cognitive and emotional experiences in context over time (e.g. episodic and semantic memories). If a recipient cannot perceive the message, although he wishes to do so, information transfer does not take place. The message prevails at sign level containing all its potentials of meaning, information and cognition hidden from that recipient. If perceived, the signs *may* develop through some or all of the processing levels from morpho-lexical to pragmatics, as guided by the recipient's world model in context - Fig. 2.1, right-hand side. The *meaning* of a message may hence be disambiguated at a semantic level into a common semantic value and sense, either because the message itself supplies adequate and understandable context, and/or the recipient adds his own context, probably but not necessarily also shared by other actors.

To reach the pragmatic or cognitive level of processing *information*, a semantic value (van Rijsbergen 1986; 1999) or sense is interpreted into a *construct* by means of *that context* the individual recipient's world model currently supplies (e.g., a belief or the emotional perception in situation B). The information resulting from this interpretation process is hence supplementary to the current cognitive model of the recipient, and may or may not be different from that intended by the generator. That depends of the actual overlap of cognitive models and contexts (situation A vs. situation B). See examples in Sect. 2.3 below. Hence, we observe the aforementioned principle of complementary social and cognitive influence in action.

In order to reach a pragmatic or cognitive level of actual information processing we deal with three kinds of *perceived context*: 1) that of which the message itself forms part; 2) that context which is supplementary to the message supplied by the receiving actor her/him/itself. This *can* be shared by a community or culture; 3) that which is highly individual and self-contained. Evidently, at a pragmatic level individual actors may share the conventional understanding or idea of a sign *and* the information interpreted from that sign; but we may also frequently expect that the actors obtain different information (and cognition) although their understanding of a sign is in agreement. This phenomenon gives raise to the notion that *information goes beyond meaning*.

This view of information processing corresponds to the *semiotic triangle* by Peirce (1955) in which a sign is defined by its 1) *representamen,* i.e., something that for somebody stands for 2) an *object*, ground or idea, and 3) the *interpretant* i.e., somebody developing an interpretation of the representamen in a social and cultural context (Brier 1996; Mai 2001). We could say that what is communicated is basically the primary sign, that is, the representamen. During the communicative act the semiotic triangle is destroyed. To facilitate successful communication, i.e., to allow the recipient to make sense of the message, the triangular relation must be reestablished.

During the recovery process the meaning of a message does *not* have to imply something *new*, in order to transform a state of knowledge (to become information). Hence, novelty does not form part of our cognitive information conception. Thus, verification as a result of an experiment indeed produces information, although perhaps nothing new surfaces. The degree of *doubt* that made one carry out the experiment in the first place signifies the information *value* obtained. On the other hand, *falsifying* a proposition, a hypothesis or theory probably results in more dramatic information or value or a higher degree of informativeness. The degree of informativeness (or drama) attributed to information is only tangible by the receiving mind(s). In conclusion: if information were conditioned always to carry something new, only positive falsification would result in real information. Negative falsification, or verification, would consequently not be seen as informative.

2.2.4 Other Central Information Conceptions

Historically there are many understandings of information. The majority of alternative conceptions pertinent to Information Science and IS&R associate to specific elements of the conditional cognitive conception and to portions of Fig. 2.1.

At The Sign Level: Shannon, Salton and Artandi. Shannon's information concept, which, to be more accurate, originally was a measure of probability for transfer of signals forming part of his mathematical theory of communication, is very limited in scope (Shannon and Weaver 1949). The measure is concerned with the *probability of the reception* of messages or signals in the form of bits through a channel, explicitly not with the semantic aspects of messages. Shannon's information conception thus deals with the signs communicated between generator and recipient. To him *information* is simply communicated *signs*. The measure cannot be applied to IS&R where meaning in general is related to information. Neither intentionality, nor any context is present during message transfer, according to the conception. We are definitively located at the linguistic surface level during communication, and condition one is not necessarily satisfied.

Salton (and McGill 1983) identifies information with text *contents*, that is, information objects as represented by the inherent features, such as, words, image colors or (automatically extracted) index keys. Context is thus limited to such features in objects. Searchers may provide relevance feedback, but this fact does not indicate any notion of effect on the searcher, only on the system. Further, it does not provide any social communicative context, see Fig. 1.1. Salton's interest lies in isolating generated messages (texts) conveyed by signs (words and other attributes) in organized channels (information systems). Hence, implicitly Salton recognizes that contents of information objects contain, carry or have *meaning* (are meaningful or have sense), otherwise the calculation of word frequencies in texts would not be meaningful. In the framework of the cognitive information conception Salton's notion of information equals the first condition only: *information is intentional signs* placed at the linguistic surface level on the generator side, Fig. 2.1. Information systems are thus real information systems, not in any metaphorical sense. In practice Salton and most other experimental researchers in IR base their feature-based search engine algorithms on independent features of objects, that is, at a morpho-lexical level. See also Sect. 4.4.

S. Artandi (1973) attempted to make use of Shannon's information measure. She assumes the measure to form the basis for a *dual* understanding of information, different from that of Salton, and each related to different components in the communication process. One approach adheres to semiotics, i.e., essentially to *meaning* which entails intentionality: a message has meaning; the other views information as a means to *reduction* of *uncertainty* at the individual recipient side of communication.

It is clear that the reduction of uncertainty is a relevant concept in the study of human actors (searchers) and their reasons for desire of information. However, it becomes unclear how this understanding of information may be related to generation processes and to non-human recipients, for instance, machines. Albeit, machines may update their probabilities of certainty as to the recognition of signs.

With Salton, Shannon and Artandi the focus of the concept of information has moved from the areas of generated messages (contents of information objects), over the message in a channel (not its meaning), to its meaning (e.g., to the recipient or sender). This drift in focus corresponds to a move from the left to the right in Fig. 2.1, but at the linguistic surface level. Only the second Artandi's concept, reduction of individual uncertainty, can be said to reach a cognitive stage, thus being connected to knowledge, and only at the recipient side of communication.

Reduction of Uncertainty: Wersig. Also G. Wersig (1971) devoted attention to a concept associated with the reduction of uncertainty or doubt and the effect of a message on a recipient. Uncertainty (or doubt) is the end product of a *problematic situation*, in which knowledge and experience may not be sufficient in order to solve the doubt. It is important to note that Wersig's information concept operates in a situational and social context. Just as for Artandi, his concept of information only vaguely deals with the senders' states of knowledge, although he extends his information concept and communication model to include the *meaning* of the communicated message, i.e. that it makes sense, in order to explain the effect on the recipient, reducing uncertainty (Wersig 1973a). In this concept a message 'has meaning', and may 'give meaning' to the recipient.

Cognitive Communication: Belkin, Machlup, Cherry, Bateson. The 'problematic situation', i.e. what is known by the recipient to be a choice between possibilities of action, of solutions to problems, or fulfillment of factual or emotional goals or interests (authors' interpretation), is re-defined in the model, Fig. 2.1. It is the *problem space* that may be transformed into a state of uncertainty as part of the actor's cognitive/emotional model. This latter state can then be seen to be identical to the notion of the 'anomalous state of knowledge' (ASK), defined by N. Belkin (1978) to be 'the recognition of an anomaly by the recipient in his/her state of knowledge'. The ASK can be solved by communication, for example by laborious experimentation, interrogation of information systems or exchange with a human actor. In 1978 however, Belkin did not operate with a 'problematic situation' or 'problem space' functioning as the trigger for his ASK. This was first brought forward in (Belkin et al. 1982a). To the authors, the transformation in problem space into a state of uncertainty is fundamental and eventually takes place when a person cannot solve a problematic situation or fulfill an interest, a perceived work task, or a goal by himself by thinking.

Belkin made a similar distinction between two levels of communication, as does later F. Machlup (1983): a linguistic level and a *cognitive* level. Belkin (1978) suggests and argues for an information concept "explicitly based on a cognitive view of the situation with which Information Science is concerned" (p. 80). Information is here seen as a structure and Belkin proposed that (1978, p. 81):

"[The] *information* associated with a text is the generator's modified (by purpose, intent, knowledge of recipient's state of knowledge) conceptual structure which underlies the surface structure (e.g. language) of that text".

We observe the source for the first condition in our cognitive information conception. He took "that [information] system to be a recipient-controlled communication system, instigated by the recipient's anomalous state of knowledge (ASK) concerning some topic" (p. 80).

The 'recipient-control' serves to include the important notion of *desire for information*, and Belkin is right in claiming his concept to be satisfactory. It is related to states of knowledge of both generators and recipients in terms of structural transformation and it takes into account an effect, by solving the anomaly in the recipient's ASK. Belkin's model is a direct forerunner to the more elaborate model, Fig. 2.1. Simultaneously with Belkin, B.C. Brookes discussed in detail his Information Equation, founded on a cognitive perspective. For further analysis, we refer to (Ingwersen 1992, p. 30-33).

In his critical essay on the semantics of information *Machlup* followed similar principles as Belkin concerning the importance of the sender in the communication processes. In addition, he provides a definition of the concept of information in communication, broader than Wersig's but useful in its distinction between information proper and 'metaphoric information'. He states (Machlup 1983, p.657):

"[Real] information can come only from an informant. Information without an informant – without a person who tells something – is information in an only metaphoric sense ... *information is a sign* conveying to some mind or minds *a meaningful message* that may *influence* the recipients in their considerations, decisions, and actions" (emphasis by the present authors).

He pointed to C. *Cherry* who states that '[all] communication proceeds by means of signs, with which one organism affects the 'state' of another' (Cherry 1957). There are rather strong similarities between Cherry's statement and G. Bateson's central notion: information is a difference that makes a difference (1973). In Bateson's elegant conception we observe how the sender creates 'a difference' that 'makes a difference' on the side of the recipient. Machlup's, Cherry's and Bateson's understanding of information clearly distinguished between the *sign level* and the *semantic level* of a message (its meaning or sense).

2.2.5 Relations to the Conditional Cognitive Information Concept

One clearly observes that our conditional cognitive information conception, Sect. 2.1, is strongly influenced by Wersig's analyses (1971; 1973a) by including the notions of problem space and uncertainty state, however, as part of a cognitive/emotional model in a context. *Both* generator *and* recipient possess such models. This constitutes an extension of the conception as originally proposed in Ingwersen (1992). Further, our information conception reflects Machlup's (1983) and Belkin's (1978) two-level communication models. However, we explicitly include the contextual/semantic information processing level as part of the linguistic surface level. Consequently, we regard that information commonly goes beyond meaning, as discussed in Sect. 2.3.1. The first condition of our conception modifies slightly the idea of information as structure proposed by Belkin (1978, p. 81).

Isolated, the first condition refers to what M. Buckland analyses as information as signs, i.e., the tangible contents of objects (1991a; 1991b). The second condition itself refers to his notion of information as knowledge, which is as intangible as what he calls information as process. The latter notion refers to the communication process of informing, the cognitive level on Fig. 2.1. A fourth concept, information processing, refers to the tangible data processes within machines or through communication channels at linguistic surface levels.

A central issue of the cognitive information conception is related to the possibility to predict/describe the state of knowledge, i.e. the *knowledge structure* of all components (or actors) participating in the communication process. Wersig doubted this. In the authors' opinion it is possible to have a (general) idea of a *group* of recipients' states of knowledge derived from empirical investigations, or better, deliberately *to induce* a specific and controlled *work task situation* into 'problem space', creating a 'state of uncertainty' in the perceiving mind. In such experimental cases the resulting effects on the recipients (considerations, actions taken, linguistic transformations observed over time, etc.) represent *parts* of the state of knowledge that can be analyzed. Controlled empirical investigations of this line have been carried out, for instance, by C.W. Cleverdon and colleagues in relation to (human) indexer consistency (1966), by Ellis and colleagues concerning (human) inter-linker consistency (1994), by Iivonen on inter-searcher consistency (1995), by Ingwersen in relation to librarians' search procedures and use of search concepts (1982), and by Borlund using simulated work task situations in IR experiments (2000a; and Ingwersen 1997). Wang and White have recently performed a longitudinal information seeking study by observing the linguistic transformations occurring in relation to actual project task solutions (1999).

What is not possible is to have an exact model of several states of knowledge, nor to predict individual effects. This is a problem of *scientific uncertainty* inherent in the cognitive approach to information.

2.3 Implications of the Cognitive Information Conception

Below we first discuss briefly the relationship between information and meaning, and the four fundamental kinds of knowledge involved in IS&R. Then the application of the cognitive information concept to the transformation of sensory data into information is discussed, i.e., its utility in every-day information acquisition and in scientific discovery.

2.3.1 Information and Meaning

Machlup's and Cherry's understanding - as that of the authors – contrast the semantic information theory by Dretske (1981; Bonnevie 2001) in which information embedded in information systems or objects leads to meaning, i.e., something that makes sense, already at a semantic communication level. To Dretske meaning hence goes beyond information. The latter is equaled to signs or data in the common sense of those terms.

At the *cognitive level* of information processing information is seen as *supplementary* or complementary to the cognitive-emotional model of the individual actor. Thus, the information is derived from or triggered by the perceived (understood) message itself. It is basically the construct by association and *interpretation* of the perceiving mind in its time-dependent situation and context. To a receiving actor information comes to existence in a situation different from that framing the message creation at a specific point in time. This conception of information vs. meaning also bears on the generation of messages. The information to be conveyed by the generator is *supplementary* to the mere semantic values or cases expressed explicitly in the message. Information comes to life by the combination of explicit semantic values, and is often the unspoken, i.e., the *implicit values,* the idea, situation or context the message tries to depict. Speaking about IS&R, and in accordance with van Rijsbergen (1990; 1996), it is not sufficient to retrieve an adequate meaning in IR, i.e., to retrieve a relevant explicit semantic value as done in machine translation. On the other hand, automatic indexing faces severe problems if required to capture implicit values or the un-spoken. In spite of its reductionistic nature, this is the advantage of human intellectual indexing.

In this conception of meaning there is no doubt that *information goes beyond meaning.* Old archives, history studies as well as archaeology or IS&R are full of problems of interpretation of ambiguous sources, due to the lack of adequate context surrounding such sources. This is the reason why modern archival practice attempts to improve future sense-making and informativeness of the archive, and to avoid too much guess work, by adding sufficient context to the sources. The issue here and elsewhere on the thin line between meaning and information is: what is sufficient context? An insufficient portion of context may require an added context, e.g., by additional communication and information seeking acts.

Socio-linguistic conventions, and collective cognitive structures, that is, the principle of social and cognitive complementarity, play a significant role. A notable example provided by Blair is the 'Mark Twain Painting Case' (1990, p. 133) in which the information object is pictorial. Thus, we do not have any textual features to extract automatically, only image features that, in this case, are not dealt with:

[Mark Twain is visiting a house giving the reader an account of what he sees and how he interprets the situation]:

"[In] this building we saw a fine oil painting representing Stonewall Jackson's last interview with General Lee. Both men are on horseback. Jackson has just ridden up, and is accosting Lee. The picture is very valuable, on account of the portraits, which are authentic. But, like many other historical pictures, it means nothing without its label. And one label will fit as well as another:

1. First Interview Between Lee and Jackson.
2. Last Interview Between Lee and Jackson.
3. Jackson Introducing Himself to Lee.
4. Jackson Accepting Lee's Invitation to Dinner.
5. Jackson Declining Lee's Invitation to Dinner -- with Thanks.
6. Jackson Apologizing for a Heavy Defeat.
7. Jackson Reporting a Great Victory.
8. Jackson Asking Lee for a Match.

... a good legible label is usually worth, *for information*, a ton of significant attitude and expression in a historical picture" (Twain 1965, p. 216), [Emphasis by the authors].

This case demonstrates what is meant by 'cognitive diversity', 'representation', 'meaning' and 'information'. The entire quote exhibits a representation of representations of representations of ... It may convey a meaning supposedly containing at least one interpretation (information), e.g., that labeling paintings is worthwhile (for the benefit of the spectator) or that one label put on paintings will fit as well as another. To obtain any meaning (sense) the reader must at least know what a '(historical) painting' means. This semantic condition fulfilled, people not knowing this particular painting may know other historical paintings of similar nature, i.e., they may recognize some of the contents of the painting from the description and for example recall 'Wellington meeting Blücher at Waterloo'. Here, they will apply a representation by association, guided by the conventions applied in the language Mark Twain has used.

The content of the painting, which the reader actually may never have seen, is represented by at least the nine labels suggested by Twain. With imagination a few others could easily be added. These labels constitute nine interpretations, some even contradictory, of what Twain thought the painter might wish to communicate. Twain acted like an indexer. Depending on the presuppositions in the reader's mind each label may convey *information*, particular to every reader in his context. Each of the nine labels plus the description of the painting may first of all provide information to Twain himself, and now to us. For example, that there might be a matchbox in the hand of Lee; that Jackson is a smoker; that he looks exhausted and lost; or that a battle has occurred which may not be in the painting at all. These are our representations of the *information* that we got from the labels, and just now conveyed to you, the reader of this account. They are themselves messages with a certain meaning carrying information associated with them.

One might go on like this. However, one should also notice that the painting itself, hanging on the museum wall, in principle *also is a representation* of one or all the labels plus the description generated by Twain – and by us. Such iconic representations are often used on the front covers of museum catalogs because they are thought to project the content or other dimensions of the collection in a semantic way. The Bookhouse by Pejtersen (1989) used iconic representations of novels exactly because of their multidimensional and disparate informative potential.

An important aspect of the Mark Twain Painting Case is its capability of demonstrating that information predominantly goes beyond meaning – especially in non-textual media.

When the meaning of a message signifies that it *makes sense* individually or is collectively (semantically) meaningful, information may indeed also simply equal meaning. Jokes told within one culture are funny due to the prevailing context, the shared semantic memory, and a recognizable and understood situation. A slight twist of the common context may create a surprise and the significance – i.e., the unexpected sense (meaning) becomes the information and the gist of the new joke – based on known context. Here, we regard information as similar to meaning at a semantic level. Jokes can only with difficulty be transferred and provide the laugh (expression of information) in other communities or cultures, although indeed linguistically understood. But the necessary context is simply lacking on the recipient side to provide the intended interpretation and construct of information: the joke turns often into a statement not even making sense. Deliberate misinformation builds often on known shared semantics (contexts) from which the expected sense ought to lead to the desired interpretation by the recipients, i.e., to the desired (mis-)construct in their minds. Similarly, misunderstanding of messages may lead to constructs different from the intended ones. In all these cases of false, wrong, or misinformation, we talk about information as such. The information construct does not have to be true to be information.

Finally, it is central to understand human-computer interaction in light of the cognitive information conception: Messages communicated *to the system*, by a human actor or via an interface, remain constantly at a linguistic surface level. The interface may interfere at a very simplistic level, e.g., as done in best match retrieval by 'analyzing' the incoming request and assigning weights. The degree of uncertainty will commonly be high as to making 'sense' of the message by the mechanisms involved. Their algorithmic structures (their 'state of knowledge') may indeed change (effect), e.g., according to frequency thresholds or alike pre-defined inferences, but they remain at a linguistic level of communication: only the first condition of the information concept defined above is satisfied. Messages communicated *from the system,* including to and from an interface mechanism, remain at a linguistic level until they conceivably transform a human cognitive state by turning into information. The human state of uncertainty may be high, depending on the degree and adequacy of context provided by the system (including the interface) and the human actor. Thus, only in case of human recipients during IS&R interaction we may talk of *information transfer*.

2.3.2 Basic Knowledge Types in IS&R

When talking of states of knowledge that become represented or changed following our conditional information conception it is of importance to distinguish between the kinds of such knowledge states or cognitive structures. We make a distinction between communication of *domain* and *IS&R* knowledge. Typically, Winograd and Flores' analyses (1986) concentrated on the system structures, such as screen features or commands, and their informativeness, e.g., in word processing. In IS&R it is vital to understand both types of cognitive structures, because the domain knowledge constitutes the original cause for seeking and retrieval behavior: the work task or daily-life task or interest and the desire for information. The IS&R knowledge reflects search task skills.

Ingwersen (1992, p. 36) suggested three kinds of knowledge: passive, active, and conceptual. The structures relate to the syntactic tool-specific knowledge, semantic tool-specific knowledge, and semantic task-specific knowledge of the Syntactic and Semantic Object and Action (SSOA) model by Shneiderman (1998). The authors feel that Ingwersen's terms (1992) are ambiguous and inconsistent with related concepts in other fields. Consequently, and for reasons of clarity, we now refer to passive knowledge as 'declarative knowledge' and active knowledge as 'procedural knowledge'.

Declarative knowledge may appear as 1) declarative *IS&R knowledge* embedded in, or about, the system setting, like database structures or information sources, essentially knowledge of how to perform searches with the system, or as 2) declarative *domain knowledge* embedded in, or about, information objects, such as text, concepts, pictures or tasks.

Procedural knowledge is inherently activity-related and includes 3) procedural *IS&R knowledge* embedded in, or about, algorithms within the system setting, like retrieval or weighting algorithms, search task execution skills, or as 4) procedural *domain knowledge*, such as problem and work task solving knowledge.

It is central for the understanding of IS&R processes that all four knowledge types are taken into account. In contrast to Winograd and Flores (1986), who concentrate their efforts on the declarative and procedural system-related knowledge types, IS&R research must involve the domain-related types too: they are concerned with the work task or interest perception, the information gap, problem and task solving as well as relevance assessments and further use of information.

2.4 Information Acquisition: From Sensory Data to Scientific Discovery

How is it at all possible to acquire information, cognition and knowledge from signals, manifestations and other alike phenomena – *not* deriving from intentional transformations of knowledge – but being products of nature? In Sect. 2.2 we proposed that the conditional cognitive information conception could be generalized to include acquisition of information from sensory data, that is, in a range of cases for which the first condition of the conception does not apply (or hardly applies). Hence, the ensuing sections attempt to deal with such phenomena. First, information acquisition is discussed for situations where the first condition just holds but the means of communication (the language) is unknown to the recipient actor. This was presumably not the intentionality of the original creator and the perception and transformation of cognitive state is thus difficult (the second condition is also problematic): the Japanese Text Case. Secondly, we examine how information acquisition may occur when no intentionality and knowledge transfer is behind the creation of signs – as may happen in nature. This case is named the Okawango Pursuit. Third, we discuss scientific information acquisition leading to knowledge discovery of phenomena for which no conscious actor, i.e., nature itself, is responsible. All cases are kinds of information seeking behavior.

K. Popper's Three-World Ontology (1973) is a quite useful framework for dealing with the different types of knowledge and data, signals or signs involved in IS&R and Information Science – as already proposed by Brookes (1977; 1980). The ontology consists of objective knowledge (World 3), i.e., man-made sign structures, such as, buildings, boats, books or computer files, made out of natural substance (World 1) as knowledge carriers by instigation of World 2. Subjective knowledge (World 2) signifies the cognitive spaces of individuals and communities. The interaction between World 2 and 3 can be said to constitute information interaction being the focus for Information Science and IS&R (as well as focus for other sciences, like archaeology, history or literature history). Brookes, however, centered on World 3. The World 1, that is, the natural artifacts, is not included and discussed in Brookes' proposal. The relation between Worlds 2 and 1 is of interest, since it is from nature (un-intentional sensory data and signals) that World 2 often deducts cognition that is stored in World 3 by means of signs. Without a World 2 World 1 absorbs the present World 3.

2.4.1 Information Acquisition from Unknown Signs

The Japanese Text Case, Fig. 2.4, demonstrates cultural contextual issue and point to how a non-Japanese visitor (World 2) may grasp the pictorial signs (World 3) in a quite cumbersome way – eventually leading to information.

A Japanese author of directive scripts has created the sign, depicted at the lower left-hand side of the Fig. 2.4, to be placed along the path in one of the temple gardens near Kyoto, Japan. There are several of them and each is mounted on a metal stick with an arrow pointing in a direction. The Danish temple visitor does not know any written Japanese. He is alone, so he cannot follow any Japanese visitors towards the exit somewhere. First he thinks that the sign may mean the bathroom and – considering himself smart – he assumes from his own cultural context (B) that the bathroom is located near the exit. By applying these pre-suppositions the visitor gambles that similarities exist between the two cultures. This shows up to be true when the signs stop. He can get out of the garden.

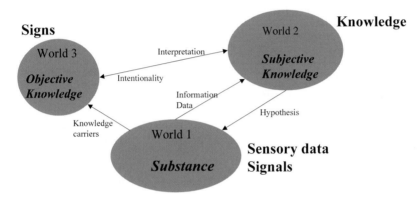

Fig. 2.3. Popper's Three World Ontology as interpreted by the authors

However, the visitor now faces the problem of remembering this vital sign for other occasions in the future. By dividing the sign into its two monadic elements the visitor may put an understanding or idea on the first element, seeing it as a tree. The second element looks like a gate – and the combination quite logically has the meaning: tree and gate/door signifies 'outside a building'. This *interpretation* is partly derived directly from the visitor's cognitive model, i.e., problem space and uncertainty state that become reduced by the current cognitive state (by deduction). Partly it originates from the visitor's interpretation of his Danish past experiences framed by his current context B.[4] This way of acquiring information by first understanding the meaning of an unknown sign (in an unknown language, but in a perceived situation in context), and then making an interpretation that supposedly fits the reality is very cumbersome. The visitor

---

[4] As a curious fact, in Denmark at Christmas time the custom is to place a Christmas tree *inside* the houses. This context might hence have altered the interpretation completely. Further, the second monadic element actually signifies a "mouth" or gate in Japan.

(recipient) moves step-by-step up through the four stages of information processing towards the cognitive pragmatic stage, Sect. 2.1.1.

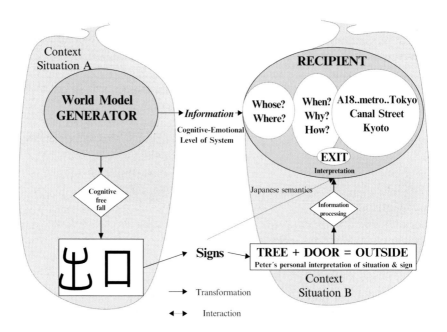

Fig. 2.4. The Japanese Text Case. Practical interpretation of the cognitive communication system, as illustrated in Fig. 2.1

The next time he observes that sign, for instance, in a Tokyo metro station, he acts with a Japanese understanding (semantics), knowing where there exists an exit. Of course, the visitor now may be in trouble, since the Tokyo metro stations are large with many exits: which to take in order to get to the Keio university? That uncertainty may also face the busy Japanese person who has the advantage of immediately knowing the significance of the 'exit' signs, due to his common cultural and linguistic context (semantics). But which exit to take? Fortunately for our Japanese friend (and unfortunate for the visitor), the street names are indicated in Japanese signs so he is not likely to be in a problematic situation for long.

2.4.2 Information Acquisition from Sensory Data: The Okawango Pursuit

The Okawango Delta is located close to the Kalahari Desert as a part of Botswana up against Northern Namibia – a World 1 representative. Rivers feed the delta running west carrying the sparse rains that arrive in Eastern Botswana every year with the tropical storms coming from the Indian Ocean, far to the East. The delta is vast, full of lagoons and river arms, but runs dry into the desert plain. Many animals and birds are found in the delta and it is consequently worth special boat safaris.

In one such safari two boats were participating (World 3), each with a local guide driving the boat and a couple of tourists (World 2). The boats left early in the morning to avoid the worst of the African heat, but one boat was rather faster than the other. After some time the second boat could not any more observe the first – and the second local guide did not know the final destination of the trip. The water surface was still and no spoor seemed to be leading to the first boat. At least the tourists could not detect any clues as to where the boat had passed through the maze-like area of reeds and water lilies under the gleaming sun. What amazed them was the speed by which the second local guide tried to catch up with the first boat. He went left, then right through the tunnels of reed without hesitation. One of the tourists asked him during the pursuit how he could be so sure where to go, which of the many channels to take. The local guide replied, still concentrating on the waterways and the boat course: 'You see the reeds to the right? They are still wet over the still water surface. The boat has passed that way turning up the water on to the reeds. Getting here before half an hour after the boat has passed will show the wet reeds and the track. Later, the water has disappeared from the reeds in the heat!' – 'Only half an hour', exclaimed the tourists to one another and looked at their watches. 'But what if we are farther behind?' – the local guide smiled: 'Then there are the water lilies, you see. They turn around with the boat screw, and turn right again after two hours – look there! – Of course, after two hours we are lost!'

In this case the tracks were made by man, i.e., his passing boat, but unintentional. We could also say that the watermarks on the reeds depended on the time of the day, the heat, and that it did not rain. In a way nature (World 1 as carrier) was responsible for the spoor (World 3) to be followed by somebody with relevant *pre-suppositions* and experiences. The tourists did not have a clue but that guide did. He also made a couple of *hypotheses* and predictions, for instance, that the higher waterline was made by the boat, and thus should be continuous, and not made by a hippo swimming across the channel at a particular spot. By concentrating on the surrounding reeds, water lilies, animal positions, etc., he constantly *tested* his hypotheses. In this daily-life information acquisition situation the experienced guide *verified* his hypotheses and received information on the course to follow. One could say that he mixed interaction with World 1 (the reeds) and World 3 as if the former was the latter. Falsification of the hypotheses by the testing (e.g. observing no up-turned water lilies) would have posed a problem that might have led to disaster.

The essential elements of all information acquisition are thus the past experiences, situations and *contexts* which, under influence of intellectual processing in a mind, produce *pre-suppositions* that in a present *situation* may serve as intentional trigger for creative *hypotheses* to be *tested* empirically, producing data that is *interpreted* – see Fig. 2.5.

The interesting consequence is that the human recipient of sensory data (the visible spoors or other natural effects not completely fulfilling the first condition of the cognitive information conception) *simultaneously becomes a sender* or generator of data on which a certain structure is superimposed by means of a hypothesis. The data structure (and flow) is conveyed to the recipient as signs due to his concentration and attention on selected sensory data framed by the hypothesis. By testing the hypotheses the person (man, a guide, a hunter, a scientist) becomes part of a communication process for which the first condition for information *then* is satisfied, by him or herself, so to speak. His/her problem is the *interpretation* of the test results and involves knowledge, experience, ethics, honesty, etc. The interpretation may lead to acceptance of the hypothesis (and theory) - but it may also lead to a degree of uncertainty or complete rejection of the hypothesis (and theory) or of the test method applied.

The Okawango Pursuit case demonstrates in addition that information *does not have to be new* – see also section 2.2.3. When verifying a hypothesis the verification is obviously hoped for. A positive outcome is information – as is a negative outcome.

Another dimension of the case is the issue of intentionally generated spoors (signs) by transformation of knowledge and experience made by non-human species, i.e., nature: elephants are well known for deliberately walking in circles in order to come up behind the pursuing hunter. Its spoors are hence intentional and based on its ideas of the recipient minds (of the hunters). Condition one of the cognitive information conception is thus satisfied. The hunter may evidently misinterpret the spoor pattern and be misinformed; yet, the second condition of the information concept is fulfilled. Similar situations exist for dolphins and their inter-dolphin communication. The observing scientist (the recipient) is located in the black box of the Chinese Room case, section 2.2.2, or in the Japanese Text case, without any clue as to what is communicated. But he or she may produce some hypotheses due to theories of observed dolphin behavior. These may be wrong or partly right or pure speculation. To the dolphin the signals are evidently information.

2.4.3. Information Acquisition in Scientific Discovery

Scientific discovery follows the same route as in daily-life situations. The difference is that the conventions nowadays for the variety of disciplines are more pointed than for common situations. Certain rules have to be followed, whether in the Humanities, the Social Sciences or in the Sciences.

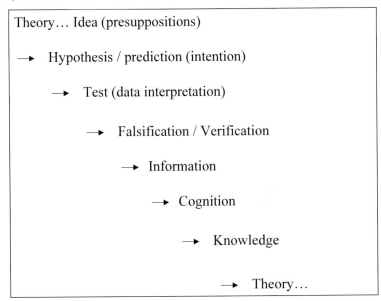

Fig. 2.5. Simplistic stages for scientific discovery

Fig. 2.5 demonstrates the basic elements in the scientific work, as introduced in the previous section. The scientist has a goal, an idea and perhaps an already established theory. From that theory he generates a hypothesis about the world. Tycho Brahe was one of the last astronomers to make observations only by eyesight. He created a vast data collection of positions of the stars and planets. At that time (late 16th Century) the theory about our universe adhered to the so-called Ptolemaic cosmology with the Earth as center and the sun and stars turning around in spheres. The problem was that the planets did not behave as they were supposed to in their orbits, according to the prevailing cosmology. Their courses were erratic. The hypothesis was that the observations available were not exact enough. Hence the cumbersome work by Tycho Brahe. In a way we may say that his data collection activity was made in order to *verify* the prevailing theory (the Ptolemaic cosmology). He did not himself manage to carry out the proper calculations of the new orbits. Copernicus did that later on and made a discovery of consequence! The observations did not suit the prevailing cosmology. In fact they suited much better an inverted cosmology, that of the helio-centric system. The original observations – made for verifying and improving the original cosmology – succeeded in *falsifying* that theory and to suggest a more suitable one. In fact, the observations were later also used by Keppler to produce his Laws.

To Tycho Brahe starlight and his observations of star positions were built on a hypothesis (albeit wrong) that guided his way of making the observations. He consequently concentrated his attention on specific patterns of starlight and superimposed *his* intentionality on them in data collection. He thus became a generator *and* recipient at the same time of the communicated signals, originally generated by nature without purpose.

The same data set may thus provide very different information constructs, cognition and knowledge, later to be put into theoretical patterns that may produce novel hypotheses. It all depends on the nature of the *presuppositions* and context that are applied as well as creativity and courage to allow a falsification to lead to unexpected conclusions.

3 The Development of Information Seeking Research

This Chapter reviews the developments in information seeking from about 1960 to 2000 and beyond. The sixties were the time when information seeking research expanded. A major event for information seeking was the 1958 Conference on Scientific Information. From 1960 to mid-1980's information seeking research produced survey type studies on information seeking in institutional contexts. The period form 1986 to 2000 was a period of reorientation in information seeking research. The critical review of information seeking research by Dervin and Nilan (1986) set forth a revolution in the area. Their main claim was that the mainstream information seeking studies were too narrowly (library) systems-oriented. Consequently, the focus of Information Seeking shifted towards human actors. Several projects based on an actor-centered approach were started and some produced empirical findings already in the 1980's. Also the theoretical understanding of the field evolved during the last part of the 1980's. In the 1990's, several process-oriented and longitudinal studies of information seeking were published.

We shall consider the research questions and major results of information seeking research in the period 1960 - 2000. We provide brief references to review literature, followed by models developed for research. The models illustrate the research done and point out the limitations of the research based on them. We shall also discuss research methodology as well as the limitations and open problems of this area. This Chapter is not intended to be a literature review and thus only representative studies and findings will be discussed. The reader wishing to obtain a better coverage of the literature is referred to the many reviews published in the Annual Review of Information Science and Technology (ARIST) as a secondary source of literature (although its coverage of essential European research literature could be better). Menzel (1966), Herner and Herner (1967), Paisley (1968), Allen (1969), Lipetz (1970), Crane (1971), Lin and Garvey (1972), Martyn (1974), Crawford (1978), and Dervin and Nilan (1986) have reviewed this period of information seeking research in ARIST. Hewins (1990), Allen (1991), Jacobs and Shaw (1998), Ingwersen (2001b) and Vakkari (2003) have reviewed the more recent period of information seeking and related research in ARIST. Some of them are discussed below and the rest in Chapt. 4. Donald O. Case (2002) contributed a recent survey of research on information seeking, needs and behavior.

3.1 Research Questions and Findings

3.1.1 Overviews of the Literature

In general, the early studies on information seeking (1960 to 1985) were limited in many ways. They provided a distorted image of information seeking, which was mainly seen from the information systems viewpoint. Thus, they typically investigated user behavior almost solely within the framework of the information systems or institutions. There was more focus on system needs than user needs. Another approach in many studies was to view people as members of sociological groups and then to assess group information needs for systems development. There were several conceptual and methodological problems (e.g., Brittain 1975; Dervin and Nilan 1986; Hewins 1990; Kunz et al. 1977a; Wersig 1973a). From the cognitive viewpoint, the bulk of early information seeking research was limited.

Elizabeth Hewins (1990) reviewed the literature 1986 to 1990 in information seeking for ARIST. She sought to find out whether the Dervin and Nilan (1986) review, with its suggested emerging research approaches had made an impact on the literature. Is there a shift from information seeking studies driven by a systems focus or by a sociological group focus to studies driven by real user studies – actors as individuals in concrete situations? She found several studies in Medical Informatics that extended to the use and impact of information in medical decision-making. Within Information Science proper she observed a clear shift of focus toward actors: while old paradigms still produce further papers, most of the literature falls under new approaches with actors in the center. The new concerns are analyzing (1) individual differences for systems design and (2) common cognitions (and behaviors) of users. These studies formed the new mainstream but still lacked well-defined conceptual frameworks. Carol Kuhlthau's work (1991; discussed below) on information seeking processes, Belkin's and his colleagues work on cognitive modeling (see Sect. 5.2.2 on user-oriented and cognitive IR), and Saracevic's and his colleagues work (1988a) on IS&R were major contributions (see Sect. 5.4.4). Hewins also pointed out the relevance of the literature of cognitive Psychology, Computer Science, Linguistics, Philosophy, and Management Science for studies of cognitive processes and IS&R. She also argued that systems or interface design should not be the primary goal of research in IS&R – it should rather be new theories and conceptual frameworks for IS&R.

Pertti Vakkari (1997) reviewed the literature on information seeking in his conclusion to the ISIC 1996 (Information Seeking in Context) Conference. He saw the conference papers, and the domain at large, reflecting positive trends in information seeking research: more varied and holistic theoretical/methodological approaches, increasingly viewing information seeking contextually or situationally embedded in other activities, increased process orientation and longitudinal approaches, and professionalization of research. Information needs were no more studied as ends in themselves but rather as embedded in the actions they support. Theoretical and methodological ideas drawn from other disciplines, management and communication studies, Social Psychology and Psychology, in particular, were used in the studies.

Linda Schamber (1994) reviewed the literature on relevance for ARIST. This is discussed in Sect. 5.7.2 on IR in more detail but is also relevant here because Schamber also reviews some relevance research outside the computerized information seeking context. Generally speaking, the literature contributes to the holistic situational view of relevance, affected by the actor and his/her knowledge and experience, task or current problems, and the context or situation in which these take place. Relevance criteria are many and they vary along task processes. Relevance is a cognitive, situational and dynamic phenomenon. Schamber's review was followed by many empirical and conceptual analyses of relevance, e.g., by Saracevic (1996), Mizzaro (1997), and Cosijn and Ingwersen (2000).

Peter Ingwersen (2001b) reviewed the literature on cognitive IR for ARIST. His focus is analytic and empirical research on the complex nature of information need formation and situation, their inherent association with the concept of relevance, and the development of cognitive and related IR theory and evaluation methods. This is discussed in more detail in Chapt. 5. Ingwersen notes that recent theoretical models, research approaches and empirical findings have increased the possibility of creating a unified theory of IS&R – or at least the possibility of a comprehensive research framework or program has increased.

Karen Pettigrew, Raya Fidel and Harry Bruce (2001) reviewed the literature on conceptual frameworks in information behavior. They look both at cognitive, social and multifaceted approaches. They conclude that a new unifying theoretical body is emerging, emphasizing the contextual interplay of cognitive, social, cultural, organizational, affective, and linguistic factors.

Finally, Pertti Vakkari (2003) reviewed the literature on task-based information searching for ARIST. His review focuses on IR and spans from task requirements to information seeking and retrieval. He makes a strong case for the argument that tasks need to be taken into account for understanding and explaining information searching (and seeking). Vakkari clarifies the differences between work tasks and search tasks, Sect. 6.2.3, and discusses dependent and independent variables in explaining IR in a useful way for task-based information seeking. The review also covers the limited literature on document selection and use, as well as the impact of searching and document selection on task outcome.

3.1.2 Information Seeking Models

In 1966 - 1981 several models for information seeking were created. They were to a large extent based on analytical thinking, drawing on different sociological and/or psychological paradigms, but also to some degree reflecting the empirical work done. It remains as a matter of argument whether they served later empirical work more as icons than really as guides to setting research problems and explaining research results. Nevertheless, the models by Paisley (1968), Allen (1969) and Wilson (1981) are examples of the best theoretical thinking in Information Seeking of their period. In these early models, the concepts of information, information need, information seeking and use were left open. These models identified many factors affecting information behavior but did not analyze work tasks and the individual's specific situation / context in detail. They were thus interpreted as legitimizing research focusing on information systems or services in isolation and providing, as icons, the theoretical foundation for such studies. This resulted in a large number of Library and Information Science studies on information seeking which have been heavily criticized later on (see Sect. 3.3). However, the models cannot be fully blamed for their questionable applications.

T.D. Wilson (1999) stated that "a model may be described as a framework for thinking about a problem and may evolve into a statement of the relationships among theoretical propositions. Most models in the general field of information behavior are of the former variety: they are statements, often in the form of diagrams, that attempt to describe an information-seeking activity, the causes and consequences of that activity, or the relationships among stages in information-seeking behavior. Rarely do such models advance to the stage of specifying relationships among theoretical propositions: rather, they are at a pre-theoretical stage, but may suggest relationships that might be fruitful to explore or test." The limitation of models, however, is that they do little more than provide a map of the area: they do not analyze causative factors in information behavior and, therefore, do not directly suggest hypotheses to be tested. (Wilson 1999)

We shall discuss in detail some *more recent* models in information behavior research. Here we focus on, e.g., Dervin's Sense-making Approach (1983; and Nilan 1986), Ellis' (1989; Ellis et al. 1993) information seeking features, Kuhlthau's (1991) process model, and Wilson's (Wilson and Walsh 1996) model on information behavior. To this we add a further model on task-based information seeking, originated by Byström and Järvelin (1995) and further developed by Vakkari and Kuokkanen (1997; Vakkari 1998), and Wilson's (1999) problem solving model. Finally, we shall introduce discourse analysis (Talja 1997; 1998; Tuominen 2001; Tuominen and Savolainen 1997). There are other recent models deserving attention, e.g., the professionals' information seeking model (Leckie et al. 1996), or an information acquisition model for decision-making (Saunders and Jones 1990). However, due to limited space we shall by pass them.

The Sense-Making Approach. Brenda Dervin and Michael Nilan (1986) called for a new paradigm for the research into information seeking processes which would view information as being constructed and information seeking as a situation-sensitive sense-making process. It should focus on the information seekers (*actors* instead of users) and assess information systems from their viewpoint. The proposed approach is known as the Sense-making Approach to information needs and seeking. Dervin and Nilan provided a model for the new approach. Dervin and others have published several studies based on the Sense-making Approach (see below).

Dervin and Nilan proposed that information seeking requires approaches that can be characterized as focusing on subjective information which is constructed by the actors; constructive, active users (or actors) as opposed to passive receivers of information from systems; situations in which the actors act (as opposed to situation-independence). Moreover, information seeking research needs a holistic view on information seeking, taking into account events/actions preceding and following information system use; internal (or cognitive) conceptions (instead on external behavior); systematic individualism (instead of considering individual features as leading to chaos); and qualitative rather than quantitative research methodologies.

Dervin and Nilan suggested that information seeking should look upon information as constructed by humans, and upon humans as actors who are free to construct, on the basis of systems and contexts, whatever they wish. Information use should be seen as situational (or contextual) and events/actions preceding and following information system use should be understood. Systems should be seen from the users' point of view, not the contrary. These views directly support the cognitive viewpoint developed in this book.

The Sense-making Approach has developed over a number of years, and consists of "...a set of assumptions, a theoretic perspective, a methodological approach, a set of research methods ..." to cope with information perceived as "...a human tool designed for making sense of a reality assumed to be both chaotic and orderly." (Dervin 1983). Later she states, that the approach is a set of meta-theoretic assumptions and propositions about the nature of information, human use of information and communicating. Sense-making itself can be defined as behavior, both internal (i.e. cognitive) and external (i.e. procedural), which allows the individual to construct and design his/her movement through time-space. Sense-making behavior, thus, is communicating behavior. (Dervin 1992; 1999)

The Sense-making Approach contains some basic assumptions about human reality, including assumptions on moving, process, discontinuity, situationality, gap-bridging, and information seeking. Individuals are assumed to continuously move through time and space, and sense-making is a process of taking steps. Reality is assumed discontinuous, and sense-making is assumed to be situational rather than explainable through personal traits. Step-taking is interrupted when a gap is encountered. This requires information to be bridged. Information seeking is an individual process of construction, not a process of utilizing ready-made information bricks.

The Sense-making Approach can be modeled as consisting of situations, gaps and helps, and outcomes. A person proceeds in her task and situation (the context of task and information problems) and runs into a gap that blocks progress. She needs to make sense of the situation in order to proceed, i.e., to find helps for bridging the gap and reaching the outcomes (Fig. 3.1).

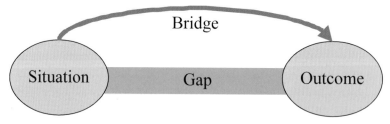

Fig. 3.1. The Sense-making Approach illustrated (based on Dervin 1983)

Dervin (1983) provides several dimensions for analyzing situations, gaps and helps that may be used depending on the goals of investigation. Some of the dozen situation dimensions are:

- Situation movement state: how was the actor's motion stopped? This one has several heuristic subcategories, like wash-out and barrier.
- Situation clarity: how unclear or fuzzy is the actor's interpretation of her situation?
- Situation embeddedness: how does the actor see her situation connected to other situations?
- Social embeddedness: how much is the actor's situation connected to other persons?
- Situation importance: how important is the situation to the actor?
- Power to change: does the actor think herself able to change her situation?

Some of the 15 gap dimensions are:

- Ease of answering – reasons for difficulty in this;
- Question connectedness (to other questions);
- Importance of answering – and reasons for this;
- Answering success – reasons for the lack of success; - and sources; and
- Gap-bridging strategies – which strategies did the actor employ in gap bridging?

Some of the help dimensions relate to the uses of information, which helped in:

- Obtaining a picture or generating ideas,
- Planning,
- Situation management,
- Getting away from an unpleasant situation, or
- Avoiding an unpleasant situation.

These dimensions are not always mutually exclusive. Nevertheless they represent dimensions of the difficulties and ways to cope with them, which one may encounter in sense-making or IS&R. Therefore they provide ideas for the cognitive analysis of situations, gaps and helps.

Dervin (1997) reviews the concept of *context* as used in social science and communication studies literature. She states that no term like context is more often used, less often defined, and when defined, defined so variously. On the one hand, context may be almost anything that is not defined as the phenomenon of interest. On the other hand, context may be assumed as an inextricable surround, always particular and thus never generalizable.

There are strongly opposing views on the concept. Dervin's findings challenge all uses of "context" as an explanatory factor in information seeking studies. Our understanding of context is described in Sects. 2.1.4, 6.0, and 6.2.2.

Dervin (1999) discusses the ontological and epistemological issues related to the Sense-making Approach, now called the Sense-making Methodology. The article seeks to exemplify how the Sense-making Methodology bridges the gap from meta-theory to research methods. The methodology tries to avoid tacit assumptions of information as inherently helpful (it may be harmful). Likewise, the methodology tries to avoid tacit assumptions of human frailties or incompetence as a barrier between an actor and information – this may or may not be the case.

Dervin's sense-making metaphor, considered as a model, is fairly broad in its attempt to cover information seeking (while not modeling work tasks). It is a process model in the basics of its metaphor of situations, gaps, and bridges. It is an abstract model since situations, gaps, and bridges are abstract and may entail many quite different objects and actors. As such, it is a summary model, not directly suggesting analyzable relationships. Finally, it is a general model, claiming applicability over a range of empirical domains.

Being highly abstract, the sense-making metaphor of situations, gaps and bridges might be applicable to many levels (e.g., individuals, organizations) of information seeking and use in all kinds of contexts. The abstractness also produces a weakness: the metaphor does not say much about information seeking in various contexts and does not suggest testable hypotheses. Sense-making does not mandate particular research questions as much as a way of *looking* at all research questions (Dervin 1999).

Savolainen (1992; 1993) discusses the merits of the Sense-making Approach as a research paradigm. He points-out the problems that the core concepts of the approach are defined metaphorically and that the approach is highly individual-centered. On the other hand, its basic assumptions regarding its research objectives are explicit and its methodological basis is elaborated. Discourse analytical approaches by Talja and Tuominen also assume a critical position toward the early Sense-making Approach while build on the more recent one (see below).

From the cognitive point of view, the Sense-making Approach was an essential step forward in Information Seeking. It draws attention to individual sense-making (problem solving) in varying situations, and focuses on the actor and process viewpoints rather than a systems (or traditional assumptions') viewpoint. It opened up the chaotic variety in real information behavior but also provided methodologies to deal with it. While focusing on individuals it did not exclude the study of sense making as a social phenomenon. It admitted that by studying individual (chaotic) variation, systematic underlying features of information seeking may be found.

Ellis' Feature Set. David Ellis (1989; Ellis, Cox and Hall 1993; Ellis and Haugan 1997) has identified eight features of information seeking behaviour, which seem to characterise the information seeking patterns of scientists, engineers and social scientists in both academic and industrial settings. These features are as follows (Ellis and Haugan 1997):

- *Starting:* activities such as the initial search for an overview of the literature or locating key people working in the field;
- *Chaining:* following footnotes and citations in known material or 'forward' chaining from known items through citation indexes, or proceeding in personal networks;
- *Browsing:* variably directed and structured scanning of primary and secondary sources;
- *Differentiating:* using known differences in information sources as a way of filtering the amount of information obtained;
- *Monitoring:* regularly following developments in a field through particular formal and informal channels and sources;
- *Extracting:* selectively identifying relevant material in an information source;
- *Verifying:* checking the accuracy of information;
- *Ending:* activities actually finishing the information seeking process.

Ellis (1989) provides a slightly different but comparable package of six features. This set of features has emerged from a sequence of empirical studies. Ellis (1989, p. 178) admits that "... the detailed interrelation or interaction of the features in any individual information seeking pattern will depend on the unique circumstances of the information seeking activities of the person concerned at that particular point in time". Also Ellis and Haugan (1997, p. 388) leave the interrelations of these activities open. Wilson (1999) proposes how the features may relate to each other temporally (Fig. 3.2).

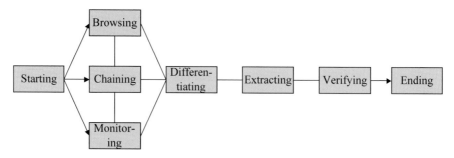

Fig. 3.2. A process version of Ellis's feature set (Wilson 1999)

Ellis calls the features a behavioural model of information seeking patterns. However, he also states that the model does not attempt to specify the exact relationships of the activities or their order, because this is likely to vary. One may *describe,* at a general level, many information seeking activities through Ellis's features. Indeed, they are general enough to fit a large number of empirical situations. However, if one is to *explain* information seeking behaviour, say, in terms of the work tasks the subjects are engaged with, or their knowledge of the task, the features fall short because they are not explicitly related to such external possible causative factors. Neither is there any possibility to predict the order in which the categories appear in an individual seeking process. In fact, Ellis and Haugan (1997) consider several project types and their relationships on information needs and sources, but do not develop this into a model to be tested.

Ellis's features provide a set of categories, which may serve the analysis of information seeking at the individual level. In our approach, based on the cognitive viewpoint, such categories need to be connected with other categories describing actors' tasks, situation, and information systems, among others. Ellis (1989) discussed the extent to which these categories are available in existing IR systems and proposed the use of the categories as a framework for organizing recommendations for IR systems design. It is desirable from the cognitive point of view to have such features at the actor's disposal as access strategies. However, the categories do not provide directly any design specifications for the systems. Instead, they represent types of activities the users of the systems might want to accomplish through the systems. Then the question becomes whether, and to what degree, the systems do support, or can be made to support, these activities.

Ellis's feature set, considered as a model, is fairly broad in its attempt to cover information seeking but narrow in not covering tasks or retrieval. It is explicitly a process model of fairly concrete process steps. As such, it is a summary model, not directly suggesting analyzable relationships. Finally, it is a general model, claiming applicability and validity over a range of empirical domains.

Kuhlthau's Process Model. Carol C. Kuhlthau (1991; 1993a) has shown in a series of longitudinal empirical studies that learning tasks and problem solving by students and library users consist of several stages. A model emerged from these studies and it maintains that people search for and use information differently depending on the stage of the process. The stages of Kuhlthau's model are as follows:

- Initiation, becoming aware of the need for information, when facing a problem;
- Selection, the general topic for seeking information is identified and selected;
- Exploration, seeking and investigating information on the general topic;
- Focus formulation, fixing and structuring the problem to be solved;
- Collection, gathering pertinent information for the focused topic;
- Presentation, completing seeking, reporting and using the result of the task.

Stages	Initiation	Selection	Exploration	Formulation	Collection	Presentation
Feelings	Uncertainty	Optimism	Confusion, frustration, doubt	Clarity	Sense of direction, confidence	Relief, satisfaction or disappointment
Thoughts	Vague			Clearer	Increased interest	Focused
Actions	Seeking background information		Seeking relevant information		Seeking pertinent information	
Appropriate tasks	Recognize	Identify, investigate	Identify, investigate	Formulate	Gather	Complete

Fig. 3.3. Kuhlthau's model illustrated (1991)

Along the stages of the process, also the actor's feelings, thoughts and actions change (Fig. 3.3). Prior to focus formation the actor feels uncertain and her thoughts are general, fragmentary and vague, and actions involve seeking background information. The actor is unable to formulate her task and express precisely the kind of information needed. After focus formation, information seeking becomes more directed and the thoughts about the task clearer and more structured. This leads the actor to seek relevant, focused information using the whole range of information resources. Feelings change from uncertainty and frustration toward certainty and confidence. At the end of the process re-checking searches are made for possible additional information. (Kuhlthau 1991; 1993a)

Kuhlthau's model is not a plain cognitive model since it also describes the changes of feelings along the stages of the process. This is based on Kelly's *personal construct theory*, which *"... describes the affective experience of individuals involved in the process of constructing meaning from the information they encounter."*(Kuhlthau 1993a). Her central thesis is that an actor's problems in information seeking are characterized by uncertainty and confusion, which may lead to anxiety (Kuhlthau 1991).

Kuhlthau's early work was based on longitudinal studies of high school students writing essays. This means that the students' tasks were fairly complex. In particular, Kuhlthau's tasks involved the pre-focus stages. This means that the actor needs to formulate the task or problem, it is not routine enough to be memorized and directly applicable. Later she has shown the applicability of her model to the work of a securities analyst (Kuhlthau 1997; 1999). Nevertheless, task complexity varies in real life, and so do the actual stages of task and information seeking processes (see below the Byström and Järvelin model, and Sect. 6.2.5.)[1]

Kuhlthau's model is fairly broad in its attempt to cover information seeking (while not modeling work tasks). It is explicitly a process model of fairly concrete process steps and associated abstract concepts (feelings, thoughts). It is an analytical model, directly suggesting relationships between process stages and feelings, thoughts and actions. Finally, it seeks to be a general model, claiming applicability and validity over a range of empirical domains, but may depend on the particular kind of work tasks ("term papers") on which it is based.

Wilson (1999) explores whether the Ellis and Kuhlthau models may be brought together, and roughly maps them to each other by associating from starting / initiation to ending / presentation – compare Figs. 3.2 and 3.3. As Wilson notes, the two models are nevertheless opposed: Kuhlthau posits stages on the basis of her analysis of behavior, while Ellis suggests that the sequences of behavioral characteristics may vary. An explanation may reside in Kuhlthau's data consisting of single-sorted processes – all being assigned term paper projects – while Ellis collected data on multi-sorted processes, that is, on work tasks of various kinds.

Vakkari (2001b) extended Kuhlthau's model in the field of IR based on a series of empirical studies (see Sect. 5.1). The explanatory factor of the model – stages in task performance – was the same, and some factors to be explained – information types needed, search tactics, term choices and relevance judgments – were specified and connected to the stages.

---

[1] Also pointed out by Elbaek and Skovvang (2003).

Wilson's Model on Information Behavior. T.D. Wilson (1997; 1999) revised his earlier model on information behavior (1981), drawing upon an extensive review of research from a variety of fields other than information science, including decision-making, psychology, innovation, health communication, and consumer research (Fig. 3.4). He proposed theories of these disciplines to be used in the analysis of information behavior.

According to the model, information seeking is activated in a context, has various modes (including passive attention), and results in information processing and use, which provides a necessary feedback loop when the needs are satisfied. The intervening variables may be supportive and / or preventive of information use. Wilson said that the model has been simplified by showing the intervening variables only at one point while some of them may intervene between context and the activating mechanism, between the activating mechanism and information seeking behavior, and between information seeking behavior and information processing and use.

Wilson (1997) claimed that the other disciplines considered in his review offer many analytical concepts, models and theories that have been ignored by information scientists and urgently need to be incorporated into Information Science. In particular, he suggested the relevance of stress/coping theory, risk/reward theory, and social learning theory as relevant theories to explore in information seeking. In Wilson's (1999) view the model remains as one of macro-behavior while the inclusion of other theoretical models of behavior makes it a rich source of hypotheses and further research.

Wilson's model is neither a process model nor directly based on empirical findings. It is a static, fairly broad, general summary model of information-behavior and thus needs specification by analytical concepts if it should to be used for the study of relationships between tasks, information seeking and retrieval.

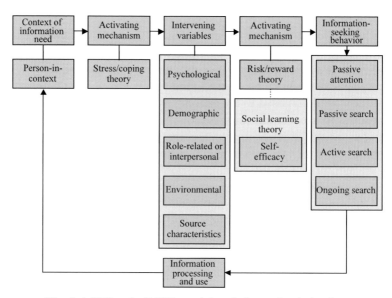

Fig. 3.4. Wilson's (1997) model on information behavior

The Byström-Järvelin Model. Byström and Järvelin (1995) consider task-based information seeking as a problem solving process. At the surface level, they modeled information seeking as a process consisting of needs analysis, selection of actions, the seeking proper (implementation of the actions), and evaluation of the results. This process was seen to depend on a number of situational, personal, and organizational factors, as well as on the actor's perceived task (Fig. 3.5; based on Feinman et al. 1976). The model was used in a qualitative empirical study on the relationships of task complexity, type of information sought and type of information source. Based on the data, a theoretical model (Fig. 3.6) emerged. This model claims systematic relationships between task complexity, type of information sought and type of information source, e.g., the higher the degree of task complexity, the more varied information types are needed and the greater the share of general-purpose sources (experts, literature).

Byström further developed the models through empirical studies (1999; Murtonen 1994). Vakkari and Kuokkanen (1997) analysed the model as a unit theory of information seeking processes. They used it as a starting point for an analysis of theoretical growth in information seeking, based on Wagner and Berger's (1985) conception of sociological theories and their growth. Vakkari (1998) analysed the growth of theories on task complexity and information seeking in detail. He pointed out that the Byström-Järvelin model meant theory growth in terms of theory precision, empirical support and the number of predictions within the research program.

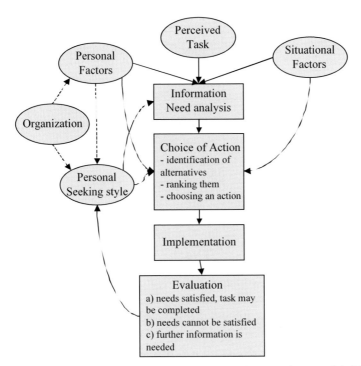

Fig. 3.5. Byström and Järvelin's information seeking surface model (1995)

Byström and Järvelin's model is valuable for the integration of information seeking and retrieval since it explicates dependencies (causality) between task complexity, information needed and information sources. The strength of their unit theory lies in that it explicitly generates hypotheses through systematically categorising the central concepts, which are discussed in the next subsection. One should bear in mind, however, that tasks have many other features than just complexity that are worth studying in information seeking and retrieval, for instance, size, urgency, reasons of difficulty, and dependencies (including cooperation) with other tasks – see Sect. 5.1.2.

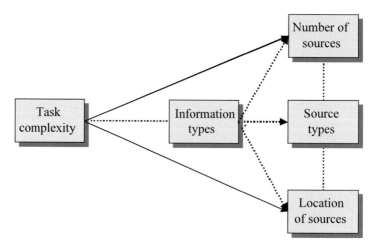

Fig. 3.6. Byström-Järvelin model of information seeking (1995)

The Byström-Järvelin model has a broad scope – from work tasks to information seeking, see also Sects. 6.2.5-7. It is an abstract and static model relating abstract concepts like task complexity and information types but not explicitly modeling a process. Moreover, it is a highly analytical model and specific to professional task contexts.

Discourse Analysis as a Meta-Model. Sanna Talja (1997; 2001; et al. 1997; 1998) and Kimmo Tuominen (2001; Tuominen and Savolainen 1997) recently applied discourse analysis (DA) in information seeking research. Their conception of discourse is based on Foucault (1972), and Wetherell and Potter (1988). They aim at proving the usefulness of constructionistic meta-theory (see Sect. 3.3.1) for Information Science. Talja and colleagues (1997; 1998), and Tuominen and colleagues (2003) apply DA in the design of digital libraries for chronically ill patients as a case.

Discourses are knowledge formations, entities that map out and organize wide chunks of our worldview. According to Foucault (1972), discourses are sets of statements about the real world that systematically formulate the objects considered in speech. Each discourse is based on a few wide background assumptions, here called *statements.* They act as preconditions behind the ways of presentation within each discourse. Each topic within a discourse is approached from the angle of the statements, and a specific state of things and relationships is assumed. Alternative, even contradictory discourses may coexist. They construct the object of presentation in different versions – thus discourses may be called *interpretative repertoires* (Talja 1997; 1999; 2001; Tuominen 1997).

The propositions of a discourse are not true or false – rather they are selective. Discourses are not 'ideological' because of the partiality of their
contents but rather because the basis of all conceptualizations is limited.
As the statements define a viewpoint for talking about a given topic, they
at the same time exclude a number of other possible constructions. Therefore the statements may lead to *absences* – there may be interpretations
that one does not come to think of because of the credibility of the dominating viewpoint. (Talja 1997; 2001; et al. 1997; 1998).

The statements and the arguments supporting them are always debatable
and relative when explicated. However, they are rarely explicated and analyzed since they are the foundation of the dominant viewpoint. Arguments
presented within a discourse are often perceived as truthful within a discourse because they seem traditional, logical and credible descriptions on
"how things are". Any given domain or interest area may have several
more or less contradictory discourses. The debate between discourses is a
debate on what kind of social knowledge is credible. (Talja 1997; 2001).

Discourse Analysis (see Fig. 3.7) treats discourses as historical phenomena. Texts are not read with the goal of understanding the speaker's or author's intentions. While authors use words to express their own intentions,
the words carry social distinctions and oppositions with themselves. Therefore the discourse overcomes the speaker by its pre-existing conceptions
even if the speaker would like to oppose this. (Talja 1997; Tuominen 2001;
Tuominen and Savolainen 1997).

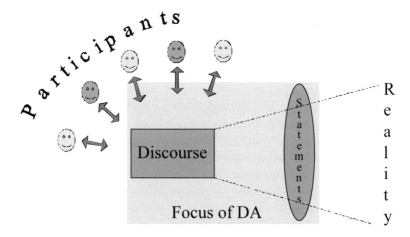

Fig. 3.7 Discourse Analysis

An individual may use several discourses as argumentation resources.
She may assume different discourses in different situations in order to pro-

mote or defend her intentions or views. DA stresses that meaning, values and ethical principles are not created individually but rather in social interaction (negotiation) between people (Talja 1997; Tuominen 2001). See also our IS&R model, Fig. 6.9, Sect. 6.2.1, for individual representations of the IS&R processes and segments, negotiated via social interaction.

Seen in this way, DA is a meta-model about how information (knowledge) is constructed in society through human social interaction (negotiation, debate). When people act, they dwell in discourses, which greatly affect the way they seek information and what they actually seek for. DA alone does not provide information directly about IS&R. Nevertheless it helps us to understand how information is used in argumentation and therefore why particular kinds of information are needed or sought for, and other kinds perhaps are excluded. Relevant information needs to support the assumed discursive viewpoint.

As such, DA does not provide a specific model on information seeking. Thus it cannot be analyzed through the model categories of Chapt. 1. However, DA is able to reveal different kinds of discourses in any domain and this can be used, not only for the understanding of communication, but for the design on information services as well.

3.1.3 Conceptual Evolution

Information Needs. The period 1960 − 85 produced several proposals for conceptual development in relation to information needs (Taylor 1968; Wersig 1973a-b; Line 1974). Robert Taylor (1968) proposed concepts, which relate to the development of an information need from an unconscious origin to an expressed request. However, how the need originally arises and how this relates to the person's situation or tasks remains unanalyzed. Gernot Wersig (1973a-b) suggested a conceptualization of information needs which accounts both for the personal and for the task aspects. An individual's task or his/her problematic situation can be understood as to require some specified hypothetical set of information, which form the task's (situation's) information requirements (Informationsanforderungen). However, task requirements cannot always be determined until afterwards when the task already has been completed. The interpretation by the individual of a problematic situation, raises his / her information needs (Informationsbedürfniss). In order to learn about information needs and seeking one needs to take into account the whole active professional role of the individuals being investigated. The cognitive viewpoint developed in this book seeks to analyze actors in their various roles − including the roles of generators and recipients – in professional communication and the social construction of tasks.

Work Tasks and Search Tasks. Although actors' work tasks had been an issue for the critics of information seeking studies already in the 1970's, work tasks (or corresponding leisure time activities) were really conceptualized as parts of information seeking studies in the late 1980's and 1990's. A work task is a sequence of the activities a person has to perform in order to accomplish a goal (Hansen 1999) – this definition covers both work and leisure related tasks. A work task has a recognizable beginning and end, and may consist of a series of sub-tasks, resulting in a meaningful product (Byström 1999). As Vakkari (2003) points out, this characterization of the task does not provide a strict operational definition. It does not indicate clearly on which granularity level of activities we should identify tasks; which sequences of activities constitute a task; and which are its sub-tasks.

Tasks may be defined as *abstract,* objective sequences of actions. This would require an agreed and complete description of the task process – which hardly is available for other than simple tasks. Moreover, such an objective description would not necessarily describe an actor's understanding of neither the task nor the process, nor the associated information needs she goes through when performing the task. Therefore *perceived work tasks* (by the actor) are reasonable starting points for studies in IS&R while the 'objective' ones, when known, may directly serve information systems design.

Some subtasks of a work task relate to information seeking and retrieval. A *search task* is a sequence of activities with the goal of finding specified information – the specification may range from narrow and detailed, e.g., a fact, to broad and vague, e.g. "something about memory problems in old age". The activities may involve the use of IR systems. However, we use the term also for "seeking tasks" involving no use of IR systems. In the real life search tasks are *natural,* emerging from perceived work tasks of real actors. In research settings, search tasks may be *simulated* (Martyn and Lancaster 1981; Borlund and Ingwersen 1997; Borlund 2000ab), involving a specified work task scenario, or just *assigned* search topics, like in typical IR experiments. (See also Sects. 5.9 and 6.2.3)

The tasks performed by a worker can be analyzed and classified in many different ways. Byström and Järvelin (1995), based on vast literature in several domains, concluded that typical job-level analysis criteria like job variety or autonomy are insufficient for the analysis of IS&R because such criteria do not describe individual (work) tasks – the basis of IS&R. Task complexity or difficulty is one of the most essential factors affecting task performance as observed in psychological experiments, in organizational studies, as well as in information seeking studies. Hansen (1999) summarizes task categorizations, which may be useful in studying information searching. Campbell (1988) reviews literature on task complexity.

We present below two frameworks, one concerning the analysis of work tasks, their change and information requirements (Järvelin 1986), and the other a framework for cognitive work analysis (Rasmussen et al. 1992). Both frameworks are models at a more general level than information seeking and retrieval per se, but have led to empirical investigations in information seeking and retrieval. Both also propose conceptual developments for task analysis and related phenomena as well.

A Framework for the Analysis of Work Tasks, Their Change and Information Requirements. Drawing on several prior studies, Järvelin (1986) analyzed tasks, information technology and information seeking/retrieval at the conceptual level. He suggested several dimensions of tasks and information that should be taken into account in the analysis of information seeking processes and in the design of information (retrieval) systems. The claim was that different types of information are supplied through different types of systems and that different types of information have different relevance and impacts on different types of work. Therefore information and work should not be treated as steady-state phenomena and left unanalyzed. Järvelin's framework was not an information seeking model but led to the development of one (see the Byström – Järvelin Model above). While being at a more general level, and emphasizing the study of tasks and information technology for the analysis of information seeking and retrieval, it nevertheless suggested taxonomies and hypotheses concerning the relations of tasks and information resources.

Tasks may be *difficult to perform* due to many reasons (Järvelin 1986; Eloranta 1974):

- *Structural reasons:* open constraints or too many alternatives to consider;
- The *information basis;* no or imprecise raw data, or much irrelevant information;
- *Ideas* in task formulation, e.g., lack of ideas or adherence to wrong ideas; or
- *Task treatment,* e.g., insufficient methods or cost of design and evaluation.

Tasks may also be classified according to one complexity dimension, which is based on the *a priori prescribability* of tasks (their outcomes, processes and necessary inputs). Simple (or routine) tasks are completely prescribable at the outset by actors working in that context whereas for difficult tasks even the type of the result is unknown in the beginning of the process, not to mention the process itself or its information requirements. Fig. 3.8 illustrates this through solid arrows and boxes for the prescribable parts of tasks, and dotted arrows and hazy boxes for the non-prescribable parts. As an example according to the classification, the type of outcome of a normal decision task may well be prescribed and most of the process as well. However, part of the process cannot be prescribed nor the majority of inputs. (*Anon.* 1974; Järvelin 1986)

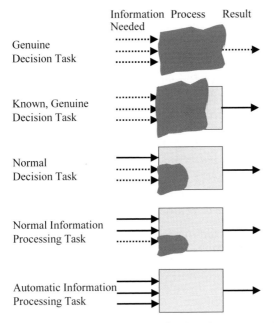

Fig. 3.8. The task complexity classification (Byström and Järvelin 1995)

The notion of task complexity remains nevertheless without a general agreement. The literature suggests many task characteristics related to complexity: repetivity, analyzability, *a priori* determinability, the number of alternative paths of task performance, outcome novelty, number of goals and conflicting dependencies among them, uncertainties between performance and goals, number of inputs, cognitive and skill requirements, as well as the time-varying conditions of task performance. Also these characteristics have been understood in many different ways. They however belong into two main groups: characteristics related to the *a priori* determinability of tasks and characteristics related to the extent of tasks.

Byström and Järvelin (1995; Byström 1999) summarize the literature on task complexity from the IS&R viewpoint.

Tasks may have different *kinds of subtasks,* which differ in their information requirements. For example, Rich suggested (1983; here as modified by Järvelin 1986) that the roles of information differ between subtasks like setting goals; designing alternative actions; analysis of situation, goals, or alternatives; selection of an action; justification of a decision; organizing or controlling; reconciling – making compromises or trade-offs; or seeking/retrieving information.

Drawing on several other authors, Järvelin (1986) proposes classification dimensions of information for IS&R. One dimension is *reliability,* where the utilization of, the need for, and seeking of hard facts vs. soft information differ in timing, channels and sources (Caplan, Morrison and Stambaugh 1975; Rich 1983). Information may have an *interest* woven into it and therefore we may differentiate between neutral vs. persuasive information, and between research vs. politics vs. advertisements. From the *problem treatment* perspective, there are:

- *Problem information,* i.e., the specifics of the problem at hand;
- *Domain information,* i.e., general facts and other knowledge in the domain (or subject field) into which the problem belongs; and
- *Problem solving information,* i.e., methods and heuristics for solving problems, or performing tasks, in the domain.

This classification originated in expert systems research (Barr and Feigenbaum 1981). Rich (1983) suggests further dimensions for information, e.g., its domain (or subject field). Allen (1991) reviewed the use of different kinds of knowledge, including the types presented above, in cognitive research and systems design.

Having several types of tasks, and information raise several questions concerning IS&R:

- Are the roles and impacts (relevance) of different types of information different in different situations, e.g., also in different phases of task solution?
- Is the access to, or seeking of, different types of information different?
- Are the sources of different types of information different?
- Do all types of information allow systematic treatment, e.g., tacit knowledge?

Tasks may also be classified as proper domain tasks and seeking / searching tasks obtaining the information for the former. The typologies and questions above apply to both equally – see further Sects. 6.2.5-7.

The relevance of task typologies for IS&R may be understood by recognizing that different kinds of tasks may be served by different kinds of information and may pose different kinds of access constraints. Different kinds of difficulties in performing tasks may be relieved by different kinds of information – at different stages – if by any information at all (e.g., under information overflow). Access to information and/or documents may differ by task type and information in a given context because frequently needed information often is supplied by permanent information systems (or other practices). Moreover, some information arrives to its recipient through passive reception and only seldom are active ad hoc efforts needed for information access.

Järvelin suggested in particular, that the categories of tasks, information, and information sources are systematically related with each other. More specifically, his analysis suggested hypotheses of the type: Different types of tasks (and difficulties in them) are supported by different types of information acquired from different types of sources. This model led later into a series of empirical studies by Byström and Järvelin, revealing the interrelationships of some of the proposed categories (see Sect. 3.1.2 above).

Technology changes tasks, and consequently, their associated information seeking and retrieval, as well, at several levels. Järvelin (1986) proposed a typology of five classes. In the simplest case, only the implementation of the method of performing the task changes without changing the input, outputs or the algorithm, e.g., when the SMART system (Salton 1968a) is re-implemented in a new programming language. At the next level, the 'algorithm' itself is changed, e.g., by moving from plain word frequencies to tf.idf in weighted automatic indexing. At the third level, the required quality of the result is raised, e.g., from muddling-through to optimal actions. This happens, for example, when Boolean retrieval is replaced by ranked retrieval. Next, the evaluation criteria may be changed, thereby posing new requirements to the whole task. For example, issues related to the particulars of retrieval engines are replaced by issues related to interfaces and IS&R strategies. Finally, the ultimate goals of work may change. This signifies a paradigm shift, for example, moving from system-oriented user studies to actor-centered study of human information access.

In simple changes IS&R is only marginally affected, if at all. Obviously, the greater the changes are in the tasks, the more thorough are the changes in the associated IS&R. Therefore there is a constant dynamic interplay or (im)balance between task goals, task processes, information and information seeking, as well as information systems (Fig. 3.9). An established practice means only a temporary balance between these factors. Sect. 3.4 discusses information acquisition generally, e.g., as part of one's task proper. In Fig. 3.9 information acquisition signifies acquisition from sources that are human (e.g., colleagues) or produced by humans (e.g., documents).

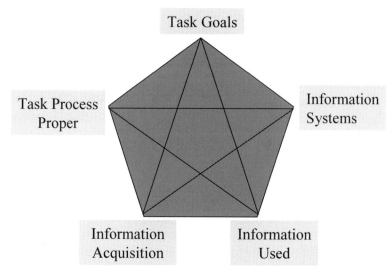

Fig. 3.9. Interaction of task goals, task processes, information and information seeking, as well as information systems (modified from Järvelin 1986)

The model of Fig. 3.9 may be seen as representing an individual worker's situation. The model would benefit from taking organizational and social factors into account – task reorganization and reorganization of cooperation often go hand in hand. These factors are contained in the next proposal. Fig. 3.9 also represents an early analysis of the reciprocal (bidirectional) relationships between information and communication technology and context – consisting of tasks, goals, information and its acquisition – currently discussed in *Social Informatics* (Fawyer and Eschenfelder 2002).

A Framework for Cognitive Work Analysis. Rasmussen and colleagues (1992) developed, based on ergonomics and cognitive engineering, a user-oriented framework for field analysis of work domains. We discuss this framework as another example of conceptual evolution related to tasks, and not as an information seeking model, since it is far more general that just an information seeking model.

The framework by Rasmussen (1990; et al. 1992) consists of seven dimensions and a substantial number of structured categories, mainly dealing with the contextual and situational factors in relation to information systems. The seven dimensions of the framework are:

- Work domain, task space.
- Activity analysis in domain terms.
- Decision analysis in information terms.
- Information processing strategies.
- Allocation of decision roles.
- Management structure, social organization.
- Mental resources, competency, and preferences of the individual actor.

Rasmussen (1990, p. 1) states that for modern work places, the ergonomic concern in design of workstations is not primarily the human-computer interaction in a separate tool or 'application'. The concern rather is the concurrent influence of technology on work conditions, work organization, management structures and, consequently, the influence on information requirements of actors in a cooperative network. In most work places, we find dynamic environments and concerns for flexibility and rapid adaptation to new requirements. In order to be useful for design of information systems in such a situation, a modeling framework should serve the representation of the work domain, the generic cognitive decision tasks, and useful strategies for such decision tasks together with subjective decision criteria. The framework seems well suited for both the analysis of IS&R and the design and evaluation of IR systems, since it makes tasks and contexts explicit dimensions of IS&R and also provides concepts for their structuring.

The framework originates, in part, from Pejtersen's design and evaluation work, based on field studies, on the Bookhouse system (1980-1990), an early icon-based hypermedia and best match system for accessing library collections (see Sect. 5.3). The framework is intended to remind the researcher systematically and explicitly about various relationships between the work requirements and the actor's resources.

This taxonomic approach also guides empirical analysis and evaluation of the use of systems and information – both conceptual information, but also the functional of other information structures, communicated for example during IR interaction, such as structures defined in the IT setting (e.g., database field codes or command language syntax). This dual approach to information use corresponds to the notions of domain and retrieval knowledge structures and work tasks vs. search tasks put forward by Ingwersen in an IR context (1986; see also Sects. 6.2.1 and 6.2.4). The approach provides means for qualitative evaluation across information systems in different work domains, and of cooperative information systems, including IR systems, in one domain.

The framework for cognitive work analysis has led to empirical work in the analysis of information seeking of engineers (Hertzum and Pejtersen

2000), and Web information retrieval (Pejtersen and Fidel 1999), discussed in Sect. 5.5.

3.1.4 Empirical Findings

The Early Years. The early empirical research into information seeking was conceptually at a moderate level. The studies were based on questionnaires, interviews, observations, and diaries, see Sect. 3.2. According to Brenda Dervin and Michael Nilan (1986), the most typical kinds of empirical studies were the following:

- *Demand on systems or resources approach:* how much do the users use various sources, media, systems, documents or channels?
- *The awareness approach:* how well aware are the respondents about the currently available services?
- *The likes-dislikes approach:* to what degree are the users satisfied or dissatisfied with various features of information services?
- *The priorities approach:* the respondents are asked to describe the kind of information they would like to receive.
- *The community profiles approach:* Demographic and environmental profiles of the user populations are created with the aim to find out service development needs.
- *The interests, activities and group membership approach:* respondents are asked to report their interests, actions and memberships in various groups in order to find out service development needs.

Findings from the early studies provide the following:

- An understanding of how people behave in the context of various services (e.g., libraries) and which demographic and other factors affect this.
- The principle of the least effort. The finding that, for users, information services seem to be of less value than might be expected from the service provider's point of view was quite frequent. This has often given rise to views that actors would be irrational, or even lazy. Such behavior can, however, be understood by approaching the actors from a different viewpoint, e.g., management studies, as pointed out by Wilson (1987) and by considering the whole information environment of the actors.
- Survey statistics on information system use and preferences of user populations.

- There were some innovative empirical studies, which suggested new approaches, e.g., by Allen (1966a-b) and Kunz and Rittel (1977b), suggesting task analysis, and by Wilson and Streatfield (1977; 1981b) and Caplan, Morrison and Stambaugh (1975), focusing on non-academic information seeking.
- We hardly learn anything new from further quantitative studies on channel and information source use, if they are not connected to the use of information.

Findings Based on the Sense-Making Approach. The Sense-making Approach is a broad approach to, or a methodology for, research in IS&R rather than a single unified theory. Therefore there is no single set of results, which would confirm or refute the Sense-making Approach as a theory. Instead one might claim, that the Sense-making Approach itself is a major result with a lot of empirical backing – a view on human sense-making, information seeking and use which challenges 'the traditional ones', treats humans as active constructors of meaning rather than as victims of various fallacies. However, one cannot prove the Sense-making Approach (as being true) by empirical studies completed under its umbrella. One may however state that the Sense-making Approach has been very relevant and useful. Moreover, it is explicit about its assumptions about human communication unlike many other approaches (Dervin 1999).

Dervin (2002; Dervin and Frenette 2001) suggests people's broad concerns and 'situationality' of information seeking as major empirical findings of the their approach.

- *Information needs vs. broader concerns of people.* Sense-Making has found people addressing all sorts of concerns which systems would not normally categorize as 'information needs' and traditional approaches may miss but which systems could assist in addressing.
- *Static vs. situational analyses.* Framing humans as across time-space consistent works best only for habitual behavior constrained by social structures and/or internal structures. Sense-making does not focus on static characterizations of individual people who are assumed to behave the same across varying circumstances. Rather, it focuses on the idea that communicating is responsive to situational conditions – the moment of sense-making replaces the person as primary focus. Sense-making has derived situational predictors that account for more variance in information seeking and use than either demography or attitudinal/life-style predispositions.

The mass of empirical studies done within the framework of Sense-making, not reviewed here, supports these views.

Ellis's Empirical Findings. David Ellis and others (1989; Ellis, Cox and Hall 1993; Ellis and Haugan 1997) investigated information seeking patterns of various professional groups including social scientists, physical scientists, and engineers. The eight categories discussed above emanate from these studies.

Ellis and Haugan (1997) analyzed information seeking of engineers and research scientists involved in incremental, radical, and fundamental R&D projects. They showed that the subjects' information seeking patterns vary in relation to the stage of their projects and can be described in terms of eight categories based on Ellis (1989). When researchers progress toward the advanced phases of their projects, and become more knowledgeable about their tasks, they are increasingly selective. The use of formal channels decreases, and person-to-person communication becomes more dominant.

Unfortunately there is no reported information about the specific tasks the subjects in Ellis and others' studies were performing when the data were collected — i.e., whether certain categories were more likely to be used with certain kinds of tasks. Nevertheless, we learn that quite different approaches in information seeking may be utilized.

Findings based on Kuhlthau's ISPs. Kuhlthau's ISP (Information Search Process) model is based a series of empirical studies, first small-scale for developing the model and then testing and verifying it in longitudinal and large-scale field studies. Her model is derived from, and verified by, the findings. This is a strong feature of her model.

Along the stages of the process, also the actor's feelings, thoughts and actions change. During the early stages, the affective symptoms of uncertainty, confusion, and frustration are prevalent and associated with vague and unclear thoughts about the task. The actor's actions involve seeking background information. The actor is unable to formulate her task and express precisely the kind of information needed. After focus formation, information seeking becomes more directed and the thoughts about the task clearer and more structured. This leads the actor to seek relevant, focused information using the whole range of information resources. Feelings change from uncertainty and frustration toward certainty and confidence. Satisfaction and relief were common at the conclusion of the ISP. While the model predicts a linear IPS process, the study participants felt the process as being a more iterative one. (Kuhlthau 1991).

Because Kuhlthau's (1991) study was longitudinal, her findings are also able to point out that the actors' topics changed and central themes evolved as information was gathered, and the task developed. This clearly supports the views that actors are *learning during information seeking* and that their information needs are dynamic.

Kuhlthau's model has been employed in a number of later empirical studies. Most of them deal with relevance judgments or web IR and are discussed in Sects. 5.2.2 and 5.5.2. However, some deal with information seeking. Based on various such models, including Kuhlthau's model, Yang (1997) observed six students during information seeking processes in hypertext and identified eight types of searching behaviors. Each stage of searching reflected the subject's mental state. They typically engaged in *exploratory searching* before they found a specific direction. At this stage they tried to establish a framework for their task. The database was searched without specific criteria or coordinated plan. *Purposive searching* occurred when they were able to find firm points of reference. They could then search for specific information, which they had identified as directly relevant to the current goals. Finally, they demonstrated *associative searching* when they looked for related and interconnected information to support arguments they already had established. Yang also showed that, as the task becomes clearer, the share of exploratory and purposive search decreases and associative increases.

Yang's (1997) study also demonstrated that the learners did not follow prescriptive, predetermined plans but were prepared to modify them. This finding echoes Suchman's situated actions (1987), Schön's reflection-in-action (1990) as well as Norman's opportunistic actions (1988). All argue that purposeful behavior is ad-hoc, rather than deterministic and logical. Actors respond adaptively to their current situation.

Byström's Empirical Findings. Katriina Byström and Kalervo Järvelin (1995; Byström 1999; Murtonen 1994) developed a qualitative method for task-level analysis of the effects of task complexity on information seeking. They found in a Finnish public administration context that these effects are systematic and logical. As task complexity increases (Byström 1999; Byström and Järvelin 1995) then the:

- Complexity of information needed increases,
- Needs for domain information and problem solving information increase,
- The share of general-purpose sources, people in particular, increases and that of problem and fact-oriented sources decreases,
- Successfulness of information seeking decreases,
- Internality of people as sources increases, and that of documentary sources decreases, and
- Number of sources increase.

The contrast between simple *vs.* complex tasks underlines the importance and consequences of task complexity: in the latter understanding, sense-making and problem formulation are essential and require different types and more complex information through somewhat different types of channels from different types of sources. The other findings include that, in general, very few channels are used to locate the sources used in all task complexity categories. The internality-externality dimension of sources indicates a large share of internal sources even in complex tasks. The findings suggest that both the task complexity and the information type - dimensions are needed in a general model of task-based information seeking and retrieval – see Fig. 6.8, Sect. 6.2.

Differences Between Experts vs. Novices. Isenberg (1986) studied information seeking and use by experts and novices in business problem solving. His goal was to find out what cognitive processes managers use when they deal with business problems, and about differences in problem solving between experts (experienced managers) and novices (business school students). The problems were presented as 7-card stacks, which the subjects could utilize as much as they wanted, and without any extra costs or penalties. Data on problem solving were collected through thinking aloud.

Isenberg found that experienced managers made less use of the information available than novices. Instead, they made more conditional conclusions, which were based on less information supporting them. Experienced managers reasoned from general to specific, based on their experience, and considered several alternatives simultaneously. Powerful deduction and interpretation was typical for them. Isenberg explained this through opportunistic reasoning: if information is valuable but scarce, and its availability unlikely, an expert has learned to distill all possible out of the information at hand. Therefore the managers made speculative but plausible inferences even on a narrow basis. In the course of problem solving the managers started outlining solutions at an earlier stage than novices and produced qualitatively better results. In other words, relating to Kuhlthau (see above), experienced managers found a focus earlier, perhaps directly without any preceding stages, while novices explored each case longer by identifying major concepts and relations before finding a focus. Regarding task complexity, the managers' perceived tasks were considerably simpler with the process, outcome and required information definable at the outset, while the novices had to construct these.

In these findings we see that even easily available information may be neglected (rightfully) as one may draw on one's experience (cognitive structures) and learned interpretation of one's situation. The way an assigned work task is perceived – and thus formed into a personal work task – depends on the actor's knowledge, which also affects the need for any additional information.

Discourses in Society. Sanna Talja (2001, 2004) applied DA in the analysis of music library users' interviews and library policy documents. She identified three discourses in music culture, one taking the general enlightenment viewpoint (e.g., national music culture in international context), the second focusing cultural alternatives (and being critical to dominating commercial music culture), and the third being demand-driven (e.g., citizens' interests should be respected). These discourses do not occur as pure in speech or text but always intermingled with each another. The result of DA is the explication and systematization of the discourses (and their features). Different discourses are relevant in different contexts. Talja and colleagues (1997; 1998) applied DA in the development of a regional digital library. They analyzed the terminology present in users' service requests in libraries, tourist information bureaus, telephone operator etc. DA was able to describe the discrepancy between the users' and the service providers' terminologies.

Summarizing Empirical Findings. Facing the same imposed work task, an expert's interpretation of it, the perceived task, is simpler than a novice's interpretation (Byström 1999; Järvelin 1986). Therefore the stages an expert goes through in the work task process are different from the ones a novice deals with. In particular, there is less pre-focus exploration and sense making in the expert's process. An expert therefore experiences less anxiety and her thoughts are clearer and she looks for pertinent information (Kuhlthau 1991). An expert needs less explorative searching while the share of purposive and associative searching is larger (Yang 1997). An expert has a simpler task and needs less information (Byström 1999; Isenberg 1986), less domain information and problem solving information, less sources, and less general-purpose sources like people (Byström 1999). In complex tasks, browsing is connected to pre-focus activities and analytical strategies, mostly querying, to post-focus (Kuhlthau 1991; Yang 1997).

Whether focusing on experts or novices, scholarly communication or cultural interests, the actors dealing with information participate in discourses, which socially construct their objects and the ways to see them and to deal with them. Discourse analysis is valuable for the cognitive viewpoint in several ways:

- DA supports understanding of communication: DA reveals the discourses in a domain, their structure and the distinctions applied. It can also reveal the foci of debate between them. Discourses have thus consequences in IS&R, e.g., in the choice of means (channels) for acquiring information, in relevance judgments, in the interpretation documents, etc. DA also reveals vocabularies of discourses, e.g., for query modification.

- DA helps to avoid individualism and radical monologism by suggesting dialogical views of (social) knowledge construction (see Sect. 3.3.1).
- DA is doable without introspection: data may be collected from interviews and documents, which are fairly easily available. Much can be analyzed without bold (and un-testable) hypotheses about processes within human minds.

While a debate between DA and the Cognitive Viewpoint, two discourses themselves, may be a good way to keep them both healthy and running, the controversies do not seem insuperable and do not prevent cross-fertilization.

3.2 Research Methods

The methodological aspect of investigations may be seen as consisting of a research strategy, data collection and analysis methods, and type of investigation (Järvelin and Vakkari 1990). The *type of investigation* can generally be grouped as empirical, theoretical and conceptual, and methodological. Moreover, the study of information systems forms a group of its own, which may utilize empirical, conceptual, etc. methods, but focuses on the constructive study of technical systems. Empirical studies can further be classified into descriptive, comparative and explanatory studies. *Research strategy* is an overall approach to the study within which, e.g., the decisions concerning data collection and the type of analysis are made. Typical strategies for empirical research are, e.g., survey strategy, qualitative strategy, case or action research strategy, and experimental strategy. Typical strategies for theoretical research may be called the conceptual research strategy (e.g., verbal argumentation, concept analysis), mathematical or logical strategy. The strategy for systems investigations may be called system analysis and design. Empirical research uses empirical data derived through many *data collection methods.* Typical data collection methods are, e.g., questionnaires, interviews, observation, content analysis, and historical source analysis. (Järvelin and Vakkari 1990; 1993).

There is an abundance of literature on research methods in Social Sciences to draw from to advance the study of information seeking. Martyn and Lancaster (1981) made a valuable contribution to the field by explaining research methodology and specific methods through sample studies completed in Library and Information Science. We now look at the research methods used in information seeking studies.

3.2.1 Research Strategies

Theoretical and meta-theoretical development in Information Seeking in the 1980's (e.g., Dervin and Nilan 1986) made a shift of emphasis in research strategies and data collection methods necessary. In general, structured data collection methods support data analysis but also entail presuppositions about the phenomena studied. This may be fatal if it leads to neglecting, in data collection, essential dimensions of the phenomena being studied. Less structured, often qualitative, methods may collect such data but may also require tedious interpretation on behalf of the researcher. Qualitative methods in data collection are a solution to the superficiality problems of survey methods but they suffer from difficulty in generalizing the results. Moreover, they are no guarantee of more valid or in-depth results if the conceptual framework of the research is not developed. Therefore, "going qualitative" is no excuse for being un-analytic. Moreover, both approaches may be combined in a single study by application of both kinds of methods (triangulation) or by processing the qualitative findings also quantitatively.

Despite of sometimes heated meta-theoretical argumentation within IS&R, the meta-theoretical assumptions made by IS&R researchers are rarely carried forward in coherent ways into a method (Dervin 1999). Dervin proposed the Sense-making Methodology as providing guidance for research methods and avoiding unattended (and untested) assumptions about the nature of the phenomena studied by making them explicit. Niels Ole Pors (2000) addressed the application of Social Science research methodology in IS&R. The design of experiments and statistical methods are covered.

Which research strategies are appropriate for cognitive IS&R research? All strategies may contribute, if properly applied. However, important contributions to IS&R during 1985 – 2000 were based on experiments, qualitative studies, and discourse analysis.

Survey Strategy. The empirical information seeking studies 1960 - 85 predominantly used quantitative surveys based on structured questionnaires and interviews as data collection methods despite their known insufficiency and often superficial results (Brittain 1982; Dervin and Nilan 1986). Surveys accounted for up to 80 % of the methodology in research articles in information seeking published in 1965 1975, and 1985 (Järvelin and Vakkari 1993). Their popularity is due to their ease of use, low cost, and support to quantitative analysis. Hewins (1990) reported that the survey methodology continued to dominate the research into information seeking in the late 1980s. There was nothing methodologically interesting here, in particular, from the cognitive viewpoint.

The early studies on information seeking were mostly descriptive; explanatory studies were rare. The dominance of the descriptive survey methodology suggests one-sided research strategies and problem formulations. For new influences in the research on information seeking, qualitative research strategies and methods, such as theme interview, participant observation, and action research, are necessary. (Järvelin and Vakkari 1993) In the 1990's, prominent studies were using other strategies.

Experiments. Isenberg's study (1986) was an example of experiments, of which there are not too many in Information Science (Järvelin and Vakkari 1993; excluding traditional IR experiments). There were two groups of actors, experts and novices, and a selected short business case to solve. The goal was to analyze the difference between the groups in their problem solving processes and in the quality of the outcome. The experts were 12 experienced general managers from six corporations, and the novices three college undergraduates. All solved the same business case. The case was presented in a controlled way on seven cards, arranged randomly to reflect real business situations where cases do not begin in orderly fashion. Data collection and analysis was through thinking aloud and protocol analysis, see below. Isenberg's methodology is an early application of *simulated work tasks* in the domain of Information Seeking (see also Sect. 5.9).

Explanation and theory development in IS&R requires experimental methodology. Experiments are invaluable for studying the relationships of work tasks and IS&R.

Qualitative Approach. T.D. Wilson (1981) suggested that qualitative methods be particularly appropriate to the study of the needs underlying information-seeking behavior and Fidel (1993) provided an overview of qualitative methods in IS&R research. Semi-structured or open-ended interview is recommended for data collection.

Grounded Theory. Grounded theory (GT) is often referred to as *the* methodology in qualitative studies, including IS&R. Glaser and Strauss (1967; Strauss and Corbin 1990) developed GT. In IS&R the GT methodology has been used, among others by, for instance, Ellis (1989), Ellis and Haugan (1997), Spink (1997a), Cole (1999) and Pharo (2002). GT is a qualitative methodology that uses induction to develop a theory about a phenomenon. GT is characterized by developing theories that are close to the data through interplay between theory and data. Concepts are developed through coding the data in several stages at the same time as working hypotheses, stemming from the researcher's theoretical sensitivity, are verified by testing them on the data. Systematic analysis, or 'coding', of the data will reveal its properties and relationships.

Coding may be divided into three different stages. The first stage (*open coding*) involves categorizing and classifying properties of the data and the identification of significant categories/concepts and their attributes/properties. *Axial coding* is used for the construction of individual categories and attributes and for identifying connections between the elements. In the final coding stage (*selective coding*) one identifies a core category and its relations to the remaining ones. Time-line interviewing and inductive content analysis are suitable techniques for GT (Schamber 2000).

Discourse Analysis. DA focuses on the constructiveness, functionality, and variability of the use of language. The focus shifts from mental objects like 'information need' or 'intention' to socially organized action among humans, which is both material and linguistic. The analyst does not reach out and beyond the text but rather focuses on the meaningful action represented by language use. The truth or falsity of the ontology constructed in speech/text is not a focus in discourse analysis. (Tuominen et al. 2002). The actual analysis in DA is discussed below (see 3.2.3).

3.2.2 Methods of Data Collection

Which methods are relevant for cognitive IS&R research? All methods may contribute when applied properly. Still, during 1985 – 2000 progressive studies in information seeking often applied methods appropriate for collecting qualitative data, such as semi-structured interviewing, time-line interviewing, critical incidence studies, observation, thinking aloud, diaries, and triangulation through several methods. Several studies integrated qualitative and quantitative data collection in a longitudinal study setting.

Qualitative Methods in Data Collection. Typical methods of data collection for qualitative analysis are semi-structured or open-ended (thematic) interviewing, observation, thinking aloud and protocol analysis (Ericsson and Simon 1984), user panels, and diaries. Interviewing requires more effort than questionnaires but provides better possibilities for thorough analysis of information needs and seeking.

Interviewing Methods. Time-line interviewing is a technique derived from anthropology, ethnography, and clinical psychology. Dervin (1983; 1992; Dervin and Dewdney 1986; Schamber 2000) developed the *micro-*

moment time-line interview technique for the Sense-making approach. This interviewing technique focuses on a relevant and critical past incident the respondent has experienced. The interview then details the person's situation, the gap preventing progress and the helps looked for. Micro-moment time-line interview involves asking the respondent in detail what happened in a problematic situation step-by-step. The respondent is then asked about any questions or confusion that emerged at each step. Finally, the respondents are further asked about these questions or confusions for aspects that relate to the dimensions of situations, gaps and helps.

The time-line interview technique is promising in its support to thoroughness of analysis and generalization of results. It seeks to open a historical window to past behavior and perceptions. The views presented by the respondents may be incomplete and distorted (Dervin 1999) but the strength is that concrete real past episodes help the respondent to report on situations, gaps and helps concretely, in a focused way, and more reliably (Schamber 2000). The interview is pseudo-longitudinal in its focus on the step-by-step development of the sense-making process – while the data are collected at a single moment in time. Tuominen (2001) suggested that the interaction of the interviewer and the interviewee have not been taken sufficiently into account and that this may affect what the interviewee report on past incidents.

Schamber (2000) noted that time-line interviewing has been useful in needs assessment and in studying actors' perceptions in different situations. She gave a detailed methodological account on the use of time-line interviewing. Its strengths are:

- Time lines are naturalistic and relatively unobtrusive ways of collecting data on cognitive perceptions.
- A structured questionnaire as the basis of an interview allows flexible discussion of any number of events, questions and sources.
- Remembering a recent event is not a problem for respondents.
- Open-ended neutrally worded questions yield rich data for analysis.
- The main disadvantage is the labor-intensiveness of the method:
- Questionnaire development, interviewer training and interviews take time.
- Interview result transcription is time-consuming.

Another data collection technique, the *neutral questioning* technique, has been used to conduct reference interviews (Dervin and Dewdney 1986; Savolainen 1993). The idea is that the interviewer understands an interviewee's need (questions) from the latter's viewpoint. Neutral questions avoid premature diagnosis of information needs and support understanding what the underlying situations, gaps and foreseen helps may be.

Ellis and Haugan (1997) used semi-structured interview to explore the information-seeking behavior of research workers within an international oil and gas company. A sample of 23 interviewees was selected to represent the company's different research areas, research project types, project phases, project working roles, and educational backgrounds. The interviews lasted 45 minutes to one hour, and were tape-recorded and then transcribed. The transcriptions were used for feedback and as a guide for further interviews. An average transcript consisted of about 6000 words. In the subsequent analysis, themes were first identified in the interviews and arranged into behavior patterns and then sorted into coding categories while attempting to keep the categories internally homogeneous and separable from each other.

Questionnaires and interviews, in general, have problems of reliability and completeness if data collection occurs long after the activities being described. Neutral questioning about an interviewee's current situation does not have such problems but neither provides such a perspective as the time-line interview.

Critical Incident Method. The critical incident method focuses on a recent concrete incident to collect data on a phenomenon. Martyn and Lancaster (1981) give a fairly elaborated account on the application of the critical incident method in the study of information seeking. The strength of the method is that it relates the use of information to the problem solving process. It is easier and more reliable to report on a recent concrete incident than to answer more general questions. The critical incident method can be used together with questionnaires or interviews – by beginning with more general questions and then focusing on a critical incident. Allen's (1966ab) solution development records may be seen as a variation of the critical incident method that has served as a basis for others, e.g., Dervin and Nilan (1986). In Allen's case an on-going project was taken as the critical incident and data were collected through diaries. An open-ended interview is valuable in validating the diary results. Also the time-line interview discussed above is a variation of the critical incident method for data collection. Hewins (1990) reviewed the application of critical incident methods in medical informatics.

Observation in Data Collection. Observation allows real time data collection. Wilson and Streatfield (1977; 1981a-b) used it in the INISS-project to collect data on some 6,000 communication events of social workers. They noted that observation is not well suited to collecting data on desk-based work. In general, observation cannot produce data on thinking processes.

Thinking Aloud. Yang (1997) used thinking aloud and protocol analysis in a field study on information seeking and retrieving in hypertext. The data were collected using audiotapes and videotapes, observations, and interviews. Think-aloud protocols involved asking the subjects (all students attending a course in classical Greek studies) to verbalize their thoughts while working on an assigned problem. The verbal data were recorded and analyzed to find the goal-oriented and information seeking patterns in the subjects' problem solving. Isenberg (1986) used thinking aloud and protocol analysis in his experiment on information seeking by experts vs. novices.

A variation of thinking aloud is *talking aloud.* Talking aloud is easier because it does not require training and requires less attention than thinking aloud. On the other hand, there are fewer guarantees that the cognitive processes of the subjects can be captured. Training sessions are mandatory prior to thinking aloud experiments (Ingwersen 1982).

The advantages of thinking aloud and recording are that everything is recorded in real time, and that the often complicated cognitive tasks, which take place over long periods of time, can be analyzed (Ingwersen 1992). Ericsson and Simon (1984) argued that thinking aloud could produce valid verbal accounts of cognitive processes, in particular, if the latter already are linguistic or conceptual processes prior to verbalization. A disadvantage of thinking aloud is its obtrusiveness (Ingwersen 1992). He pointed out that this leads to a validity problem – there is uncertainty about the degree to which the protocols reflect actual thoughts or the intentionality of actions, and bring forward reliable data. He outlined how experiments should be set up to reduce these problems.

User Panels. A user panel is a group of individuals who are consulted for information more than once and who have agreed to provide responses on such a basis. Martyn and Lancaster (1981) suggested panel studies when changes in behavior or performance over time are in focus. They also describe the use of *simulated work tasks* (initiated by problem statements given to panelists) as a means of studying work and information seeking processes, relevance judgments and information use – see also Sect. 5.9.

Diaries in Data Collection. Diaries have throughout the period, but not often, been used for data collection in information seeking research. They are kept by the participants of the study and also allow real time data collection. This enhances reliability and completeness of the data. The tediousness of diaries requires that the participants are motivated and willing to cooperate (Allen 1977). Allen (1966ab) collected data through diaries filled in by the respondents (scientists and engineers). They recorded their activities in a diary (a solution development record) listing all possible solutions to a problem encountered and the information used to choose between them. Martyn and Lancaster (1981) described the use of diaries and recommended as simple and structured diaries as possible. Vakkari and Hakala (2000) collected, among other data, research diaries from students preparing their research proposals for a term-long seminar – see under longitudinal studies. Kuhlthau (1991) also used diaries – see also longitudinal studies. Byström (1999; and Järvelin 1995) used structured diaries, among other data collection methods, in her study of civil servants' information seeking – see also triangulation below.

Multiple Methods – Triangulation. Multiple methods may be used to collect data on complex phenomena. The advantage is that even if each data collection method delivers only a partial evidence on the phenomenon, several methods together may cover multiple aspects. In addition, multiple methods allow cross-checking the results by each of them thus increasing the reliability and validity of the data. This cross-checking gave rise to the term triangulation. Byström (1999), Kuhlthau (1991), Yang (1997), and Vakkari and Hakala (2000) are prominent among those, who have used triangulation in IS&R. We shall consider Byström here and the others later, see under the section on longitudinal studies.

Byström (1999; and Järvelin 1995) used multiple data collection methods like theme interviews, observation, and diaries in her study on civil servants' information seeking. The subjects filled out questionnaires for background information, they were interviewed for tasks and information behavior at the general level, and they filled-out structured diaries describing their current tasks and information access while performing their tasks. The diary form is in Fig. 3.10. The idea of structured diaries was to simplify diary keeping and thus encourage the subjects to fill them. The diary form seeks to attain the subjects' cognitive state at the beginning of the task and through its stages.

DIARY   Date :   Time started :
1.   Describe your task in detail :
2.   Describe the situational factors affecting the task :
3.   What is the ambition level you aim at in the task : good, nearly good or satisfactory ?
4.   Describe in detail what kind of information you think you need in order to perform the task.
    (a)   thoughts in the beginning of the task :
    (b)   thoughts emerged later during the task :
5.   Which channels and sources do you consider (mention also those you won't use)
    (a)   thoughts in the beginning of the task :
    (b)   thoughts emerged later during the task :
6.   How much time did you use in planning information seeking ?
7.   Which channels and sources did you use ? (Include yourself ; mention the names of any colleagues consulted ; mention channels used no matter whether or not you obtained the sources) :

Source	Why chosen	Channel	Why chosen	Success	Applicability

Success : you got the information (a) wholly, (b) partly, (c) not at all
Applicability : the information was (a) well-applicable, (b) partially applicable, (c) not applicable at all

8.   Was the whole of the information obtained (a) sufficient for the task or (b) insufficient for the task ?
9.   Estimate the time spent (a) on information seeking (b) on the whole task.

Fig. 3.10. Byström and Järvelin's diary form (1995)

Byström developed *work charts* to organize the data delivered by questionnaires and diaries (Byström and Järvelin 1995), see Fig. 3.11. Each sample task was first abstracted into a work chart based on the information-seeking model employed. The sample task in Fig. 3.11 is a normal decision task, which must be performed in hurry. The worker in this case was a lawyer (i.e., with a university degree) with 12 years experience and had the ambition level "good". Both problem and domain information were needed.

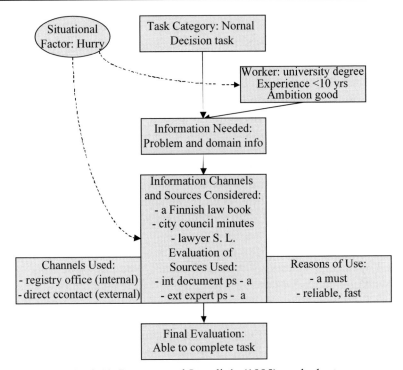

Fig. 3.11. Byström and Järvelin's (1995) work charts

The worker did not consider any channels in the beginning but rather three sources: a standard Finnish law book, the city council meeting minutes and the lawyer S. L. The evaluation of channels and sources used is coded. The code "int document ps – a" describes the search and use of the city council minutes, i.e., that an internal (official) document was used. The code "ps – a" denotes that information seeking was partially successful and that the information obtained was well applicable. On the right, the reason for using this document is given as a must, and on the left the channel for this document is given as the city registry office, which is an internal channel. Similarly, the contact to the lawyer is coded as external expert yielding partial and well applicable information. He was contacted directly due to known reliability and fast response.

The lowest box gives the final evaluation. In this case the outcome was positive, the worker was able to complete the task. The situational factor 'hurry' may have had influence on the ambition level and the choice of sources (e.g., neglecting the law book). The workers' thoughts about the task, channels and sources, which could not be fitted into the boxes of the work charts, were recorded beside the work charts.

The work charts were used to organize the findings – the data. In the analysis, the charts were combined in *process tables* for each task category (see next subsection).

Longitudinal Studies. In longitudinal investigations, study subjects are followed over a longer period of time, beyond the single interaction or session level. This allows identification of possible patterns regarding types of information needed, channels and sources used, their way of use, as well as other cognitive aspects – and how these evolve along a longer process. Byström's studies (see above) were longitudinal: she followed each task from its initiation to completion. Most task processes were however short – from a few minutes to a few hours while some lasted a couple of weeks (Byström and Järvelin 1995). In her later study, tasks lasted from a week to one year (Byström 1999).

Kuhlthau (1991) developed her information seeking process model (see Sect. 3.1) through a series of five field studies. The first three were qualitative with an aim to develop her ISP model. In the initial study, high-school seniors kept diaries and recorded in them their actions, thoughts and feelings about their search process in libraries due to a term paper project. Also search logs were kept with data on sources used, procedures for finding them, and their usefulness. The participants also wrote a paragraph length text on their topics shortly after the initiation, and again, at the end of their projects. Teachers assessed students' final papers. Further, questionnaires were used to collect data on students' library use, and an in-depth case study (interviews at six separate occasions) was conducted to verify and explain the data collected by other means. The second study used the same questionnaire and population after four years of college to obtain longitudinal comparative data. The third study continued the case study (one interview) also after four years of college.

The last two of Kuhlthau's studies were quantitative with an aim to test the ISP model. In the fourth study, high, middle and low achieving high-school students (N=147) were studied at three points during a four-week research paper assignment (initiation, middle and closure) – and teachers assessed their papers. The fifth study sought to validate the ISP model in broader empirical settings with 385 academic, public and school library users in 21 sites. A similar process survey at three points (initiation, middle and closure) was administered to each participant.

Vakkari and colleagues (Vakkari 1999; Vakkari 2000; Vakkari and Hakala 2000) used multiple data collection methods in a coordinated way: interviews, observation, diaries, transaction logs, as well as talking aloud. The participants of the study were 11 students attending a term long seminar for preparing research proposals for a master's theses. The students made IR searches in the beginning, middle and end of the seminar. Data for describing their understanding of the task, search goals and tactics as well as relevance assessments were collected through pre- and post-search interviews after each session. The students were also asked to talk aloud in the sessions. The transaction logs were captured and talk aloud was recorded. In addition, research and search diaries were collected. Among the many findings, change of relevance criteria according to shifting knowledge levels of the problem at hand was observed.

Also Wang and Soergel (1993) and Wang and White (1999) have studied IS&R processes in longitudinal research projects from a cognitive viewpoint, beyond the role of seeking activities, and into information selection, use, and writing. King and Tenopir recently reviewed the reading aspects of information use in science contexts (2001). Tang and Solomon have analyzed one information seeking actor over a longer period (1998), and in specialized contexts. Kuhlthau and Tama studied search processes of lawyers (2001), also explored by Sutton with respect to case relevance judgments (1994).

3.2.3 Methods of Data Analysis

Which analysis methods suit cognitive IS&R research? All methods may contribute when applied properly. Still, during 1985 – 2000 the dominance of quantitative analysis of survey data was replaced by more varied analytical methods including inductive content analysis, protocol analysis, triangulation, and discourse analysis. Several studies integrated qualitative and quantitative data analysis in a longitudinal study setting. Below we shall discuss some non-standard approaches to analysis that are relevant for cognitive IS&R. Standard quantitative analysis methods are covered well in text-books.

Inductive Content Analysis. Inductive content analysis is particularly appropriate in studies based on a grounded theory approach, or studies which derive theory from data rather than verify existing theory. Inductive content analysis helps the researcher to interpret interview responses (or other qualitative data) in a way that does not compromise the original expression of the subject (Schamber 2000).

Inductive content analysis is labor-intensive. Obtaining the data, e.g., interview responses through time-line interviews, may require much effort. Coding schemes and questionnaires must be developed together through extensive pre-testing to guarantee reliability. However, the amount of effort may be reduced in explorative studies by limiting the number of respondents in a study. For example, as few as 10 respondents can serve in eliciting cognitive perceptions like relevance criteria. (Schamber 2000).

Schamber (2000) concluded that time-line interviewing and inductive content analysis were successful methods for learning about relevance criteria in real-life information problem situations. The methods would be useful in exploratory research. She believes that the value of discussing relevance criteria outside some situation in context is not worthwhile. More generally, inductive content analysis of interviews is one means to learn about actors' cognitive processes in various IS&R situations.

Protocol Analysis. Protocol analysis is another name for content analysis, particularly, when the data (protocols) are transcribed thinking-aloud accounts of cognitive processes. Isenberg (1986) discussed the efforts needed in developing and testing the coding schemes for reliable data analysis. A scheme of 17 content categories was developed for thinking aloud transcripts. The scheme's categories registered instances of various types of cognitive processing, e.g., inference from specific to general or vice versa, reasoning by analogy, and summarization. The category scheme was developed through a pilot rehearsal analysis and subsequent refinement by two researchers. Their inter-coder reliability was 86 %. Moreover, an action plan was outlined from each protocol. This described how the subjects planned to solve the business problem at hand. Specialists subsequently rated the plans (on a 7-point Likert scale) over 6 dimensions, e.g., completeness, and overall effectiveness.

Protocol analysis (or verbal interaction analysis) is also a major analysis method for user-oriented and cognitive IR research (see Sect. 5.8.3).

Triangulation. Byström and Järvelin (1995) used predominantly qualitative analysis in the study of task-complexity and information seeking. This began with a purposive selection of 25 out of 94 task processes with an aim to retain maximal variety among processes and to collect equally many processes for each complexity class. Work charts (see the preceding section) were used to organize the findings. In the analysis, the charts were combined in *process tables* (Table 3.1) for each task category. The practical process tables summarized respondent background information (from interviews/questionnaires) and the actions performed during task performance (from diaries). The thinking process tables summarized the sources considered during the processes and those actually used. The coding of the table columns is as in the work charts above.

Any patterns emerging from the data were looked for. In order to support qualitative analysis, and further summary analysis, several quantitative summary indicators were computed. Among others, the following indicators were computed:

- In order to characterize roughly the complexity of information needed in each task category, the *Information Complexity Index* was constructed. For that purpose, the information category of each task was quantified as follows: PI = 1, DI = 1, PSI = 2, PI & DI = 2, PI & PSI = 3, DI & PSI = 3, and PI & DI & PSI = 4. The mean of these quantifications was then computed in each task category. This quantification was motivated as follows: PI and DI can most often be presented in the form of simple factual statements — either descriptive in the case of DI or prescriptive in the case of PI. Thus the value 1. PSI, on the contrary, is more complex and not simply factual: it is often in the form of frameworks and procedures in relation to PI and DI — thus the value 2. The quantifications for the combined classes follow in an obvious way.
- To characterize the patterns among the sources and channels supplying them, they were classified into fact-oriented (registers, databases), problem-oriented sources (people concerned, documents), and general-purpose sources (experts, literature, personal collections). The percentage shares of these classes were computed among sources considered and actually used as the indicators *Fact-oriented %, Problem-oriented %* and *General-purpose %.*

Table 3.1 (a). The practical process table for two normal decision tasks (Byström and Järvelin 1995)

Task No	Ambi- tion	Work- er	Info Type	Chan- nel	Sourc- e	Suc- cess	Rea- son	Eval- uat.
				none	int lit	s - pa		
				none	int lit	s - pa		
1	good	uni, ≤ 15	PI & DI & PSI	none	int ex	s - pa		
				none	int ex	s – pa	-	posi- tive
				none	int ex	s - pa		
				none	ext ex	s - pa		
				none	int do	ps - a	indisp	
				none	int per	ps - a	indisp	
2	satis- fact	poly, ≤ 15	PI	none	int per	ps - a	indisp	posi- tive
				none	int ex	ps - a	neces- sary	

Table 3.1 (b). The practical process (a) and thinking process (b) tables for two normal decision tasks (Byström and Järvelin 1995).

Task	Sources and Channels		Task	Sources and Channels	
No	Considered	Used	No	Considered	Used
1	• literature	int lit	2	• employm decisions	int do
	• literature	int lit		• personal calculation	int per
	• expert	int ex		• personal notes	int per
	• expert	int ex		• a colleague	int ex
	• expert	int ex		• other branches of	-
	• expert	ext ex		city administration	

Legend: In the Success-column, s = successful, ps = partially successful, ns = not successful, a = applicable, pa = partially applicable, and na = not applicable. Positive in the Evaluat -column means that the worker was able to complete the task. PSI = problem solving information, DI = domain information, PI = problem information. Uni = univ degree; poly = polytechnic degree. Indisp = indispensable.

Qualitative analysis was used to assign tasks into complexity categories. While all explanation remained qualitative, the summary indicators provided quantitative insight into the data. This exemplifies triangulation through multiple analysis methods.

In a subsequent study, Byström (1999) employed a significantly larger data set, which allowed quantitative explanation. Her project is a recent example of research that combines personal and task features with information seeking and source utilization.

Discourse Analysis. DA analyzes texts often collected through interviews. Another source of data consists of published texts within a domain. The subjects' opinions and conceptions as such often are interesting and useful. However, they should not be taken as facts describing how they really think or act. Views presented in an interview are interpretations about the current focus of attention and this interpretation is more complex and varied than usually assumed in Social Sciences or qualitative research. A longer text normally contains varied viewpoints, which are not easy to summarize. The result often remains in the form "on one hand ... on the other hand ...". The text may thus appear variable and inconsistent. When a single topic is considered from multiple viewpoints, different aspects will be emphasized. This is the reason for the variance. Commonly accepted interpretations and logical, well-argued opinions may be mutually conflicting. A summary therefore often misses the contextuality and viewpoint-dependence of interpretations. In each speech (text) context, one interpretation is given as the correct one and supported by substantial and logical arguments (Talja 1999).

Discourse analysis focuses the variability of interpretations concerning a given topic (or object of interest). Interpretative repertoires (or discourses) are identified by analyzing the regularities in this variance. As cues one may use conflicting views on the topic in the speech of a single speaker, and the occurrence of similar positions in the expression of different speakers. The presence of different discourses is revealed by the conflicts in interpretations as expressed in the speakers' view. All differing views that are present in the data are taken into account. Thereafter they can be grouped by viewpoints (approaches) generating them. The result of the analysis is a summary on different interpretative repertoires concerning the object of interest. (Talja 1999).

Tuominen (2001) argued that all interpretative repertoires (or discourses) present in an interview or text are equally valuable for analysis. He argued that the analyst need not check her interpretations with the subjects (authors) – as often done in qualitative research – since they are not the sole authorities for interpretation. The subjects' speech varies by context and they cannot control their use of language to the degree assumed by conventional analysis. Therefore they may in their speech, or with their speech, do things unconsciously or even things they later would deny.

3.2.4 The Methodology in Non-Empirical Studies

Information Seeking research produced, among the non-empirical type of investigations, new models and concepts. It is difficult to describe their construction, from the methodological point of view, in more detail than by stating that they were based on analytical thinking and synthesis of earlier empirical findings. Many papers proposing new models and/or concepts are not explicit about their methods and there are no common well-defined methods.

Vakkari and Kuokkanen's study (1997) on theory growth in task-based information seeking was however a landmark in its genre, being very methodological, and explicit about this. Vakkari and Kuokkanen introduced tools for analyzing theory growth and theory reconstruction, starting from Wagner and Berger's (1985; Wagner et al.1992) conception of sociological theories and a structuralist theory of science (e.g., Stegmüller 1976). The conceptual and methodological tools proposed include systematization and formalization of theories, and help in (1) stating the central concepts and their relations in a theory, (2) revealing implicit restrictions of the theory, and (3) facilitating the derivation of additional hypotheses from the theory's axioms.

The analytical exercise in Vakkari and Kuokkanen's study is the reconstruction of the unit theory by Byström and Järvelin (1995, see Sect. 3.1), which was formalized. Subsequently, the unit theory was refined by introducing new hypotheses, which connect some of the concepts in the unit theory that had remained unlinked. Finally, integration of both an actor's situational and personal factors into it through the introduction of new hypotheses expanded the unit theory.

Applying the tools Vakkari and Kuokkanen proposed on cognitive IS&R is necessary for the analysis of its theoretical growth as a research area but also very demanding.

3.3 Limitations and Open Problems

3.3.1. Theoretical Developments and Limitations

Evolution of Frameworks. The early studies on information seeking from 1960 to 1985 were limited. They provided a marginal and distorted image of information seeking, mainly seen from the information systems viewpoint. Thus, they typically investigated user behavior almost solely within the framework of the information systems focused on in each study. There was more focus on system needs than user needs.

Dervin and Nilan (1986) summarized the critique also voiced by many others (e.g., Brittain 1975; Herner and Herner 1967; Kunz et al. 1977a; Wersig 1973a) by stating that the first 30 years of IS studies focused on objective knowledge, considered users mechanically and as passive, did not take the user situations into account, had only a narrow view on information seeking (as atomistic users of systems). Moreover, the studies focused only on observable behavior, considered the study of individuals as leading to chaos, and were predominantly quantitative. Further, the focus was on questions based on the system viewpoint: the use of the system, explained through demographic and/or other sociological variables, knowledge of systems, likes and dislikes, *what*-questions instead of asking *why* the actors behaved as they did.

Theoretical understanding of the interaction of situations or contexts, work tasks, information seeking and information systems increased in 1986 - 2000. A major change was the shift of focus from systems-oriented studies to actor-oriented ones – individuals in concrete situations. This was reflected in several new models of information seeking, which explicitly focused on situations or contexts, work tasks, actors and/or information seeking processes. The frameworks discussed provide tools for investigating:

- *Contexts* of information seeking, e.g., Dervin's Sense-Making Approach;
- *Processes* of information seeking, e.g., Kuhlthau's process model;
- *Work task* based information seeking, e.g., Byström and Järvelin, Vakkari and Kuokkanen; and
- *Actors* engaged in information seeking instead of *users* of institutions or systems.

There are broad and narrower models, analytic and summary models, abstract and concrete models, and static and process models. However, in all of them the theoretical connection between information seeking and IR, or information systems more generally, is by and large still missing.

The shift of focus of frameworks toward individuals in concrete situations perhaps resulted in too individualistic frameworks. Jacobs and Shaw (1998) called for a more social view and Ingwersen (2001b) for a holistic approach. Indeed, although some frameworks presented the category of context / situation, the (theoretical) social science elaboration of contexts / situations was often thin.

Conceptual Evolution. Most of the research community agrees that the basic concepts in information seeking research – such as information, information need, information seeking, and the use of information – are quite vague in meaning. These concepts are nevertheless used as (undefined) primitives in many studies. The evolution of the concept of *information,* and the discussion around it, was presented in Chapt. 2.

The concepts of *information need, information seeking* and the *use of information* were not addressed in 1986 – 2000.[2] There is a vague working understanding of information seeking as the activity related to formulating and explicating information needs (or interests), and actually gaining access to the sources of information, getting them at hand. Similarly information use roughly means using – that is consuming, reading, attending, watching – documents, interpreting them, formulating answers and conceptions based on them. Such distinctions are only partly analytical but still needed. Further, one may discern the utilization of what was constructed from documents in ensuing documents, presentations, etc. Issues

---

[2] Donald Case (2002) discusses the concepts information need, seeking and information behavior.

of how seeking and use intermingle with other aspects of task performance are not understood nor analyzed in the literature of IS&R.

Work tasks and *search tasks* were commonly proposed as different and relevant concepts for information seeking. However, the distinction between them was not always clear and they are sometimes used interchangeably – in a confusing way – see Sect. 6.2.3. No widely accepted definitions exist.

Although there was a lot of discussion of information seeking in various contexts, studies seldom explicitly conceptualize the context at organizational or societal levels, not to mention empirical analysis.

Development of Theories. Vakkari (1997) reviewed information seeking literature up to mid-1990's and concluded that nearly all proposals by Dervin and Nilan in 1986 regarding information seeking meta-theory have been met in the literature. Vakkari also summarized the work up to mid-90s as suffering from several shortcomings, including: lack of theoretical growth, weak specification of meta-theories into substantive unit theories, unspecific definitions of basic concepts and their relations, lack of cumulative findings, and little interest in organizational or societal level, or information use.

Vakkari and Kuokkanen (1997, p. 512) discussed the consequences of such shortcomings. First, they pointed out that without a clear conceptually structured description of the research object, one's ability to create a specific and valid picture of the domain is impossible. Secondly, lack of theoretical structure with discriminating power hampers the utilization of the results of the research in future studies. Third, the implication of this is a slow or nonexistent theoretical growth in the field.

The work by Byström and Järvelin (1995) on task-based information seeking and its extension by Vakkari and Kuokkanen (1997), and Vakkari (1998; 1999) are examples of theoretical growth in information seeking through explication of basic concepts and their relationships. This development however covered only a narrow slice of the research area. Overall, there was no comprehensive theory of information seeking that would be analytic and process-oriented – neither general nor specific.

Progress in Information Seeking Research. The progress in Information Seeking Research after 1980s may be discussed through Bunge's (1967) functions for theories (see Sect. 1.5): Systematization of knowledge, guiding research, and mapping of reality.

Without going into details, framework-by-framework, one may claim that Information Seeking has progressed in all the major areas of knowledge systematization, research guidance, and mapping of reality. This progress, however, is still fragmented with the broadest frameworks lacking power in the systematization of knowledge while still guiding research. The frameworks capable of systematization of knowledge are narrower (e.g., they focus just on seeking) or cover only some aspects (like task complexity) of a broader context. The progress that has taken place in the 1990's is very promising but a lot needs to be achieved for a (cognitive) theory of IS&R.

Limitations and Open Problems in Information Seeking. Considering the frameworks proposed for the research area, one may state that there still are no frameworks that are *broad* – from work task to information retrieval – *abstract* – specifying theoretical concepts and their relationships rather than concrete stakeholders – *analytical* – suggesting hypotheses – and explicitly *process-oriented*. Such frameworks remain to be created and empirically validated, first in specific domains and contexts, and then more generally. Current research does not provide a sufficient knowledge basis *for engineering in information seeking* that would enable one to infer from actor, task and context descriptions the kind of information seeking environment needed for task performance.

There is too little theory-driven research although recent work suggests that there is progress toward this goal. A great number of empirical domains remain unexplored.

Meta-Theoretical Challenges. The mainstream (cognitive) research in information seeking has been challenged by discourse analytic approaches, which criticize the individualism of early cognitive and other actor-centered work in information seeking. At a deeper meta-theoretical level, the individualism of mainstream (cognitive) research in IS&R has been seen as a consequence of monologism, when dialogism would provide a more social account. These criticisms are treated in the following.

Discourse analytic approaches (Frohmann 1990; Talja 1997; 2001; Tuominen and Savolainen 1997) considered knowledge production through language and therefore the individual no more is the unit of analysis. Rather, the resources that languages provide (within a discourse) for the formation of knowledge are in focus. Each discourse provides for, and limits, a particular way of speaking about a topic. At the level of empirical phenomena, in any domain of communication, all actors producing, mediating, seeking and using information may share a discourse, at least partially. This is a prerequisite of successful communication, real gap-bridging. Knowledge is created, renewed and maintained socially, in human interaction. It is therefore important to study the socio-cultural aspects of actors and systems in information seeking or communication.

The protagonists of discourse analytic approaches have been quite critical toward the cognitive viewpoint (Frohmann 1990; 1992; Talja 1997;

Tuominen et al. 2002), the main criticism being against the supposed un-warranted individualism of the cognitive viewpoint and the erasure of the social. As stated in Chapt. 2, this criticism is pertinent regarding the period ending in the 1980's. We consider DA as a valuable contribution to the cognitive viewpoint proposed in the present volume, because it clarifies the knowledge formations individuals have jointly created and renewed, and thus have at their disposal when advancing their cognition in various (social) contexts. Individual sense-making or cognition is to a great degree bound by (social) discourses. Really new sparks, we believe, stem from individuals and then develop through social interaction.

Monologism vs. Dialogism. Tuominen and colleagues (2002) consid-ered prevalent meta-theories in Information Science and argued that they are based on the *subject – object dualism* (Capurro 1992; Talja 1997). In their view this approach may be called *monologism* since it focuses on a human individual – a traditional way of thinking in western scholarship. Here the subject makes rational observations about an object and can thus arrive at an understanding of, not just the surface of the object, but also its deep structure. Language provides a window both to mind and to reality, which it mirrors. Without this view it would be difficult to maintain the subject – object dualism. It is believed that language may obscure thinking and represent the reality in a distorted way. However, it is also believed that this influence can be avoided.

Tuominen and colleagues (2002) further argued that both the *informa-tion transfer model* and its *constructivist challenge* (e.g., Dervin 1983) in Information Science represent monologism. In the former, the focus is on information that objectively represents reality. Therefore the subject needs to be an objective observer. She should also focus on the essence of the ob-jects, not their surface. So derived, the representation is coded as a mes-sage and sent through some channel to some receivers who assimilate it and obtain an identical representation of reality (Tuominen et al. 2002).

Constructivism challenges this by understanding knowledge formation as an individual mental-conceptual process. The subject dominates the ob-ject. She may receive potential information, which turns into real informa-tion when her knowledge structures are affected by her interpretations. In-formation no longer is an objective thing but an object of conscious individual interpretation, construction and sense making. Systematic scien-tific methods help to avoid radical individualism or even solipsism. Never-theless, constructivism is a theory about individual knowledge formation. (Tuominen et al. 2002)

The information transfer model and constructivism in Information Sci-ence are opponents, which need each other: Both are based on the same subject – object dualism. To postulate objective knowledge requires a subject's individual mental worlds – and vice versa. (Tuominen et al. 2002)

Modern Social Science suggests *dialogism* as an alternative to monologism (Sampson 1993). The monologistic focus on human individuals is replaced in dialogism by knowledge formation through dialogue. Tuominen (1997; Tuominen et al. 2002) argued for a dialogistic meta-theory called *constructionism,* which is a theory on social formation of knowledge. Constructionism claims that our interpretations are linguistic constructions that are based on dialogues within communities (e.g., organizations) or traditions (e.g., paradigms). We use such constructions to (re)create social reality – which monologism projects out. These constructions are regarded as knowledge when they become commonly accepted. When such a consensus becomes wide enough, the underlying constructions become Talja's (1999; 2001) statements, which act as unchallenged preconditions within each discourse. When people apply the constructions in dialogue, they construct the social reality, which monological approaches exclude from discussion.

Constructionism meets constructivism in assuming knowledge formation as perspective-bound. The difference between them lies in that constructivism assumes individual perspectives while constructionism assumes dialogical perspectives. The information transfer model assumes freedom from all perspectives: feelings, ideologies and the like are disguises, which need to be distracted to see the truth. (Tuominen et al. 2002).

Our approach in this book is closer to monologism than dialogism (see Chapt. 6). We aim at a reasonable compromise between the information transfer model and constructivism. We think that documents are objective (as information objects) but their creation and assimilation are based on subjective interpretation, which is context-bound (see Chapt. 2). While the model we suggest in Chapt. 6 has a certain focus on individual actors, context is far from neglected. We see no irresolvable contradictions between our cognitive approach and dialogical approaches.

3.3.2. Empirical Developments and Limitations

Recent empirical findings of information seeking research provide new insight into actor-centered information seeking. Information seeking was seen as associated with work (or other primary) processes. Information seeking itself was understood as a process where the actor's understanding of his/her tasks/problems, information needs, relevance criteria, and the available information space evolve. The actors being studied became more varied, now including various professional groups and also lay people.

These studies provided rich and realistic descriptions on how people encounter discontinuities or gaps and how they try to make sense of them.

However, despite of the progress in theoretical understanding, empirical studies of information seeking provided only few empirical answers to research questions that relate characteristics of contexts and situations to characteristics of tasks, actors, information, seeking processes, sources, systems and use of information. It also remained difficult to apply the findings to information system design. Allen (1991) came to the conclusion that the process of merging system development with user studies begins to produce results, but substantial research gaps remain. We believe that this conclusion still is valid. While the understanding of task effects on information seeking has advanced, the understanding on how to derive and apply design criteria for information (retrieval) systems has not advanced correspondingly. For the most, IR system design is not informed about the situations and conditions of their use. There is shortage of studies that relate (IR) system features to features of task and/or seeking processes (see Chapt. 7).

In part the above limitations are problems of vision – in eyes of the critics. When the literature to be analyzed is defined as the (Library and) Information Science literature on information seeking, the research has apparent problems. With a broader approach, e.g., by including the literature on research management in engineering (e.g., Allen 1966a-b; 1969; 1977; Allen et al. 1980), the picture is cognitively more interesting: the work tasks and processes, performance level, interpersonal communication, and the utilization of various sources – not just printed ones – are not neglected while information seeking is considered. However, this vast literature deserves its own bound volume.

3.3.3. Methodological Developments and Limitations

The period 1986 – 2000 meant an increase in the application of qualitative methods (e.g., qualitative interviews, thinking aloud, and discourse analysis), longitudinal methods, and triangulation. Learning about the relationships of contexts, situations, task processes, actors, information, seeking processes, sources, systems and use of information would also require explanatory research methodology, i.e., design of field experiments and controlled experiments. In the field studies, careful elaboration of the research settings to contain variables on context, task, information, source, and other characteristics would also facilitate explanation of information seeking. The methods were available but not used to a sufficient degree.

Vakkari (1997) noted that qualitative approaches to information seeking usually have not aimed at explanations. Qualitative research rather aims at understanding the actors and their actions. However, Vakkari claimed that, also within qualitative approaches to information seeking, it is possible to scrutinize the relationships of constructs (or variables) of information seeking phenomena and the activities they support. We consider qualitative methodology a necessity in order to further develop the understanding of cognitive actors in the IS&R process.

In our view, session-dependent as well as longitudinal investigations of IS&R should not be limited to focusing on retrieval or seeking activities and behavior only. Since the same individual during IS&R may alter his/her cognitive role, due to the nature of the perceived work task or interest in context, other cognitive actors or processes taking part in IS&R ought to be as serious objects for research. Already Wersig (1973a) stressed this idea. Later, several investigations assumed a longitudinal approach allowing for the interplay of various cognitive actors in the IS&R process.

Triangulation, the use of multiple methods, is also necessary to capture complex cognitive phenomena of IS&R.

4 System-Oriented Information Retrieval

This chapter discusses the development of systems-oriented Information Retrieval research from 1960 to present time. The sixties were a decade when IR research expanded. Major events for IR were the ASTIA and Cranfield experiments in the 1950s and '60s (see e.g., Cleverdon 1967; Ellis 1996) laying down the model for much of experimental information retrieval research. Also the first operational automatic (non-interactive) retrieval systems were developed in the early sixties. The period 1960 - 90 produced three major approaches to IR: Systems-Oriented IR, User-Oriented IR, and Cognitive IR. The evolution of the latter two is discussed in the next chapter.

During the period 1960 – 90, the systems-oriented approach contributed several major mathematical retrieval models, including several best-match models, and the paradigm of laboratory based evaluation for IR (see Chap. 1). Evaluation experiments based on best-match IR methods were carried out in small test collections. On the practical/industry side, the online IR industry developed systems utilizing Boolean logic that provided global access to large bibliographic and later full-text collections.

The beginning of the 1990's with the start of the TREC (Text REtrieval Conference; Voorhees and Harman 1999) Conferences meant scaling up of IR systems and was a major landmark in IR. The scope of developments during this decade is astonishing both theoretically and regarding IR techniques and their practical application.

In the 1990s IR research expanded into many new areas. These include text retrieval in the form of text summarization, question answering, filtering, cross-language retrieval, and topic detection and tracking, foreboding text mining. Also IR in new media such as speech, music, images and video, as well as hypermedia developed. Along with multi and hyper media, document structures and mark-up gained attention both in document representation and access. The platforms used for document access developed from remote access to dedicated databases to ubiquitous access, through the Web and its search engines, to publicly available material and the dedicated (proprietary) databases as well. The systems-oriented approach contributed new mathematical retrieval models, including logical and language models. The paradigm of laboratory evaluation of IR methods was solidified by the extension of the approach to new types of document collections and evaluation settings and by scaling up from small test collections to very large ones.

On the practical/industry side, the Web with its search engines revolutionized IR by supporting ubiquitous access, by integrating searching, browsing and navigation, and by making web browsers the *de facto* standard access platform. Increasingly, search engines provided ranked retrieval while sometimes allowing Boolean queries as an advanced feature. Information overflow became concrete in a new way – often a short query of one to five words returned hundreds of thousands of documents. However, searchers were mostly happy and only interested in the first page or two of retrieved links, thus voting for precision rather than recall as a desired attribute of search results.

All these developments make it very difficult to produce an overview of developments even if one focuses on developments from a single perspective – the cognitive viewpoint. Here we have an inherent problem – the cognitive viewpoint seeks to cover all aspects of IR. Ingwersen and Willett (1995) is an introduction to systems-oriented and cognitive approaches to IR. Like the preceding chapter, this chapter is not intended as a literature review and thus only representative studies and findings, relevant to the cognitive viewpoint, will be discussed. The reader wishing to obtain a better coverage of the literature is referred to the many reviews published in the Annual Review of Information Science and Technology (ARIST). The following ARIST reviews are useful sources for readers wishing to go deeper into the literature: Bates (1981), Belkin and Croft (1987), Allen (1991), Kantor (1994) on IR techniques, Haas (1996), Blair (2002a) and Chowdhury (2002) on natural language processing, Efthimiadis (1996) on query expansion, Spink and Losee (1996) on feedback issues, Rasmussen (2002) on Web IR, Marchionini and Komlodi (1998) on user interface issues, Hjørland and Nielsen (2001) on indexing/access point issues, and Harter and Hert (1997) on evaluation. The textbooks by Salton (1968a), Rijsbergen (1979), Salton and McGill (1983), Salton (1989), Ellis (1996), Korfhage (1997), Losee (1998), Baeza-Yates and Ribeiro (1999), and Belew (2000) discuss the development of systems-oriented IR research in the 1990s. Sparck Jones and Willett's contribution (1997) is a selection of key IR papers set in context of the core development of best match IR methods from late 1950's to mid-1990.

The goal in real-life IR is to find useful information for an information need situation. Therefore IR is one means of information seeking. In practice, this goal is often reduced to finding documents, document components, or document surrogates, which support the user (the actor) in constructing useful information for her/his information need situation.

Documents, which facilitate the construction of needed information, are relevant.

Consequently, the goal of IR research is to develop concepts, methods, systems and algorithms that make all information, regardless of its form or location, as easily available as possible for any actor requiring it and in a form that is as accessible as possible for this actor. According to Peter Ingwersen (1992), IR research is concerned with the processes involved in the representation, storage, searching and finding of information that is relevant to a requirement for information desired by a human user.

The goal of systems-oriented IR research is to develop algorithms to identify and rank a number of (topically) relevant documents for presentation, given a (topical) request.[1] Research seeks to construct novel algorithms and systems, and to compare their performance with each other, finding ways of improving them. On the theoretical side, the goals include the analysis of basic problems of IR (e.g., the vocabulary problem between the recipient and the generator, document and query representation and matching) and the development of models and methods for attacking them. Systems-oriented IR research provides several such models and methods.

While being essential for the history and present stage of IR, most of the systems-oriented IR is at the monadic and structural levels (see Chap. 2) when processing texts or requests. It focuses on using individual text words as indexing / matching features. We therefore rather focus on research and efforts lifting IR systems and research toward the structural, contextual and cognitive levels. In this section we shall focus on the following systems-oriented IR research areas:

- Documents, requests, and relevance.
- Indexing, classification and clustering.
- Interfaces and visualization.
- Interaction and query modification.
- Natural language processing.
- Expert systems and interfaces for IR.

However, we shall begin with models in IR research and briefly review major developments and trends in the 1990s. We shall close the section by a discussion of research methods in IR, mainly IR evaluation, and limitations and open problems in IR research.

---

[1] This is, of course a somewhat narrow view regarding the goal, neglecting slightly different goals of some research domains. For example, in question answering one ranks potential answers to a question, in filtering one accepts/rejects documents, and in topic detection and tracking one seeks to identify new news topics and follow their development as accurately as possible.

4.1 Models in System-Oriented IR Research

There are several inherent problems, which make IR difficult and challenging. First, all relevant documents are not easily found because the search requests always are incomplete with respect to the searcher's needs. Moreover, even the incomplete requests can often be expressed through very many possible expressions in documents – sometimes indeed implicitly – that is, there is semantic openness in documents. Also some of the expressed requirements may be ambiguous, either due to conceptual fuzziness (e.g., what does 'new' mean – at most one year old?), or due to lacking a unique structural data element (e.g., title, abstract, index term), where to look for the information. Secondly, the retrieval results also contain unwanted documents because the very same keys used as evidence of document relevance also appear in unwanted, irrelevant documents. This is unavoidable due to the properties of natural language (see Sect. 4.7), and the use of context-free – monadic – keywords (text features) for searching. Thirdly, retrieval results are often indirect, i.e., documents (or passages or surrogates) are retrieved instead of information. To obtain the required information, the user has to construct it, i.e., go through document acquisition and interpretation. Consequently, we may conclude that text and, generally, all feature-based retrieval is inherently fuzzy.

The Laboratory Model of IR set the general framework within which these problems were studied. Several retrieval models have been developed within the laboratory model to handle these problems as well as possible.

The Laboratory Model of IR is the single dominant model of research for the entire system-oriented IR research (see Fig. 1.1, which extends the original Fig. 4.1 below). The basic laboratory model has no user involvement. This model suggests documents, search requests, their representation, the database, queries, and the matching of the two latter as foci of research and development. Methodologically, it also suggests relevance assessments, recall base construction and query result evaluation as foci of analysis.

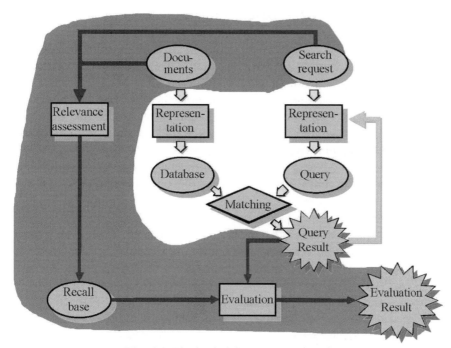

Fig. 4.1. The basic laboratory model of IR

In its focus on documents, requests and their matching, the scope of the Laboratory Model of IR is narrow. Users or cognitive actors, their situations and tasks fall outside the model. Therefore IR design issues cannot be related to the actors' worlds. Moreover, the model has mainly served studies on computational and/or formal aspects of IR. It is explicitly a process model of two representation steps and one matching step. Moreover, it explicitly focuses on evaluation, which has achieved a prominent status within IR research. The Laboratory Model of IR is a summary model – as such it does not suggest variables of the entities or processes, or their relationships. It is a very general model – applicable over a range of entities or processes, e.g., over any kind of document collection (mass communication, scholarly) in any language (or even any media), for any query representation, etc. It therefore allows for a broad range of research.

However, the full potential of the Laboratory Model of IR has not been used. In particular, documents, search requests, and relevance were seen in standard ways that support controlled experiments – see Sect. 4.3 below.

A *retrieval model* consists of the specification of document representation and request representation, and of the definition of the matching algorithm for comparing the two representations. In principle, *document representation* may concern the representation of the document content, its layout, its structure, and its metadata. Up to 1990, the main focus of retrieval models was in content and metadata representation. Content representation meant document indexing through an indexing process that was either intellectual (manual) or automatic. The index keys were derived either from a controlled source, such as a thesaurus, or from the document content itself. Metadata representation, e.g., in the form bibliographic citations, often augmented by the texts of document abstracts, had the same choices but less content. Sect. 4.4 discusses indexing in more detail. *Request representation* meant selecting the search keys for the request and determining their mutual relationships through query language operators. Again, either an intellectual (manual) or an automatic process was involved.

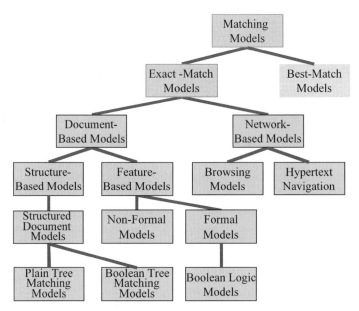

Fig. 4.2(a). Exact matching methods (extended from Belkin and Croft 1987). New boxes with a solid frame.

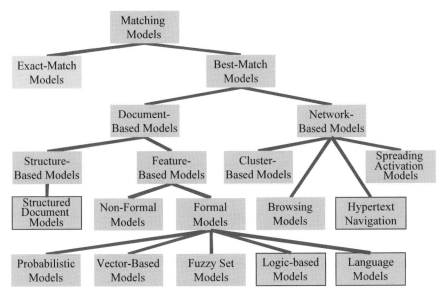

Fig. 4.2(b). Best match methods (extended from Belkin and Croft 1987). New boxes with a solid frame.

Belkin and Croft (1987) classified the matching methods as *exact match methods* (e.g., Boolean logic), and several *partial match* (or best match) methods. New retrieval models and matching algorithms were introduced in the 1990s – based on novel ways of representing documents and/or requests, or on novel matching algorithms for comparing the two representations. Among them were novel structure-based models, hypertext network-based models, language models, and logical models. Some were definitively best match approaches, some both exact and best match approaches (see Fig. 4.2).

We do not go into details regarding these models and methods. Readers interested in the novel methods in Fig. 4.2 are advised to other sources as follows:

- Structure-based models: Basically these models represent documents as tree-structures and queries as path-expressions and associated conditions on subtree similarity and/or content feature similarity.
  Kilpeläinen and Mannila (1993), among others, proposed a tree pattern matching which allows easy expression of queries that use the structure and the content of the document. Macleod (1991), building on SGML text representation, proposes a query language supporting structural and content conditions. Kuikka and Salminen (1997) proposed a grammar-based model for structured text document represen-

tation and retrieval. Järvelin and Niemi (1995; 1999), based on an NF2 data model,[2] combined structural and content conditions with deductive capabilities. These approaches were based on exact match retrieval (Fig. 4.2a). Fuhr (1992; and Rölleke 1997; and Großjohann 2001), and Chinenyanga and Kushmerick (2001), and Lalmas (1997), among others, sought to integrate structural and probabilistic matching (Fig. 4.2b). The recent papers extend the capabilities of the XQuery query language (XQuery 2001). Since 2002, the INEX evaluation campaign (http://inex.is.informatik.uni-duisburg.de:2004/) has developed XML-based retrieval. Structure-based models are relevant for the cognitive viewpoint because they allow the use of cognitively different components of documents in a coordinated way to refine/constrain result document structures, to improve precision by matching within semantically appropriate components, and to support poly-representation (see Sect. 5.2.3).

- Hypertext network-based models: Hypertext IR models often represent, as one layer, the document network and, as another, a concept network. Links relate concept nodes and document nodes together. Searchers may browse either network, and move back and forth between them (e.g., Lucarella and Zanzi 1993). Salminen and colleagues (1995) propose a model with a grammar-based schema and exact match IR capabilities (Fig. 4.2a). Agosti and Smeaton's (1996) book is an overview of hypertext IR systems and covers hypertext construction, retrieval and visualization. Among the articles, various best match IR techniques are integrated with spreading activation, structure traversal and link processing techniques (Fig. 4.2b). These are precursors of Web retrieval techniques employing link information, such as Page Rank (Brin and Page 1998; Page et al. 1998), and examples of utilizing cognitive poly-representation. Hypertext retrieval models integrate cognitively different access approaches: browsing, navigation and retrieval.
- *Language models* represent queries and documents directly as probabilistic models and integrate document indexing and retrieval into a single model – see Hiemstra (1998a-b), Ponte and Croft (1998), and Berger and Lafferty (1999).
- *Logical models:* Van Rijsbergen (1986) proposed the Logical Uncertainty Principle and for the first time explicitly connected logic and IR modeling. In logical IR models document relevance is identified with the probability that the document logically implies the query. Van

---

[2] NF2 – non-first normal form data model, i.e., unnormalized or nested relations data model.

Rijsbergen (1989) argues that mathematical, linguistic and algorithmic IR theories can be unified under a logical model. Lalmas (1998) discusses the weaknesses of classical logic for information retrieval and introduces several non-classical logics, such as Modal Logic, Logical Imaging, Terminological Logic, and Situation Theory, that are more appropriate for IR.

The development of various best match retrieval models was an attempt to avoid inherent problems of the Boolean Model, which are (Belkin and Croft 1987; Ingwersen and Willett 1995):

- Making a sharp distinction between the retrieved and the non-retrieved documents;
- Providing the result documents in an arbitrary order (a set);
- Providing only a weak control of the result set size;
- Not allowing weighting of search keys to tell their importance for the request;
- Requiring a good command of Boolean logic which is difficult for human users; and
- Discharging relevant documents when applying the not logic (or set difference).

On the contrary, best-match models can be characterized as providing:

- Flexible and graded distinction between the retrieved and the non-retrieved documents;
- Relevance ranking in the result list, i.e., documents expected to be the most relevant are listed first;
- Full control of result list size;
- Weighting of search keys; and
- Simple user interface through natural language queries.

All best-match models do not provide all of the features listed above. We do not review the best-match models in this book. They are covered in the textbooks cited in the beginning of this chapter.

The most positive features of Boolean logic, e.g., that queries can be structured by operators (conjunctions, proximity operators) and that content and metadata elements, like publication years or author names, can easily be combined in queries, have not been superseded by the best match IR models.

The operational IR systems and the experimental IR systems research and development communities have been rather separate, not communicating much with each other. See, for instance, the author co-citation maps of Information Science and IR by White and McCain (1998) and Ding,

Chowdhury and Foo (1999). The experimental IR systems research and development community produced a vast majority of the systems-oriented research literature. We will now discuss the developments by both communities.

4.2 Major Developments of System-oriented IR Research

In general, systems-oriented IR research and development continued to be technology-driven. Through the years, computer technology has constantly provided more powerful systems and new approaches for solving problems in information processing. Research and development in IR has investigated possibilities for developing more powerful IR systems to fully utilize the technological potential of each era. (Saracevic 1990; 1992) Increased computation power made novel IR applications practical also in the 1990s.

The early results of the experimental IR systems research may be outlined, in broad terms, as follows:

- Development of various best-match retrieval models to provide ranked retrieval output, including the Fuzzy Set Model, the Vector Space Model, and the Probabilistic Model (in 1960-70), and logical models (in 1980s);
- Development of various weighted indexing methods for the above (in 1960-70);
- Development of methods for automatic classification and clustering (in 1970-80);
- Development of methods for relevance feedback and query expansion (in 1970s);
- Application of NLP methods on IR (morphology, surface syntax; in 1980s);
- Development of the distributed expert systems approach and expert systems for information retrieval, e.g., systems like I^3R, Coder, MedIndEx (in late 1980s);
- Development of methods for 2D and 3D presentations for feedback and results (in late 1980s);
- Development of the IR evaluation methodology based on the Laboratory Model (or Cranfield paradigm; in the 1960s and later).

The main results of recent experimental IR systems research may be outlined as follows:

- Development of novel IR models: structure-based models, hypermedia IR models, language models, and logical models to better handle increasingly complex documents as discussed above;
- Scaling up the laboratory evaluation paradigm to manage collections of gigabyte size;
- Consolidation of the laboratory evaluation paradigm in new systems-oriented IR research areas, such as speech retrieval;
- Expansion of IR research to new systems-oriented research areas;
- Development of visual interfaces, interactive IR evaluation and the criticism of the Laboratory Model from the cognitive viewpoint, among others (Sects. 4.5, 4.6);
- Semantic information retrieval and the Semantic Web (Sect. 4.6);
- Further integration of IR with NLP and database management research.

The laboratory-oriented IR research extended in the 1990's into many areas beyond monolingual document retrieval, such as Question Answering, Topic Detection and Tracking, Cross-language IR, Music IR, Spoken Document Retrieval, Multimedia Retrieval, Web IR, and Interactive IR. Also research in older areas, such as, Filtering and Routing, Text Categorization/Classification, and Summarization flourished. Many of these had their own sessions, tutorials, and workshops at ACM SIGIR conferences, sometimes even their own independent workshops and conferences. In these special areas the tasks were cognitively different and often required their own evaluation metrics and methods. We will not cover these areas in any systematic way in this section.

The *operational IR systems,* forming the backbone of commercial information retrieval services, were mainly based on Boolean logic. By the end of the 1960s research had formulated the basic methods of preparing queries through Boolean operators, of representing document metadata in computer files (the basic document file and the inverted index), and of matching the queries through the inverted index with the document representations. The mega-trends in the development of the operational IR systems have been:

- Moving from batch processing systems to online systems by early 1970s;
- Improving the accessibility of online systems through increasingly better computer networks – first through dedicated networks and later through the Internet;
- Developing various online search aids, for example, search key truncation, proximity operators, multiple database searching, inverted index

look-up, online thesauri, frequency ranking and other system feedback
(in the 1980s);

- Improving interaction and interfaces through feedback mechanisms
(both human and system feedback);
- Scaling up from bibliographic retrieval systems to full text retrieval
systems; and development of special application domains like chemical IR.

The Web and its precursors (Gopher, Veronica, WAIS) changed the operational IR landscape in the 1990s tremendously. The mega-trends in the
development of the operational online information access became the following:

- Improving the accessibility of the online bibliographic and full-text databases through increasingly better computer networks – the Internet,
the Web;
- Moving from dedicated online IR systems (the "Deep Web") to open
Web-based IR applications using Web browsers as standard interface;
practical integration of searching, navigation and browsing;
- Expansion of the number of online documents up to billions of documents and expansion of document types – HTML and XML coded
home pages, among others, often in no way edited or controlled for
neither format nor content, serving quite diverse and varied (cognitive
and social) communication needs in comparison to traditional scholarly documents;
- Expansion of user populations of (Web) IR systems: from mainly (edu-
cated) IR system users to tens of millions of lay users lacking searching (and specialized domain) skills and reluctant to learn such; pre-
dominance of extremely short queries, often of factual types;
- Expansion of digital libraries from local to regional and nation-wide
networks encompassing both traditional and several non-traditional
types of materials like digital maps and satellite imagery; digital libraries having an important role as proxies negotiating access licenses to
their user communities;
- Increasing involvement of the users in electronic environments, including not just IR but also electronic mail (with file attachments), news-
groups, IRC (Internet Relay Chat) as well as other (organizational)
communication and information systems; and
- Expansion of electronic commerce and online marketing – including
spam – and the consequent need for filtering.

4.3 Documents, Requests and Relevance: Issues and Findings

4.3.1. Documents

Originally systems-oriented IR research dealt with document metadata – bibliographic references. The first laboratory databases, like the Cranfield Collection, and the first operational databases, like the MEDLARS database in medicine, were bibliographic databases. The document types of real life IR evolved significantly in the 1990s. Document *genres* changed from predominantly scholarly documents or their surrogate representations to full text and multimedia (hypermedia) in all genres of communication – news, popular articles, music, image collections, film, discussion lists, and personal views / opinions – also making publicly accessible previously publicly non-accessible or even censored documents such as personal / organizational home pages, porn and ads of diverse kinds. Also document *domains* became more diverse – moving from a dominance of various domains of science, technology and other scholarship to all domains of human life – religion, sex and crime included. Finally, documents evolved also *structurally,* already from the 1980's (see Goldfarb 1991) – that means from plain text / bibliographic records to structured textual and hypermedia documents marked-up on the basis of the SGML, HTML, XML, or HyTime standards that became an essential part of online IR during that decade.

Citation indexes expanded and the web of documents, based on their citation relationships, could be browsed online (Lawrence and Giles 1999; ResearchIndex, http://www.researchindex.com; WebofScience, http://isiknowledge.com). Web document link structures gave rise to page ranking in search engines (PageRank, see Page et al. 1998; Rasmussen 2002) and a new research area – Webometrics (Almind and Ingwersen 1997; Ingwersen and Björneborn 2004).

The most important document genre and domain in modern *laboratory oriented IR* research in the 1990s was *news documents.* This is because the major test collections used in the TREC conferences consisted of news articles – with some US governmental reports included (Harman 1993). The documents were furthermore predominantly *structurally simple* with little or no structural mark-up in addition to simple attributes like document ID, author, date, source, etc. An early interesting collection was the cystic fibrosis database which contained 1239 documents with their references and the number of citations each document had received over a long citation window and 100 test topics with extensive relevance assessments (Shaw, Wood and Tibbo 1991). However, toward the new millennium, novel types of test collections were created. The IEEE Computer Science collection contained fully XML marked-up scholarly Computer Science documents (12107 documents, 494 MB, 60 test topics, Gövert and Kazai 2002), and the W10T collection of general Web documents, links included (10 GB, 50 topics, Voorhees 2001b)[3]. Documents were no more seen as collections of independent indexing features – the features had at least structural relationships (in addition to increasingly recognized linguistic relationships, see Sect. 4.7). These developments were reaching out from the narrow boundaries of the traditional test collection approach.

Salton and colleagues (1993; 1994) investigated *passage retrieval* – breaking up the approach of retrieving full documents as responses and retrieving, instead, text passages of varying granularity. Low scoring long documents, covering a range of themes, may contain passages highly relevant to a query. These may be identified through local passage-level matching after global document level matching. Retrieval effectiveness was shown to improve through passage retrieval. Callan (1994) found that passages based on paragraph boundaries were less effective than passages based on overlapping text windows of varying sizes. Further, it seemed always best to combine document-level evidence and passage-level evidence. Question answering (e.g., Voorhees and Tice 1999) went deeper in text analysis, trying to elicit from texts answers to factual questions.

Non-text media were also experimented with. The TREC conferences started a track on video retrieval (TREC Video Track[4] in 2001) and spoken document retrieval (TREC Spoken Document Retrieval Track[5]; Garofolo et al. 2000). Several teams also worked on image retrieval (e.g., Rasmussen 1997; Markkula and Sormunen 1998). However, no large standard test collections emerged from these latter efforts.

In the *operational IR research* arena, it is difficult to say which document types were most important. Typically the operational systems research did not analyze the diverse genres of Web documents while emphasizing log analysis of document access.

---

[3] The VLC2 Collection contains 100 GB of data (http://trec.nist.gov).
[4] http://www.itl.nist.gov/iaui/894.02/projects/trecvid/ [Cited February 27, 2004].
[5] http://www.nist.gov/speech/tests/sdr/sdr2000/sdr2000.htm [Cited March 9, 2004].

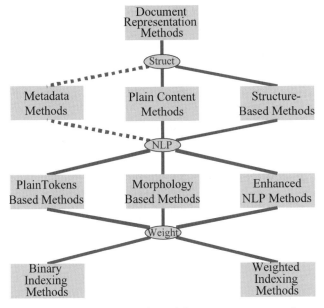

Fig. 4.3. A classification of feature-based document representation methods

Many methods were used in document representation. Analogously to the classification of matching methods, Fig. 4.3 classifies methods of feature-based document representation, where one needs to make three essential decisions: whether document structure is represented, whether NLP techniques are used for manipulating document text before indexing, and whether binary or weighted indexing is used. Regarding structure, in metadata-based methods, just the metadata, e.g., bibliographic elements and keywords are represented as indexing features – this holds for the most traditional online databases and for indexing of non-text media collections. Alternatively, the document may be processed as plain content, with just the running positions of indexing features retained as in traditional full-text indexing. In more recent efforts, the hosting structural element, such as, an XML path of a document, may be indexed with each indexing feature. Regarding NLP (see Sect. 4.7), the most traditional way is plain token indexing, that is, using text-words as such as indexing features without any manipulation. Morphology-based methods cover traditional stemming and lemmatization of text words to turn them into indexing features. Enhanced NLP methods include, in addition, for example phrase processing and anaphor resolution. Weighting in traditional online systems was binary whereas best-match systems employ real non-binary weights. These representational choices affect the cognitive load and possibilities searchers have.

In summary, documents have three dimensions: content, explicit structure, and layout (e.g., text styles, number of columns). Essentially, these are dependent on domain, media, and social discourse community. Much of IR research has dealt with document content only – with the exception of online IR research dealing with short structured bibliographic items. Recent efforts in IR have shed light on document structure and its application in retrieval. Layout has not been used as a retrieval dimension in IR. The plain document content may also be seen to have a structure, e.g., a rhetorical structure (Paice 1991b), or based on the dimensions and distinctions made, which can be identified by semiotic analysis (Suominen 1998) or discourse analysis (see Sect. 3.1.1). This type of research was rare.

Documents are seen in systems-oriented IR research as collections of independent indexing features. In principle, each word in a document is considered as an indexing feature and stored as an access point in an inverted index. From the cognitive point of view, such indexing remains at the monadic level, the index keys have neither structure nor context.

4.3.2. Requests

Systems-oriented IR research dealt with requests as collections of searching features. In the laboratory research, these features were either used as such, or often after some morphological processing such as stemming (e.g., Salton and McGill 1983) and phrase recognition (e.g., Croft, Turtle and Lewis 1991), as bags of search keys without further structural relationships. This fostered automatic query construction from request texts – and allowed natural language queries. However, operational systems were based on Boolean logic and therefore searching features were treated as logically related.

The change of user populations toward predominantly lay users (or the general public) resulted in the change of the distribution of request types. Formally, queries representing requests turned extremely short, containing often just one or two words and having hardly any structure or query language operators (e.g., Jansen and Pooch 2001). Content-wise, all domains of human life, interests and desires became request topics in contrast to scholarly topics of the preceding decade. In addition, conscious topical and well-defined requests, Sect. 6.2.6, lost their dominance, at least now, if they ever had such in the real life. The many search engine log studies (e.g., reviewed by Jansen and Pooch 2001) performed in the late 1990s or in the beginning of the first decade of the new millennium have not informed the community about the distribution of various request types, including muddled, variable and/or factual ones.

In laboratory-oriented IR research, however, conscious topical and well-defined requests (topics) dominated. Query length[6] was devoted some attention. Longer topics (TREC 1-3) and shorter requests (TREC 4) were tested (Harman 1995b; Voorhees and Harman 1997). However, even the short topics of TREC contained on the average 10 (non-stop) words, well above the real life practice of about two key words, or less, in Web IR. Ill-defined, variable requests were not considered. Even in interactive IR (IIR) experiments in TREC, the topics were conscious topical, stable and well-defined, not properly representing the situation of an unknowledgeable searcher facing a complex search problem.

In operational systems-oriented research, log analyses do not easily reveal any search strategies or moves when users issue two-word queries, examine some links on one or two topmost pages – and perhaps change their access mode to browsing / navigation, only to return several minutes later (if ever). Thus the log analyst cannot easily know whether the much later issued new queries belong to the former context or not. This problem remains largely unsolved within any simplistic log analysis approach at the search engine side. See Pharo (2002) for alternatives. See also Sect. 5.5.

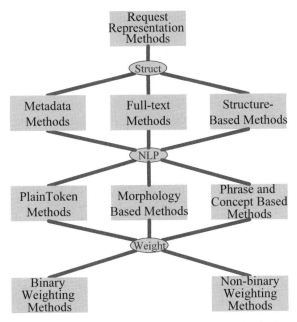

Fig. 4.4. A classification of request representation methods for text retrieval

---

[6] TREC terminology employed – this really means topic specification length in some TREC experiments.

Many methods were used in request representation. Analogously to the classification of matching methods, Fig. 4.4 classifies methods of request representation for feature-based retrieval. As above, but now regarding requests, one needs to make three essential decisions: whether structural search criteria are represented, whether NLP techniques are used for manipulating request text before indexing, and whether binary or weighted search keys are used. Regarding structure, in metadata-based methods, just the metadata, e.g., bibliographic elements and keywords are used as search keys. Alternatively, the request may be represented as plain content, as full-text keys. In more recent efforts, the required structural element, such as an XML element, of a document may be indicated for each search key. Regarding NLP (see Sect. 4.7), the most traditional way is to use plain tokens as search keys. Morphology-based methods cover traditional stemming and lemmatization of text words to turn them into search keys. Phrase and concept based methods include, in addition, for example phrase marking in queries and synonym set marking for keys representing the same request concept or aspect. Weighting in traditional online systems was binary whereas in best-match systems it is real-valued. These representational choices affect the cognitive load and possibilities searchers have. Of course, request representation must be compatible with document representation.

Fig. 4.4 classifies explicit request representation methods. The methods may also be implicit. The searcher may for example in relevance feedback state that certain documents are relevant – likewise regarding images retrieved in a collection. However, even the implicit methods translate to explicit ones. Even if the searcher points just to a document or image symbol without specifying any of its features as relevant, the system uses their representations to derive a novel request representation.

In the case of (primarily) *non-text* documents, textual elements of the documents were often used for retrieval – e.g., image captions, video subtitles. This approach allows textual requests. Alternatively, image structure, texture and color scheme were popular in CBIR (content-based image retrieval). However, such image (or video) elements are semantically very open and thus challenging retrieval criteria. Therefore the most accurate semantic access continued to be either through image captions, which may be indexed text-wise, or through assigned metadata, like Dublin Core (see Sect. 4.4). A part of the metadata may be organized as ontologies (see Sect. 4.6).

4.3.3. Relevance Assessments

In user-oriented / cognitive IR research, non-binary relevance assessments became popular in the 1990s (see Sect. 5.7). Also other aspects of relevance than plain topicality were considered. However, the laboratory-oriented IR research continued using predominantly binary relevance assessments based on static topicality without assessor saturation effects Even in interactive IR (IIR) experiments in TREC (Hersh and Over 2000), relevance assessments were ordinary binary TREC assessments, based on conscious topical and well-defined requests, and not leaving room for searchers' cognitively differing interpretations and needs (even if facing the same assigned work task / search task). Toward the new millennium there was, however, progress toward graded assessments in test collections, an early one being – since the original Cranfield Collection – the Finnish TUTK collection with a four-point assessment scale (50 K documents, 35 topics; Kekäläinen 1999; Sormunen 2000a-b)[7]. Later came the TREC WT10g collection (three-point, 50 topics; Voorhees 2001b), the WT100g collection (binary assessments 10,000 topics of which less than 100 used in evaluation; Hawking 2001; Voorhees 2001a) and the TREC Multi Grade Collection (four-point, 38 topics; Sormunen 2002a-b). The INEX test collection (12107 Computer Science documents, 60 + 66 topics for 2002-3) also used four-point relevance assessments inspired by TUTK and the TREC Multi Grade Collection and was the first to contain full documents in XML (Fuhr et al. 2002). These developments affected the methodology of laboratory-oriented IR evaluation, see Sect. 4.9.

Sormunen and colleagues (2001) studied empirically the interaction of document text characteristics, document relevance level and query formulation. Statistical differences in textual characteristics of highly relevant and less relevant documents were investigated by applying a facet analysis technique. The facets were identified from requests. In highly relevant documents a larger number of facets of the corresponding request were discussed. Moreover, searchable expressions for the facets were distributed over a larger set of text paragraphs, and a larger set of unique expressions were used per facet than in marginally relevant documents. However, even at the highest relevance level, only two thirds of the facets were present in all relevant documents. This supports directly best match retrieval since a Boolean query on all facets would automatically fail in retrieving many highly relevant documents. The strategy in Boolean retrieval used to fight this problem is to reduce the exhaustivity (number of facets) of queries.

---

[7] This test collection was originally designed and constructed by Sormunen in 1990-91.

This fails because the searcher does not know which facets are missing from relevant documents – and this varies. Therefore a less exhaustive query fails to use the evidence *for* relevance existing in documents but for the dropped facets (Sormunen 2000).

A query expansion experiment verified that the findings of the text analysis could be exploited in formulating more effective queries for best match retrieval in the hunt for highly relevant documents. The results revealed that expanded queries with concept-based structures performed better than unexpanded queries or 'natural language' queries (see Sect. 4.6). Further it was shown that highly relevant documents benefit essentially more from the concept-based QM in ranking than marginally relevant documents. (Sormunen et al. 2001).

4.4 Indexing, Classification and Clustering: Issues and Findings

Indexing. Text indexing is a process that creates a short description of the content of the original text (Moens 2000; Rowley 1988; Lancaster and Warner 1993). The result is the representation of the text. In particular in intellectual indexing the representations are short whereas in automatic indexing all words in the text may serve as indexing features. Indexing can derive index keys from document texts or assign index keys from a controlled vocabulary source. Intellectual indexing and automatic indexing are the main approaches in systems-oriented research.

Automatic Indexing. Salton (1968a-b; 1989; Salton and McGill 1983) summarizes several experiments in automatic indexing where stop-lists, stemming, phrase processing and statistical thesaurus processing have been evaluated. Belew (2000, Chap. 3) is a modern introduction to statistical automatic indexing techniques with keyword stemming, discrimination power and document length normalization included. Language models (Sect. 4.2) integrate document indexing and retrieval into a single model. The basic automatic indexing techniques remain at the *monadic level* (Sect. 2.1.1) and are not discussed further. Sect. 4.7 deals with NLP in IR and *structural level* approaches in automatic indexing – like word form inflection, phrases, and compound words – and techniques that are relevant especially when dealing with languages other than English.

Some *structural* to *contextual level* approaches toward automatic conceptual indexing have been proposed. Efforts at knowledge-based text representation (representation of the meaning) for indexing or abstracting, e.g., by Rau and colleagues (1989), and Hahn (1990), suffered from poor prospects of broadening such systems to cope with a wider variety of input. They were effective in narrow domains and with a specific document genre. These were based on frame representation with frame slots representing important concept types and their relationship types in a specified domain. Paice and Jones (1993) suggested that indexing and abstracting may be performed as interrelated activities. In their proposal source texts are scanned, and stylistic clues and constructs are used for extracting candidate fillers for various slots in frames. Subsequently, an actual concept name is chosen for each slot by comparing various candidates and their weights.

Marti Hearst and Christian Plaunt (1993) explored subtopic identification in full text documents and proposed two-level indexing into main topics and subtopics. They suggested TextTiling as an approach to identification of subtopics in a longer document – to partition texts into coherent multi-paragraph units that represent the pattern of subtopics that comprise them. They claimed that the main topics of a text occur throughout the length of the text while the subtopics are of only limited extent. Thus they proposed an index to be built consisting of two parts: the global main topic index, and a set of local subtopic indexes. This separation facilitates a retrieval paradigm in which a user can specify both the main and the subtopic to retrieve on. Hearst and Plaunt noted that the subordination relationship between main and subtopics is different from logical conjunction. The identification of subtopics was experimentally shown to improve retrieval effectiveness. Their work shows that higher-order (than monadic word-level features) discourse features can be used for the benefit IR – automatically.

Carol Tenopir (1985) and McKinin and others (1991) compared full-text indexing to controlled vocabulary indexing in Boolean IR and found that full-text indexing greatly improves recall while precision may dramatically deteriorate. Recall may also deteriorate because the searcher does not use search keys that match the index keys of relevant documents (Croft, Krovetz and Turtle 1990; Blair and Maron 1985; 1990). Raya Fidel further investigated empirically the application of controlled vocabulary versus natural language search keys during operational online IR in a comprehensive study (1991b).

Edie Rasmussen (2002) reviewed both automatic and intellectual indexing in the Web. Automatic indexing techniques include traditional keyword indexing techniques and structural techniques, e.g., weighting specially tagged text more heavily. Also text in link anchors and around them may be used to locate related pages. However, the hypertext link structure of the Web might also be indexed and used to improve search results. PageRank (Page et al. 1998) is one such technique, used e.g., by Google (http:

//www.google.com), allowing a retrieval engine to characterize the importance of a web page by its position in the link graph, i.e., the in-links it re-
ceives from other pages of varying importance and their anchor texts. Here
the Web user / publisher community collectively votes for page importance – a social source of (socio-) cognitive evidence.

The MedIndex system (Humphrey 1991) represented an approach to indexing medical literature that mediates between automatic and intellectual
approaches. It employed frames to represent documents and medical
knowledge, and scripts to represent the indexing process. The latter guide
the indexing process and propose knowledge frames to be instantiated for
the document to be indexed. The system also suggested fillers for the
frame slots. When reviewed and accepted, or otherwise filled in by the
human indexer, demons were automatically launched to check and infer
additional frames and/or slot-fillers for the document. The MedIndex system combined automatic inference and book-keeping, based on the MeSH
thesaurus (Medical Subject Headings), with human expertise in indexing.
See also UMLS (Unified Medical Language System) in Sect. 4.6.

Intellectual Indexing and Classification. Intellectual indexing involves human indexers, but may be most often considered nevertheless
systems-oriented – the indexers and the indexing language being part of
the system and indexing aiming at serving no narrowly defined user group.
F. W. Lancaster (1968a; 1972; 1998; and Warner 1993) gives overviews of
intellectual indexing. W.J. Hutchins (1975) and Claire Beghtol (1986) consider intellectual indexing from a linguistic viewpoint and cognitive viewpoint. A.C. Foskett (1996), among others, explains semantic relationships
like synonymy, hierarchy and association, and their presentation in
thesauri and classification schemes, later to be also called ontologies. He
also discussed the syntax of assigned indexing – how index terms or class
notations are related to each other, e.g., through role indicators, in order to
express more complex semantic relationships than just plain coordination.
Mainstream automatic indexing approaches, or intellectual indexing approaches for online IR, do not express richer relationships than simple coordination (co-occurrence) of index keys. Richer representations would be
welcome from the cognitive viewpoint – meaning contextual and even
cognitive level representation and serving also polyrepresentation. Richer
representations are, however, difficult to apply reliably under economic
pressure and, if used alone, not sufficiently exhaustive compared to full
text. The IR community has more or less disposed the techniques already
developed in the 1960s and often for card catalogs – perhaps tossing off
the baby with the bath water. Interesting semantic relationships, long studied in classification theory, *do not disappear* from texts or requests just by

ignoring them. However, we expect progress in semantically richer representations to mainly come from application of taxonomies and ontologies in retrieval, Sect. 4.6, and the NLP – IR area, Sect. 4.7.

F. W. Lancaster (1968b) made a landmark evaluation of an operational IR system: the MEDLARS batch mode service. The evaluation also looked at the indexing of the database and analyzed recall and precision failures attributable to indexing – due to index language, indexing exhaustivity, specificity, and processing. About 10% of recall failures and 36% of precision failures were attributable to index language, 37% of recall failures and 13% of precision failures were due to indexing. Among the 37% of recall failures due to indexing, 30% units were due to indexer omissions and insufficient indexing exhaustivity. Among the 36% of precision failures due to index language, nearly 20% units were due to lack of index language specificity. The influence of the intermediary in the process was not found to be always positive. These findings are not surprising – the problems are typical to intellectual indexing based on a controlled vocabulary.

Table 4.1. Access points classified by kinds (examples from Hjörland and Nielsen 2001)

Access point dimensions
• Verbal vs. nonverbal (e.g., words vs. images as links)
• Long forms vs. short forms (e.g., abstracts vs. class codes)
• Controlled vs. uncontrolled forms (e.g., journal names from authority files)
• Derived vs. assigned forms (e.g., title words vs. thesaurus terms)
• Explicit vs. implicit forms (e.g., descriptor vs. reference)
• Content-oriented vs. question-oriented forms (e.g., descriptive–evaluative)
• Pre-coordinated vs. post-coordinated forms (e.g., phrases vs. individual words)
• Syntactic vs. syntax free forms (e.g., roles and links vs. term lists)
• Intellectually vs. automatically generated forms

In the current practice of full-text indexing, the author of a document intellectually indexes the document by authoring its title, style and structure, text, references or links, and other components. Other actors in the document communication / distribution process may add value through other access points – see Sect. 6.1. Hjörland and Nielsen (2001) review subject access broadly. They cover various types of access points, such as titles, classification codes, and full text, of various origin – whether generated by authors or other actors – or whether assigned or derived. While Table 4.1 lists intellectual indexing as one end of the last dimension, intellectual indexing may produce access points that represent any combination of the other dimensions. In the 1990s there was much pressure toward developing automated (and thus low-cost) indexing systems and therefore also research in intellectual indexing was under pressure. Nevertheless, cost is a secondary issue in the evaluation of the potential of various subject access points (while being essential for practical solutions). The strengths and weaknesses of each type of access point in content representation should be understood for effective polyrepresentation, see Sect. 5.2.3.

Dublin Core. The current *de facto* standard for metadata on Web documents is Dublin Core. The elements of Dublin Core are Title, Creator, Subject, Description, Publisher, Contributor, Date, Type, Format, Identifier, Source, Language, Relation, Coverage, and Rights (ANSI/NISO Z39.85-2001). The elements describe three dimensions of metadata – the content or *data*, the *source*, and the *collection process* to collect the content (Cosijn et al. 2002). This subdivision describes the aboutness, isness and processing of information objects, and is related to topical and known item requests (Sect. 6.2.6).

Edie Rasmussen (2002) reviewed intellectual indexing in the Web. She pointed out that indexing for Web retrieval can be produced by document authors through the HTML META tags, especially the keywords and description tags. However, tags can be purposively misused for keyword spamming – repeating them to affect document ranking – which may be the reason to not indexing them by several search engines. Rasmussen also points out that the adoption rate of META tags for content description was low, and in the case of Dublin Core very low. Thus, effectively, one needs to rely on automatic methods in indexing Web documents.

Automatic Classification and Clustering. Automatic text classification is about deciding which of several predefined classes (or groups) a text belongs to. Automatic clustering is about identifying similarities between texts and putting reasonably similar texts into the same clusters, without employing a predefined set of classes/clusters. Rijsbergen (1979), Salton and McGill (1983) and Salton (1989) provide overviews of the methods. In general, findings suggest that clustering may not be effective in comparison to plain best-match searching (Willett 1988).

Automatic classification / clustering have many application areas. These include improving matching queries to text, organizing search results in interfaces by classes / clusters, alerting and awareness control for new documents (i.e., routing), and blocking unwanted content (i.e., filtering). Automatic classification may also be used to identify document style and genre so that proper NLP tools may be applied on them. Further applications allow the classification of real-world entities based on their textual (or attribute-based) representations. Automatic text classification and clustering are popular themes in recent IR research (see Belew 2000, p. 267-281). They are clearly IR techniques at the monadic level although NLP preprocessing may entail the structural level.

4.5 Interfaces and Visualization: Issues and Findings

Gary Marchionini and Anita Komlodi (1998) reviewed in *ARIST* user interface issues for information seeking. Pejtersen (1991) summed up work on interface design, in particular with respect to associative semantics for browsing during IIR based on empirical investigations. She returned (1999) to the Bookhouse iconic principles in a more general sense for interface design concerned with domain knowledge. In a seminal paper Bates developed ideas on interface design for standard Boolean-based online searching (1990). A decade later she puts special emphasis on the interaction processes associated with the digital library interface (2002). Here Bates presents the so-called Cascade Model, which has similarities to the models by Ingwersen (1992, p. 16) and (1996), Fig. 4.10. By doing so she drew upon the comprehensive results of the investigations in relation to the Getty Museum online searching project 1993-96 (Bates, Wilde and Siegfried 1993). Lunin and Rorvig (1999) is a collection of papers on visual IR interfaces. Vickery and Vickery (1993) is a review of literature on online search interface design.

In this section we look at IR systems interfaces with a system feature focus. Interaction with interfaces is discussed in Sects. 4.6 (systems viewpoint), 5.3 – 5 (cognitive and user-oriented viewpoint). We first discuss interface design and then their evaluation.

Interface Design. Interfaces can be analysed along the three dimensions: objects of representation, the offered functionality, and the HCI technology employed. The first two are shown in Fig. 4.5.

Representation Objects. First of all, an IR interface will normally represent somehow the functions it offers (e.g., a text box for entering search keys and the search button to activate searching). In addition, it may represent the search process explicitly or implicitly as consisting of several stages. For example, the standard web search engine interfaces explicitly represent query formulation and result examination. An interface may represent the information need explicitly, e.g., as a sequence of keywords, or implicitly in the form of one or more relevant documents (for similarity search). Either representation may retain request history over session time or even between sessions (Campbell 2000). The interface may explicitly represent the topical organization of some domain(s) or its database(s), e.g., in the form of a thesaurus or ontology (MedLine, INSPEC), or just the database index contents. Several online IR systems had this facility. Further, the search result (set or ranked list) or the entire collection may be represented as a plain ranked list or along a combination of other dimensions (Nowell et al. 1996; Olson et al. 1993). Finally, the interface may represent individual documents with more or less content and structure concretely or abstractly. For example, Tilebars (Hearst 1995) is an abstracted representation of document content supporting fast identification of documents, which have paragraphs containing search keys. Traditional online databases allow an abridged representation of document content (bibliographic data), whereas Web browsers allow representation of full documents linked to by a search engine. XLM interfaces allow structured document representation.

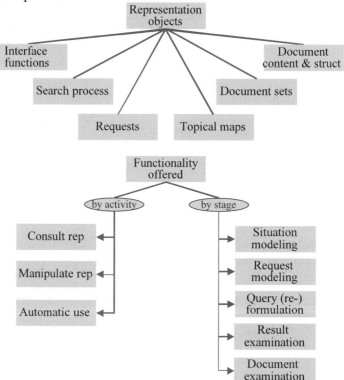

Fig. 4.5. Dimensions for the analysis of interfaces: the types of representation objects, and the types of functionality offered.

Functionality Offered. The functionality offered by an interface may be seen in two ways – by the types of actions the searcher may perform, and by the stage of retrieval process supported. The simplest *action type for the searcher* is consulting a pre-designed representation as it is. For example, the searcher might examine a thesaurus, a ranked list or a document as it is. A more demanding functionality is the manipulation of representations – adjusting display formats or document structure for display, zooming in or out in a topical map, etc. Finally the representations may be automatically used for performing (parts of) the search, for example, expansion on a broad subject heading in MeSH or requesting relevance feedback on a set of documents marked relevant.

Marcia Bates (1990) classifies the interface actions from the interface's viewpoint into classes 0 to 4 of increasing system involvement. At level (0) there is no system involvement, at level (1) the systems lists alternatives the user may perform, at level (2) the system acts upon user's command, at level (3) the system observes user's actions and recommends further actions, and finally at level (4) the system acts upon its own initiative. Bates called for more interface support on tactical and strategic aspects of searching, not just moves. She criticised the popular aim within IR research to strive toward level (4). In her view, searchers need to be in command of searching – like driving a car – in the information space. At the time of writing, professional searchers still were perhaps the most important IR system user group. It is questionable whether real end users (or lay users) would value anything else than full automation – being often disinterested in searching as such.

The interface may seek to offer functionality that explicitly *supports all stages* of search performance, as the intelligent IR interfaces of late 1980's and early 1990's did (Sect. 4.8). Current web search engines only support query formulation and result list examination, leaving it to the browser to access and display the linked documents. Not surprisingly, Beaulieu (2000) states that current interface environments offer a user dialogue, which falls far short of the rich discourse required for task sharing between the searcher and the retrieval system. The two-level model of hypermedia (e.g., Agosti and Smeaton 1996) integrates request / query formulation and collection / result examination through the link structure of the conceptual layer, the document layer and the links between them. In an integrated environment not dedicated to retrieval alone, a further stage could be document manipulation for, e.g., deriving new documents / information. This however leads to document / information management and informetrics (see, e.g., Kuikka and Salminen 1997; Järvelin et al. 2000).

The *HCI technology,* not shown in Fig. 4.4, which is employed in the interface may be a textual one, a graphical one supporting direct manipulation, multimodal, i.e., supporting interaction based on text, speech, and gestures (eye movements), and virtual reality in 3D.

Specific Interfaces. The most traditional type of interface is the command-language based textual online IR system interface. Current versions of these, and the search engine interfaces, are mostly simple graphical versions of the former – with search engines not providing clear separation between different types of access points. All these are based on *query-document similarity*. The VIBE IR system (Olsen et al. 1993) also employs query-document similarity but visualizes clustering patterns in a document space. This space may be formed of the keywords of a query. By arranging (through direct manipulation) the keywords on the screen the position of each document with respect to each of the keys is represented.

The Envision system (Nowell et al. 1996) seeks to provide some alternatives to query-document similarity. It displays search results as a matrix of icons, with layout semantics under user control. Envision graphically presents a variety of document characteristics – author, relevance score, publication year, index terms, document type, citations, etc. – which the searcher may use pair wise in any combination. Envision was based on interviewing prospective users on how they would like to work with literature. The interviewees wanted to:

- Identify trends in the literature, spotting emerging topics of research, as well as identifying peaks and valleys of research interest in topics.
- Locate frequently cited highly influential documents.
- Identify relationships among research topics that were not apparent.
- Discover communities of discourse in which authors regularly cite and respond to one another's work.

Envision supported a range of such user tasks.

Another approach to searching uses *implicit queries.* Kohonen's self-organizing maps (SOMs) may be used to visualize semantic associations in a collection. A notable application of this is the WebSOM system by Honkela (1997; http:// websom.hut.fi/websom/). Based on word co-occurrence statistics, a two-dimensional map is drawn with density and distance between documents coded by color. The map may be organized in several layers where the searchers can zoom in and out – documents at the bottom-most. For every point on a map, they may see keys representing documents in the vicinity. WebSOM thus allows implicit queries and semantic navigation of a collection. There is no published IR type of evaluation of WebSOM.

Another interface supporting implicit queries is by Golovchinsky and colleagues (1999). Their interface, XLibris, supports users in free form annotation of documents while they read them. They claim that annotation can reveal readers' interests with respect to a particular document. It then becomes possible to construct full-text queries based on annotated passages of documents. XLibris interprets readers' annotations as selections of underlying text, constructs queries from this text, runs the queries against a full-text database, and presents links to retrieved documents. This is an example of a composite system where IR is embedded in other activities – in work tasks. For a set of TREC topics and documents, queries derived from annotated passages were found to perform significantly better than queries derived through relevance feedback.

Interface Evaluation. Preece and colleagues (1994) discussed interface design and evaluation in general. Much of interface development in IR is based on a pure engineering approach – "we have this fancy idea based on latest technology – isn't our interface immediately pleasing!" Rigorous user-based design and usability tests are less frequent. This may be in part due to the rapid development of technology and user tests requiring much effort. Pejtersen (1991) was a careful user-based design and evaluation. The Envision system's (Nowell et al. 1996) design was user-based and it was also tested for its usability. Its formative usability evaluation results show great user satisfaction with Envision's style of presentation and the document characteristics visualized. Hancock-Beaulieu and colleagues (1995) evaluated graphical interfaces for QM in a naturalistic environment and compared automatic QM to user's selection of expansion keys.

Visualization and Mapping. Mapping of domains of professional academic or user-defined nature for visualization purposes was an aspect of IIR that in addition became enhanced during the 1990s. Ding, Chowdhury and Foo (1999) demonstrated how the IR field could be mapped for the purpose of IIR; however, the maps were stationary when once created. Also Lin (1997) reviewed the visualization opportunities for IIR and White and McCain provided a kind of visual dynamic view (1998) of how real-time cluster presentations might look by means of periodic maps of Information Science. Cole, Cantero and Ungar developed a tool to allow undergraduates seeking information for assignments to carry out diagnostics on their work tasks (2000). However, first with Lin, White and Buzydlowski we see a real-time visualization interface for interactive online IR (2003). There exist a natural, but often forgotten direct bridge to Informetrics and Scientometrics, for which domain mapping by clustering methods of a variety of representation types of (academic) documents has been done for several decades – as demonstrated by Noyons and van Raan (1998).

4.6 Interaction and Query Modification: Issues and Findings

Query modification (QM), often also called query expansion (QE), means query reformulation by changing its search keys (or modifying their weights) in order to make it better match relevant documents. Query formulation, reformulation, and expansion have been studied extensively because the selection of good search keys is difficult but crucial for good results. Real searchers' requests and/or queries often do not contain the best expressions about their information needs. Moreover, requests are typically short. (Lu and Keefer 1995) Therefore query modification is needed. The first query formulation often acts as an entry to the search system and is followed by browsing and query reformulations (Marchionini et al. 1993). Efthimiadis (1996) reviewed QM research. QM can be based on external, collection independent knowledge structures (such as thesauri), collection-dependent knowledge structures (e.g., word co-occurrence statistics) or search results (Fig. 4.6). Lancaster (1968a, p. 112) pointed out that also citation networks and authorship might be used for QM. In fact, all available representations of information objects maybe applied in QM.

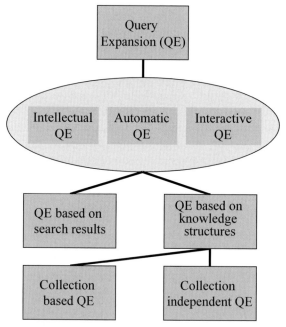

Fig. 4.6. Query expansion types (Efthimiadis 1996)

In this section we shall discuss relevance feedback, query modification and expansion, ontology-based retrieval, and operational systems interaction studies. Drawing the line between systems-oriented research and user-oriented research here is very difficult. Savage-Knepshield and Belkin (1999) review trends over time in IR interaction. The following discussion owes a lot to Kekäläinen (1999, Sects. 5.1-5.3).

4.6.1. Relevance Feedback as Query Modification

Spink and Losee (1996) reviewed feedback issues in IR in general. Efthimiadis (1996), and more recently, Kekäläinen (1999) reviewed relevance feedback as a query expansion method. Rocchio originally developed automatic relevance feedback (1971).

Relevance feedback is a query modification technique based on search results. The idea is that, after an initial query formulation, the searcher examines the search result and identifies a number of relevant and irrelevant documents in it.[8] Information about the occurrences of possible search keys in relevant and non-relevant documents is used in the selection of new search keys or in key re-weighting. The IR system automatically reformulates the initial query to be more similar to the identified relevant documents and less similar to the irrelevant ones. Such relevance feedback should result in retrieval result re-ranking where the already identified and previously unseen relevant documents are ranked closer to the top of the result list. Typically search keys are added from relevant documents in the retrieval result. All words of relevant documents may be added, but usually some algorithm ranks expansion keys. The optimal number of added words varied from a few words to several hundred between studies (e.g., Harman 1992; Efthimiadis 1996, p. 134–135; Buckley et al. 1995; Beaulieu et al. 1997). Harman (1992) argues that several feedback iterations in retrieval are beneficial.

The searcher may be asked either to judge the relevance of the results or to choose the expansion keys from a ranked list of words, or he may do both. Efthimiadis (1992) investigated real searcher' selection of expansion keys that were obtained from relevance feedback. The searchers chose about one third of the words offered. They were asked to state the relation of the five best expansion keys to the original search keys. For 34% of ex-

---

[8] So automatic relevance feedback is not really automatic – only the query modification bit is, since the searcher judges relevance. This is proper interaction. *Pseudo*-relevance feedback – assuming top-N of the retrieved results as relevant – is fully automatic but does not support dynamic information needs.

pansion keys there was no relation to the original search keys. Of the remaining two thirds, most keys (70%) were hyponyms of the original search keys, 5% were hyperonyms, and an associative relationship held for 25%. The overall search results provided some evidence for the effectiveness of interactive QM based on relevance feedback. The searchers seem to be fastidious in QM, thus, automatic QM has given greater improvements. (Efthimiadis 1992.) However, Magennis and van Rijsbergen (1997) suggest that experienced searchers are able to improve retrieval performance through interactive expansion whereas the inexperienced ones are not. Their findings were based on simulated searchers. However, there is evidence that real experienced searchers are better able to articulate their needs in proper terms and to recognize relevant vocabulary when confronting it (Sihvonen and Vakkari 2004). The inexperienced have a hard time recognizing relevant vocabulary because of deficient domain knowledge (see Sect. 5.4.5).

Hawking and colleagues (Hawking et al. 2000; Hawking, Thistlewaite and Craswell 1997) tested QM based on relevance feedback and concept identification at TREC-5. The main idea was that in order to be relevant a document should contain evidence for the presence of all search concepts, not just one. In the TREC-5 study, search concepts were intellectually selected from requests and then search keys were generated for each concept without using information from the collection. Queries consisted of *concept intersections*. The queries were then expanded by words from the top ranked documents retrieved by initial queries. The expansion words had to be allocated to the right concepts because of the query structure. This was achieved by computing association strengths between concepts (their representatives) and candidate expansion words. Compared to unexpanded queries, expansion increased recall significantly. The performance of the concept-structured queries was also superior to automatically constructed queries. (Hawking, Thistlewaite and Craswell 1997.)

Hawking, Thistlewaite and Craswell (1997) tested three relevance scoring methods: (1) a frequency based matching; (2) concepts scoring, in which the final score of a document was a product of the concept scores of request concepts for the document; and (3) distance scoring, also used in TREC-5. Five types of queries were constructed: (1) automatically formulated from requests; (2) intellectually refined versions of the former queries without consulting the collection; (3) interactive queries; and (4) automatically expanded queries using 20 top ranked documents as a source for 30 expansion words. The performance of all queries with concept-based structure (expanded and interactive) was better than the performance of the unexpanded or automatically expanded queries. In addition, concept scoring worked significantly better than frequency scoring; distance scoring was the worst method. The authors argue that concept scoring improves the ranking of documents that contain expressions for all search concepts.

Mitra, Singhal and Buckley (1998) discuss the problem of *query drift* in relevance feedback, when no relevance judgments are available, and *n* top ranking documents are assumed to be relevant. If a large proportion of these *n* documents is not relevant, bad expansion keys will be added to the query. Apparently such a blind feedback approach is not the best possible. The researchers suggest that all aspects of a request should be represented, through Boolean constraints, in documents assumed to be relevant and used as a source for expansion keys. Human constructed constraints were compared to automatic constraints. Both increased the effectiveness of relevance feedback. The studies by Hawking and colleagues, and Mitra and colleagues indicate that structural and contextual levels are needed in QM and some means to approach that automatically.

While the automatic relevance feedback operation is at the monadic level as such, it relies on the searcher's cognitive (pragmatic) interpretation of the retrieved documents. This interpretation is at the contextual and cognitive levels but drops to monadic feedback in query reformulation.

4.6.2. Query Modification Based on Collection-Dependent Knowledge Structures

Jing and Croft (1994), and Callan, Croft and Broglio (1995) tested QM with an automatically constructed co-occurrence thesaurus (PhraseFinder). In QM nouns, verbs, adjectives, adverbs, numerals, and different phrase combinations of these were added into queries. The number of expansion words and phrases varied, and different weights for search keys and expansion keys were tested. Jing and Croft (1994) report that a phrase-based thesaurus yielded better performance than a word-based thesaurus, but both improved performance compared to unexpanded queries in a small collection. The shorter (original) queries gained most from QM, while still performing, overall, worse than longer queries. Callan and colleagues (1995) confirm the results showing that QM by PhraseFinder improves performance overall and with different document cut-off values (DCV[9]). QM was more effective with short queries constructed from the concepts of the TREC topics only, compared to long queries constructed with words from all topics fields (title, description, narrative and concepts).

---

[9] DCV, document cut-off value indicates the number of documents in a result list in best match retrieval. Precision scores may be calculated at several DCVs, and then averaged over these points (Hull 1996).

The PhraseFinder thesaurus is based on expression co-occurrences in the whole collection, whereas typical relevance feedback uses *n* top ranked documents as search key sources. Xu and Croft (1996) combined these techniques into an approach called local context analysis. Noun phrases were selected on the basis of their co-occurrence with search keys in *n* top ranked passages of 300 words. The phrases were ranked, and 70 top ranked phrases were added into a query. The expanded query included the original query as one part and the expansion keys as another part. Xu and Croft showed that local context analysis was more effective than relevance feedback or PhraseFinder-based QM alone: the unexpanded baseline average precision was 25.2%, PhraseFinder gave 26.0%, relevance feedback 27.9%, and local context analysis 31.1%, respectively.

4.6.3. Query Modification Based on Ontologies

Doyle's (1962) semantic road maps were early examples of the idea of QM based on thesauri. Lancaster (1972, p. 150) proposed searching thesauri for intellectual QM. Piternick (1984), Strong and Drott (1986), and Bates (1986a) discuss possible forms and use of thesauri in IR and QM. Many experimental systems that include intermediary functions for query formulation, maintain a knowledge structure, e.g., a thesaurus (see below Sect. 4.8). Here we focus on query modification based on collection independent knowledge structures, such as thesauri, formal ontologies, or the WordNet. The name ontology is adopted from the philosophical study of the nature of being, i.e., Ontology. Ontologies are models showing concepts and their relations (in some possible world). (Guarino 1995). They are used as unifying framework for communication between people with different viewpoints and needs, and for inter-operability among systems with different paradigms, languages and software tools. (Guarino, Masolo and Vetere 1998; Uschold and Gruninger 1996.) Kekäläinen (1999, p. 13-18) discusses concepts and semantic relations from the viewpoint of IR. UMLS (Unified Medical Language System) is a large ontological source in Medicine, combining terms / concepts from more than 30 vocabularies, including the MeSH (McCray and Nelson 1995; UMLS-KS 1995).

The study of *formal ontology* is the basis for ontology construction. Formal ontology is defined as "the *theory of a priori distinctions* within [1] (our perception of) the entities of the world, or particulars (physical objects, events, regions of space, numbers of matter...); [2] the categories we use to talk about the real world, or universals (concepts, properties, qualities, states, relations, roles, parts...)" (Guarino 1997). Guarino states that ontologies include formal definitions, which are mostly lacking from thesauri, thus, the latter are 'simple ontologies'. Guarino and colleagues (1998) criticize WordNet for undifferentiated relations (e.g. mixing disjoint and overlapping concepts). However, formal ontology provides tools for elaborating conceptual relationships further for IR.

Voorhees (1994) expanded queries through WordNet (Fellbaum 1998), which includes types of semantic relations similar to those of a thesaurus and is general in scope. Test requests were TREC-3 requests and the retrieval model was the vector space model. Three kinds of unexpanded queries were constructed: (1) queries based on the full TREC request, (2) queries based on the description and concept fields, (3) queries based on the description only. Voorhees selected WordNet word groups (synsets) that she found appropriate for QM on the basis of the request. Thus, she disambiguated polysemous words. Four expansion strategies were tested: expansion by synonyms only; expansion by synonyms and all descendants in the *is-a* hierarchy; expansion by synonyms and all parents in the *is-a* hierarchy; and expansion by synonyms and any synset directly related to the given set of synonyms. Queries were vectors composed of n sub vectors of different search key types, e.g., original query words and expansion keys representing synonyms or different hierarchical levels in WordNet.

QM in Voorhees' (1) and (2) type queries did not prove useful. For type (3) queries the performance of expanded queries was significantly better than performance of the unexpanded queries (35% improvement in the 11-point average precision), but the overall performance was lower than the performance of unexpanded type (1) queries (39% decrease in the 11-point average precision). (Voorhees 1994.) The impact of the length of the unexpanded query on the effectiveness of QM is very clear in this study. The early TREC requests were quite long compared to typical end-user requests or queries (Sparck Jones 1995; Lu and Keefer 1995) – cf. Jing and Croft (1994) as discussed above. In TREC-4 the requests were much shorter and the overall performance in that round dropped notably (Harman 1995; Voorhees and Harman 1997).

Järvelin and colleagues (1996; and Kekäläinen and Niemi 2001) developed a tool, the ExpansionTool, for ontology-based QM and tested its effects in a Boolean and best match retrieval system using a manually constructed domain-specific thesaurus. The tool allowed QM in different ways regarding the extent of expansion, different types of semantic relationships used for expansion, different types of morphological processing in document indexing and request representation, and different types of structure in the resulting queries. The tool is based on the three abstraction levels discussed below. The empirical tests showed that the tool successfully constructs, upon request, very differently behaving queries.

Kekäläinen (Kristensen 1993) tested ontology-based QM in a Boolean IR system. The results indicated a remarkable increase in recall with a small decline in precision. Roughly, she found that one may double recall with only 10% decrease in precision. Semantically different expansions (synonyms, hierarchical, and associative) had very low overlaps while their combination gave clearly the best recall. Interestingly, paragraph-based proximity operators combined with maximum expansion delivered roughly the same performance as unexpanded queries without the proximity condition.

4.6.4. Structured Queries in Query Modification

Later Kekäläinen (1999; and Järvelin 1998; 2000) tested ontology-based QM using the best-match retrieval system InQuery. She found that the effects of QM depend on query structure, i.e., the use of query operators is critical for QM. Prior work, while largely using bag-of-words type of expanded queries, hinted toward the importance of query structure. Fig. 4.7 summarizes the typology of query structures developed in Kekäläinen (1999). It depicts three decisions made in query formulation. The first one is about explicitly representing the concepts of the request through query language operators. This can be done, in a Boolean environment for example, by expressing a disjunction of the search keys representing each concept and connecting these by conjunctions. In a best-match environment one may use, e.g., a synonym operator. If concepts are not represented explicitly, keywords are listed without marking their mutual relationships in any way. The second decision is about weighting the search keys. If some keys are considered more valuable in representing the request, they may be given higher weights. Alternatively, all keys are weighted equally. The third decision is about marking phrases explicitly. Search keys may be used on a word-by-word basis or marked as phrases through proximity operators. The bottom of the figure presents two abstracted queries, which have the same search key content (keys a – e) using the InQuery query language. The query on the left is a weakly structured bag-of-words query, i.e., neither concepts nor phrases are marked nor weights employed. The query on the right presents two concepts by synonym operators (e.g., #syn(d e)) and gives the first one the weight 3. The latter has weight 1. The adjacency requirement of the keys b and c is given as #3(b c).

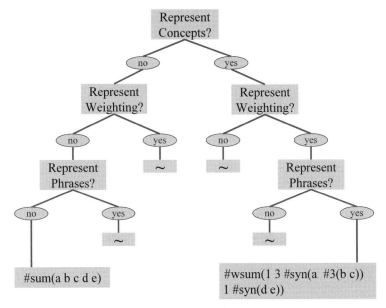

Fig. 4.7. A typology of query structures. The branches ending with tilde (~) are cut short for saving space.

In all, Kekäläinen experimented with 13 different query structure types, five different expansion types and two query length levels (the number of concepts of the request included in the query). As all possible combinations were not tested her setting generated 110 queries with different structure and expansion combinations for each of the 30 requests of the test collection. Queries with strong structure, i.e., with elaborated relations expressed between search keys by means of query operators, performed much better than unexpanded queries, and gave the best performance of all query structure types. QM with probabilistic Boolean queries and queries with weak structure (bag of words) were not effective. The best performing query structures however resembled the (Boolean) facet structure – but in a probabilistic guise. When expanded, they performed 16% to 18% better than unexpanded bag-of-words queries[10]. Kekäläinen (1999) analyzed the effects of query expansion, query structure, complexity and length in detail. Concurrently with Kekäläinen (Kekäläinen and Järvelin 1998),

---

[10] Average precision over DCVs 1-50 for the query structures at varying QM levels, N=30 requests,

Pirkola (1998) found that similar query structures, based on InQuery's synonym operator, were effective in dictionary-based cross-language IR.[11]

The semantic division of relationships – typical for thesauri – was not particularly useful in QM in Kekäläinen's experiments. In most cases the best performance was obtained by the largest expansion including all semantic relationships. However, all the relationships were nevertheless semantic and this is compatible with the approach of treating the expansion keys of any particular key as synsets. Here, an ontology as the source of QM keys is cognitively very different from a statistical association thesaurus. (Kekäläinen and Järvelin 1998; 2000)

Kekäläinen and Järvelin also looked at graded relevance assessments and how different query structures and expansions are able to rank relevant documents of different relevance grades, the highly relevant documents in particular (Järvelin and Kekäläinen 2000; 2002; Kekäläinen and Järvelin 2002). Their test was run with a best match retrieval system (InQuery) in the Finnish TUTK collection of newspaper articles (see Sect. 4.3). In general, their findings were that strongly structured queries, expanded through a domain-dependent ontology, rank highly relevant documents better toward the top of the retrieval result than queries with other structures, whether expanded or not (Fig. 4.8).

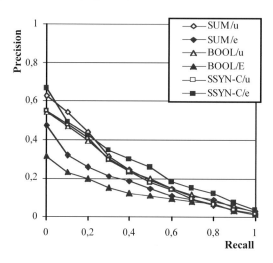

4.8(a) Marginal documents

---

[11] Dictionary translation by synonym sets, incorporating all word senses both in the source and the target languages into a single synset for each source language word is known as the *Pirkola Method* in CLIR.

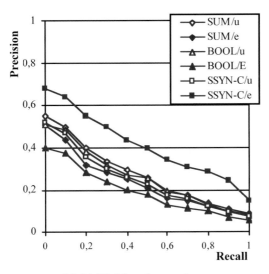

4.8(b) Highly relevant documents

Fig. 4.8. P-R curves of SUM, BOOL, and SSYN-C queries at relevance degrees 1 and 3. Three query structures: bag-of-words (SUM), probabilistic Boolean (BOOL) and concept-as-synonym-sets (SSYN-C) and two expansion types: no expansion (u), and full expansion (e) (Kekäläinen and Järvelin 2002).

In Fig. 4.8 (a) we observe that the expanded Boolean and bag-of-words structures perform clearly worse than the others, which again do not have marked differences at the relevance degree 1. When retrieving highly relevant documents (b), the expanded concept-based structure is by far better than the others. The authors argue that in order to gain insight into the retrieval process, one should use both graded relevance assessments *and* suitable effectiveness measures (Sect. 4.8) that enable one to observe the differences, if any, between retrieval methods in retrieving documents of different levels of relevance. They also point out that due to information overload, one should pay attention to the capability of retrieval methods retrieving highly relevant documents.

Ontology-based query formulation is convenient when a searcher is not willing or able to articulate proper search keys. For example, the searcher might not be knowledgeable in the topic or would need too much effort in entering all pertinent search keys. The IR interface could support a searcher by showing her the ontology from which she could select the search concepts. Then search keys representing the concepts could be incorporated automatically into a query or be shown to the searcher for selection. Keys for concepts could be collected by a statistical approach, intellectually, or they could be elicited from existing vocabularies or thesauri. The structure for a query could be chosen on the basis of the number of selected search keys, or some strong facet / concept structure could be used as a default, unless the searcher selects a structure for her query.

4.6.5. Query Modification in Operational Systems Interaction Studies

In traditional Boolean IR systems, also query modification was intellectual – it remained the searcher's responsibility to expand queries by new search keys through consultation of intermediate results and/or index and thesaurus display. Web search engines provided automatic QM ("find similar"). Studies of operational Web IR to a large degree have used log analysis (see review in Jansen and Pooch 2001) or surveys (e.g., GVU's WWW user surveys (2001), and the Nielsen surveys (Nielsen netratings 2003)) as their data collection methods. Log analysis can provide researchers with data on large numbers of searcher-system interactions focusing on searchers' actions. Most often log analysis has been used to see how searchers formulate and reformulate queries (e.g., Spink et al. 2001). The user surveys have focused on demographics of web users and collected information on the use of different kinds of web resources, time spent on web use, e-shopping etc.

4.7 Natural Language Processing: Issues and Findings

A number of reviews cover natural language processing (NLP) issues in IR, see Salton (1968), Salton and McGill (1983), Salton (1989), and Sparck Jones and Kay (1973). Haas (1996) reviewed NLP techniques in machine translation, text generation, text summarization, and IR. Sparck Jones (2001) discussed the historical development of NLP. Pirkola (1999) discussed natural language problems in IR at various levels of analysis with particular focus on anaphors and ellipses, as well as CLIR. Arampatzis and colleagues (2000) discussed linguistic variation in IR and NLP methods to handle the variation mainly from the viewpoint of phrase-based searching. Chowdhury (2002) covers recent research on NLP tools, applications and interfaces, and evaluation.

The text box on *Natural Language Features* lists natural language features that cause problems in IR. Techniques to handle spelling errors, derivations, inflection, affixes, compound words and phrases became available in the 1980s and were fairly easy to apply – at the monadic and structural levels. However, algorithmic handling of ambiguity, synonymy, anaphoric references, hyponymy and metonymy, and paradigms remained very difficult, in some instances intractable – they require processing at the contextual and cognitive levels.

Natural Language Features as IR Problems

NL is social construction – NL is variable, rich, flexible and constantly evolving. It contains many subcultures or discourses based on age, class, race, profession, or context of use.

Ambiguity – NL is ambiguous due to homonymy (homography) and polysemy. Thus it allows a large number of expressions through a smaller number of words. Every reader brings his / her own interpretation every time he or she reads a text.

Synonymy – there are many synonymous expressions for many concepts. Acronyms, abbreviations and antonyms may be considered special cases of synonymy. Also *paraphrasing* may also be used in lack of a specific concise word.

Anaphoric references – anaphors are often stopwords while their antecedents may be key expressions for the document and the query.

Hyponymy and metonymy – textual expressions may be hierarchically related to the concepts intended either due to anaphoric use or inaccurate expression. *"John's car* broke down. You know, this *chap's vehicle* wasn't in very good hands."

Paradigms – a theme can be discussed from multiple, even contradictory viewpoints, which do not share all concepts nor expressions, e.g. "globalization" from the viewpoint of large enterprises vs. Greenpeace.

Compound words and phrases – when compounds are spelled together, their headwords may be inaccessible in retrieval. Compounds and phrases carry meaning that is more than the product of the meaning of their constituents. There often is instability in expression – "seatbelt" vs. "seat-belt" vs. "seat belt".

Affixes – prefixes and postfixes modify the meaning of the root and may hide it in retrieval.

Inflection – in most languages singular and plural forms differ and there may be several grammatical cases (nominative, genitive) and genders which all cause inflection of word forms.

Derivations – a root may produce several derivations, which sometimes should be conflated in IR but which sometimes have lexicalized to the degree that the connection to the root is only formal.

Spelling errors – insertion, omission, substitution, and transposition errors occur in all texts and may be fairly frequent and difficult to handle if they are proper names not recognized by spelling checkers.

NLP in IR can be discussed at several structural and linguistic levels. We shall first look at these levels and then briefly at the application areas of NLP in IR, level by level.

4.7.1. NLP Processing levels

Document collections may be analyzed and parsed *structurally* at the collection level, at the individual document level and at document component level. Indeed, there is a whole continuum from smallest marked-up (or otherwise identifiable) elements to the whole collection and one may, in principle, define at what level one's documents are. This yields entities of cognitively varying granularity for analysis while not specifying how the entities are processed. Belew (2000, p. 40-48) discussed parsing a collection into documents (i.e., identifying documents) and parsing documents for indexing, including tokenization, stemming, and identifying stop words - see also the discussion on structure-based models in 4.1. *Linguistic processing* takes place at one or more levels – phonological, lexical, morphological, syntactical, semantic, discourse and pragmatic. Below the lexical level, at the sub-lexical level words and texts are treated as character strings of varying lengths without trying to identify lexical words. Yet another proposal (Järvelin et al. 1996; 2001) deals with three *abstraction levels* of character strings, natural language expressions and concepts. We shall discuss the linguistic processing levels and abstraction levels in more detail below. From the cognitive viewpoint, language processing at the lexical, morphological (i.e., monadic) and syntactical (i.e., structural) levels is a pre-requisite for cognitively more demanding processing.

During 1960 – 90, the main applications of NLP in IR were clearly at the morphological and lexical levels. The main approach was stemming of document and query keys for improved recall in best match systems. Various stemmers were developed and applied in IR, e.g. the Porter Stemmer, Lovins Stemmer, and the simple S-algorithm (Salton 1989; Harman 1991). Indexing and retrieval remained at the monadic level – processing of individual words. Stemming was shown to generally improve performance. While the majority of the IR community developed stemming for English, the first studies of IR effects of morphological lemmatization of morphologically different, more complex languages began to appear (Koskenniemi 1985; Nurminen 1986). Below we focus on research on NLP in IR in the late 1980s and beyond.

The Sub-lexical Level – Approximate String Matching. Words and texts may be treated simply as character strings of varying lengths for matching – without attempting the identification of lexical words. Techniques for phonetic string matching (Zobel and Dart 1996) and n-grams (Robertson and Willett 1998) are useful in spelling error correction and cross-language name identification (e.g., Keskustalo et al. 2003; Pirkola et al. 2003). From the cognitive point of view, these techniques are quite mechanistic, even below the monadic level as they treat sub-word character strings. Still, they may be linguistically informed. For instance, phonetic string matching with SOUNDEX is based on pronunciation similarities between words and the technique by Pirkola and colleagues (2003) on transliteration statistics between word pairs in two languages.

Phonology is relevant in speech IR systems but this research really began in the 1990's. Nevertheless the HEARSAY I – II project at the University of Massachusetts (Erman et al. 1980) is worth mention. While the main goal of the project was to explore the Blackboard Architecture for Expert Systems (see Sect. 4.8), the application area was IR with spoken requests in a bibliographic database. In HEARSAY I – II, processing took place at several levels – signal processing, phonology, morphology, syntax, semantics and pragmatics – and levels were not isolated from each other. Instead, experts at multiple levels cooperated in problem solving. This was a unique feature of the system.

The Lexical Level – Tokenization. Recognizing individual words in running text is fairly easy for English and most European languages. One only needs to define all word separators like space, comma, full stop, etc. The handling of character strings containing diacritical characters, mixtures of alphabet and numbers or special alphabet, however, may require more care. Even several Western European languages, e.g., Germanic and Romance languages, have "non-standard" characters with umlauts, accent marks, etc., which must not be counted as word separators. In many Asian languages tokenization is a serious problem since words in running text are spelled together (Huang et al. 2003). Cognitively higher level processing requires first recognizing the elements.

4.7.2. Morphology in IR

Morphology studies word structure and formation. It consists of *inflectional morphology* and *derivational morphology* (e.g., Karlsson 1994). The former focuses on the formation of inflectional word forms from lexemes. The latter is concerned with the derivation of new words from other words or root forms. Inflectional word forms indicate grammatical relations between words. Therefore syntax analysis depends on the analysis of inflectional word forms. English and Chinese have a simple morphology whereas many other languages, e.g., Germanic languages, are morphologically more complex. The expansion of IR research into languages other than English in the 1990's caused an expansion in morphological studies in IR in the same period.

Stemming has been the most widely applied morphological technique. With stemming, the searcher does not need to worry about the correct truncation point of search keys. Stemming also reduces the total number of distinct index entries. Further, stemming causes query expansion by bringing word variants, derivations included, together. (see, e.g., Alkula 2001; Krovetz 1993; Pirkola 2001). Some early research results with English collections questioned the effectiveness of stemming (Harman 1991). Later results by, e.g., Krovetz (1993) and Hull (1996) find stemming useful especially when long enough retrieved sets of documents are analyzed. Hull also found out that stemming is always useful with short queries. With short queries and short documents, a derivational stemmer is most useful, but with longer ones the derivational stemmer brings in more non-relevant documents. Stemming increases search key ambiguity and greedy stemming may be counter-productive: with long queries and documents, relevant material can be identified with conservative stemming. In languages other than English, stemmers have been even more successful than in English text retrieval – e.g., in Slovenian (Popovic and Willett 1992), French (Savoy 1999), Modern Greek (Kalamboukis 1995), and Arabic (Abu-Salem et al. 1999).

Lemmatization is another conflation technique: for each inflected word form in a text, its basic form, the lemma, is identified. The benefits of lemmatization are the same as in stemming. In addition, when basic word forms are used, the searcher may match an exact search key to an exact index key. Such accuracy is not possible with truncated, ambiguous stems. Homographic word forms cause ambiguity (and precision) problems – this may also occur inflectional word forms (Alkula 2001). Another problem is owing to words that cannot be lemmatized, e.g., foreign proper names, because the lemmatizer's dictionary does not contain them. Such problem words need special handling.

Compound words form a special problem area in lemmatization. A compound word (or a *compound*) is a word formed from two or more component (or *constituent*) words (Matthews 1997). Often no difference is made between the compounds in which the components are spelled together and the compounds in which the components are spelled separately. In IR this distinction is however essential. Therefore we refer by *compound word* to the case in which the components are spelled together. In the other case we use the term *fixed phrase* (see below at section on syntax).

Several languages, Germanic and Finno-Ugrian languages included, are rich in compounds in contrast to English, which is phrase-oriented. For example, The Dictionary of Modern Standard Finnish contains some 200,000 entries, of which two-thirds are compound words (Koskenniemi 1983, p. 68).

Compounds may be split into their components in lemmatization. When indexing a text collection, both compounds and their components may be recorded in the database index thus enabling retrieval through all combinations of compound components. Based on Krovetz (1993) and Alkula (2001) it seems beneficial to use words instead of stems. This may not be the case in all languages, but seems a reasonable conclusion, considering how different Finnish and English morphologically are (Alkula 2001). Alkula's findings also suggest that compound splitting is beneficial for retrieval.

Handling compounds in different languages affects the NLP tools needed: in compound-rich languages the morphological problem of compound splitting corresponds to the syntactical problem of phrase recognition in non-compounding languages. Morphological NLP tools for stemming, lemmatization and compound splitting, while working at a monadic level, are – cognitively – an aid to the searcher. The searcher need not consider all word form variation or compounding and may use simple words or plain natural language text in query formulation. The user is greatly relieved if she need not consider potential expressions like "Verkehrswegeplanungsbeschleunigungsgesetzveränderungsentwurf"[12] when interested in legislation on road planning. In best match IR systems, which lack the search key truncation operator, the normalization of index word forms is essential for users, if the collection language is morphologically complex. However, a query in a basic word form index has to be constructed with care in order not to loose derivatives, which one may cover by truncation in a traditional index. Word form lemmatization is also needed in dictionary-based Cross-Language IR. While lemmatization with compound splitting seems to improve retrieval performance in Boolean (Alkula 2001) and best-match retrieval (Kunttu 2003), their most important effects may be the cognitive simplification of query formulation.

4.7.3. Syntax and Disambiguation in IR

Salton (1989) is a good overview of early techniques for syntactic analysis in IR, e.g., phrase-structure grammars and augmented transition networks. Syntax as a field of linguistics studies the structure of sentences. There are three important aspects in the structure of sentences: (1) the linear order of

---

[12] In German – a proposal for changing the law on speeding up the planning of roads – here no compounds.

words, (2) the organization of words into part-of-speech categories, and (3) the grouping of words into the constituents of a sentence (Akmajian et al. 1990). For IR the most important syntactic feature of sentences is *phrases*. Another area of recent attention is *word sense disambiguation*. Both may benefit from *part-of-speech tagging* and *shallow syntactic parsing*. We discuss these briefly below. The following text owes a lot to Pirkola (1999) and personal communication with him.

Phrases. In IR literature, the term phrase has three senses: (1) *fixed phrases*, (2) *syntactic phrases*, and (3) *statistical phrases* (Mitra et al. 1997; Strzalkowski 1995). A fixed phrase is an established combination of words, e.g., *data mining*, *seat belt*, and *hot dog*. Like in the case of compound words, there is no clear-cut well-established definition of a fixed phrase. In a syntactic phrase, the components have a relation in a given sentential environment, e.g., the phrase *"Peter's red old car"* in the sentence *"This is Peter's red old car."* A statistical phrase is a combination of words in the case where the words often occur together – as determined by word co-occurrence (*collocation*) statistics. With the exception of statistical phrases consisting of non-adjacent words, fixed and statistical phrases are also syntactic phrases.

In IR, the most important phrase type is the *noun phrase*, because search keys often are nouns. A noun phrase consists of a noun or pronoun head, and modifiers, which are usually adjectives, determiners (such as articles) or other noun phrases. For example, "phrase-based representation of documents and queries" is a noun phrase.

Phrases are often regarded more meaningful lexical units than words, and therefore phrase-based representation of documents and queries is often preferred to word-based representation (Arampatzis et al. 2000; Strzalkowski 1999). In the case of non-compositional fixed phrases, such as *hot dog,* the phrase components as separate search keys may be misleading. In the case of general syntactic phrases the components taken alone may be too general (Zhai et al. 1997). For example the keys *junior* and *college* separately are not specific enough to distinguish between the phrases *college junior* and *junior college*. The identification of phrases is important both in monolingual IR (Strzalkowski 1995) and cross-language IR (Hull and Grefenstette 1996; Ballesteros and Croft 1997). Strzalkowski (1999), Buckley and colleagues (1995), and Arampatzis and colleagues (2000) discuss methods of phrase identification and representation.

Part-of-speech Tagging. In part-of-speech (POS) tagging words are assigned POS in their sentential context. In this way meaningful sequences of words, such as phrases, can be recognised. POS tagging may be used for phrase recognition – identifying sequences of adjectives and nouns – and word sense disambiguation (Ballesteros and Croft 1998).

Shallow syntactic analysis is more demanding than POS tagging and aims at detecting phrases and head-modifier relations within phrases (Sheridan and Smeaton 1992; Strzalkowski 1995). Some shallow syntactic analysers identify the functional roles of words in sentences, such as verbs and their arguments. Typical syntactical phrase algorithms extract noun phrases from syntactically parsed texts.

Many studies using sophisticated linguistic analysis or statistical methods have shown retrieval performance improvements when the word-based representation of documents and requests is augmented with phrase-based representation (Buckley et al. 1996; Strzalkowski 1997; Zhai et al. 1997). However, the improvements in retrieval performance owing to phrase recognition have been modest. For example, Mitra and others (1997) found that the use of phrases did not help to improve retrieval performance at high precision levels. Small improvements were found at low precision (high recall) levels. No difference was found between syntactic and statistical phrases.

Lexical ambiguity consists of *homonymy* and *polysemy* (Lyons 1984). A word form with two or more distinct meanings is said to be *homonymous*. Thus homonyms are different lexemes with the same form but unconnected senses. Homonymy covers both *base form homonymy* and *inflectional homonymy*. An example of the former is the word form *bank,* which represents the base forms of two lexemes. In inflectional homonymy an inflectional form of one lexeme matches an inflectional or base form of another lexeme while their base forms differ. For example the form *being* is a base form noun, and a second participle form of the verb *be.* A single lexeme with several related senses is *polysemous.* The word *board,* for example, has several senses, e.g., (a) *a thin plank,* (b) *a tablet,* (c) *a table,* (d) *food served at the table,* (e) *a committee,* and (f) *go into an aircraft.* A polysemous word may belong to two or more POS categories.

The sense of a word in a sentence depends on its context. Out of context a word may have many senses, as in a dictionary, but in a sentential context often just one sense. Therefore word-by-word lemmatization in document indexing, and word-by-word translation through a dictionary, often produce ambiguous results, which may undermine retrieval performance.

Word sense disambiguation (WSD) aims at finding correct senses for word occurrences. Most IR studies on WSD have reported no or minor improvements in retrieval performance owing to WSD (Krovetz and Croft 1992; Sanderson 1994; Voorhees 1993). Pirkola (1998) found that in dictionary-based CLIR one may neglect WSD in request translation and database indexing, and incorporate all translations of request words into the target language query if it is structured appropriately (Sect. 4.6). Although in principle WSD seems attractive in IR, in practice it does not necessarily contribute significantly to retrieval performance, since several other factors affect this as well. For instance, in case of long queries, disambiguation is of minor importance. On the other hand, a short query with an ambiguous but essential search key is a good candidate for a positive WSD effect. Even if WSD does not seem essential in document retrieval it may have high potential in other areas of IR such as question answering. These findings also suggest that IR is concerned with information beyond meaning – see Sect. 2.3.1.

4.7.4. Semantics and Discourse in IR

Semantics. Handling synonyms (including acronyms, abbreviations and antonyms), hyponyms and metonyms, as well as other semantic relationships in request and query formulation constitutes a focal semantic problem – sometimes called the vocabulary problem – in IR (see Sect. 4.6). The variability of possible natural language expressions in documents that are relevant to an information need (or request) requires that semantics be handled in IR somehow. There is also lots of evidence suggesting that the set of documents retrievable by query formulations based on distinct sets of search keys often have minor overlaps (e.g., Kristensen 1993).

The most popular approach in *experimental IR* for handling semantics is statistical association thesauri, but they have given mixed evaluation results (Sect. 4.6).

A popular approach in *operational IR* for handling semantics is based on thesauri, such as the MeSH (Medical Subject Headings; http://www.nlm.nih.gov/mesh/meshhome.html) and the INSPEC Thesaurus (physics, engineering; http://www.iee.org/Publish/Support/INSPEC/Document/ Thes/index.cfm). Index term relationships in them are created intellectually, and in good-quality thesauri such as the above, there is a guarantee that the semantic relationships between index terms are as indicated. Their semantics are rich since they are created intellectually. Cognitively they reflect their creators' contextual and cognitive level views, which other people may interpret differently. The *salto mortale* of intellectual thesauri is the connection between the thesauri (of whatever type) and the documents in the collection. There is no easy way to guarantee matching semantics between the thesaurus entries and document words – unless the documents are severely restricted in their domain and their textual expressions. Past experiments in intellectual indexing (Lancaster 1972; and

Warner 1993) also suggest that intellectual document annotation based on ontologies is no magic wand to solve the problems.

Currently there is no simple way of automatically handling semantics in IR in the general case. So far only small-scale applications in narrow domains may be successful. Therefore handling semantics in IR remains a challenge. David Blair (2002a) makes this understandable by pointing out, based on Wittgensteinian philosophy of language, that meanings are not directly linked to words and understanding the meaning of words is not based on having definitions in one's mind – context matters.

Discourse / Pragmatic Levels. At discourse and pragmatic levels, the issues of recent interest in IR research have been anaphor and ellipsis resolution, the analysis of topical structures – discussed below – and collection level linguistic analysis (bypassed, see Pirkola and Järvelin 2001). Anaphoric and elliptic references affect text retrieval since search keys may occur in a text indirectly through their references.

Liddy and colleagues (1987) presented perhaps the first broad and coherent classification of anaphora with classes: (1) central pronouns (personal, possessive, reflexive), (2) nominal demonstratives, (3) relative pronouns, (4) nominal substitutes (e.g., 'former'), (5) the pro-verb 'do', (6) indefinite pronouns, (7) pro-adjectives (e.g., identical), (8) pro-adverbials (e.g., similarly), (9) subject references, and (10) the definite article 'the'.

Liddy and colleagues (1987) also developed a manual resolution method and found that the average frequency of anaphora per scientific abstract in the PsycINFO and INSPEC databases was 4.49 and 2.86, respectively. Their resolution method achieved 83%-99% correctness depending on anaphor class. Bonzi and Liddy (1989) found that anaphora refer to central concepts of scientific abstracts and their resolution increases the term weights of their correlates in statistical IR. However, anaphor resolution did not help to differentiate between relevant and irrelevant documents because query keys had higher weights than other words already prior to resolution. Therefore, the relevance of anaphora (or their resolution) to IR remained an open question (Liddy 1990).

Later, various *anaphor and ellipsis* resolution algorithms based on syntactic, semantic, and discourse level language analysis have been proposed (Pirkola 1999). In general, anaphor and ellipsis resolution is difficult. Lappin and Leass (1994) developed an anaphor resolution algorithm for third person pronouns, reflexives and reciprocals. The algorithm identified the correct antecedent for 86% of the pronoun occurrences.

Pirkola and Järvelin (1996a) investigated the effects of anaphor and ellipsis resolution in proximity searching in Finnish newspaper database using a Boolean retrieval system. In the categories of single words, compound words, and common noun phrases resolution effects were minor. However, then the case of proper name phrases, the effects were significant. A follow-up study (Pirkola and Järvelin 1996b) was based on test requests (n=28) and a relevance assessment corpus. Again, anaphor and ellipsis resolution effects were significant in the category of proper name phrases, in the other categories the effects were small. Resolution improved *both* recall and precision.

The analysis of *topical structures* of texts is important in the fields of document summarization, categorization, and segmentation. In these text-processing tasks the identification of discourse topics is one of the core issues (Lin 1997). Both statistical methods and semantic analysis are used to determine topic words.

4.7.5. Three Abstraction Levels of NLP in IR

Järvelin and colleagues (1996; 2001), Fig. 4.9, proposed three levels of abstraction for information storage and retrieval. The *conceptual level* represents concepts and conceptual relationships (e.g., hierarchical relationships) – typically handled in ontologies. The *linguistic level* represents natural language expressions for concepts and their relationships (e.g., synonymy). Typically there are many expressions – including basic words, compounds and phrases, and common codes and abbreviations – for each concept. Each expression may have one or more matching patterns at the *string level*. Each matching pattern represents, in a query-language independent way, how the expression may be matched in texts or database indices built in varying ways, e.g., with or without stemming, lemmatization, and compound word splitting. Query expansion can be performed at all levels of abstraction. The three abstraction levels are well founded in the IR literature (e.g., Croft 1986, Paice 1991a, UMLS 1995).

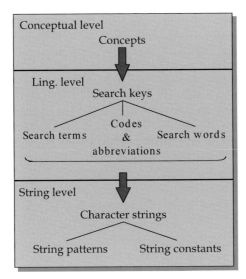

Fig. 4.9. Abstraction levels for query formulation and expansion

Summary of NLP processing. NLP has provided advances in IR at several fronts. Still its effects are far from dramatic. They are rather small improvements here and there, and depend on particular situations – collections, document genres, document languages, information needs and requests. Searchers are relieved in many cases by tools freeing them from considering inflected word forms, compounds or phrases. Nevertheless, fairly simple techniques work surprisingly well. Moreover, many tough problems in NLP, e.g., word sense disambiguation and anaphor/ellipsis resolution, may not be critical in IR – and there are other ways around the problems. On the other hand, handling semantics in query formulation (the vocabulary problem, expansion) is an important searcher problem for which NLP does not yet offer sufficient support.

What are the NLP goals in IR, then? Should IR deal with 'truly unrestricted natural language'? Is it mandatory for IR systems fully to understand user requests and texts (or other multimedia materials) in order to perform effective retrieval?

Firstly, IR systems and their interfaces cannot 'understand', and will never come fully to understand, user requests and document texts. Neither do human intermediaries always understand them (Brooks and Belkin 1983). Secondly, document or request text understanding has not been the goal in IR. Already in 1979 van Rijsbergen put forward this principle in IR as he stressed (1986, p. 194): "It has never been assumed that a retrieval system should attempt to 'understand' the content of a document". Thirdly, an NL understanding component is not required as part of an IR system. If an IR system translates requests and texts into meaning representation, it will be on the premises of its knowledge base, which either is implemented by another individual, mirroring his conceptual structures, goals, etc., or it is acquired by some rules via processing document texts or (other) users' requests. Thus the translated meaning will tend to be any other meaning than that of the actual searcher (Ingwersen 1992). Therefore, IR is concerned with information beyond meaning. A text does not have a single meaning. IR systems should supply information for transforming the recipient's knowledge structures.

4.8. Expert Systems and Interfaces for IR: Issues and Findings

Intermediary systems to aid users in accessing operational Boolean IR systems were developed from early 1970's onwards (e.g., Marcus 1971; 1982; Meadow et al. 1982). Due to progress in Artificial Intelligence, Expert Systems research in particular (Sowizral 1985; Waterman 1986), there began very active development of expert systems for IR in the 1980s. The idea of an IR expert system, or an (intelligent) intermediary system for IR, was to act as an intermediary between an end user and the IR mechanism – and perform similar functions as human expert intermediaries used to perform. The logical placement of an IR expert system (intermediary) is depicted in Fig. 4.10. The interface mediates between the searcher and the IR system, helping the searcher to express his/her information need and use the system properly, to select appropriate document collections, to provide the system feedback, and finally to retrieve relevant / pertinent documents. Belkin and others (1987), Ingwersen (1992) and Vickery and Vickery (1993) are good overviews on the approaches, issues and ideas in developing expert systems for IR. This section draws much on the above overviews.

We shall briefly look at the knowledge employed in IR expert systems, their functions, their types, a sample system (I^3R), and major issues and findings of the research. Interestingly, not much happened in this research area after Ingwersen's book 1992, at least not under the titles 'IR expert system' or 'intelligent intermediary systems'. The topic did not get into Salton's book (1989) and it no more was important in 1997 (see Korfhage 1997, Losee 1998, or Belew 2000, where this topic is hardly mentioned).

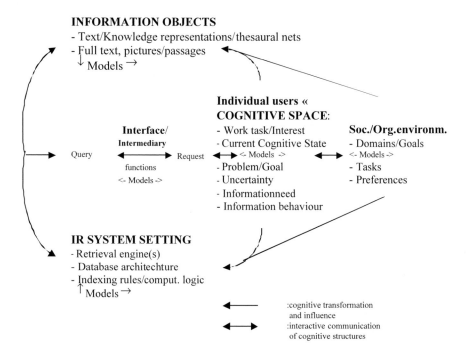

Fig. 4.10. A cognitive model of information transfer (Ingwersen 1992; 1996)

4.8.1. IR Expert System Knowledge and Functions

Knowledge structures for IR expert systems were drawn from empirical user-oriented and cognitive studies. Ingwersen (1992) reviews these studies in detail (see also Sect. 5.4). The major knowledge structures of expert systems for IR may be summarized as in Fig. 4.11.

The specified types of knowledge were seen to serve as a framework for designing elaborate expert intermediary systems for IR, consisting of larger and smaller building blocks. An expert intermediary system requires that the design contains at least the three blocks: Intentionality (with expectations, etc.), IR System Setting, and IR Processes. Without causality, means to act, and objects for action, the system cannot function.

The key-block in the design was the User Model. This component, as well as the associated 'domain and task' knowledge, were the most difficult to organize, since they required rather profound field studies, or tightly controlled transfer from other, similar domains, in order to function properly. Domain complexity complicates inferential rules and processes. On the other hand, the installation of a 'conceptual map' in the system, e.g., in the form of a thesaurus, was a moderately demanding task in a well-defined domain. A conceptual map as well as the 'Setting' and 'IR Process' blocks were seen suitable to implement in systems. The research interest in expert intermediary systems consequently concentrated on the four remaining major components, their contents, functionalities, and interaction with one another as well as with users and the IR system(s).

System setting, i.e. various IR systems and information sources, IR techniques, software features (incl. feedback facilities), database structures, methods and rules for representation, actually applied indexing, database producer policies;

IR processes, i.e. search strategies (incl. system selection), tactics, system interrogation;

User model, i.e. seeking behavior, user preferences & values, user expectations, user intentionality, IR knowledge, domain knowledge;

Actual user & request model building, i.e. search interviewing on: information need, terms, underlying problem, User Model attributes;

Domains and domain tasks, including subject & affective areas, concepts and concept relations (conceptual maps), paradigmatic structures;

Intentionality, expectations and experience, values, imagination, and planning.

Fig. 4.11. Major knowledge structures of expert systems for IR. (Ingwersen 1992)

IR Expert System Functions. IR expert system functionality was also based on several empirical studies on user – intermediary interactions in library and information retrieval settings. The first major model on IR expert system functionality was the MONSTRAT model (Belkin, Seeger and Wersig 1983; Belkin et al. 1987; Belkin, Brooks and Daniels 1987).

Ingwersen (1992) found the MONSTRAT model limited in scope due to its focus on the user – intermediary functions and overlooking of some intermediary – IR system functions. He also suggested several additions and improvements to the MONSTRAT functions. The outcome was the MEDIATOR model for expert intermediary systems in multi-domain and multi-IR system environments. We use the latter model's functions as a summary on IR expert system functionality, see Fig. 4.12.

Function	Description
1. Domain Model	Contains knowledge of *work task* in the domain(s), major subject (and affective) areas, possible paradigmatic views, and *conceptual map(s)*;
2. System Model	Contains knowledge of *IR systems* and other information sources relevant to the domain, *IR techniques*, database structures and description (coverage), rules for representation, and *(host) software*, incl. feedback facilities;
3. User Model	Contains general knowledge of *seeking behavior, user preferences, values and expectations*, user *intentionality* in relation to work tasks in domain(s), as well as user *knowledge status and levels*;
4. System Model Adaptor	Generates knowledge of remote database structures, etc., by *interrogation* using *System Model* properties, leading to system *learning*;
5. User Model Builder	Generates analytic knowledge of *actual user* characteristics, based on attributes in the *User Model* or associated to the *Domain* and *System Models*;
6. Retrieval Strategy	Chooses and carries out (or provide to user) appropriate IR strategies in local and/or remote IR systems, based on *System* and *User Models* as well as the actual user model from the *User* and *Request Model Builders*, i.e., to carry out *matching*.
7. Response Generator	Determines and examines response to user appropriate to situation, i.e., evaluates result of *Retrieval Strategy* leading to *Feedback* generation, *Transformation* or *System Model Adaptor* (interrogation);
8. Feedback Generator	Generates *internal* or *external* conceptual feedback according to situation;
9. Request Model Builder	Generates analytic knowledge of *actual information need* and *problem* in form of concepts and concept relations;
10. Mapping	Generates, updates and *stores* relevant knowledge from individual *User Model Builder* and maps *conceptual associations* between contents in *Request Model Builder* and the *Functions 6-8*, i.e., saving searches and conceptual relations by user;
11. Explanation	Describes mechanism and remote IR system operation, capabilities, etc. to user, depending mainly on *User Model Builder* and *Mapping*;
12. Transformer	Determines *dialogue mode*, based on *User* and *Request Model Builders* and *Mapping* knowledge; *converts* input and output data from users as well as from IR system(s);
13. Planner	Processing rules for all other functions based on *intent, expectations,* and *values*, implemented in the intermediary.

Fig. 4.12. The 13 major functions of the Mediator Model (Ingwersen 1992, p. 204). Words in *italics* refer to major or sub-functions of the model.

4.8.2. I³R – a Sample IR Expert System

I³R (Intelligent Interface for Information Retrieval; Croft and Thompson 1987; Belkin et al. 1987) came at the same time as Fox's CODER design (1987), and is based on the blackboard architecture (or the cooperative experts' paradigm of HEARSAY II – Sect. 4.7) that was popular in expert systems research in 1980's. It consists of a collection of independent experts communicating indirectly using a shared global data structure (the blackboard). As shown in Figs. 4.13-4.14, I³R is a good representative of a comprehensive IR expert system. However, it did not go beyond the *stand-alone* system approach, i.e., that one IR system is directly contained as part of the intermediary system in one narrow domain. This approach implies that System Setting, Information Objects as well as Intermediary functionalities are contained together in *one* physical and conceptual configuration.

The domain of I³R is AI in the form of stored references to some 2500 articles on the subject, including their cited papers. The latter are in order for the user to apply citation searching. Fig. 4.13 presents the architecture of I³R and Table 4.2 displays the models and data structures accessed by its expert rules, controlled by a scheduler. The Request Model serves to obtain knowledge of the actual information need in pseudo-NL, i.e. that the user types his request in NL and then selects important phrases from this formulation as search concepts. Concepts are compared with the contents of the Domain Knowledge Model's semantic net (an elaborate AI synonym thesaurus). If recognized, the concepts are validated or replaced with preferred terms. If not recognized, the concepts may still be used for retrieval as individual query keys. Domain knowledge is collected from the users (Croft 1986; Croft and Das 1990).

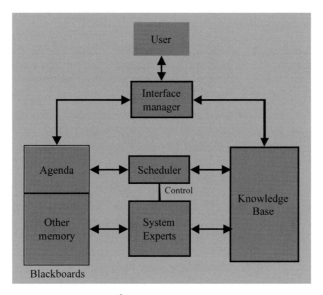

Fig. 4.13. I^3R architecture (Croft 1986)

Expert Name	Function
User Model Builder	Collects knowledge on users to match stereotypes
Request Model Builder	Builds a model of the users' current information need
Indexing Expert	Preprocesses both document and query texts
Domain Knowledge Expert	Utilizes domain knowledge acquired from the user or stored in the knowledge base for recognition of concepts that are presented to users
Search Controller	Chooses and executes the search strategy for each query
Browsing Expert	Provides a browsing possibility with any document, author name or index key as the starting point
Explainer	Explains system actions and knowledge to the user

Fig. 4.14. I^3R experts (Croft and Thompson 1987)

Table 4.2. Models, data structures and implementations used in I^{3}R (Belkin et al. 1987)

Model Name	Conceptual Structure	Data Structure
Request Model	Probabilistic request	Hash Table
Domain Knowledge Model	Semantic Net	Hash Table
User Model	Stereotypes and Expectations	Association List
Document Representation	Network of Documents and Terms	Relational Database
Browsing Model	Semantic Net fused with Net of documents and terms	Hash Table

In I^{3}R the User Model and the Request Model have several components. User Goal in the User Model holds two possibilities: precision-oriented searching (i.e., search outcome = few, highly relevant references) or recall-oriented (i.e., outcome = several relevant references). User's background knowledge (in the User Model) related to actual topic holds a detailed model of knowledge level options the user may point to, for example, from 'have read a news magazine article about subject', ..., 'have read scientific article', ..., 'have written scientific article about subject', to 'have written textbook about subject'. The option(s) selected by the user determine the number of searches to be run by the scheduler. User's IR and computer experience is similarly determined, for instance from the option 'use word processing', over 'knows programming' to the option 'have used online IR systems'. Such knowledge is used to determine the mode of response in I^{3}R to users. I^{3}R remembers the user profile and applies it during the following sessions, adjusting it accordingly. Its User Model and User Model Builder rely on rather simplistic user attribute stereotypes, but were more universal than in the MONSTRAT Model. I^{3}R demonstrated an advance into mixed-initiative dialogue with a nice explain function providing relevant support in IR situations.

I^{3}R also provided several IR techniques, the use of which was inferred in user and request model building. The implemented IR techniques were partial match, i.e., probability-based search and clustering techniques, as well as exact match Boolean logic. The two former techniques were mixed according to the knowledge on user goal and domain knowledge. For example, precision-oriented searching by a subject specialist suggested clustering, since it provided slightly higher precision than probability-based search. If in recall-oriented mode, the two techniques were combined, since they gave slightly different results for the same query. Search outcome was ranked and queries could be modified after user validation of their results. In addition, I^3R demonstrated hyperlinked navigation means, e.g., by use of nearest neighbor cited works or documents associated by content feature similarity to the current document.

4.8.3. IR Expert Systems Issues and Findings

The IR expert systems research aimed at bringing together several lines of research, empirical user-oriented (Chap. 5), theoretical, and systems-oriented. It was closely connected to the development of the individual Cognitive Viewpoint, i.e., not taking social interaction between actors into account. Findings from empirical research on users and user-intermediary interaction, knowledge on IR processes and systems were coded into several models and knowledge based experts of expert intermediary systems. The prototype systems demonstrated that it is indeed possible to develop IR expert systems incorporating various kinds of knowledge. None of the prototype systems developed a high degree of user's work task modeling as a separate facet from search task modeling.

Ingwersen (1992, p. 175) points out three dimensions or issues that may be used to organize the research:

- Whether the IR expert system simply provides support to users vs. also containing proper user modeling
- Whether the IR expert system is integrated with a local IR system and database as a stand-alone system vs. serving multiple IR systems in remote locations.
- Whether the IR expert system simply supports exact match retrieval vs. also including best match retrieval.

Research on stand-alone systems took place in all the possible combinations of model building and use of matching techniques, and was in general regarded as the area for 'intelligent IR' research, since the systems were capable of dealing with NL requests in some way. By maintaining full control of design parameters, several progressive techniques can be tested. However, the stand-alone approach is confined to simple IR situations. More realistic IR system combinations would require combining several exact and best match IR systems under one umbrella. Database selection problems and adaptation to more than one system and one narrow domain would have to be taken into account. We prefer to see the stand-alone systems as test-beds, trying out specific functionalities in controlled settings, to be applied later in other more complex designs.

Another cluster of IR expert system research focused on intermediary design connected to operational exact match IR systems. By means of various knowledge-based techniques, these system prototypes attempted to cope with rather complex IR situations, involving a variety of differently implemented, remote knowledge structures. This research area displayed rather applied research characteristics, e.g., regarding retrieval support and database selection problems.

The most challenging IR expert system context would however be the multiple remote IR systems context, with varying retrieval paradigms. This incorporates the highest complexity, most support problems, and the most realistic future IR environments. Ingwersen's Mediator Model (1992) developed the specifications for the functionality of a general IR expert system for such IR environments. The model however, was not implemented as an IR expert system.

What was left – cognitively? Systems-oriented research on IR expert systems stopped in the early 1990's. However, this research gave a boost to holistic cognitive IR research in the 1990's. Some of the issues and solutions have gained new relevance in the new millennium in the research and development toward the Semantic Web.

4.9 Research Methods

The *types of investigation* in systems-oriented IR research cover empirical, theoretical and conceptual, methodological, and constructive. Empirical studies can further be classified into descriptive, comparative and explanatory studies. *Evaluation studies* dominated empirical studies in systems-oriented IR research. Also these were descriptive – e.g., performance evaluation of a single operational IR system – comparative – e.g., performance evaluation of several indexing algorithms – and explanatory – e.g., explaining anaphor resolution performance through statistical characteristics of document texts. Within the general evaluation approach, popular *research strategies* were case studies and experiments. The former, and field experiments, dominated operational systems studies while, not surprisingly, lab experiments dominated the lab IR studies.

Lots of theoretical research was involved in the development of IR models – their research strategies may be called the conceptual (e.g., verbal argumentation, concept analysis), mathematical and/or logical. The specific methods fall outside this book.

The development of the laboratory IR evaluation methodology involved many studies of requirements on test collections (Spark Jones and van

Rijsbergen 1976), experimental set-up (Sparck Jones 1981; Tague-Sutcliffe 1992), evaluation measures and their calculation (van Rijsbergen 1979; Salton and McGill 1983), and statistical inference (Salton and McGill 1983; Harter and Hert 1997). Specific methods of these studies varied from verbal argumentation and concept analysis to mathematical modeling and empirical experiments. Lancaster and colleagues (1996) proposed a methodology for the evaluation of interactive knowledge-based systems. Ellis (1996) discussed the dilemma of measurement in IR research – realism is lost when relevance assessments are fixed.

The strategy for systems type of investigations may be called system analysis and design. We do not cover constructive Computer Science methods of IR systems development – whether through formal methods or other – in this book.

Due to the significance of evaluation in IR, we shall in the following discuss the evaluation methodology of both the laboratory IR studies and the operational systems studies. Our viewpoint is critical – we look at the methodology (-ies) to assess the contribution of systems-oriented research to cognitive IS&R. We focus on the study setups, evaluation measures and data collection.

4.9.1. Laboratory Evaluation Studies

Test Collections in the Laboratory Model. Test collections consist of a document collection, test requests, and relevance assessments. The *document collections* were very small until in 1990s, ranging in size from less than one hundred documents to a few thousand documents. *Test requests* typically were well-defined topical requests that give the algorithms much more data to work with than typical real life IR situations do. *Relevance assessments* were binary and topical.[13] In early test collections, real users or real work tasks were not seen as necessary. See the discussion in Sect. 4.3.

The experimental laboratory methodology developed especially owing to the TREC Conferences that also challenged research methodology by requirements for scaling up to large collections. Building reliable test collections required developing the *pooling approach*, whereby the research groups participating in a research campaign each produce for each request a ranked list of results of a given length (say top-1000). These lists (or

---

[13] Interestingly, the original Cranfield Collection had graded relevance assessments on a 5-point scale. This original *realism* was neglected in later studies for a long time. See Sect. 4.3.

their top-*n*, *n* < 1000, for example *n* = 100) are then merged, duplicates removed and the resulting pool sent to relevance assessment. Any relevant documents in the collection *not* found by any participant group in their top-1000 (or top-*n*) result will not belong to the recall base of a query. The recall pools may be reliable, when there are many participating groups, and they use quite different query formulation and retrieval techniques. The individual retrieval results may then be evaluated against the recall bases. Strictly speaking, recall assessments are in this case relative to the combined results by participants. Voorhees, Buckley, and Zobel made extensive analyses on the reliability and robustness of this approach (Voorhees 1998; Buckley and Voorhees 2000; Zobel 1998). Zobel argues that the TREC pools only cover 50 to 70 % of all relevant documents in the collection. Blair (2002b) seriously questions the validity of pooling.

Experimental Setup in the Laboratory Model. The overall goal of IR experiments following the Laboratory Model has been empirically to test a theory of IR, or at least novel algorithmic components. The specific goal of IR experiments has been to evaluate the algorithmic components – document and request representation and matching – of IR systems in the retrieval task of identifying and ranking a number of topically relevant documents for presentation, given a topical request. In a typical experiment a number of algorithms (e.g., for automatic indexing) or full-scale IR systems (employing varying algorithms) are compared for their performance in a test collection. Each algorithm or system is evaluated by running a set of test queries derived from the test requests, against the document collection and measuring its performance for individual queries and averaging over the query set. The experiments have mainly been batch-mode experiments – queries are run automatically in a batch without searcher interaction or focus on individual query results. Often the tests are repeated in several test collections to enhance the external validity of findings. Table 4.3 illustrates the experimental set-up.

Table 4.3. Experimental set-up in IR experiments. Two or more methods or systems are compared over a range of treatments or techniques in a test collection for a given set of topics and measured for average precision over defined recall levels.

	Method/System I	Method/System II
Technique A		
Technique B	*Average Precision over Recall Levels for a Set of Topics ...*	
Technique C		
Technique D		

The main strengths of this experimental setup are control of experimental parameters and the possibility of running repeated tests economically. Documents and their representations, as well as requests and (automatically derived) queries representing them, are all objective as texts. Therefore the algorithms can analyze whatever among their explicit features to produce a document ranking. Various parameter combinations for running the algorithms are economical to test. Even if computationally demanding with the available computer resources, they do not require crowds of test persons to counteract learning effects. It is possible to test each system component in isolation or in combination with others. As the assessments are independent of any retrieval systems being tested, experimental results are impartial.

The main weakness is the lack of realism in the laboratory experiment approach: the experiments are not unquestionably valid representations of real-life IR situations. In particular, it do not reflect the interaction of cognitive actors in the IR process.

Evaluation Measures in the Laboratory Model. The major effectiveness measures are recall and precision, the former giving the share of relevant documents retrieved by a query and the latter the share of relevant documents in the retrieved result. These measures can be seen to correlate in a meaningful way with the quality of, and effort required in, analyzing the retrieval result from the user's point of view.

Numerous other effectiveness measures have been developed – fallout, generality, normalized recall and precision, the E-measure, expected search length, and sliding ratio to mention a few (van Rijsbergen 1979; Salton and McGill 1983; Harter and Hert 1997, p. 10-12) – but these have never reached the status of recall and precision.

Also other user-oriented performance criteria, efficiency criteria, and cost have been discussed in the literature (e.g., Salton and McGill 1983). However, these were never essential in the laboratory setting. Saracevic and Kantor (1988) showed the weaknesses of recall and precision, see Sect. 5.4.4.

Data Collection and Analysis in the Laboratory Model. To test a retrieval algorithm it is run with each test request in the collection. The ranked order of retrieved documents is observed and the relevance files are consulted to obtain the sequence of relevant and non-relevant retrieved documents. Standard methods (e.g., Salton and McGill 1983) may be employed to derive the recall statistics and curves for each query. These are then averaged over the request set of the experiment. When the document and request representations and matching algorithms are available, the batch mode test cycle can be fully automated from retrieval to effectiveness statistics and significance tests.

While supporting experimental efficiency, the non-interactive approach to testing / data collection fosters one-pass batch-mode queries and overlooks many real-life interactive IR strategies and tactics (e.g., Bates 1979a-b; 1989).

By typically averaging the request-level results over the whole request set, and only analyzing and testing for significance of this average result, one looses the possibility of identifying requests (and consequently, request types) which yield excellent or poor performance in the test collection (Hull 1993).

4.9.2. Operational Systems Evaluation Studies

Systems-oriented evaluation of operational systems roughly followed the laboratory test collection approach in the collection and formulation of test requests, defining the document collection, and obtaining relevance assessments. However, due to the sheer size of the operational environments, obtaining relevance assessments required different solutions. Operational systems in 1960 – 1990 were based on Boolean logic which also affected study designs – there was no automatic way of deriving queries from requests.

Operational Systems Study Designs. F.W. Lancaster's evaluation of the MEDLARS demand search service (1968a-b) was the first comprehensive evaluation of a large-scale operational IR system. Among others, the evaluation sought to determine how effectively the (batch-processing) MEDLARS service met users' requests and which factors affected ad-

versely its performance. The latter included factors like indexer performance, indexing policy, index language features, and query formulation (by
professional searchers). (Lancaster 1968b, p. 8-10) Lancaster's approach
emphasized realism in evaluation but yet sought to keep it under control.
The setting was systems-oriented but included intermediaries as a system
component.

The MEDLARS evaluation looked at some 300 real end user requests.
In order to establish precision figures, these users assessed the relevance of
a 25-30 document random sample extracted from the search output. A
three-point scale was used (a document being of major, minor or no value).
The assessments were in relation to the actor's *information need,* not just
topical assessments. To establish recall, various searching means (outside
MEDLARS) were used in an attempt to identify documents relevant for
the requests and contained in the database – to form a recall base of relevant documents. The users similarly assessed the relevance of such documents. In this way one obtains *relative recall* of retrieval, since a large file
might contain further relevant documents not identified in the construction
of the recall base. (Lancaster 1968b, p. 11-21)

Search failure analysis looked at each retrieved non-relevant article and
each known relevant article not retrieved. In each case, the article itself, its
indexing record (i.e. representation in the system), the request by the user,
the search formulation, and the user's filled-out relevance assessment were
examined. Decisions regarding whether a search failure was attributable to
indexer performance, indexing policy, index language features, or query
formulation were made by the investigator. The failures were classified in
detail and numbers of searches or results affected were given where appropriate. (Lancaster 1968b, p. 23-29)

The STAIRS Study by David Blair and M. Maron (1985; 1990; Blair
1986; 1996) was the first large-scale evaluation of an operational full-text
IR system. The end users in the test were two lawyers helped by paralegals. The lawyers issued 50 requests. It was their requirement to find all vital documents and 75% of all relevant documents before the paralegals
should stop retrieval. The latter were allowed to use full functionality of
the retrieval system and search until the results were satisfactory. Also interaction between the searcher and lawyer was encouraged. The lawyers
judged the relevance of retrieved documents on a four-point scale (non-
relevant, marginal, satisfactory, and vital).

The investigators went into great trouble in finding relevant documents
for each request in order to arrive at correct absolute recall estimation. In
addition to the retrieved results, sections of the database likely to contain
relevant documents for each request were sampled in order to enhance the
recall bases. These documents were interspersed with the retrieved results

for blind assessment. Consequently, the investigators were able to estimate the maximum recall for the searches.

The methodological strengths of the STAIRS Study are graded relevance assessments by end-users with real information needs, full natural interaction with the IR system, and the estimation of maximum recall of retrieval results – instead of much weaker relative recall. The findings were also tested for statistical significance in the study.

Tenopir (1985) is an example on the comparison between bibliographic data fields and full text in an operational IR setting. The database was Harvard Business Review Online (HBRO) with some 900 full text articles (with bibliographic descriptions). The IR system, BRS, allowed for Boolean operators, wild cards, and proximity operators. The requests were real requests in the business domain obtained from two information service units. The researcher did all searches by herself. To avoid problems due to learning the database contents, all query versions on full text and bibliographic fields were developed before running any queries. Further, the queries were run like in batch mode, without any interaction or modifications. The query versions for each topic were the full text only query, title only, abstract only, index term only, and the bibliographic union query on title, abstract, and index terms. All text queries (i.e., on full text, title, or abstract) were identical except that the full text queries had a paragraph proximity condition on all keys. Three domain experts assessed the relevance of retrieved documents. The assessments were topical and binary. Major evaluation measures were relative recall – calculated against the union of results of query versions of each request – and precision.

Tenopir's study is a field study version of laboratory experiments. Essential features of real-life IR – interaction, query reformulation, and real relevance assessments – were sacrificed to obtain control of the phenomenon studied. Even the database was fairly small. The same queries should not be applied on different document representations. This was a problematic feature in some other studies as well (Sormunen 2000a).

Operational Systems Evaluation Measures. Numerous other effectiveness and efficiency measures were developed for operational studies. For example, Lancaster (1968a) and Salton and McGill (1983) proposed criteria for assessing user's effort, system's response time and form of output, as well as document input policies (database coverage, indexing). Both also discuss system cost evaluation.

The experimental laboratory approach was also adapted in novel areas of IR like question answering, topic detection and tracking, music IR, spoken document retrieval, multimedia retrieval, filtering and routing, text categorization / classification, and interactive IR. This meant adaptation of evaluation measures and set-ups – not discussed here.

The user-oriented and cognitive IR research (Sects. 1.3 and 5.1) challenged the systems oriented IR research in the 1990's. While laboratory experiments provided good control in research design, the main shortcoming was seen to be the lack of realism (or of real searchers, real dynamic information needs) – that is, test designs were seen artificial and thus not producing results that translate back to real life. The lab IR community tried to respond to these problems in several ways. The interactive track of TREC was established with its own methodology. Secondly, novel test collections with graded relevance assessments and/or task-based relevance assessments were developed. Finally, novel evaluation measures based on graded relevance assessments were proposed.

4.9.3. The Interactive Track of TREC

Beaulieu and colleagues (1996) discussed the methodological issues involved in the evaluation of interactive systems within the experimental approach. They also consider how the methodology evolved from TREC 1 to 4[14]. They bring up issues in (1) relevance judgments (differences in judging interactively vs. for a recall base), (2) recruiting searchers suitable for the search topics, (3) organizing the retrieval task (e.g., query construction, feedback, and selection of expansion keys, running the final query), and (4) diagnostic evaluation and significance testing (e.g., which comparison baselines). As a major issue in interactive experiments remained the use predefined topics and associated relevance judgments vs. real searchers with real search tasks and personal relevance judgments. The former fosters control in experimentation, the latter realism.

The TREC-7 and TREC-8 Interactive Track introduced *instance recall* as an evaluation measure. A searcher was to find in a limited time (15 - 20 min) as many distinct answer instances as possible to a given question. The effectiveness of each search was evaluated in terms of the fraction of total instances found for a topic. The track imposed an experimental matrix (Latin square design) that defined how searchers and topics were to be divided among experimental and control systems being tested. This ensures that the findings are not contaminated by interaction between searcher and topic. The participating groups found little difference in effectiveness between their experimental and control systems. (Over 1999; Voorhees and Harman 1999).

---

[14] Officially, the Interactive Track started at TREC 4.

At TREC 2001 *observational studies* were carried out in order to increase the realism of evaluation. Searchers were allowed to use publicly accessible data and tools in the Internet and to choose tasks (16 tasks in four domains) and tools they find appropriate. Each searcher made four searches, two fully specified and two partially specified ones. (Hersh and Over 2001).

The TREC Interactive Track shows progress in the realism of research design. The many results show the difficulty of observing significant differences between systems in interactive experiments even if such differences are present in laboratory experiments.

A part of methodological developments in the 1990's was the development of novel test collections and performance measures. These are discussed in the next section.

4.10. Novel Test Collections and Performance Measures

In the 1990's, several test collections employing graded topical relevance assessments emerged – see Sect. 4.3. This was based on the view that all documents are not equally relevant – often some are highly relevant while others are marginal. When any query easily produces a flood of documents in response, one should focus on retrieving the best documents first. In part these efforts were a reaction to the standard relevance criteria that had been quite liberal. For example, TREC guidelines stated (TREC 2001):

> "Only binary judgments ("relevant" or "not relevant") are made, and a document is judged relevant if any piece of it is relevant (regardless of how small the piece is in relation to the rest of the document)."

In the construction of the TREC Multi Grade Collection (four-point, 38 topics), Sormunen (2002) found that, among the 2266 documents considered relevant in a secondary analysis of TREC documents, only 16% were highly relevant while 34% were fairly relevant, and 50% marginally relevant. This suggests that in any set of IR systems, the systems' relative performance may differ if evaluated by the retrieval of all relevant vs. only by the retrieval of highly relevant documents. Voorhees (2001b) actually found – using the TREC WT10g collection (three-point, 50 topics) – that this is the case. Kekäläinen (2005) got a similar result using the TREC Multi Grade Collection.

Sormunen (2002) describes in detail the process of setting up a test collection with graded relevance assessments. Cormack and colleagues (1998) proposed two methods, Interactive Searching and Judging and Move-to-front Pooling that yield effective test collections while requiring many fewer judgments. Interactive Searching and Judging selects documents to be judged using interactive retrieval. It may be used by a small re- search team to develop an effective test collection using minimal resources. Move-to-Front Pooling improves on the standard pooling method by using a variable number of documents from each source depending on its re-trieval performance. However, collections developed in this way still employ topical and static relevance assessments and do not take document overlaps into account.

Image and video-retrieval (e.g., Markkula and Sormunen 1998) pose problems to the laboratory paradigm because here it becomes obvious that document relevance depends heavily on situational interpretation and there is no agreed vocabulary (or text features) to support it. Sormunen and col-leagues (1999) proposed a methodology for the evaluation of content-based retrieval algorithms, which was based on the relevance perspective of photojournalists performing their illustration tasks in newspapers. In this approach the roles of photo search based on caption text for finding a superset of relevant documents, say on President Yeltsin, and of the image content-based retrieval (using a sample photo) within this superset for similar photos were carefully delineated.

Borlund and Ingwersen (1998; Borlund 2000b) on the one hand, and Kekäläinen and Järvelin (2002; Järvelin and Kekäläinen 2000; 2002) on the other, proposed new evaluation measures for IR experiments when graded relevance assessments are available (Sect. 4.3).

4.10.1. Evaluation Measures: Relative Relevance and Ranked Half-Life

Borlund and Ingwersen (1998; Borlund 2000b) proposed two evaluation measures for interactive information retrieval experiments based on graded relevance assessments. One is the relative relevance (RR) measure, which is a measure of correlation between relevance judgments of different types or given by various actors. The other is the Ranked Half-Life (RHL) indi-cator and denotes the degree to which relevant documents are located on the top of a ranked retrieval result. The measures are proposed to be ap-plied in addition to the traditional performance parameters, such as, preci-sion and/or recall in connection with evaluation of interactive IR systems.

The RR measure describes the degree of agreement between different types of relevance (e.g., algorithmic, topical, situational – see Sect. 5.7) applied in evaluation of information retrieval (IR) systems in a non-binary assessment context. The measure has potential to bridge the gap between subjective and objective relevance, as it makes it possible to understand and interpret the relation between these two main classes of relevance used in interactive IR experiments. Further, it informs about how well a search engine retrieves, for instance, topically relevant vs. situational relevant objects useful to the work task (Borlund and Ingwersen 1998). Owing to scaling differences comparisons across engines are not feasible.

When two or more types of graded relevance assessments in IIR are available, *comparisons* of retrieval rankings become critical. By taking into account the algorithmic *rank position* and the various assigned relevance values of the retrieved objects one takes advantage of two parameters: 1) the algorithmically ranked order which represents a list of decreasing degrees of *predicted* objective relevance to the user's request; *and* 2) the applied subjective types and values of the relevance assessments representing the assessor's or user's interpretations of the ranked documents. The proposed *Ranked Half-Life indicator* (RHL indicator) directly uses both parameters. The statistical method applied to calculate the RHL value corresponds to the computation of the median of grouped continuous data. The RHL value is the median "case", i.e., the point that divides the continuous data area exactly into two parts. Hence, it informs about how far down in the ranked positions a searcher must look in order to retrieve half of the relevant documents. It is analogous to the cited half-life, the time taken to accumulate half the citations given to a particular document, in Bibliometrics. For the RHL indicator the time dimension is substituted by the continuous ranking of documents produced algorithmically by a retrieval engine. Each ranked document represents a class of grouped data in which the frequency corresponds to the graded relevance value(s) assigned the document (Borlund and Ingwersen 1998). The RHL is related to the expected search length (Cooper 1968) and average search length (Losee 1998).

4.10.2. Evaluation Measures: Generalized Recall and Precision

Kekäläinen and Järvelin (2002; Järvelin and Kekäläinen 2000; 2002) proposed new ways of using traditional evaluation measures (recall and precision) and new evaluation measures for IR experiments when graded relevance assessments are available. Among the former they proposed evaluating IR systems separately for each relevance degree, e.g., marginal, fair and highly relevant documents. Because an ordinal scale assessment does not directly allow inferences like "a document of relevance degree 3 is three times as relevant as a document of relevance degree 1", separate recall bases may be constructed for highly relevant documents (relevance degree 3), fairly relevant documents (relevance degree 2), and marginally relevant documents (relevance degree 1). This allows the examination of research questions like the following: Do measurements by different levels of relevance yield different results? Are performance levels, the order of methods, or statistical significance of findings affected by the recall base used? Do the findings yield new insights into the retrieval process, e.g., the scoring of documents during matching? See Fig. 4.8 for an example of such an evaluation.

Among the new measures proposed by Kekäläinen and Järvelin are generalized recall and precision, and novel cumulated gain-based measures.

The generalized, non-binary recall and precision. These measures were defined as follows. Let R be a set of n documents retrieved from a database $D = \{d_1, d_2, \ldots, d_N\}$ of N documents in response to a query on some topic, $R \subseteq D$. Let the documents d_i in the database have relevance scores $r(d_i)$, being real numbers ranging from 0.0 to 1.0 with as many intermediate points as used in the study in question, with respect to the request behind the query. Generalized recall gR and generalized precision gP may now be computed by:

$$gP = \sum\nolimits_{d \in R} r(d) \, / \, n \qquad gR = \sum\nolimits_{d \in R} r(d) \, / \sum\nolimits_{d \in D} r(d) \qquad (4.1)$$

These measures can be computed and used like the traditional binary recall and precision, e.g., they allow averages over queries, precision averages across recall levels or at various document cut-off values, and drawing performance curves. If the original document relevance scores are, say, from 0 to 3 points, they can be scaled down to the interval [0, 1] by dividing by the highest possible score (3). The generalized measures allow for any number of ranks on an ordinal scale, or a continuous scale of relevance assessments. They also allow reweighing of ordinal measurements to produce non-linear relationship of document value to its assessment rank. The weights only need to be multiplied by suitable non-linear coefficients. By using several such schemes the experimenter may gain insight into the performance of various IR methods in relation to various document relevance degrees. Therefore, generalized recall and precision provide performance measures, not far from the traditional ones employed in IR evaluation, which handle graded relevance assessments and rewards IR methods the more, the better documents they are able to find. The generalized P-R approach extends to DCV (Document Cut-off Value) based recall and precision as well.

4.10.3. Evaluation Measures: Cumulated Gain

The *cumulated gain-based measures* (Järvelin and Kekäläinen 2000; 2002) are based on graded relevance assessments and the ranked result list of a query. Examining the list it is obvious that:

- Highly relevant documents are more valuable than marginally ones, and
- The greater the ranked position of a relevant document, the less valuable it is for the searcher, because the less likely it is that (s)he will ever examine it.

The first point leads to comparison of IR techniques through test queries by their cumulated gain by document rank. In this evaluation, the relevance score of each document is somehow used as a gained value measure for its ranked position in the result. The gain is summed progressively from ranked position 1 to n. Thus the ranked document lists (of some determined length) are turned to gained value lists by replacing document IDs by their relevance scores. Assume that the relevance scores $0-3$ are used (3 denoting high value, 0 no value). Turning document lists up to rank 200 to corresponding value lists gives vectors of 200 components each having the value 0, 1, 2 or 3. For example:

$$G' = <3, 2, 3, 0, 0, 1, 2, 2, 3, 0, \ldots >$$

The cumulated gain at ranked position i is computed by summing from position 1 to i when i ranges from 1 to 200. Formally, let us denote position i in the gain vector G by $G[i]$. Now the cumulated gain vector CG is defined recursively as the vector CG where:

$$CG[i] = \begin{cases} G[1], \text{if } i = 1 \\ CG[i-1] + G[i], \text{otherwise} \end{cases} \quad (4.2)$$

For example, from G' we obtain $CG' = <3, 5, 8, 8, 8, 9, 11, 13, 16, 16, \ldots>$. The cumulated gain at any rank may be read directly, e.g., at rank 7 it is 11.

The second point above stated that the greater the ranked position of a relevant document, the less valuable it is for the user, because the less likely it is that the user will ever examine the document owing to time, effort, and cumulated information from documents already seen. This leads to comparison of IR techniques through test queries by their cumulated gain based on document rank with a rank-based discount factor – *Discounted Cumulated Gain* (DCG). The greater the rank, the smaller share of the document score is added to the cumulated gain.

A discounting function is needed which progressively reduces the document score as its rank increases but not too steeply (e.g., as division by rank) to allow for user persistence in examining further documents. A simple way of discounting with this requirement is to divide the document score by the log of its rank. For example $^2\log 2 = 1$ and $^2\log 1024 = 10$, thus a document at the position 1024 would still get one tenth of it face value. By selecting the base of the logarithm, sharper or smoother discounts can be used to model varying user behavior. Formally, if b denotes the base of the logarithm, the cumulated gain vector with discount DCG is defined recursively as the vector DCG where:

$$DCG[i] = \begin{cases} CG[i], \text{if } i < b \\ DCG[i-1] + G[i]/^b\log i, \text{ if } i \geq b \end{cases} \tag{4.3}$$

The discount is not applied on ranks less than the logarithm base (this would give them a boost). This is also realistic, since the higher the base, the lower the discount and the more likely the searcher is to examine the results at least up to the base rank (say 10). For example, let $b = 2$. From G' given above we obtain DCG' = <3, 5, 6.89, 6.89, 6.89, 7.28, 7.99, 8.66, 9.61, 9.61, ...>.

The (lack of) ability of a query to rank highly relevant documents at the top of the result list should show on both the CG and the DCG vectors. By averaging over a set of test queries, the average performance of a particular IR technique can be analyzed. Averaged vectors have the same length as the individual ones and each component i gives the average of the ith component in the individual vectors. The averaged vectors can directly be visualized as gain-by-rank–graphs (e.g., Fig. 4.15)[15].

The actual CG and DCG vectors by a particular IR method may be compared to the theoretically best possible – see the *ideal vector curve* in Fig. 4.15. The latter vectors are constructed by sorting the relevance scores of all documents in each request's recall base in descending order and then forming them into vectors of the same length as for the retrieval methods being tested (filling the tail by zero-values, if needed), e.g., I' = <3, 3, 3, 2, 2, 2, 1, 1, 1, 1, 0, 0, 0, ...>. The ideal CG and DCG vectors, as well as the average ideal CG and DCG vectors and curves, are computed as above. Note that the curves turn horizontal when no more relevant documents (of any level) can be found.

---

[15] The graphs are based on reweighing the relevance levels 0-1-2-3 by ratio-scale values 0-1-10-100. Through such reweighing one may investigate what the effects of smoother vs. sharper gains of relevance levels have on IR performance.

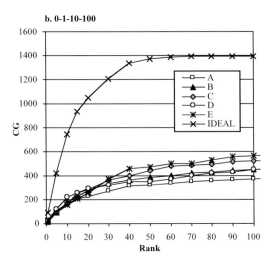

(a) Cumulated gain (CG) curves, non-binary weighting (0-1-10-100)

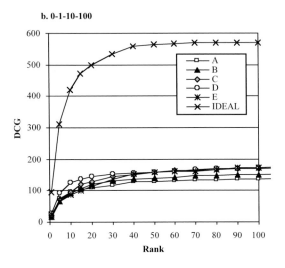

(b) Discounted cumulated gain (DCG) curves, non-binary weighting (0-1-10-100)

Fig. 4.15. Sample average CG and DCG vectors visualized. Data: 20 topics by five participants A-E from TREC-7 ad hoc manual track and ideal curves; four-point relevance assessments with weights 0-1-10-100. (Järvelin and Kekäläinen, 2002)

The *normalized (D)CG* curves test whether two IR methods are statistically significantly different in effectiveness from each other when evaluated through (D)CG curves. The (D)CG vectors for each IR method can be normalized by dividing them by the corresponding ideal (D)CG vectors, component by component. In this way, for any vector position, the normalized value 1 represents ideal performance, and values in the range [0, 1) the share of ideal performance cumulated by each technique. Normalized (D)CG vectors for two or more IR techniques also have a normalized difference. These can be compared in the same way as P-R curves for IR methods in statistical tests. Fig. 4.16 visualizes average normalized DCG vectors.

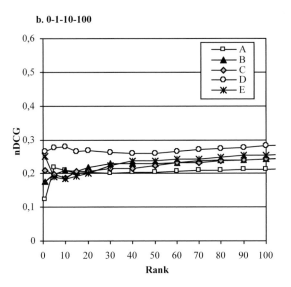

Fig. 4.16. Sample average normalized DCG vectors visualized. Data: 20 topics by five participants A-E from TREC-7 ad hoc manual track; four-degree relevance assessments with weights 0-1-10-100. (Järvelin and Kekäläinen 2002)

The proposed CG, DCG, nCG and nDCG measures have several strengths in common as discussed in (Järvelin and Kekäläinen 2002). In addition, the DCG measure has the following further advantages:

- It realistically weights down the gain received through documents found later in the ranked results.
- It allows modeling user persistence in examining long ranked result lists by adjusting the discounting factor.
- Further, the normalized nCG and nDCG measures support evaluation:

- They represent performance as relative to the ideal based on a known (possibly large) recall base of graded relevance judgments.
- The performance differences between IR techniques are also normalized in relation to the ideal thereby supporting the analysis of performance differences.

The cumulated gain-based measures are directly searcher-oriented in calculating the gain cumulated by consulting an explicit number of documents. P-R curves tend to hide this information. The cumulated gain-based measures directly reflect the dynamism of information needs and grades of relevance, which are important in the cognitive view.

4.11 Limitations and Open Problems

The systems-oriented approach to IR is theoretically limited. It has been confined in many ways, including the scope of the approach and even the work performed within its scope. It is theoretically ad-hoc since it is not based on any theory of text or communication other than statistical occurrence of words – except for the probabilistic retrieval model. These limitations are discussed below.

The Scope of Systems-oriented IR. The mainstream systems-oriented IR explores the relationships between IR techniques (i.e., query formulation, NLP, document indexing, matching methods forming the independent variables) and recall and precision type-of variables as the main dependent variables, with request, and document types as constant controlled variables. This is reflected clearly in the laboratory model, see Fig. 1.1. The widespread agreement on the model has been a real strength to IR research: it allows building on each other's work and thus supports growth of knowledge. This was not the case in Information Seeking studies. However, by continuously subscribing to the same model, theoretical development may also stagnate.

In fact, the laboratory model excludes many variables, e.g., task types, information need types, or searcher types are not controlled – they are completely neglected and outside the model. If the only variables in the mainstream IR models are the ones related with IR techniques, recall and precision, with everything else being either fixed or excluded, there is no possibility to explain why some IR systems are successful, and some others not, in specific real situations characterized by specific types of tasks, needs, actors and environments. Is it owing to clever document selection, innovative indexing, the choice of access points, the lack of any other means of acquiring information, trained and motivated searchers, the kinds of frequent questions they pose, or specific IR techniques employed? The critical questions of Sect. 1.3 are worth considering although some answers were also suggested. Therefore we believe that:

- Systems-oriented IR research is too narrowly systems-oriented – running the risk of being development of technology with no carefully analyzed use contexts;
- There is no guarantee that what seems to produce a significant effect in an automatic laboratory experiment would have a similar impact in a real life context;
- We do not need *less* engineering – quite the contrary: we need *more* engineering with a view on particular realistic work / search contexts, e.g. the patent domain.

It is not that laboratory IR should stop – it should just not be the only type of IR research conducted. In the laboratory IR research there is no theoretical connection between IR techniques and the real situations where those techniques are employed. Thus nobody among the IR technology developers may claim much about the strengths or weaknesses of IR techniques (whether Boolean or best-match) in real life situations, as parts of whole systems and among other available means of IS&R, which they do not know about. Perhaps some proposed leading edge precision technique is marginal when faced with the actor's situations?

Ad-hoc Approach vs. Theory. The Boolean approach – with its enhancements – is completely ad-hoc. Nevertheless, it involved a human component for query formulation, for deriving a logically acceptable query from a request formulation. However, even this process remained an art rather than science. The Boolean Model scaled up to large settings and was shown empirically to work fairly well (by IR standards). The Vector Space Model is also completely ad-hoc. Weighted monadic indexing features and monadic query features represented as vectors, and vector similarity comparison was empirically shown to perform fairly effectively (by IR standards). However, for neither model was there a theoretical justification on why they work.

The probabilistic model is theoretically stronger. The Probability Ranking Principle (Robertson 1977) provided an optimal ranking for documents, given their probabilities of relevance and non-relevance (based essentially on human relevance assessments). The model also related, with some simplifying assumptions, probabilistically the occurrence of request and document words to document relevance and non-relevance. However, even this model is at the monadic level dealing with independent binary word occurrences (the binary independence model) or independent quanti-fied word occurrences (the non-binary independence model; Salton 1989) in texts.

Therefore one may say that the probabilistic model seeks to explain the probability of (binary) topical relevance by the probabilities of independent character strings occurring in documents without resorting to syntactical or semantic relationships – a *direct jump* from statistics of occurrence to topical relevance. This is a nice parallel to the view that "it has never been assumed that a retrieval system should attempt to 'understand' the content of a document" (see 4.7). Why does this work? – It is simply due to the fair correlation between semantics and monadic character string occurrences (see Fig. 1.2 and Sect. 7.5.2).

The above limitations leave open three important questions:

- What is the utility of IR systems in regard to real IR situations? Even an IR system of high recall-precision performance in batch mode retrieval with well specified topical requests and binary topical relevance assessments may, at least in principle, be far from perfect for its users in real settings where they were never tested.
- Toward which directions should IR systems be developed? The laboratory model only suggests more varied document and request collections, better document and request representations (e.g., through increased NLP), and improved matching methods. Being a summary model, it does not suggest classifications of the former or interesting relationships or hypotheses between them. What if the key to more effective IR systems lies outside the model?
- Is the probabilistic explanation of the probability of (binary) topical relevance by the probabilities of independent character strings occurring in documents – the direct jump from statistics of occurrence to topical relevance – the ultimate theory of IR?

It is the critic's responsibility to try to point out a way out of the problematic situation. This is something we aim at in Chaps. 6 to 8. Stephen Robertson, in his Salton Award Lecture (2000), finds in IR research a lot of commercial and theoretical pragmatism. Theory has not been so highly valued. Nevertheless he discusses two kinds of theory: theory and Theory. The problem with Theory is the range of different domains such a theory would have to encompass – Linguistics, Cognitive Science, Probability, Statistics, Epistemology, and Ontology.

> "It seems unlikely that we can find a Grand Theory that will tell us exactly when we should be worrying about the linguistics and when, by contrast, we should take the linguistic entities we have

identified by their face-value and treat them as statistical clues. I'm not claiming that such a theory is impossible – just that's a tall order. This is not at all to say that the search for theory is futile – far from it."

Robertson nevertheless believes that present models can be extended by theoretical argument and experimentation. Therefore we dare to propose extensions, from the cognitive point of view, of current models and theories in Chaps. 6 to 8.

Other Limitations and Open Issues. There were other, consequent limitations and open issues in the systems-oriented approach as well. These include limitations and issues related to the handling of incompleteness (or overlaps), handling of aboutness and relevance, application of findings in design, and learning about users and their situations / work tasks. These are discussed briefly below.

Handling of Incompleteness (or Overlaps). Cleverdon (1984), Saracevic and Kantor (1988), and Ingwersen (1992) pointed out the incompleteness and differing judgments of various actors in the IR process. Two indexers do not provide alike indexing results; similarly, two searchers do not produce two alike queries. Two end-users judge different sets of documents relevant. Ingwersen (1992) points out that such differences of judgment and the resulting overlaps have not been sufficiently employed as poly-representation in the IR process see also Sect. 5.2.3.

Handling of Aboutness and Relevance. Ingwersen (1992) argued that the systems-oriented approach emphasized the generator's (document author's) aboutness instead of the recipient's (the user's) aboutness.

Application of Findings in Design. While the research in IR accumulated a pile of results obtained under varied conditions, no understanding emerged on how to apply different design parameters when deploying IR systems in practice (Ingwersen 1992). This is a nice parallel to the Laboratory Model not containing components or concepts representing the context of IR systems use.

Learning about Users and Their Situations / Work Tasks. The Laboratory Model does not support learning about users and their situations / work tasks since these are not included in the model. Ingwersen (1992, p. 81) points out the need for a platform to learn about such matters.

5 Cognitive and User-Oriented Information Retrieval

Chapt. 5 discusses the development of cognitive and user-oriented IR research from 1970s and onwards under one umbrella. When the systems-oriented IR research could be seen to neglect information seekers in its modeling and experimentation, user-oriented IR research focused precisely on them. The complementary nature of these two areas may be seen in the light of Fig. 5.1.

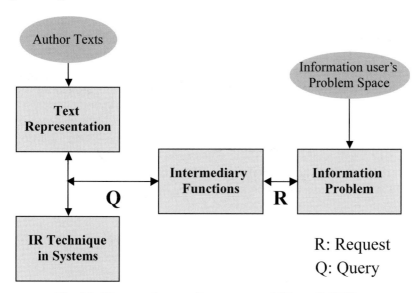

Fig. 5.1. IR research areas (Ingwersen and Wormell 1989).

The systems-oriented IR research focused on the left side of the figure, on authors' texts, their representation, queries, and IR techniques – yet from the 1990s in various media and scaled up to large collections. The user-oriented and cognitive IR research focused on the right side, on users' problem spaces, information problems, requests, interaction with interme-diaries, interface design and query formulation but hardly on analyzing au-thors' texts, their representation, queries, or IR techniques. Since its start in

1977 the cognitive approach to IR could briefly be characterized as user- and intermediary-oriented. First during the recent decade the approach has gained momentum and turned into a holistic view of *all* the interactive communication processes that occur during information transfer, as discussed in Sects. 2.1.2-3. This went along with the understanding of the limitations of the laboratory evaluation approach, increased focus on human actors in complex IS&R situations, the role of work and search tasks, and revived interest in relevance. It coincided with the start of the interactive TREC track and, in particular, with the interactive OKAPI experiments incorporating human test persons. From the 1990s this development led to an increased focus in cognitive IR research on searchers interacting with best match retrieval systems seen in context – at least on analytic levels and in some cases also in experiments, e.g., concerned with relevance feedback and query modification.

Simultaneously, user-centered IR research shifted focus from exploring traditional (scientific) online interaction to Web-based IR. Characteristically of the new realism invoked by the Web environment intermediary studies almost disappeared, to be replaced by an increasing number of longitudinal empirical studies of IS&R processes, progressively more based on cognitive models and research approaches. Studies and empirical investigations of issues of *relevance* and *modeling* of IIR processes became the trademarks of the approach during the decade.

In this chapter we shall discuss the central developments in cognitive and user-oriented IR research, but with emphasis on the 1990s. We do include, albeit very selectively, some discussion on the developments during the first years of the new millennium. Some research that was reported in the 1990s but is close to the present authors will be discussed only briefly here and more thoroughly in Chapts. 6-8.

The cognitive and user-oriented approaches differed from the systems-oriented approach in the following respects in the 1970s and 1980s (Ingwersen 1992, p. 87-90):

- *Concept of information:*
  - o User-centered: all types of cultural, popular and scientific information were included;
  - o Cognitive perspective: seen as perception and interpretation of document contents (a construct) by a person;
- *Nature of information need:*
  - o Cognitive and user-centered: needs were not always seen as well-defined and topical, they may be complex, muddled, verificative; problem-based rather than topical; with Label Effects (see Sect. 6.2.7);

- *IR system setting:*
  - o Cognitive and user-centered: the system setting was by and large assumed to be an operational Boolean IR system;
- *IR system boundaries:*
  - o Cognitive and user-centered: the searcher and intermediary were seen as parts of the IR system, not just the technical components;
- *Role of intermediary:*
  - o Cognitive and user-centered: an intermediary, whether automatic or human, was seen as necessary between the end-user and the system;
- *Interaction:*
  - o Cognitive perspective: seen as the central process for harmonizing different cognitive structures in documents, systems and searchers during IR.

The 1990's differ basically in the following respects, in particular concerning the cognitive perspective of IR research:

- *Concept of information:* seen as a result of interpretation processes and vital in relation to human cognition and to understanding formal systems in which potential information is seen as functioning at low linguistic processing levels – Sect. 2.2;
- *Task dependency:* The perceived work task (or daily-life task or interest) situation is seen as the underlying reason for information need development;
- *IR system setting:*
  - o User-centered: by and large assumed to be a hypertext supported, operational and Web-based Boolean IR system, increasingly with some best match properties, e.g., relevance ranking;
  - o Cognitive perspective: increasingly also including best match systems in experiments and investigations;
- *Role of intermediary:* the role of human intermediaries is re-defined and the research in the area was sparse; novel interface approaches, with the exception of visualization, are scarcely developed or evaluated;
- *Interaction:* seen as the central process for cognitive IR. But interaction is applied to benefit from the cognitive differences between cognitive actors in IS&R; harmonizing such differences is regarded futile;
- *Context:* IR is placed in context in a holistic way: all components/cognitive actors and structures of IS&R are contextual to one another;

- *Conceptual relationships:* Strong situational relationships between information need development, relevance assessments and perceptions of document representations and presentations during IR interaction;
- *Cognitive and related IR theory:* the development of evaluation methods.

In this chapter we first review some central models of cognitive and user-oriented IR research. Then we discuss issues and findings in:

- Cognitive theory building – ASK – polyrepresentation;
- Searchers' cognitive styles and models;
- Standard online IR interaction;
- Web IR interaction;
- Searcher-associated best match IR interaction;
- Relevance studies.

At the end of the chapter we shall discuss research methods in cognitive and user-centered IR, before closing by considering the achievements, limitations and open problems of this research area.

Literature Overviews. All developments in the area make it very difficult to produce an overview even if one focuses on developments from a single perspective – here the cognitive viewpoint. We have an inherent problem – the cognitive viewpoint seeks to cover all aspects of IR.

Ingwersen and Willett (1995) is an introduction to systems-oriented and cognitive approaches to IR. In addition there are early *ARIST* reviews on search techniques (Bates 1981), cognitive research (Allen 1991), and the user-oriented perspectives of IR research and analysis methods (Sugar 1995). Further reviews and discussions of the cognitive approach to IR during the 1980s can be found in Belkin's (1990) overview, Ellis's (1989; 1992) critical essays on the cognitive paradigm, and in Ingwersen's (1992) book. Belkin outlined the major contributions of analytic and empirical nature that have been rather explicitly based on the cognitive approach. We also refer to Sect. 2.1 for a detailed discussion of the cognitive viewpoint in a historical context of research. The latest period sees the review on relevance research by Schamber (1994), while Efthimiadis (1996) and Spink and Losee (1996) provide in-depth discussions of models and empirical results of (human) query expansion and feedback issues, respectively. Harter and Hert (1997) review the approaches and methods for the evaluation of information retrieval systems, also of relevance to user-oriented evaluations. Vakkari reviews the issues addressed in research on task-based information searching (2003). Web searching studies during the period and comparisons to more traditional (I)IR studies are reviewed by

Jansen and Pooch (2001). Studies of the reading and use of academic literature is discussed by King and Tenopir (2001). Further reviews and discussions of the cognitive approach to IR during the 1990s can be found in Ingwersen's (2001) ARIST chapter. The textbook by Donald O. Case (2002) looks at research on information seeking, needs and information behavior during the period, hence overlapping to IR, but does not explicitly adhere to a cognitive view.

5.1 Models for Cognitive IR Research

There are not that many models for early user-oriented IR research. There were some process models of online searching used in education and training for online searching (Henry et al. 1980). Fidel and Soergel (1983) developed an analytical model on factors affecting online bibliographic retrieval. Ingwersen and Wormell (1989) presented an overall model for IIR – Fig. 5.1. These models are briefly discussed below before turning to the more recent development of several competing models.

5.1.1 Early Models of IR Interaction

Process Models. Henry et al.'s model (1980) served pure user-oriented IR research. It was a teaching model of online IR processes. It presented the overall online search process as well as the detail of the search preparation sub-process. Similar detailed sub-process descriptions may be given for, e.g., search execution. Bates (1981, p. 153) reviewed several other flowchart models.

Such explicit process models are narrow models of search sessions. They describe Boolean online IR. Due to frequent use in Library and Information Science education, they heavily influenced thinking about IR – also in user-oriented research. An intermediary's professional competence included methods for handling each step, how to interview, where to find search keys, or which query plan (or strategy) to employ. This knowledge provided an analysis of the phases and suggested some relationships between them. However, no theory emerged. One should note the so-called 'pre-search interview' sub-process step, which clearly demonstrates how the research was applied in scope, as well as being technology and online cost-dependent.

Another process model by Belkin and Vickery (1985) looked at the main phases of the overall online search process given by the former model. In addition, it provides the associated types of data one may obtain from each step in investigations. Actors may move back and forth between the steps in each major phase, as shown by Ingwersen (1992, p. 86). This model may be used to organize the research done – point out the foci of individual studies – but otherwise the critique of the succeeding model, generated by Ingwersen and Wormell (1989), also applies. Saracevic and colleagues (1988, p. 164) depicted an online process model for IR.

Factors Affecting Online Searching. Fidel and Soergel (1983) developed a comprehensive model on factors affecting online bibliographic retrieval. They classified hundreds of searching variables into eight categories such as the *retrieval setting* (the organization, the status of online searching within it, the user group), the *user* (e.g., personality, education and experience), the *request* (e.g., domain, complexity, and specificity), the *database(s)* used for searching (like coverage, structure, and cost), the *search system* (e.g., searching aids and output formats), the *searcher* (e.g., various personality features, education, and experience), the *search process* (e.g., interaction with the end-user and query formulation), and *search outcome* (recall, precision and other measures). This model suggests a large number of variables and their possible relationships. The authors also noted that, taken individually, the variables seem to have little influence on search outcome. Their model is a narrow and static model of the online retrieval process. It is an abstract model and analyzes to some degree the relationships of categories and their proposed variables. It is a specific model for all online (bibliographic) IR.

IR Interaction. Fig. 5.1 is a rough model of IR interaction by Ingwersen and Wormell (1989, p.80). It derived from Ingwersen and Pejtersen (1986, p. 113) and is a forerunner for the more elaborated model, Fig. 4.10. Also, it leads up to the cognitive framework, Fig. 6.1. It displays the components and the interactive processes in IR. We focus on the middle and right side components, based on Ingwersen's description (1992, p. 56).

On the right-hand side we have the user's problem space, e.g., as part of a process of interest fulfillment or problem solving. If not solved by the user himself, this 'problem space' may lead to an information problem or need, i.e., a state of uncertainty (see Fig. 2.1), that results in a request for information, often formulated for an IR system.

In the middle the intermediary functions consist of the entire system's capacity to understand and support the information problem of the current searcher as well as the search possibilities and logic of the source system. These functions form part of the professional knowledge of the human intermediary (librarian/information specialist), or may be skillfully adapted to a front-end to the system as a user interface, in order to support retrieval. See for instance Fig. 4.10, Sect. 4.8.

On the left side components consist of author texts to be represented through indexing and of IR techniques that determine the behavior of the IR system.

Interaction takes place between an intermediary and an actor having a desire for information, whereby request formulation and reformulation (R) may occur. The query denotes reformulation or transformations (Q) of the request(s) for information, in the form required by the actual IR technique. At search time, the IR technique and user request and query (re)formulation interact.

This model is fairly broad since it covers the user's problem space, request and query formulation and retrieval proper. It is a static model of cognitive structures, which are understood to interact in an IR process. However, it is a summary model at a high abstraction level – as such it does not suggest variables of the entities or processes, or their relationships. It is a very general model – applicable over a range of situations, users and processes. In user-oriented IR research however, the left side components of the model were seen as constants – reflecting the assumed Boolean context of IR.

The same Fig. 5.1 (and the more elaborate Fig. 4.10) also demonstrates what the cognitive view of IR regarded as *central areas of research*, aside from interaction.

First of all it assumes a variety of individual differences in cognitive structures. According to Ingwersen (1982), the task of IR was to bring into harmony the cognitive structures of authors, systems designers, and indexers with those of the intermediary (human or computer) and the user, in order to cope with the actual information need. Ingwersen emphasized that collective cognitive structures as results of social interaction and discourses in various domains, also influence the structure of indexing systems and the relations of topics and concepts treated in the body of literature and in information needs. This can be observed in Fig. 4.10, with the collective cognitive structures located at the right-hand side in the form of a social or organizational environment.

5.1.2 Models for Cognitive IR Research

Wilson's Model. T.D. Wilson (1999) summarized the central user-oriented or cognitive research models associated with information behavior studies, including interactive IR. His overall model, Fig. 5.2, demonstrates the nesting of the central concepts, hereby also showing their contextual nature.

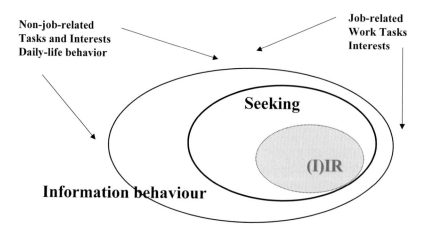

Fig. 5.2. Nested model of information behavior. Modified from Wilson (1999).

Wilson's original model did not contain the notion IIR but 'information searching'. We regard IIR more appropriate in the present context, and it is in this form that it underlies the cognitive framework put forward in Chapt. 6. The central idea behind Wilson's model is that IIR (and thus algorithmic laboratory IR as well) is always in context of information seeking processes that again constitute one of several information behavioral activities. As Wilson saw it, models like those of Ingwersen (1992; 1996), Fig. 4.10, or Saracevic's stratified model (1996), could rather be placed in the innermost nested part of the model. They were basically seen associated with (or limited to) IIR – not considering information seeking process. This is probably true. Since these two models do contain strong elements of IR systems, they did not explicitly point to softer seeking processes *not* involving formal information channels. However, several other models generated in the 1990s sought to deal with both the informal seeking activities, for instance, when persons are applied as knowledge sources, as well as the more formal processes involving IIR systems. Also Belkin (1993) advocated for viewing information retrieval in context of information seeking behavior.

We have added the underlying situational reasons for information (seeking and IIR) behavior to Wilson's model in order to demonstrate that the notion 'work task' is closely associated with common daily-life tasks and situations, including emotional interests, whether job-related or not[1].

Search Stage and Process Models – Kuhlthau. C.C. Kuhlthau's stage model or framework (1991; 1993a), presented in Chapt. 3, Fig. 3.3,

---

[1] Modification to Wilson's model (1999) suggested by Danish LIS students 2003.

was one such central model, also pointing to the central *emotional properties* of IS&R. The importance and strength of Kuhlthau' model lies in the inspiration it has given to other researchers also concerned with IIR during the 1990s. These studies made use of the model in different domains and validated its utility, e.g., Bateman (1998) on relevance criteria in a longitudinal study and Yang (1997) in connection to problem solving.

Vakkari's Models. During the 1990s Vakkari (2001a-b) extended the Kuhlthau model in the field of IR, based on a series of longitudinal empirical studies and framed by a cognitive approach.

His first model (2001a) is structurally related to the original information seeking model by Wilson (1981), but in Vakkari's shape one observes a strong drift towards IIR and – most essential – relevance criteria and assessment. The same mental model is responsible for what happens during the searching activities, including IIR, and during the simultaneous relevance assessment process. This interdependence of seeking, information need development and relevance assessment was previously put forward by Ingwersen and Borlund (1996) but in a less stringent way.

What was missing from the model was the aspects of *use of information* as a result of IS&R. A more recent model also by Vakkari (2001b), Fig. 5.3, incorporated this and other central aspects of IIR. It incorporated Kuhlthau's searching stages as a part of task performance, leading to the choice of channels or systems, and further extended Kuhlthau's model. Some additional factors to be explained, information types needed, search tactics, term choices and relevance judgments, were specified and connected to the stages. Vakkari showed that phases in task performance were systematically connected to the information searched for and the search tactics and usefulness of the information retrieved. These results are described in more detail in Sects. 5.4.5 and 5.7.

The strengths of the model are three-fold: 1) There is a clear-cut and necessary distinction between domain knowledge associated to (work) task performance, and IS&R knowledge, as will be further discussed in Sect. 6.2.4 – see also Sect. 2.3.2. 2) The work task stages and use of information in work task solving are clearly separated from search task execution. The latter can be regarded instrumental to the former – see also Sect. 6.2.3. The end product of the search task, that of relevance assessments, bridges back to the use of information in task execution. 3) There exists the concept of 'expected contribution', which refers to the experience gained by the actor in a historical sense.

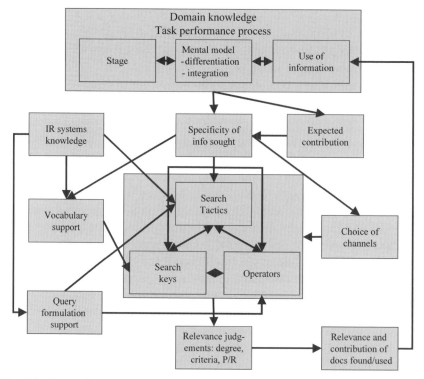

Fig. 5.3. Stages in work and search task performance (Vakkari 2001b). Legend: Arrows represent direction of impact.

The drawback of the model is its specific association to operational (non-best match) IR systems, but it can be made more general in scope. To a certain extent Vakkari's model (2001b) owed also to empirical findings and quite contextual models by Byström and Järvelin (1995) on work task complexity and information seeking, Sect. 3.1.2.

The Wang – Soergel Model. Moving into the details of using information resulting from IIR, Wang and Soergel produced their document selection framework (1998). It was based on a longitudinal empirical study of 25 self-selected faculty and graduate students in Agricultural Economics. The framework, Fig. 5.4, was also a stage model. It observes in greater detail than Vakkari, Fig. 5.3, the decision stages by applying 11 relevance criteria and five document value dimensions for the decision to select (and potentially later to use) retrieved documents. In addition, it succeeds in combining the criteria, values and decisions with so-called 'document information elements', that is, author-generated document structures and data elements as well as significant data connected to the 'isness' of information objects. These are representations of additional cognitive actors responsible for the being of documents – see further Sect. 6.1.4. It supplies highly interesting and novel possibilities of hypothesis generation on relationships between *structured* document *features*, searcher knowledge, multiple relevance criteria, *and* perceived value(s) of documents.

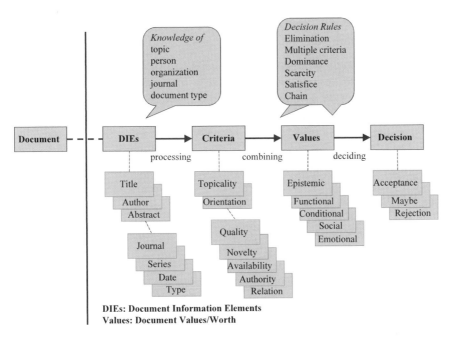

Fig. 5.4. Document selection decision stages. (Wang and Soergel 1998, p. 118).

Conceptual Models – Ingwersen. One of the main contributions in the monograph by Ingwersen (1992) was a model of IR interaction that incorporated the socio-organizational environment (context) of the current individual information searcher (p. 148). That context includes the scientific or professional domain(s) with information preferences, strategies and work tasks that influence the current perception of the user or searcher. This model became enhanced (1996), Fig. 4.10, to include the work task (or cultural-emotional interest) and corresponding situation as perceived by a searcher. Also, it emphasized central elements of a cognitive IR theory and the cognitive variation or poly-representation in documents, search engines and in the cognitive space of users at a given point in time – see Sect. 5.2.3-4. Further, the model introduced the influence of context on the information and system spaces and the social interaction between socio-organization factors and searcher over time.

Although depicting different kinds of interaction during IR events neither model versions explicitly demonstrated the relevance and information use dimensions of IIR. Hence, they did not bring into attention the flexible role changes of the cognitive actor, e.g., from searcher into generator. Later, these models led to a more sophisticated model of the cognitive communication system (Ingwersen 2001, p.14), Figs. 2.1 and 2.4, and the research framework behind the present work, Fig. 6.8.

Conceptual Models - Saracevic. Saracevic' stratified model of interaction levels (1996) was like Ingwersen's inspired by the idea of users placed in a situation in context – named the 'environment'. The model served dual purposes. First, it pointed to three communication levels. Secondly, it led to a revised and firmer grasp of the types of relevance involved in IIR. The communication levels consisted of a surface processing stratum dealing with computational data processing between sources and interface – based on a query; this stratum is hence concerned with morpho-lexical and syntactic linguistic levels of information processing – Sects. 2.1.1 and 4.7. The second stratum is the interactive cognitive communication level embracing the processes of perceiving information during human-machine interaction in relation to the perceived need for information, i.e., the searcher-query-interface negotiation. A third stratum is named 'situational' and refers to information use with respect to a perceived work task in context of the environment. The two latter strata necessarily also rely on semantic and pragmatic (or epistemic) levels of information processing. This stratified dimension of the model is probably nested, as are the information processing levels, Sect. 2.1.1. The other dimension of the model, different strata or types of relevance, is outlined below in Sect. 5.7. However, it is doubtful whether that dimension displays nested properties.

Saracevic' model is clearly associated with those by Ingwersen (1992; 1996). The advantage of Saracevic' model is its emphasis on adaptation from both the system and the searcher side during interaction to the other components and situations. In particular the former line of adaptation, that technology ought to fit the human, is fundamental to Saracevic' view of information transfer and IIR – and of Information Science. Further, information use is central as an end product of the interaction processes, and implies relevance assessments by the searcher in context.

Other Models. Slightly later Saracevic' model (1996) became enhanced with time and relevance scaling dimensions by Spink, Greisdorf and Bateman (1998) in a seminal contribution. Like the Kuhlthau model above (1993a), Saracevic' model, and later modified versions, have been important stepping-stones for generating hypotheses for empirical studies towards the turn of the 20th Century and beyond.

The seven-dimensional design and evaluation framework for cognitive systems engineering (CSE) and work analysis, developed by Rasmussen and Pejtersen and others during the 1990s (Rasmussen, Pejtersen and Goodstein 1992; 1994; Pejtersen and Rasmussen 1997; Pejtersen and Fidel 1999), viewed work tasks in professional contexts as the starting point for analysis – see also Sect. 3.1.3 for more details.

Belkin, Marchetti and Cool (1993) and Belkin and colleagues (1995a) categorized a list of information seeking strategies (ISS) into a comprehensive multi-dimensional model. In total, the model consists of 16 types of behaviors or 'episodes' within a four-dimensional classification of IR modes. Thus, the fundamental idea is that people commonly engage in multiple searching behaviors during IR sessions as well as across sessions. The model attempts to point to the types of search an IR system should support. However, it might be considered a model of IR interaction behavior rather than an 'episodic' model of ISS. That depends on the level of generalization at which one regards it. It was implemented in the so-called MERIT system and has also been applied to Web searching and navigation studies, for instance, by Pharo (1999). Pharo's analysis seemed to demonstrate a certain in-exhaustivity of the model (p. 211).

5.2 Cognitive IS&R Theory Building: ASK – Polyrepresentation: Issues and Findings

Aside from the obvious theoretical developments directly connected to the models discussed in Sect. 5.1, theory building was heavily concerned with the notions and understanding of relevance and related conceptions during the period, see Sect. 5.7. However, some general analytic theory construction, central to understanding IIR, took place. Initially, Robert S. Taylor's significant analytic approach (1968) to information need formation and his five filters is a central contribution – although Taylor did not refer to cognitive theories as such. Foremost, the ASK hypothesis (Anomalous State of Knowledge) by Belkin and colleagues (1978; 1982a-b) represents the most influential progress in the theoretical developments during the initial part of the period. During the 1990s we observe further detailed developments of cognitive IS&R theory – in particular concerned with the principle of polyrepresentation.

5.2.1 Taylor's Stages of Information Need Formation – and the Five Filters

Taylor (1968) proposed a linear model on how an information need or problem may develop in the mind of an actor – from a particular psychological state of mind to an expressed need. The model has four stages – Q1 to Q4 – the last one named the compromised need. Q1, Q2 and Q3 are named the visceral, the conscious and the formalized need, respectively. An intermediary interviewing a searcher should seek to work back from Q4 toward Q3 and Q2, the conscious need. However, how the need originally arises and how this relates to the person's situation or tasks remains unanalyzed. In this process the intermediary needs to pass through five central filters:

- Subject definition
- Objective and motivation
- Personal characteristics of inquirer.
- Relationship of enquiry description [request] to file organization.
- Anticipated or acceptable answers.

Ingwersen (1984; 1992, p. 113-115) discussed the significance of these proposals in the development of IR intermediary systems. He empirically verified the compromised need (1982) – and demonstrated how it leads directly to the concept and issues concerning the Label Effect: searchers do rarely express all what they actually know about their information gap, see details in Sect. 6.2.6-7. Hjørland saw the stages as development phases of cognition rather than concerned with information needs (1997).

However, Taylor's filters are more important than the four-stage assumption. In particular the second and fifth filters are concerned with the *intentional cause* (the work task, interest, problem or goal) underlying the information need. In an intriguing way the filters anticipated the functions of the MONSTRAT and MEDIATOR interface models (Fig. 4.12) with respect to problem and (work) task description, problem stage, and user and request model building.

5.2.2 The ASK Hypothesis

Directly from a cognitive point of view, Belkin, Oddy and Brooks (1982a-b) conducted empirical investigations in a university library setting with access to the local online information service. As in Ingwersen's (1982) investigations, they applied tape recording and protocol analysis, although basically of the pre-search interaction. They based their empirical studies partly on the experiences gained from the THOMAS system (Oddy 1977a-b), partly on a further development of the theory and hypotheses of ASK (Anomalous State of Knowledge) and Belkin's concept of information (1978).

In the preliminary design study, 27 novice clients, who were going to access information in the service, "[w]ere asked to discuss the problem with which they were faced prior to presenting a more formal request to the system" (1982b, p. 145). The focus was on the Pre-information searching behavior stages. These real-life problem statements obtained via interviews were recorded and went through a simplistic (surface-level) text analysis, producing structural representations, e.g., in the form of association maps. The idea was that the searcher narrative should provide context to the ASK. In addition, selected abstracts were analyzed, and their corresponding generators, i.e., clients and abstract authors, assessed the similarity of both representations to the original sources.

The searchers' problem statements (their ASKs) were analyzed for characteristics and patterns, leading to two basic types of ASKs, a *well-defined* one and a *more-or-less ill defined* one. The well-defined ASKs corresponds nicely to the two well-defined information need types proposed by Ingwersen (1986), based on novel analyses of his protocols from (1982): the verificative and the conscious topical needs; and the rather ill-defined one to his muddled information need type. Also Bates (1989) noted the essential issue that a substantial portion of information requirements are *not* simply 'known item' searches or precise topical information needs but frequently rather vague or fuzzy in the mind of the searcher or blends of topical and metadata inquiries.

In relation to retrieval, the idea was to evaluate the degree and patterns of overlap between the structured representations of abstracts and problem statements, in order to define means to improve existing IR strategies and techniques. These analyses led to the suggestion to interview the user more about what he knows to be *his problem*, than what he wants to know but is more or less unable to formulate, i.e., what he does not know yet. Hence, it seems important to the intermediary mechanism to build a model of the user's problem space. Although the results of these comprehensive experiments were unsatisfactory, they later led the IR community to new fundamental knowledge concerning the formation and development of the personal information need, situated in a problematic situation, the role of the intermediary mechanism and systems design.

5.2.3 The Principle of Polyrepresentation

The principle of polyrepresentation (or multi-evidence) originated from Ingwersen (1992; 1994) and Pao (1993) and was further developed by Ingwersen (1996, p. 25-41; 2001b; 2002) as a *consequence* of a cognitive theory for IIR. Initially polyrepresentation was advanced as a tool for high precision retrieval to improving the intellectual access to knowledge sources. Representation implies commonly subject access in various forms concerned with the contents of documents. However, representation in addition implies access to document contents *beyond* subject matter – e.g., by form, colors, structural elements, reference or outlink structures and contents (anchors), citations or inlinks, and a variety of metadata elements like author, employer or journal (carrier) name, mainly dealing with the existence (isness) of objects – see Sect. 6.1.4.

The principle derives partly from the experimental results gained in mainstream algorithmic IR research on best match principles, as represented by Salton and McGill (1983) and Belkin and Croft (1987): that various best match IR techniques retrieve different but overlapping results: The more alike the retrieval algorithms, the larger the overlap. The I^3R prototype (Croft and Thomson 1987) was based on this experience, featuring two different search engines – Sect. 4.8.2. The idea also drew upon plausible inference techniques applied on document representations (Turtle and Croft 1990).

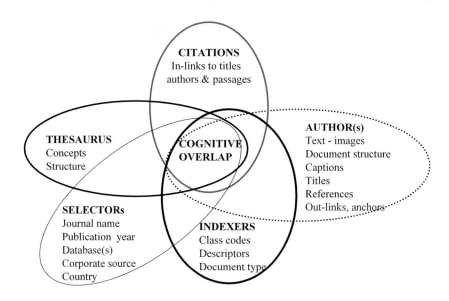

Fig. 5.5. Principle of polyrepresentation or multi-evidence in academic documents. Overlaps of information objects retrieved by cognitively and functionally different information structures, by means of one search engine via search keys associated with one searcher statement (e.g., a work task description). Elaborated from (Ingwersen 1996, p. 28; 2002, p. 294).

However, the *real novelty* in the principle of polyrepresentation is *also* to apply it to the cognitive space of the information seeker in order to extract a richer context of statements to be used as search keys during IIR – not just problem and information need representations but also work task representations.

Thus, as a third source of inspiration, the empirical studies by Ingwersen (1982) and proposals like ASK (Belkin et al. 1982a-b) had already shown that *different* underlying cognitive reasons existed for the development of information needs. Conceivably, this multidimensionality of the cognitive space can be further exploited in building request models and algorithms (not user models) that extract such evidence of searcher perceptions. For an exhaustive list, see Sect. 7.3.1.

Polyrepresentation constitutes one of several consequences of a cognitive view on IIR and IS&R – Sects. 2.1.3 and 2.3.1. Polyrepresentation directly employs the diversity of different actors' pre-suppositions and interpretations of their situations and objects over time. Further, they may be derived from the same actor but being of different *functional* nature, for instance, author generated text, diagram captions, and references or out-links (anchors) – Fig. 5.5. *Selectors* are special actors more or less directly responsible for the existence and availability of the information objects, such as, editors, publishers, employers, etc. See Sect. 6.1.4. In addition, document representations are made from different presentation *styles* according to the conventions of discourse in domains and media. In a cognitive sense, the same group of actors, e.g., indexers, may demonstrate inconsistency or interpretative variation among its members when facing identical information objects.

The principle of polyrepresentation is based on the following *hypothesis*: the more interpretations of different cognitive and functional nature, based on an IS&R situation, that point to a set of objects in so-called cognitive overlaps, and the more intensely they do so, the higher the probability that such objects are *relevant* (pertinent, useful) to a perceived work task/interest to be solved, the information (need) situation at hand, the topic required, or/and the influencing context of that situation (Ingwersen 1996; 2001; 2002). In contrast to the belief during the 1980s, that harmonization of this diversity was possible via interaction, the divergence is deliberately used as an asset. This suggests that overlaps of sets of objects created by such divergent cognitive representations be found. We name this type of overlaps 'cognitive overlaps'. The associations between polyrepresentation of information objects and cognitive space of actors are treated in Sect. 7.5.2, which also discusses the application of more than *one* searcher statement by *several* search engines, thus extending Fig. 5.5.

The principle of polyrepresentation originally associated with Boolean logic. However, polyrepresentation may be extended into a best match retrieval environment, as discussed further in Sect. 7.5.2.

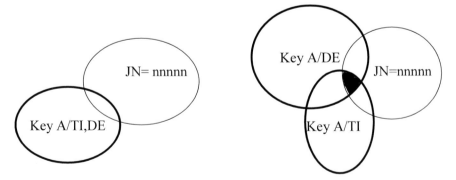

Fig. 5.6. Traditional Boolean online IR (left) vs. retrieval based on polyrepresentation (right) for one facet, Key A, and another document feature.

Polyrepresentation goes beyond the simplistic well-known Boolean intersection of topical facets as applied, for instance, to online searching of bibliographic databases or the Web (Ingwersen 1996; and Björneborn 2004). Fig. 5.6 demonstrates the difference. We have a mix of topical searching (represented by search key (A)) and metadata retrieval, represented by a journal name (nnnnn). Traditional Boolean searching is shown to the left. The key (A) is searched by *union* logic of the descriptor field (/DE), defined by the indexer, and title field (/TI), derived from the author, in a basic index. The retrieved set is intersected with the journal name (nnnnn). Documents in the overlap contain 'nnnnn' *and* key A in *either* the title *or* the descriptor field. The cognitively different indexer and author interpretations, signified by 'key A', are *not* necessarily present in the same documents in that overlap.

The right-hand side of Fig. 5.6 demonstrates how this retrieval overlap of cognitively different representations can be achieved by polyrepresentation. The key (A) is searched *independently* as descriptor (/DE) *and* as title key (/TI). The two retrieved sets are then intersected and finally simultaneously intersected with the journal name (nnnnn) into a fourth set. That set contains the 'cognitive overlap'. In case of several facets, represented by keys (B...n), the same procedure should be followed *for each facet*, prior to intersecting between all the facets themselves. Although the principle is very simple, this is highly complicated to human searchers, in particular when synonyms are involved, but doable by algorithmic retrieval – both in Boolean and best match systems.

5.2.4 Empirical Evidence for Polyrepresentation

Polyrepresentation, and its underlying hypothesis, was originally based on very few experiments carried out in the domain of citation analysis, for instance, by McCain (1989) and Pao (1993; 1994). Already Katzer and colleqagues (1982) had empirically studied retrieval overlaps between different document representations, but neither distinguishing between cognitive differences nor by involving relevance assessments. Also Tenopir (1985) studied retrieval overlaps between different document representations and their effectiveness in terms of relative recall and precision but not distinguishing between cognitive differences and origins of the representations (Sect. 4.9.2). There are, however, several combinations of divergent representations to select from to form promising polyrepresentative structures, across domains and media and over time, some of which have been carried out and empirically supporting the hypothesis:

- Using different *document features* of different functional or cognitive nature, including metadata, such as indexing, in addition to references (outlinks) and contextual data, like, citations (inlinks) or thesaurus concepts;
- Using different *algorithmic retrieval principles* (different search engines);
    - Different *weighting* schemes;
    - Different *relevance feedback* and/or *query modification* algorithms;
- Using different *databases* (document collections) combined;
- Using functionally different *searcher statements* simultaneously, e.g., of perceived work task, problem, or information need; (Belkin et al. 1993);
- Using the *previous divergent structures* in combinations including the time dimension.

Both Pao and McCain did deliberately choose combinations of *citations* and author-derived *text representations* to be combined. They involved citation databases and domain databases, and were based on seed documents (i.e. known relevant documents). In Pao's thorough investigation (1994) sets of bibliographic records were retrieved by intersecting sets formed through index and title keys with sets retrieved by citation analysis based on an initial pertinent seed document. The intersection, i.e., the document overlap made of three distinct cognitive actors, authors, indexers, and citing authors, was then evaluated by domain experts for topical relevance. The experts did not know from which sets the documents derived. Pao found that the odds for finding relevant documents in the overlap was more than six times higher than in the original separate sets. Basically, McCain's studies showed similar patterns. However, no theory building was made based on the results.

In a study similar to that by Pao, Christoffersen (2004) applied Medline, Embase and SCI in order to test the relevance proportions in any of the overlaps created online between indexer of MeSH (Medline), author text (Embase) and citing authors (SCI). Expert assessments were used. He found that "[t]he degree of overlap strongly correlates with the percentage of relevant items in a set" (p. 391). The results were statistically significant.

Peters et al. (1995) studied empirically the so-called *cognitive resemblance* between citing and cited documents by means of different similarity measures based on keywords and class terms from the Chemical Engineering domain. The study demonstrated "[that] publications with a citation relationship are significantly *more content-related* than other publications. It also showed that highly cited documents are mainly cited within their own research area ... Word-profile similarity *within* the group of publications sharing a citation [reference] to a highly cited publication, is significantly higher than [within] publications without such relationship" (p. 133, italics in original). Similarly, the chance of overlaps among such *coupled* publications increases notably.

Nielsen blind-tested two different pharmaceutical *thesaurus constructions* as search tools against one another, with relevance assessments made by domain expert users (2001). One thesaurus was of traditional academic design by an academic expert. The other was created by means of term associations by pharmaceutical researchers. As expected from the cognitive view both thesauri complemented each other during interactive retrieval, depending on the searcher context, work task and search goals, although individually displaying similar performance results.

Polyrepresentation in the Retrieval of Structured Documents.

Larsen and colleagues (2003) applied different document representations from the INEX test collection and INSPEC thesaurus terms (synonyms and narrower terms) added to the former in experiments on polyrepresentation, also involving *citation cycling* strategies, i.e., backward chaining followed by forward citation chaining, the so-called Boomerang Effect (Larsen 2002; 2004; Larsen and Ingwersen 2002). The investigation was inspired by the Pao (1993; 1994) and McCain (1989) investigations – but did not apply seed documents. It relied also on a simultaneous study of the application of highly structured queries, graded relevance assessments and polyrepresentation by Skov and colleagues (2004) – see also Sects. 4.6.4 and 4.10.3.

Results of the experiments showed, as expected, that by adding thesaurus terms to the document descriptors (not to the query search keys), performance decreased owing to increased noise. The best precision result was achieved by other tests combining functionally different representations, such as article titles, section headings and the cited titles in the references. Reasonable effectiveness was obtained by combining those representations intersected with descriptors and the Boomerang Effect.

Different *weighting schemes* were tested, e.g., by application of the frequency of documents cited. Unstructured queries were used. The effect was compared to clean polyrepresentative and bag-of-words baselines in the INEX test collection. The results showed that the Boomerang Effect did not decrease performance, but pure polyrepresentation was slightly better. However, bag-of-words obtained the best overall performance. *Structured queries* seem to be of importance in polyrepresentation and when applying citation-chaining strategies – see also Fig. 7.4 for the continuum of polyrepresentation.

Polyrepresentation and Query Representation. The issues of query structure, value adding of search keys by thesaurus terms (MeSH) and the application of the list of references in scientific documents as well as the number of citations to such documents were the central objects of the investigation by Skov and colleagues (2004). They applied the Cystic Fibrosis test collection with graded relevance assessments (Shaw *et al.* 1991) indexed in the InQuery IR system, version 3.1. They used 29 queries and searched by means of both unstructured natural language (bag-of-words baseline) and highly structured queries based on the Kekäläinen and Järvelin findings (1998; 2000) and tested 15 different overlap combinations. Their results were very promising from a polyrepresentation point of view. The more cognitively different the representations, the higher the precision obtained, both in structured and unstructured search modes. In particular, retrieval from the reference titles contributed to the high-precision results. For all 15 overlaps highly structured queries result in higher precision than queries in natural language – also supporting the Kekäläinen and Järvelin (1998; 2000) findings (see Sect. 4.6.4).

The highly structured queries tend to ensure that documents identified in an overlap have identical or synonym search keys present from *all* the representations searched. The weak structure in the natural language queries does not ensure that the search terms (or synonyms) are present in each of the document lists generating the overlaps. Therefore, proper polyrepresentation in the true sense of the concept cannot be achieved with weakly structured queries in natural language. These findings stress the importance of including representations that are both cognitively dissimilar (e.g., TI/AB; MeSH-headings) and functionally different (e.g., references). We observe two kinds of 'query structure': search keys logically structured and value added by synonyms from an ontology – the Kekäläinen and Järvelin approach (1998) – and the structural dimensions adhering from the polyrepresentation principle (Ingwersen 1996).

The two previous investigations both refer to the Rajashekar and Croft paper (1995) that investigated combining results from multiple index representations, query formulations (Belkin *et al.* 1993) and retrieval strategies (engines) by application of the plausible inference network model of IR. They saw the variety of representations (indexes, query formulations, IR principles) as multiple sources of evidence about document and query content. The combinations were used to make estimates of relevance probabilities. A significant trait was the fact that they deliberately used document and query information typical of commercial text databases and information services in their best match experiments. Their results circumscribe the utilisation of cognitively different representations of documents as well as very different search engine designs. They also indicate that substantial real benefits are possible and urge further research. Also Smeaton has experimented with the fusion of different search engine rankings (1998) with positive outcomes.

Belkin and colleagues (1993) applied multiple query formulations from *different searchers* but based on the same TREC topics in interactive TREC. As expected from a cognitive view, the combinations outperformed the individual query versions and one query version was always far the better than others. The issue here is that one cannot predict the most powerful query version beforehand and, in realistic terms, several persons might not search the same 'topic' within a short time window. However, search profiles referring to the similar popular 'topics' might be effectively combined – for instance in Web searching and recommender systems.

During the OKAPI experiments on relevance feedback and query modification Jones and colleagues (1995) reported on applying *hybrid query types* (from the same searcher) made by combining original search keys with thesaurus terms in a weak structure. Their performance was slightly better than the original search key query and better than queries applying keywords alone.

Polyrepresentation and Relevance Feedback. Relevance feedback during best match IR interaction and use of information over time is associated with searcher perceptions of information objects. Ruthven, Lalmas and van Rijsbergen (2002) based their automatic relevance feedback experiments on ideas similar to polyrepresentation. In their case various combinations of different *weighting* and *indexing algorithms* were tested experimentally with end-user participation providing evidence for algorithmic adjustments. Each algorithm can be regarded as a particular representation of a cognitive interpretation made by a designer. Combinations seemed to outperform the separate individual algorithms. See further Sect. 5.6.2.

Polyrepresentation Issues in the Web Environment. Web links and anchors are special features. Because *anchor texts* are nonstandardized they may, as outlinks to other Web entities, signify different cognitive descriptions (contexts) of such remote entities, see e.g., the Google PageRank feature by Brin and Page (1998). Google also applies the volume of inlinks to Web sites in its ranking algorithm. Inlinks are seen as features of authority – similar to scholarly citations below – as in Kleinberg's approach on 'hub' and 'authority' Web pages (1999). However, the Web information providers are not following the principle of polyrepresentation. The additional types of representations are simply applied in pragmatic and often obscure ways.

In academic communication the citing context surrounding a reference embedded in an author's text may act the same way as anchor text: for each reference its context may contribute something cognitively new to a cited object and be used for various retrieval and ontology purposes (Schneider 2004). The received *citations* can be regarded as socio-cognitive representations of use, recognition or authority by (scientific) actors of the documents over time. In contrast, the outgoing references on the list of references in academic documents are commonly regarded as *alternative descriptors* of the citing object and thus useful for IR (Garfield 1979). One should note that might not have the same significance as scholar citations, as stated recently by Thelwall and Harrier (2004) and Jepsen and colleagues (2004). Both studies recommend not applying inlinks as ranking tool if the search is on academic issues. Indeed, the functionality of Web inlinks and outlinks, references and citations is different (Björneborn and Ingwersen 2004) and should be taken into account for retrieval purposes.

5.3. Searchers' Behavior, Cognitive Models and Styles – Issues and Findings

Regardless of belonging to standard operational online or Web-related IIR research certain issues of common interest were studied, for instance, cognitive strategies, styles and expertise.

Fiction Retrieval and Strategies. A.M. Pejtersen (1980) recorded 300 intermediary – end-user interactions in fiction retrieval in a public library context. The results display important dimensions around which clients develop their desire for emotional experiences and information, and demonstrate 5 basic cognitive strategies by which they attempt to retrieve information in the system, supported by a librarian. Clients frequently employed dimensions like 'author intention' with a novel, the 'plot', the 'genre', 'time, place and environment ', 'main characters', 'emotional experience', 'ending', and 'front cover colors and pictures'. The five search strategies applied to fiction were:

- *Browsing*, in which the searcher picks out books from shelves at random, asking about their content;
- *Bibliographical*, asking for a specific known title or author;
- *Analytical*, in which one or several of the dimensions above are employed;
- *Empirical*, the intermediary selects books based on user stereotyping;
- *Analogical*, where the user wants books similar to a known one.

The empirical studies led later to the development of the Bookhouse IR system (Pejtersen 1989).

Experience in Online Searching. C. Fenichel (1980; 1981) looked at the relationship between experience and performance of online searchers. Novices did very well, and experienced searchers often searched very simply – even without modifying the initial strategy at all. These and alike investigations from the early online age are very useful for comparison to present day Web-IR studies.

The importance of distinguishing between levels of IS&R knowledge (from novices to experts) and status of conceptual or subject knowledge (domain knowledge) – so essential for understanding IS&R behavior – was originally analyzed in Marcia Bates' doctoral dissertation (1972) on catalog search success. The effect of the two distinctive types of knowledge was confirmed – also as a result of Christine Borgman's and Gary Marchionini's detailed studies of user-system interaction. Borgman (1989) investigated online searchers with different knowledge levels while Marchionini focused on novice users of full-text encyclopedias (1989), later generalized in 1995.

Fidel – Moves, Styles and Heuristics in Online Searching. In a range of studies from 1984 onwards Raya Fidel investigated basic dimensions of online searching. In an early study, Fidel (1984a) observed five experienced online searchers doing their regular job-related searches, 10 to 13 searches each. These searches were then analyzed to characterize *operationalist* and *conceptualist searchers* at pre-search, search proper and post-search stages. The former tended to use a large range of IR system capability in interaction (operational moves), focus on precision, but tended not to modify the specific meaning of the requests. On the contrary, 'conceptualist searchers' tended to map requests into a faceted structure, focus on recall, and to use conceptual moves and thus modify the specific meaning of the requests.

A year later she published the moves or changes in query formulation that are used to cut down or enlarge, or to move a search to better target it (1985). It was based on observations of about 90 searches by seven experienced online searchers in a Boolean environment. She identified eighteen operational moves and a dozen conceptual moves. The former keep the meaning of a search formulation intact but affect the result size or target, e.g., by limiting a search key to an index term field, adding a synonym, or by limiting by year of publication or language. The latter change the conceptual content of a search formulation, e.g., by intersecting the formulation with a new conceptual facet, by using broader or narrower descriptors, etc.

Fidel's series of large-scale studies culminated in her articles on searcher's selection of search keys and searching styles during operational online IR (Fidel 1991a-c) – see also Sect. 5.4.3. Fidel found that searching style had a primary effect on retrieval behavior over three dimensions: level of interaction; preference for operational or conceptual moves; and preference for text words or descriptors. The *operationalist searcher* preferred to employ operational moves and was less concerned with recall than the *conceptualist* counterpart. The *free-text searcher* preferred to apply text keys and avoided consulting thesauri – and was more likely to deal with practical questions. Fidel's findings also indicated that searchers in general had difficulty in achieving satisfactory recall – regardless of searching style.

The latter result is not identical to but associated with the central findings by Su (1994), based on a large empirical study in a Boolean context, i.e., that searchers in general attempt to pursue *recall* rather than precision when searching online. Although Su did not categorize her searchers like Fidel, it is highly probable that in *standard online IR* people wish to obtain as many relevant/useful items as possible. This is not always an easy task when searching with exact (Boolean) match and confined sets of references (or full documents).

Cognitive Style. Ford and colleagues (Ford, Wood, and Walsh 1994; Ford 2000) investigated cognitive styles during search sessions. The research continued in (Ford, Miller and Moss 2002; 2003) with special emphasis on strategic patterns of searching Boolean, best match or combined strategies in Web IIR. Three assigned search tasks of different complexity given to 65 test persons produced queries of which 500 were treated by factor analysis. The results were, for instance, that Boolean searching was consistently associated with a reproductive approach, anxiety (fear of failure), and high levels of active interest; best match searching was more linked to less anxiety and to a more meaning-oriented study approach, but the searchers were less actively interested in the search task.

Borgman (1996) looked into how end-users (still) had difficulty in using OPACs effectively, hence continuing her studies of individual cognitive differences affecting the IIR outcome (1989) and mental modeling (1986a-b). Her results were continued by, for example, Drabenstott and Weller (1996), Drabenstott (2003) and Sloane (2000; 2003), by shifting into Web-based library IR systems and catalog studies. The impact on Web search performance of online search expertise and cognitive style was investigated by Palmquist and Kim (2000), and Hong Xie looked into shifts and patterns of IIR strategies as well as evaluated Web and non-Web-based interfaces providing access to online databases (Xie 2000; Xie and Cool 2002). The influence of domain and IS&R expertise on information seeking and searching became the focus for Marchionini and colleagues (1993).

Cognitive style, intentionality underlying search strategies, expertise and other cognitive factors in IIR increasingly underwent empirical examination during the 1990s. With the exception of intermediary research they were increasingly in Web contexts.

Wang and colleagues (Wang and Tenopir 1998; Wang, Hawk and Tenopir 2000) were interested in the cognitive styles and affective states of Web searchers, associated to the Kuhlthau approach to information searching outlined previously (1991; 1993a). One conclusion they made was that many searchers develop a general mental model that covers all Web search systems (p. 243). Thus, searchers may for example use the same syntax in different systems. They also found that there is a group of Web searchers who use advanced features of the search systems – erroneously. There was no significant relationship between search time and computer and search experience.

Also concerned with cognitive pre-understanding and its possible effect, Hölscher and Strube (2000) focused on how search (IS&R) and background (domain-related) knowledge affect Web search strategies. Hsieh-Yee (1998) compared simulated searches for text with searches for graphic information as well as known-item and subject searches using Alta Vista. The author suggested that a hierarchical approach often seemed to have been used as an additional tactic to traditional tactics like keyword and author searching, owing to the structure of the Web. Such an approach means that the searcher actively manipulates the URL of a page to access a particular level in the hierarchy of a resource in order to explore it. The ideas put forward should be further investigated with data taken from actual Web sessions.

5.4. Standard Online IR Interaction – Issues and Findings

At the end of 1970s appeared some influential analytic works on online tactics, and again towards the end of the 1980s a couple of large-scale investigations were published of the online IR interaction processes. Human intermediary studies were popular but became later rather scattered. This is typical of IT-dependent research environments in which the most comprehensive achievements seem to be published just prior to major advances in exactly the IT, here: large-scale online databases during the 1980s and the arrival of the Web in the 1990s, respectively. Yet, we believe they are all of central importance also to the present Web-IR studies since they were conducted with methodological rigor. During the last decade we also observe comprehensive empirical studies on work task-based interactive IR, which, like Web-IR, fundamentally exclude human intermediaries from the studies.

Beaulieu (2000) and Savage-Knepshield and Belkin (1999) provided thorough reviews of interactive IR research, mainly concentrating on the online and experimental IR approaches. Empirical studies of end-user searching were discussed in Sutcliffe, Ennis and Watkinson (2000). The general trend over the period signified a shift from studying IIR in connection with standard (academic) bibliographic databases turning into investigating online Web IR in a range of professional and user-defined domains. The same researchers simply drifted away from traditional online studies and into the Web retrieval research. The latter is discussed in Sect. 5.5.

5.4.1 Search Tactics and Berry-Picking – Bates' Approach

Marcia Bates (1979a-b) proposed information search and idea tactics, which were intended for use in teaching and facilitating searching – seen as an interactive process in a (Boolean) IR system. In all, 29 search tactics in four categories, and 17 idea tactics were proposed. The tactics can be used to analyze what happens in a search process and to facilitate further steps in an on-going process. The tactics themselves do not contain factors that would connect the search process to its context – for analysis and explanation.

A decade later Bates (1989) criticizes the narrow view of IR (traditional online and laboratory non-interactive) as searching based on a stable topical need. To Bates real (operational online) IIR was like *Berry-Picking*. She developed Berry-Picking as a principle for searcher behavior that became very influential during the 1990s. The principle entails that each new piece of information that searchers encounter provides them potentially with new ideas and direction to follow, and consequently a new conception of their information need. At each stage of the search, the user may identify useful information items leading her or him onwards. We may here not simply talk of alternative versions of the request but of modifications of the underlying cognitive structures due to the information context faced with. She called this mode of retrieval an evolving search. The information need situation is hence not satisfied by a single final retrieved set, but by a series of selections on the road, so to speak, of individual references.

Based on findings in the literature on information seeking, like those by Ellis (1989), and the emerging hypertext-based IR possibilities, Bates suggested several capabilities that might support users better in their various information seeking strategies than current systems at that time.

Clearly, Bates' berry-picking behavior enhanced her ideas of the so-called 'exploratory paradigm' published in (1986b). Further, it forestalled the typical Web surfing strategies yet to come by emphasizing browsing and navigation as searching modes for which explicit queries do not have to exist. *Browsing* is here seen as intentional but undirected searching whilst *navigation* is intentional and directed towards a goal. Exploration of an information space and serendipity were central notions in the berry-picking mode of searching, with more realistic fuzzy information needs as instigators.

5.4.2 Human Intermediary Behavior

In the area of human intermediary behavior, early research looked at, among other aspects, intermediary behavior in libraries and during online searching interacting with end-users. Interface design models, like the MONSTRAT Model by Belkin, Seeger and Wersig (1983), were developed based on such empirical research.

Studies in Library Environments. Independently of Belkin, Oddy and Brooks (1982a-b), see Sect. 5.2.2, Ingwersen (1982) studied information retrieval in libraries, based on written assigned questions. In all, 23 thinking aloud protocols were collected. The study subjects were librarians who were told to act as if the requests represented inter-library loan requests. Ingwersen's observations of the situational influence of context on information need descriptions and perceptions, for instance in the form of reasons for having a knowledge gap, confirmed the problem conception in the ASK hypothesis, Sect. 5.2.2. Also, the investigations pointed to perceptions of users leading to problem situations, e.g., perceived goals or interests, and a certain randomness and non-rationalism in the cognitive behavior of searchers. The study revealed the Label Effect – Sect. 6.2.7.

The study also found that an *open search mode* implies that the intermediary is curious and attempts to extend her domain knowledge, to find out about the subject area given in the request. IR systems, documents and tools are used to learn about the conceptual characteristics surrounding the request. In a *fixed search mode* the intermediary immediately begins to search for the information required by the client. This mode is effective only when the intermediary actually possesses substantial domain knowledge. Otherwise the intermediary would begin to search in circles, i.e., returning to the same retrieval tools previously used. Random associative searching may be a consequence. This search mode illustrates the stable but ill-defined information need situation, Table 6.3. A *semi-fixed search mode* implies starting as in the fixed mode – but mainly due to retrieval problems, and inadequate IS&R knowledge, the mode may change momentarily into open mode in order to learn about the topic.

The same searching tools can be used differently, depending on the mode of searching. In addition, the study demonstrated a difference in perceived and remembered new concepts related to search mode. Later studies, e.g., those above by Fidel (1984; 1985) and Ford on cognitive styles (2000) confirm the findings. The mode depends on the actual combination of IS&R and domain knowledge.

Traditional reference work underwent investigations in a cognitive context and in light of the novel IT environments in which such activities take place in libraries, for instance, by Nordlie (1999) and White (1998).

Interface Design – The MONSTRAT Model. Belkin and his colleagues followed up the study on the ASK conception (Belkin, Oddy and Brooks 1982a-b) by a functional analysis of six rather extensive pre-search user-librarian interactions. The results of discourse analysis were presented by Belkin (1984), Brooks (1986) and Daniels (1986), and demonstrate an analysis scheme consisting of 10 categories and a number of sub-categories. Fundamentally, the meta-categories of the scheme are identical to the intermediary functions that constitute the analytic MONSTRAT Model (MOdular functions based on Natural information processes for STRATegic problem treatments) developed by Belkin, Seeger and Wersig (1983). According to Ingwersen (1992, p. 108-111) the MONSTRAT model can be seen as aiming at:

- *Supportive IR intermediary design,* i.e., a highly interactive intermediary mechanism that relies on implicit user and domain models, based on extensive field studies of actual domain, tasks and actor preferences.
- *'Intelligent' IR intermediary design,* i.e., an intermediary mechanism that relies on both implicit models and interactive, actual and explicit actor and problem modeling, see also Sect. 4.8 on expert systems.
- *Education,* i.e., be the framework for training future information specialists in IR interaction.

The model led to the Mediator Model (Ingwersen 1992), outlined Fig. 4.12.

The Saracevic, Wu, Spink and Associated Research Groups. Saracevic, Mokros and Su (1990) continued their design study (Saracevic and Su 1989) providing a large qualitative analysis of user-intermediary interaction. The studies stress in a very detailed manner the importance of extracting information from the user on search keys, domain knowledge level, previous information searching experience, and search task knowledge.

These central studies were followed up later by various US research groups: Spink and colleagues concentrated on how the elicitation of information from end-users by intermediaries takes place during standard online IIR and its implications for IR systems design (Spink et al. 1996; Spink, Goodrum and Robins 1998). In particular, the latter study exemplified a large-scale empirical investigation of 40 mediated IR interactions and more than 1500 elicitations. It established a categorization of purpose and strategies for mediated questions from users with real needs and monitored the transition sequences from one type of questions to another. Their conclusions were compared to previous studies and models of the issue. Lately Wu and Liu continued the trend in an empirical study of intermediaries' information seeking and elicitation styles (2003). Confirming previous studies, they found that the mediators demonstrate three different styles: 1) trying to detect the underlying information problem of the patron; 2) catching search keys for the query formulation process; and 3) more stereotypical inquiries on databases. Seen in an information and knowledge management context Ellis and colleagues (2002) viewed information seeking and searching, i.e. IIR, in holistic manner and carried out a large quantitative as well as qualitative study which among other issues concentrated on patron-searcher interaction.

5.4.3. End-user Online IR Interaction Studies

Quite comprehensive empirical investigations of end-users' interactive communication with online systems by Fidel (1991a-c) led to a detailed understanding of interactive processes and use of feedback during IIR by end-users – and to a number of ensuing research projects on central cognitive aspects of IR interaction. As briefly described in Sect. 5.3 in relation to searching styles, Fidel (1991c) used verbal and log protocols as well as observation of 47 expert searchers in their own realistic job-related environment (N = 201) searches. Fidel (1991a) examined how the searchers apply intuitive rules when selecting between text word and descriptor-based search keys. The rules, or routines, are determined by the nature of requests, database requirements or their own beliefs. The statistical analyses (1991b) denoted reasons for the selection of each search key and search modifications. Results showed that the use of thesauri and controlled indexing depended on their perceived quality and availability as well as on other database-associated reasons. Multi-database searching induced the use of free-text search keys without consulting thesauri.

Peiling Wang studied the development of information needs, request descriptions and search key application in a longitudinal real-life setting (1997). Both information needs as well as the nature and richness of the search keys applied changed over time according to the experiences gained (learning effects). This happened not only during searching, but in particular also when selecting and making use of information objects in a work task environment (Wang and Soergel 1998; Wang and White 1999). Shifts in focus of the perceived information need during IIR, owing to influence of document structures and contents, was looked into by Robins (2000) whereby early work on such shifts by Belkin (1984) was continued. *Collaborative information retrieval* (CIR) studies surfaced in increasing numbers, e.g., Fidel and colleagues (2000), Hansen and Järvelin (2004; 2005) or Hyldegaard (forthcoming), the latter investigation of longitudinal nature.

Feedback Studies. Spink and Saracevic continued investigating searchers' interaction with standard IR systems (1997; 1998), with special emphasis on the nature and manifestations of feedback during online IR sessions. For instance, they found that search keys identified from system's feedback, and later applied to query expansion, were likely to be highly productive, as were interactive sessions in *teams* of users. Spink initiated research on the application of feedback from online IR systems (1997a-b), also of interest to Fidel (1991b-c) in relation to application of thesauri, in association with her investigations on multiple search sessions over time (1996). The latter study produced a model of end-user behaviour in longitudinal retrieval situations. Based on the holistic cognitive approach and cybernetic theory Spink (1997a) analyzed three different feedback models applied in Information Science research. Central to the present work, she suggested enhancing the feedback concept within the cognitive understanding of information, thus illuminating the information seeking and IR *context*. An entire issue of Information Processing and Management was later dedicated to IR in context, edited by Spink and Cool (2002). The feedback investigations also produced a comprehensive ARIST chapter on that issue (Spink and Losee 1996).

5.4.4 Explaining Online Search Effectiveness

Trudi Bellardo (1981; 1985a-b) reviewed the opinionative literature and more rigorous studies on investigated online searcher traits and their relationship to search outcome. Her general finding for that period was that there was much of hype and overstated assumptions about the demands of online searching, while findings based on reliable analysis were much weaker. Her study, with graduate library school students as subjects, did *not* support the then common assumptions that exceptionally high intelligence or other specific personality traits would be necessary for high performance in online searching. Nor seemed experience influential.

Central Interactive IR Studies. Slightly later, Saracevic and colleagues (1988; 1988a-b) reported a large field study on information retrieval with the aim to obtain scientific evidence on how users, requests, searchers, searches and effectiveness relate to each other. In particular, the research investigated how the cognitive context and human decisions act in the process. Users posed their requests based on their own work and assessed the results – they got a free search but no payment for participation. Searchers were professionals searching Dialog databases (Boolean IR) and retrieving full bibliographic records. There were 9 searches for each of the 40 requests, five by external professional searchers and four by the research team. The former were based on the same written request text. The latter were based on a tape-recorded problem statement, the written request text, and terms from the request text with and without thesaurus elaboration. The union of the results (or its most recent 150 items) was assessed for relevance on a three-point scale. In all, nearly 18000 items were retrieved, nearly 12000 among them unique. Data were collected on users, requests, (professional) searchers, searches and effectiveness.

A major point in the study was to analyze the chances that a retrieved item be relevant as affected by other variables. Likewise, recall and precision were used as dependent variables affected by the other, independent variables.

Saracevic and the group tested correlations between many meaningful pairs of variables but very few significant correlations were found and their explanatory power regarding the variance of item relevance or search recall and precision were low. One reason to this may be that random phenomena (specific to users, questions, or searchers) affect effectiveness. However, the authors did not analyze interaction effects involving several (>2) variables. This might have revealed some significant correlations.

In general, taped problem and intent statements by users achieved the best performance. We observe an association to the ASK hypothesis investigations, Sect. 5.2.2. The poorest performance was achieved with written questions and no elaboration. This suggests that automatic query formulation, based on a user's written request (with eventual Label Effects – Sect. 6.2.7), as such may be a poor way of searching. Moreover, the user's context provided in the taped problem and intent statements turned out as valuable resources for query formulation. (Saracevic and Kantor 1988a). If multiple searchers retrieved an item for the same request, its chances of being relevant grew significantly. (Saracevic and Kantor 1988b).

Saracevic and Kantor (1988a) questioned proper evaluation measures of IR systems from the user point of view, i.e., recall and precision at search level. This research theme got more attention in the 1990's and beyond – see Sects. 4.10 and 7.1. The findings on the significance of problem and intent statements, overlaps and multiple retrievals directly support the principle of polyrepresentation: that the interplay of several cognitive actors and their interpretations supports effective retrieval, Sect. 5.2.3.

5.4.5 Findings on Task-based IIR

Borlund and Ingwersen (1997) investigated empirically in a small-scale experiment the application of work task situations in best match IIR performance evaluation. The study was based on the idea that a work task (or daily-life situation) serves as an instigator for ensuing information problem and need generation. They used simulated work task situations given to test persons who assessed relevance using a tri-partite scale – see Sect. 5.9. The work led later to novel performance measures and a complete evaluation package for IIR (Borlund and Ingwersen 1998; Borlund 2000a; 2003b) – Sect. 4.10.

Vakkari (1999; 2000; 2001a-b) and Vakkari and Hakala (2000) analyzed (work) task-based IS&R in a number of empirical longitudinal studies. The data were collected by observing 11 MSc students from Library and Information Science and 22 undergraduates from Psychology through their seminars over 4 months. The students' task was to prepare a research proposal for a thesis. Vakkari with his team investigated the students' understanding of their tasks and associated changes of search terms and tactics during task performance. When the tasks got more structured, the associated searches became more diverse: more keywords were included, and their conceptual richness increased. This is in line with Wang's observations (1997). In the exploration phase actors try to shape the task by categorizing and relating its major components. When that has been accomplished, they move to the task formulation phase and are ready to make inferences for solving the task. The relevance aspects of these research efforts are treated in Sect. 5.7.

Vakkari worked out a theory of task-based IR (2001a) and reviewed the literature on task-based information searching for ARIST (2003). He makes a strong case for work and search tasks as essential to be taken into account for understanding and explaining IS&R. He clarifies the differences between work and search tasks and discusses dependent and independent variables in a useful way for task-based information research.

5.5. Web IR Interaction

The majority of studies of Web interaction focused on single sites and was based on server log analysis. For a detailed overview of Web searching research we recommend the Jansen and Pooch review (2001).

There were surprisingly few studies that focused on user-centered surveys, e.g., on the:

1. *Searcher side* of Web transactions (Catledge and Pitkow 1995; Wang and Tenopir 1998; Wang, Hawk and Tenopir 2000, Hölscher and Strube 2000);
2. *Children's and high school students' use of the Web* to solve assigned specific search tasks (e.g., Fidel et al 1999; Large, et al. 1999; Bilal 2000; 2001); or on
3. *Pre-Web hypertext systems* (e.g., Marchionini, Lin and Dwiggins 1990; Rada and Murphy 1992; Qui 1993a-b).

Below, investigations in the categories a) and b) are briefly discussed after three central large-scale server log studies. The Digital Library research program, associated with the Web technology, is briefly depicted at the end of the section.

5.5.1 Large-scale Search Engine Studies

These were based on log analysis. The Excite studies reported by Jansen, Spink and Saracevic (2000) and in (Spink et al. 2001) were preceded by the Alta Vista study (Silverstein et al. 1999). Lately, Wang, Berry and Yang reported the longitudinal study of an academic Web server over 4 years 1997-2001 (2003). In addition, there were several smaller studies focusing on the client side of interaction[2]. The major limitations of these studies include that they only catch a narrow facet of the searcher's Web interaction. The searcher, his/her intentionality, strategies, and motivations are hardly known. On the other hand, log analysis is an easy way of getting hold of data that can be treated with quantitative methods. We can use the studies to obtain statistically significant data about searchers' selection of search keys and use of syntax in queries.

---

[2] This discussion is elaborated from Pharo and Järvelin (2004).

Jansen and colleagues (1998; 2000) analyzed more than 50,000 queries in the Excite query log. They found that searchers use *few terms* when searching the database (2.21 per query). This is in accordance with the Label Effect phenomenon discovered decades earlier, see also above and Sect. 6.2.7. The phenomenon indicates that the searchers *spend little effort* per search task in a single search engine. However, the paper says nothing about whether searchers search for different topics during a session, i.e., one does not know if they tried to solve more than one task in one session. The survey also shows that only approximately 5% of the searchers use advanced search features like the Boolean AND-operator (very few use OR and AND NOT) and relevance feedback (the latter is used in 5% of all queries). The result is in accordance with studies of advanced online facilities used by search *experts* (e.g., the Zoom and Limit All commands on ESA-IRS) made more than two decades ago (Wormell 1981b). A third important result concerns the examination of search results. Only 20% of the searchers looked beyond the first two result pages. On average each searcher looked at 2,35 pages.

A follow up study based on analysis of one million queries in Excite (Spink et al. 2001) showed that searchers moved towards *even shorter queries* and that they viewed *fewer pages* of results per query (Wolfram et al. 2001).

Silverstein and colleagues (1999) performed a similar analysis of approximately 1 billion requests, or about 575 million non-empty queries – from Alta Vista. Their findings support the notion that Web users behave differently from searchers of traditional IR systems – they use few query terms, investigate only a small portion of the result list, and rarely modify queries. It is, however, impossible to tell what the situation would have been like if the search engines had similar response times and the same (set) features as professional IR systems. The domains in question, scientific ones vs. all kinds at all conceptual levels also separate the two search environments. The 'hidden Web' much more mirrors traditional online IR. Aside from known-item searching by means of URLs and fact-finding via names, it is difficult to directly assess the kind of information needs that underlie the queries posed to the systems.

The method used for distinguishing between searchers was a combination of the use of cookies by the searchers and IP addresses. That method is not perfect since cookies can be disabled, different searchers can apply the same browser, and floating IP addresses can be assigned to computers. Another method to separate sessions is to define a session – as done by Silverstein and colleagues (1999) as a "series of queries by a single user made within a small range of time". After 5 minutes of searcher inactivity a session is timed out.

The third large *longitudinal* investigation by Wang, Berry and Yang (2003) analyzed more than 540,000 user queries submitted to an academic Web server from 1997-2001. Their log file and queries did not include IP addresses of individual searchers owing to privacy concerns. Hence, the sessions of the individual searchers could not be identified from the log data (p. 744). Nevertheless, the study demonstrates valuable results on query level statistics that reveal searchers' search activities, as well as the actual queries that uncover both topics and linguistic structures. The observations reported are thus on the searcher population as a whole. They reported, in line with Shneiderman, Byrd and Croft (1997), the *30% zero-hit problem* that seems quite consistent in Web searching. More than 25% of the zero hits were caused by misspellings. Queries are also short: on average 2 words over the period with almost 38% as one word and 41% as two-word queries. Three-word queries did increase over the period (from 12.3% in 1997 to 17.3% in 2001), while four-word queries counted for 6%. Empty queries were scarce, compared to the two studies above, but were observed to increase. The study demonstrated that 'sex' and alike terms are decreasing as most frequent search keys – at least in academic Web environments. In addition, the study analyzed the Zipf distribution of search keys over the years surveyed.

The lack of standards in determining session boundaries and individual searchers in logs makes comparisons of results from different studies very difficult, as pointed out by Jansen and Pooch (2001) who suggested a framework for future Web log studies.

If one wishes to compare differences in use between Web search engines and traditional IR systems, one should take into account both the searchers, the system and the interface, i.e., the diverse human computer interaction (HCI) dependencies like bandwidth, features of the client program, etc. To obtain such knowledge it is necessary to study interaction also from the searcher side.

The search engine effectiveness studies, for instance made by Bar-Ilan (1999; 2000), are related to the log analyses but belong to the systems performance traditions. They bridge into the realm of bibliometrics, informetrics and Webometrics.

5.5.2 User-centred Surveys

User-centered evaluations of human interaction with Web search engines started to evolve by assessing effectiveness as well as usability factors, such as screen layout, as was done by, for instance, Spink in an exploratory study involving 22 test persons (2002). She built her research design on her four-dimensional model of situated actions (p. 404) that extended the Saracevic (1996) stratified relevance framework and Kuhlthau's information seeking stage model by adding a longitudinal dimension and graded relevance judgments.

Among the user-associated investigations Wang and colleagues (1998; 2000) and other research groups specifically looked into searchers' cognitive styles and affective states, see Sect. 5.3.3. Catledge and Pitkow did an interesting longitudinal survey at the Georgia Institute of Technology (1995). In all 107 persons belonging to the Institute agreed to have their client logs captured over a period of three weeks. The client logs contained the URL of the searchers' current and target page, as well as information on the technique they used to access the target. The data were analyzed to compute path lengths and frequency of paths. Three kinds of Web users were found:

- *Serendipitous browsers,* i.e., searchers who avoided repeating long sequences;
- *General-purpose browsers*, i.e., searchers performing as expected. These users had a 25% chance of repeating complex navigation sequences.
- *Searchers*, i.e., actors who repeated short sequences infrequently, but often replicated long navigational sequences.

The survey also gave some insight into which techniques and tools are being used to browse the Web. They found that in 93% of the cases following links (52%) and using the back button (41%) was the method being used to access Web pages. Later associated studies looked into three different interactive search approaches on the Web (Dennis, Bruza and McArthus 2002) and cognitive task influence on searching behavior (Kim and Allen 2002). The former investigation studied assisted query reformulation of query-term based, directory supported and phrase-based searching, including aspects of cognitive load. Although search time increased slightly the query-term based and phrase-based reformulation assisted search modes were superior to directory-based Web IR in terms of searcher-estimated relevance. A longitudinal 10-month study of 206 college students' searching behavior showed that searchers adopted a rather passive or browsing approach to Web IR – but became more eclectic in the selection of Web hosts with growing Web experience (Cothey 2002).

Credibility and Authority. An interesting and central aspect of Web IIR is the quality, credibility, trust and cognitive authority in the Web, since searchers are heavily dependent on what the search engines actually find and presents during retrieval sessions. Wathen and Burkell (2002) have carried out a review of investigations of credibility and trust while Rieh

(2002) investigated 16 scholars' judgment behavior and the characteristics of quality and authority assessments in the Web. Rieh used assigned search tasks simulating realistic work task situations. The study found that central factors affecting the assessments were characteristics of information objects and sources, background knowledge, the current situation, ranking of retrieved objects, and general assumptions concerning the sites.

5.5.3 Children Searching the Web

Large, Beheshti and Moukdad (1999) investigated the moves (or actions) made by primary school pupils during Web searching. Later, they studied children in order to produce relevant design criteria for Web portals (Large, Beheshti and Rahmin 2002). Hirsh (1999) studied how (work) tasks affect children's searching behavior in digital environments and their relevance criteria. The study by Fidel and colleagues (1999) centered on high school students and found that they were focused and flexible searchers, but that training and search support was necessary to release the great potential of the Web as an information gathering resource.

In her three studies on 12-14 year old children's use of the Yahooligans! Web search engine Bilal examined the young searchers' cognitive, affective, and physical behavior when using the search engine (2000; 2001; 2002). The first two studies were based on fully assigned search tasks. Among other factors Bilal compared how they used the search tool for solving tasks of different complexity and found that "children had more difficulty with the research task", i.e., tasks that are open-ended, "than with the fact-based task" (Bilal 2001, p. 135). Further, children performed so-called fully self-generated search tasks, i.e., searches based on their own information problems (2002). In comparison to the former assigned search tasks she found that the children were more successful on the fully self-generated tasks, than on the assigned ones. Also, they felt on average more satisfied with the results. Further, children were more successful in all search tasks when browsing than when searching on keywords; however, the Yahooligans! Web search engine has a poor keyword searching mechanism. Bilal relies on the Kuhlthau model as well as on other seeking approaches, including the Borgman and colleagues study (1995) on children's searching behavior on browsing and keyword searching in online catalogs, a prelude to the digital library era.

In a later study Bilal and Kirby (2002) compared 22 secondary school students' (the children) and 12 university graduate students' Web searching performance applying the Yahooligans! Search engine and one fact-based search task, inspired by Vakkari's work on task complexity and problem structure (1999). They applied Bilal's so-called Web Traversal Measure that examines the weighted traversal effectiveness, efficiency and quality of Web moves (2000). The study is very instructive, also in respect of adult Web IR, in investigating searchers' perceptions of events and discussing implications.

5.5.5 Digital Library Studies

Borgman (2000) carried out the most comprehensive treatment from a holistic and human-centered perspective of the state in the digital library (DL) development, often seen as a complementary area to IR and with its own agenda. The monograph departs from the stand of a global information structure and covers almost all aspects of digital library R&D, in particular why DL are hard to use *and* providing suggestions as to making them easier to use. Although there exist several studies of the digital environments from user perspectives, like Spink and colleagues (1998), Bishop and colleagues (2000) and Park (2000) on effectiveness and user behavior in digital contexts, most work on digital library usability is theoretical or laboratory-oriented. Chen's special issue on digital libraries provides a typical sampling of (technical) papers (2000).

Borgman states "As tasks become more complex, and as the relationship between task and action becomes more abstract, technologies become more difficult to use. 'Real-world' analogies disappear, replaced by commands, menus, displays, keyboard, and pointing devices." (2000, p. 140). She suggests a research agenda that involves taking account for social *context*, e.g., incorporating digital libraries into work, seeing human–computer interaction rather as a set of relationships between *many* people and many computers, tailoring the library to communities *and* also spanning community and work task (interest) boundaries (p. 163-168). One may regard this agenda also to be of common value for Web searching behavior and IIR research. It implies a transition from metadata libraries to full object digital libraries; a transition from stand-alone systems to linked systems, including other applications; a shift from relying on query submission only to true navigation through information space. This calls for renewed research on interface design (see also Greene et al. 2000), ontology, and task modeling as well as human evaluations; and a transition in research focus, from the individual searcher to the *group of processes* (activities and actors) involved – like in the holistic cognitive framework proposed in Sects. 6.1-6.2. Research must account for the social context of Web and digital library use.

5.6 Searcher-Associated Best Match IR Interaction

Towards the turn of the Century new researchers, mainly from IR-related computer science, initiated novel empirical alternatives to the traditional best match test environment. The ensuing section highlights the research on *searcher*-associated best match IR interaction, mainly completed outside TREC.

5.6.1 The Interactive OKAPI Experiments

The OKAPI experiments played a central role (Robertson 1997a). Relevance feedback, human query modification and experiments with retrieval algorithms are valuable for the cognitive view of IIR. In all three aspects of IIR one must assume that experimental algorithmic IR research may benefit from results from the searcher-related research in order to design better performing IR systems. This happened with the OKAPI experiments (Beaulieu 1997; Beaulieu and Jones 1998) and also with the Rutgers-Amherst University IIR results, for instance, Belkin and colleagues studying relevance feedback and ranking mechanisms in IIR (1996a) or multiple query representations (1993; 1995b).

One of the central dimensions of OKAPI was its design with searchers in mind that do not possess IR expertise. In the various relevance feedback (RF) and automatic query modification (AQM) experiments the system acted as a black box. As long as it produced useful results searchers regarded AQM with satisfaction. But the problem with AQM is the difficulty in changing its search path. With human QM the level and way of active searcher control was (and is) the central issue. Manual query modification during experimentation, combined with relevance feedback on the outcome, demonstrated highly interesting results from a cognitive view. The outcome does not have to be monolithic, that is, one simple ranked list, but might also contain pointers to several conceivable routes into information space, for example, hypertext links, condensed or structured lists of concepts, and alike means of conceptual feedback. Efthimiadis (1993) evaluated the structures of monolithic term lists empirically from a cognitive and user-centered view. Simple frequency-ranked term lists seem less valuable than lists ranked with the 'best' (weighted) search terms first – see also Sect. 4.6.

In the variety of IIR experiments done with OKAPI and other systems, for instance, by the Belkin team, Iivonen (1995) or Hersh, Pentecost and Hickam, (1996), it became clear that the interface functions concerned with RF and QM are important to investigate. How should the searcher browse and evaluate results and modify search keys? Which kind of search keys to modify: single keys, composite keys, elements from key sentences in documents, most frequent keys or keys that are sorted by special QM weighting schemes? How to obtain *new* discriminating terms to avoid circular searching. What is characterizing the best balance between human and system control? Thus, we may detect the problem that arises when AQM, well-functioning during single runs in the laboratory, performs less well in realistic settings over *several* runs with searcher participation – see contra-arguments, Sect. 1.3.

Jones and colleagues (1995) reported on thesaurus-based QM done by users. The test collection was the INSPEC database searched through the probabilistic OKAPI system (see Robertson 1997b). Twenty searchers entered their queries and obtained a list of best matching terms from the INSPEC thesaurus. The users selected terms they found accurate as expansion keys. Then, four versions were constructed and run for each query: (1) – original query containing the keys from the user only, run as a text search, i.e., on all fields, (2) – controlled query containing selected thesaurus terms only, run as a controlled vocabulary search on descriptor fields only, (3) – query containing thesaurus terms only, run as a text search, (4) – hybrid query containing original keys and thesaurus terms, run as a text search. The queries had weak structure. On average the users saw 67 terms from which they selected 6.5 for QM. The top 20 documents of each query type were first pooled and judged for relevance by the users. The overall performance of the queries (2) – (3) was slightly poorer than the performance of the original query (1), while the hybrid (i.e., quite polyrepresentative) query (4) had fractionally better effectiveness. An interesting notion was that QM had a reordering effect: the overlap in top ranked result sets of the hybrid and original queries was very low. (Jones et al. 1995.)

Often results of the OKAPI experiments seemed to show that the cognitive load on the searchers is too extensive with increased control. Searchers then tend to make much less than optimal use of the RF and QM facilities. This in turn diminishes the effectiveness of the system and causes decreasing performance. It is consequently a question of finding a balance between interactivity and cognitive load, control, and functional visibility (Beaulieu 1997, p. 15; Beaulieau and Jones 1998, p. 245). For instance, it is cognitively easier to select from a prepared list of keys than to generate them self; and it is probably a more effective task to deselect keys not to be used than actively to select such elements. Automatic RF may probably better support searchers performing human QM for more effective IR – see below.

5.6.2 The New Generation of Interactive Best Match Experiments

Towards the end of the 1990s, a new generation of researchers from experimental IR surfaced in collaboration with old hands with several novel approaches to laboratory IR. First, Campbell and van Rijsbergen (1996) and Campbell (2000) experimented with the so-called 'ostensive model' for probabilistic IR. Borlund experimented with graded relevance. She applied simulated work task situations given to test persons and compared to real information need situations, as well as designed her IIR evaluation package (2000a-b; 2003a-b). Simultaneously, Ruthven (2001) and Ruthven, Lalmas and van Rijsbergen (2001a-b; 2003) evaluated ways of altering relevance feedback and query modification algorithms – depending on the behavior of the user at a given point in time during retrieval sessions.

Campbell's contributions took as their starting point that information needs indeed are *variable over session time* – as found in realistic cognitive IIR situations. This implies intuitively that when the user points to a document as relevant, this means *currently* relevant. Accordingly, the probabilistic search algorithm should mirror this fact by down-weighting documents (and their terms) selected as relevant earlier during the session. The longer time since the selection, the less the weights. Logically, the weighting scheme might follow an opposite principle if the searcher is moving within the structure of a particular document, e.g., the longer time staying in the structure, the higher the initial weights. Campbell did not follow up on this. He also designed a visual interface of the bird-view type that tracked the search process. His database consisted of naturalistic photos.

Ruthven (2001) and colleagues (2001a-b; 2002; 2003) built on top of Campbell's findings and added new dimensions to the direct applications of findings from the user-related cognitive IIR research and information seeking studies.

Ruthven (2001) argued for and tested the assumption that it is not sufficient simply to consider only what documents the searcher has marked as relevant, as done in standard RF and QM algorithms. One should also take into account the behavioral information of *how* the searcher assessed relevance, for instance, how the searcher interacted with the system, how many documents (s)he marked relevant, where in the ranking the relevant documents occur and the (non-binary) relevance scores given to documents by the searcher. Also, the positions of keys in relevant documents should be taken into account in the RF process. Further, Ruthven and colleagues (2001a-b; 2002) suggested and tested the use of multiple RF and QM weighting schemes, also in combinations, since each scheme may produce different rankings of the documents for the same query. This idea is in line with the polyrepresentation hypothesis discussed in Sects. 5.2.3-4. Other kinds of behavioral information from users might come into action, e.g., the proportion of highly relevant vs. less relevant documents assessed at a given point in time – in line with findings by Spink, Greisdorf and Bateman (1998) on online IIR. In Ruthven's study we see a fruitful awareness and use of cognitive IS&R research results applied to best-match algorithmic and laboratory tests.

From a cognitive stand it is an important point that the more information (evidence) that can be provided by the searcher in IIR to the IR system – *explicitly* or *implicitly* – and processed by it, the better the system can support the searcher with useful information.

5.7 Relevance: Issues and Findings

The concept of relevance has been a difficult issue in Information Science and IR through the years. It received a lot of attention in the 1960s and 1970s – as reflected in Saracevic's (1975) review. The main orientations in the notion of relevance were found very early: on the one hand, one may speak about topical relevance; on the other hand about user-oriented relevance. See, for instance, the seminal works on relevance by Cuadra and Katter (1967), Rees and Schultz (1967), Cooper (1971), and Wilson (1973) – the latter on situational relevance. The interest in relevance declined after the 1960s until Schamber, Nilan and Eisenberg revived it in 1990.

5.7.1 The Early Relevance Research

Already Cleverdon (1967) discussed the notion *user relevance*. Cooper (1971) proposed *utility* as the top concept for anything that is valuable for a user in search results. He identified a number of notions that affect utility, including informativeness, preciseness, credibility, and clarity. Perhaps with some frustration, Saracevic (1975) identified from literature notions like usefulness, match, informativeness, satisfaction, pertinence, and correspondence. He used these as one facet (the aspect of relevance) in a proposed generator of the literature's relevance concepts: Relevance is <any of measurement instruments>, which measures <any aspect of relevance>, which exists between <any object to be assessed> and <any scope of assessment> as seen by <any assessor>. For example, "Relevance is the *quantity,* which measures the *match,* which exists between a *text* and an *information need* as seen by the *inquirer.*" By producing all combinations one obtains thousands of notions of relevance – actually more than the literature provides.

Relevance was also early on found to be a *multi-graded* phenomenon, i.e., some documents are more relevant than others to a searcher. Cuadra and Katter (1967) and Rees and Schultz (1967) studied multiple degrees of relevance and their expression in laboratory settings. These groups experimented with multiple point rating scales (from two to eleven), both empirically and analytically. Katter (1968) experimented with category (ordinal), ranking and ratio scales. Rees and Schultz (1967) compared graphic rating scales to a ratio scale, and Eisenberg (1988) proposed a magnitude estimation scale as a challenge to category scales. Saracevic and colleagues (1988 1988a-b) employed a three-point ordinal relevance judgment scale in their field study outlined above: relevant, partially relevant, and not relevant. The Mother of all Test Collections, the Cranfield Collection, had five-point graded relevance assessments.

In summary, these findings based on pioneering theoretical studies, experimental laboratory studies, and field studies suggested that the degree of document relevance obviously varies across documents, and document users can distinguish between them.

5.7.2 The Dimensionality of Relevance

Schamber, Nilan and Eisenberg (1990) initiated the New Wave of relevance research to come during the next 15 years. This landmark article re-examined the literature made during 30 years. Essentially, the conclusions by Schamber, Nilan and Eisenberg were:

- *Relevance is a multidimensional cognitive concept.* Its meaning is largely dependent on searchers' perceptions of information and their own information need situations. Relevance assessments have multi-dimensional characteristics;
- *Relevance is a dynamic concept.* It can take many meanings, such as, topically adequate, usefulness or satisfaction. But relevance is also dynamic as assessments of objects may change over time. It depends on users' judgments of the quality of the relationship between (perceived) information and information need at a certain point in time; *and*
- *Relevance is a complex but systematic and measurable phenomenon* – if approached conceptually and operationally from the searchers' perspective.

Schamber, Eisenberg and Nilan (1990) stressed the importance of context and situation in IS&R. These bring the dimensions and dynamism into relevance. They re-introduced the concept of 'situational' relevance derived from Patrick Wilson's concept in 1973, originating from Cooper (1971). Context may come from the information objects or knowledge sources in systems, but may also be part of the actual information-seeking situation. Situation also implies a series of dynamic cognitive (and affective) states in the mind of the searcher during an IR session. Essentially, this means that if relevance is dynamic, the corresponding information need is dynamic as well – and *vice versa*. During an IR session, an information object may thus be (intellectually) topically relevant in the sense of laboratory IR experiments, but may not be perceived as useful to the particular situation the searcher is facing at that time. Obviously, only the searcher can assess this type of subjective (situational) relevance. In a cognitive sense, it is associated with a job-related or daily-life task or event placed in a specific context.

In line with Saracevic (1975), Swanson above (1986) and Harter on 'psychological relevance' (1992), Borlund (2003a, p. 914) divided relevance into *two basic classes.* They were: (1) *objective* or system-based relevance; and (2) *subjective* or human (user)-based relevance. These two classes are quite different in nature and by default imply different degrees of intellectual involvement. Each corresponds to the understanding of relevance employed by the laboratory and the cognitive user-oriented approaches – respectively. The system-driven laboratory approach treats relevance as static and objective as opposed to the cognitive approach that considers relevance to be a subjective individualized mental experience or construct that involves cognitive restructuring (Swanson 1986, pp. 390–391).

Multiple degrees of relevance and their expression have been studied in laboratory settings (Tang, Shaw and Vevea 1999) as well as in field studies of information seeking and retrieval (Lancaster 1968; Saracevic et al. 1988; Borlund and Ingwersen 1997; Spink, Greisdorf and Bateman 1998; Vakkari and Hakala 2000). Tang, Shaw and Vevea (1999) investigated empirically how people coped with different scales of relevance, from a binary to a 12-valued scale. They found that a 7-point ordinal scale was the optimum choice in terms of the assessors' confidence of their judgments. Sormunen (2000; 2002) as well as Kekäläinen and Järvelin (2002) applied a well-defined four-graded scale of relevance: highly relevant; fairly relevant; marginally relevant; non-relevant, which has been adopted in the TREC and INEX evaluation procedures – see Sects. 4.3.3 and 4.6.4.

Two tracks of relevance research initiated very fast. One track pursued the theoretical developments of relevance types, criteria and measurements, thereby bridging over to laboratory IR evaluations. The second track performed empirically based studies involving searchers in realistic settings.

5.7.3 Analytic and Theoretical Relevance Developments

Different kinds of *relations* can be expressed between (retrieved) information objects and query, request, information need, or the underlying situation – also over time (Saracevic 1996; Cosijn and Ingwersen 2000).

The relevance experiments, discussions and investigations, probably including those associated with TREC, led finally Saracevic to produce his comprehensive stratified model fundamentally dealing with communicative aspects of IR interaction (1996). He applied the model to define a range of relevance types in IR interaction, suggesting five increasingly subjective types of relevance: (1) 'algorithmic' relevance (*a*), which is similar to the ranked output processed by the search engine, and refers to the relationship between request (or query) and retrieved objects – Fig. 5.7; (2) 'topicality' (symbolized by *Int.t*) – basically dealing with the aboutness relationship between document contents retrieved and request, as assessed by a person. Owing to the human assessment (interpretation) this type of relevance is not objective. It is of subjective emotional and intellectual nature; (3) 'pertinence' (*p*), associated between the nature of retrieved objects and the information need as perceived by the searcher at a given point in time; and (4) 'situational' relevance (*S*), corresponding to the relation between the retrieved objects and the work task (or daily-life) situation as perceived by the individual searcher.

Saracevic also introduced a fifth type: an emotional/intentional type of relevance. In a later analytic discussion of the model and types of relevance (Cosijn and Ingwersen 2000) saw the emotional/intentional type as forming a natural part of *all* the subjective relevance categories (2) – (4); they replaced it by a 'socio-cognitive' relevance category referring to domain, context and collective situational preferences, also over time. The latter type originates from Hjørlands 'epistemological' relevance (1997 2000b), taken up by Ørom in a social and cultural setting (2000), but put into a cognitive perspective by Cosijn and Ingwersen (2000).

Socio-cognitive relevance is objective and tangible. It signifies situational relevance assessments and interpretations made by *several* cognitive actors, simultaneously (like in a team or program committee) and/or over time. Program committee or editorial board members negotiate their individual (situational) preferences and reach decisions based on the present context, domain influence and the tradition (or culture) of the particular event. Conference programs, or a journal's table of contents, etc., are hence objective results of socio-cognitive relevance decisions. Citations (or inlinks) given to the objects are also manifestations of socio-cognitive relevance judgments made by people over time. They imply a certain degree of recognition, acceptance and use, and may increase cognitive authority of the cited or inlinked person, journal, institution or conference.

The topical relationships (t) between a real work task (W) and documents (O-O^n) have not been analyzed in IS&R research. However, in many domains there exist guidelines as to which documents and procedures to consult in performing a work task, e.g., good laboratory practice.

It is worth noticing that there seems to exist a notable but probably *false correspondence* between the four evolutionary stages of information processing, as viewed by the cognitive viewpoint (de Mey 1977; Smeaton 1992), and the levels of interaction as well as manifestations of relevance proposed by Saracevic (1996). Whilst the four information processing stages are nested this may *not* be the case for all manifestations of relevance. As a matter of fact, investigations Cosijn (2003) indicate that algorithmic relevance, (intellectual) topicality, and pertinence as well as socio-cognitive relevance seem nested, with an increasing inclusion of different features of documents, complexity of assessment and time as the nesting criteria. Situational relevance falls outside this pattern. The question is, *what* in the information objects judged situational relevant does reflect the individually perceived work task situation? If this information is hidden from the system the situational relevance assessment is operationally impractical for relevance feedback purposes. Cosijn (2003) also models work and search task processes on to the variety of relevance types stipulated above. From a logical stand, Mizzaro (1996; 1997) analyzed the variety of conceptualizations of relevance, including cognitive contributions in IR. Borlund (2003a) provides a further detailed discussion of differences between the relevance types.

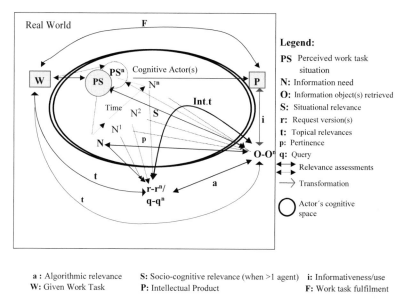

| a : Algorithmic relevance | S: Socio-cognitive relevance (when >1 agent) | i: Informativeness/use |
| W: Given Work Task | P: Intellectual Product | F: Work task fulfilment |

Fig. 5.7. Illustration of main types of relevance relationships, including situational and socio-cognitive relevance types, involved in IS&R activities over time. Extension of (Ingwersen and Borlund 1996; Borlund 2000b, p. 31, p. 44). The superscripts X^n signify versions of X over time.

In Fig. 5.7 the perceived work task (or daily-life task or interest) situation (PS-PS^n) is regarded dynamic over sessions of IS&R activities, but may remain stable over shorter time periods (PS), like a single search session. The information need situations triggered by PS may alter much faster, e.g., over a session, depending on the impact and relevance of the observed information objects. In accordance with the Kuhlthau stage model (1993a) there might be produced a product (P) which might be compared by a third person to a) the original work task (or interest) situation (F), e.g., like markings of student assignments; or to b) the information objects assessed by the searcher during the search sessions leading up to producing the product (i). This measure corresponds to the Tague-Sutcliffe 'informativeness' measure (1992): how many objects and which objects judged 'relevant' during IS&R did *actually* become *used* in the end product.

Assessment of Relevance. While assessment of topicality seems quite easy in text documents, owing to either algorithmic similarities between search keys and retrieved object contents or judged aboutness, topicality assessment is not easy for objects in other media. For instance, in music it gives no meaning. However, as long as there are some content features available such features can be used for topicality measures – by the seeking actor or by some third party in quite objective ways.

The assessment of *pertinence* is also feasible. Aside from topicality pertinence criteria are, for instance, novelty to the searcher and currency of information objects or perceived cognitive authority of author, affiliation, website or journal and other isness features. Only the seeking actor can assess pertinence.

Socio-cognitive relevance assessments are tangible, e.g., by means of the citations (or inlinks) given to the objects. The citations by scholarly colleagues imply commonly a certain degree of recognition, acceptance and use, and degrees of cognitive authority. In this respect one should note the difference between academic citations and inlinks on the Web. The former seem to correlate statistically with peer assessed scientific quality whilst the latter does not (Ingwersen and Björneborn 2004). In fact, the number of inlinks seems to correlate with academic productivity and size of staff. Also, on the Web commercial websites seem to attract more inlinks than do other domains.

Situational relevance is different. Topicality, pertinence and socio-cognitive relevance, per definition, signify the use of tangible features of the objects. Situational relevance concerns usefulness of sought objects. In a way all the features up to the point of assessment of an object are potential keys to situational relevance. However, we may not know exactly which features or which specific *combination of features* determine relevance of an object at a given point in time. References or outlinks are objective features, and at least *situational to the author* at publishing time, and probably often also situational to searchers in their context. Monitoring the relevance feedback behavior of the searcher may probably indicate something about the features in question. It might, for example, be a figure or a methodological description or results that triggers the situational usefulness of a passage or information object. The conception of 'implicit' and 'explicit' *semantic values*, Sect. 2.3.1, may help to understand the problem. 'Implicit' values are assumed to surface via interpretations made in context by the searcher when observing a passage(s) of an information object retrieved by means of 'explicit' semantic values or features. Such interpretations may lead to situational relevance assessments at a given point in time. Inconclusive experiments on this issue were actually carried out by Croft, Turtle and Lewis (1991). Nonetheless, if we cannot establish the kind of keys that give raise to situational relevance, it is not an operational kind of relevance. In other words, situational relevance tends to make use of the same features that are used for topicality and pertinence.

First when several situational judgments have been made on the same objects over time, like in recommender systems or indexed in citation databases, do we possess tangible and objective criteria, but then in the form of socio-cognitive relevance assessments.

A last facet of relevance deals with the issue: what makes a document appear relevant at first encounter vs. in the longer run? This is a highly subjective element of relevance but of importance for the validity of relevance feedback and query modification processes during best match IIR.

5.7.4 Central Empirical Relevance Studies

Schamber studied relevance assessment criteria from a cognitive view in a multimedia professional work setting (weather forecast situations) (1991). Others continued the empirical track, like Park (1993), Barry (1994) and Bruce (1994) attempting to isolate and define criteria for relevance assessment and factors influencing such processes. Park (1993) investigated the criteria employed by 10 academic users making selection decisions when presented with lists of bibliographic records. The study (pp. 330–341) acknowledged the following criteria: (1) interpretation of record including title, author name, affiliation, journal name, etc.; (2) internal (historical) context including the searcher's previous experience and perceptions, and his/her level of expertise in the problem area; (3) external (IS&R) context; (4) problem (work task) context, including the searcher's intentionality underlying the intended use of a record (document).

Barry (1994, pp. 153–157) also looked into scholars' evaluation of (printed) documents during searching. She found 23 criteria that she grouped into seven classes: (1) the information content of documents; (2) the searcher's previous experience and background; 3) the searcher's belief and preferences; (4) other information and sources within the information environment; (5) sources of the documents; (6) documents as a physical entity; and (7) the searcher's situation. As can be observed the four classes of relevance criteria in (Park 1993) correspond to or overlap the groups discussed by Barry (1994).

As a logical follow-up to the various empirical investigations of relevance issues, Schamber published (1994) a compiled list of 80 relevance criteria, proposed by the relevance studies. Barry and Schamber (1998) combined efforts in a comparative analysis of the degree of overlap of criteria identified by Schamber (1991) and Barry (1994). They found substantial overlap of criteria originating and shared by the test persons from the two studies. The criteria common to both investigations were categorized into a taxonomy of 10 classes. Some few criteria were unique but could be associated with the differences in the work contexts, search situations and the research requirements (Barry and Schamber 1998, p. 234). According to Borlund (2003a, pp. 918) the important finding of this comparative study is that two different groups of searchers in different work environments share relevance criteria. This provides evidence for the existence of a *finite range* of criteria, applicable across types of searchers, problem and task contexts, information situations, and information sources.

Tang and Solomon (1998) carried out a highly detailed task-based longitudinal study of a single actor's information seeking behavior and relevance assessments. The searcher applied three values of relevance: relevant; non-relevant; and possibly relevant. The research methods were a combination of pre-interviewing, log of Boolean online searching, talking aloud and post search discussions. The mental model of the information need was the focus of the investigation. It demonstrated that the model changes over search time, and different relevance values become used, depending on the firmness of the model.

The Spink, Greisdorf and Bateman Study. Also Spink and colleagues (1998) investigated non-binary (graded) relevance. They used a four-value relevance scale (relevant; non-relevant; partially relevant; partially non-relevant) and the model of situated actions that extended Saracevic' model (1996). However, at the end they did not apply the 'partially non-relevant' type of relevance. They used students as test persons and Dialog Knightridder online databases. In particular, they studied how the number of partially relevant documents relates to the phase of searchers' problem solving process.

Spink and colleagues (1998) showed that the number of items judged partially relevant was positively correlated with the searchers' assessment of a *change* in their own information problem definition during the search session process. Moreover, the quality of a searcher's specific task knowledge was negatively correlated with the number of partially relevant items. One can interpret the finding so that in the pre-focus phase most of the documents, which seem to have some connection to the task, would be evaluated as partially relevant. The (few) highly relevant documents might be those that topically are pertinent. In human QM experiments one might thus test whether to use search keys from the highly relevant documents only, or a mixture of keys (randomly) selected from highly and partially relevant documents. In the post-focus phase the actors obtained a structured understanding of the task and were more certain in relevance assessments. This might lead to a decrease in the number of partially relevant documents. The major variables were stages in task execution and relevance assessment of the found bibliographic records.

Vakkari (1999; 2000; 2001a-b) and Vakkari and Hakala (2000) analyzed, among other issues, Sect. 5.4.5, how changes in relevance criteria are related to changes in problem stages during task performance. One may hence compare to the findings by Bateman (1998) and Spink, Greisdorf and Bateman (1998) above. Relevance was understood as task- and process-oriented searcher constructs. The assessment of relevance was based on both retrieved bibliographic information as well as the entire documents acquired and read on the basis of this information. The investigation was longitudinal and used binary assessments. The study objects were students who were asked to perform searches in a bibliographic database at three different times during their seminar. Data for describing their understanding of the task, search goals and tactics as well as relevance assessments were collected during the search sessions through multiple methods. The findings support to a certain extent the overall hypotheses that a student's application of relevance criteria in assessing retrieved bibliographic records and documents is related to his/her problem stage during task performance. There is a connection between an individual's changing understanding of his/her task over time and how the relevance of bibliographic data and full texts is judged. The more structured the task in the process, the more able the person is to distinguish between relevant and other sources.

However, in contrast to the Spink, Greisdorf and Bateman study (1998), Vakkari and Hakala (2000, pp. 557) found that "[the] share as well as number of relevant items decrease as the individual's knowledge of the problem [work task] grows. The difference might reflect the dissimilarities in methodology. Spink's study was not longitudinal; the users' knowledge of the problem-at-hand at a certain time was measured. The measurement indicates only the level of knowledge, but not the stage in task performance." The different research conditions thus produced different relevance estimations. However, in realistic research settings with real searchers the researcher ought to be informed about at *what stage* in a work task process each test person is or sees him/herself.

The relevance criteria of documents changed more than the criteria of bibliographic records during the process. Moreover, it seemed that topicality was understood differently depending on the phase of the process. Owing to the small number of data in the studies by Vakkari and Hakala, the findings are only tentative. However, topicality accounted for 40 % of the relevance criteria. This is consistent with the findings by Wang and White (1999). Otherwise, the results were in line with the findings by Kuhlthau (1993a) and Bateman (1998).

In a later study on 12 Social Science students' document assessments Maglaughlin and Sonnenwald (2002) applied a three-partite relevance scale (relevant, partially and not-relevant) and revealed 29 criteria that could be grouped into six classes. The central finding was that *multiple cri-*

teria – of positive as well as negative nature – were applied when making graded relevance assessments.

5.8 Research Methods

During the period 1970 to present the *types of investigation* in cognitive and user-centered IR research covered empirical and theoretical approaches. Empirical methods can further be classified into descriptive and explanatory studies. Descriptive studies dominated empirical studies up through the 1980s – e.g., case studies of moves in online searching (Fidel 1984b; 1985). However, some explanatory studies (Saracevic et al. 1988; 1988a-b) sought to explain IR effectiveness. During the 1990s descriptive studies became less dominant in IS&R research. However, owing to the Web investigations descriptive log analyses flourished, Sect. 5.6. Increasingly, explanatory studies, for instance, on relevance issues or interactive IR, surfaced towards the end of the century.

From 1970 popular empirical *research strategies* were case studies and field experiments in naturalistic settings, while survey was not. *New strategies* evolved, involving longitudinal research designs and controlled but realistic IIR performance evaluations in laboratory settings. The latter evolution is discussed in Sect. 5.9.

Fundamentally, the single data collection methods, and their combinations by means of triangulation, were the same during the entire period. Data analysis methods are briefly dealt with below. Wang (2001) produced an overview of methods for information behavioral studies that are useful also to investigations of IS&R.

Methodologies in Non-Empirical Studies. There were also theoretical and conceptual approaches see Sects. 5.1-2 and 5.7 above. Many studies relied heavily on results from (colleagues' previous) empirical investigations, e.g., the various developments of modeling IS&R, while some were predominantly analytic experience-based, e.g., Bates' identification and classification of online retrieval tactics (1979a-b).

With respect to alternative analytical methods Hjørland and Albrechtsen (1995) proposed domain analysis as a 'new horizon in Information Science'. In their approach domain analysis is not at all related to domain analysis or domain modeling in Computer Science. In their sense domain analysis is opposed to the individual cognitive view as it was in the pre-1990 era – Sect. 2.1.2. It assumes that scientific domains and epistemological discourses are the determining factors of communication. Methodologically speaking, Hjørland suggests epistemological factors should be applied in order to understand IS&R phenomena, like knowledge organization, information seeking, relevance, the concept of topic, etc. (1997; 2000b; 2001).

The methods of non-empirical studies often remain unclear and at least are not well-known named techniques. Often one may only say that the methodology consists of analysis and synthesis, carried forward by scholarly argumentation. Taylor (1968) refers to no particular methods in his postulation of information need stages. In Bates' (1979a-b) proposals for information search and idea tactics there are no particular methods producing (or identifying) the tactics. As the author states, the tactics are adapted from her own experience and thinking, literature, and comments by colleagues. Nevertheless, the tactics are comprehensive and organized – so there is good analysis behind them.

5.8.1 Variables and Strategies in Research

Especially in experimental and investigative research, including case studies, one is interested in the effects observed in *dependent variables* as a consequence of variation in *independent variables.* Since multiple variables may affect the dependent variables, one may have to seek to neutralize the effects of some variables, the *controlled variables.* This is a typical Social Science research methodological approach. Already Fidel and Soergel (1983) elaborated this standard variable typology in a useful way, also applied to the proposed research program, Chapts. 7-8:

- Variables affecting the outcome
  - *Independent variables*
    - Variables for which predetermined values are fixed
    - Variables for which any occurring value is measured
  - *Controlled variables*
    - Variables that are held constant
    - Variables that are measured and the effect of which is statistically neutralized
    - Variables whose values are randomized over the sample being studied
  - *Hidden variables* – Variables not considered at all
- Dependent variables
  - Variables describing the outcome of the experiment

Essentially, the cognitive research framework presented in ensuing Chapts. attempts to make use of this notation and, in particular, Chapts. 7-

8 demonstrate which *hidden variables* that potentially are involved in various research settings.

The *survey strategy* may be used to study IR system searchers' conceptions about information retrieval, their preferences in using various services, the frequency of use, encountered difficulties, etc., in addition to personal / demographic attributes. Bellardo (1985b) reviewed some studies of this kind. However, surveys are not effective in studying interaction or the retrieval process. To this end, field studies and experiments are more appropriate.

Case Studies. Case studies with appropriate data collection methods like observation, talking/thinking aloud, etc. – e.g., Fidel (1984b; 1985) – are relevant field studies. One observes the subjects systematically when doing their regular real-life searches. Their search logs are collected with any other available documents for data analysis. This may consist of writing up a description of each search, discussing it with judges and validating it with the original subjects via interviews – clarifying issues and adding any further information that have not been observed. Case studies in IR allow one to go out from a laboratory and study IR processes in naturalistic and realistic settings, but at the same time sacrificing at least some aspects of control of the study setting.

Field Experiments. Field experiments also seek to retain realism of the study setting. One may study real IR processes and real actors in the process in natural setting and context, as far as possible. However, the experimental setup commonly allows more control on the test persons and their procedures, e.g., by means of assigned search tasks, and thus supports *explaining* phenomena in addition to just describing them. The field study by Saracevic, Kantor and others (1988) is a landmark study also in its methodological thoroughness. The methodology is carefully explained in the study, which is an example of multiple data and analysis collection methods (triangulation).

Longitudinal Research Designs. Longitudinal investigations were mainly done as quantitative studies (Bilal 2000; 2001; 2002; Spink 1996; Vakkari and Hakala 2000; Vakkari 2000; 2001a-b; Wang 1997; Wang and White 1999). Their number increased substantially in the 1990s and demonstrated one of the innovations of cognitive and user-oriented IR research. This is an interesting development since longitudinal studies are cumbersome to carry out. Kuhlthau's success in applying this methodology probably reinforced its utility during the following decade, see Sects. 3.1.2 and 3.2.2.

5.8.2 Data Collection Methods

Direct observations, recordings of thinking/talking aloud, videotaping and transaction logs, and post-search interviews became widespread. However, one should note that they are inherently obtrusive methods, also in combination. This implies that the subjects know of the investigation and their behavior becomes influenced. Hence the mandatory use of enough test persons to assure statistical validation of results in quantitative studies.

Observation, Thinking Aloud and Videotaping. Aside from Fidel (1985; 1991a-c), Pejtersen (1980) recorded 300 intermediary – end-user – system interactions in fiction retrieval in a public library context. The recordings were by an observer who wrote down the often-short dialogue sequences. Such direct observations are associated to videotaping. Videotaping search sessions – both the searcher and the screen – is a relatively obtrusive data collection method. While it may affect the search process it provides on the other hand a rich data set for analysis. Plain screen capture (perhaps with voice recording) is less obtrusive but yields poorer data. Saracevic, Mokros and Su (1990) used videotaping, search logging and observation in their data collection. Plain search logs can be collected unobtrusively and economically – which may explain their popularity especially in the 1990's for Web retrieval logging – see below.

Thinking (or actually talking) aloud recordings were very popular from the start of the applications of case studies, field experiments and other kinds of quantitative as well as qualitative investigations – see further Sect. 3.2.2. As for observations and videotaping, the recordings end up in verbal protocols to be analyzed, Sect. 5.8.3.

Interviewing in Data Collection. Interviewing, e.g., in the form of post-search interviewing of study subjects, may effectively augment and validate data collected through other methods. The investigator's observations may be incomplete and interpretations of, e.g., search logs or video biased or incorrect. Therefore a clarifying interview used as triangulation of data may be very helpful. Interviewing can be open-ended or employing closed questions and is structured to various degrees – depending on the purpose of study and the environment in which it takes place.

Web Retrieval Investigations. Web search engine performance investigations from a user perspective were comprehensively reviewed and discussed by Su (2003) in one of the rare *meta-analyses* in IR (and Library and Information Science), covering ten major studies from the 1990s. Su based the discussion on a systematic and very useful model for user evaluation of search engines, consisting of 7 research methodological tasks to perform or develop (2003, p. 1176). The model can be generalized to cover other research objects than search engines.

The many *search engine log studies* (e.g., reviewed by Jansen and Pooch 2001) performed in the late 1990s and in the beginning of the first decade of the new millennium display some serious limitations. As stated, log analysis is an easy way of getting hold of data that can be treated with quantitative methods. One can use it to get statistically significant data about searchers' choice of search keys and use of syntax (or lack of operators) for querying search systems. On the other hand, they hardly inform anything about information need situations or request types. The data are poor if used alone, since they lack most traces of searcher's intentions and thoughts during Web interaction.

Therefore logs and observation in naturalistic settings, combined with interviews, seem more scientifically informative, as carried out by Pharo (1999; 2002; Pharo and Järvelin 2004). He divided protocols from the logs/observations into *search situations* and *process transitions* (the SST method) whereby a quantitative micro-analysis as well as a qualitative macro-analysis may be performed.

5.8.3 Data Analysis Methods

The richness of the data required for cognitive and user-oriented IR research is a major problem in the analysis of the data. From the 1970s micro as well as macro protocol analyses and discourse analyses of various kinds were used both at qualitative and quantitative levels. Cognitive researchers thus produced both descriptive results and causal cognitive explanations of, for instance, user-librarian interactions (Belkin and Vickery 1985; Pejtersen 1989) or later searcher-system IR interaction (e.g., Spink and Saracevic 1997; Spink, Goodrum and Robins 1998; Pharo 1999; 2002).

Standard (quantitative) analysis methods are covered well by textbooks. However, we briefly outline protocol analysis below as a major analysis method for IS&R research – see also Sect. 3.2.3 – and point to innovative approaches to qualitative analysis proposed and applied in interactive IR.

Protocol Analysis. Protocol analysis (or verbal interaction analysis) relies either on a pre-defined coding scheme for analysis, like the MONSTRAT model as used by Belkin and colleagues (Brooks and Belkin 1983; Belkin 1984; Brooks 1986; Daniels 1986), or it leads to the detection of behavioral patterns of interaction, like turn-taking.

OBSERVATION REMARKS in PROTOCOL	Subject 05/1/UL/761020-rev. 1 – Observer: SK Q1: WHICH MARKING SCALE IS USED IN THE ASSESSMENT OF (TECHNICAL) DRAUGHTS-MEN?
1) Subject begins at the reference desk; 2) $\mid^5$ walks to doc. in reference room $\mid$ (there are 2 *EK*: a) one for reference purpose; b) one for lending; Subject employs first a). $\mid^6$ reach *EK* and picks up the index card $\mid$. (2a): looks up 'tech. draughtsmen' in index 3) Looks trough the *EK* without finding the card 4) Looks up in *EK b)* 5) Looks through *EK b)* 6) Picks up the card concerning 'tech. draughtsmen' 7) Subject scans the text	1) $\mid^1$ Which marking scale is used in the assessment of technical draughtsmen? $\mid^2$ /4/ yes /3/ then I in the first place rather have to find out which . training the draughtsmen get $\mid^3$ err which high school they consult I don't know that immediately . $\mid^4$ and uhmm that I think I will look up in the *ErhvervsKartotek* $\mid^{5+6}$ 2) /12/ $\mid^7$ in .. *EK* 's index .. one can look up (2a) $\mid^8$. technical draughtsmen $\mid^9$ 3) /26/ $\mid^{10}$ but the article is not in its place $\mid^{11+12}$ ... 4) $\mid^{13}$ I'll try the other *EK* $\mid^{14}$ 5) /24/ $\mid^{15}$ yes that was really embarrassing that . there is a mess in the *EK* $\mid^{16}$ ... there it was 6) .. $\mid^{17}$ 'technical draughtsmen' $\mid^{18}$ 7) /11/ $\mid$ --- ---
	Key: $\mid^1$ $\mid^2$: a statement .. : two seconds pause /4/: four seconds pause *EK* : *ErhvervsKartoteket* – an archive with information on cards on different professions.

Fig. 5.8. Passage of a verbal protocol concerning the retrieval of information on 'technical draughtsmen'. The left column lists observational remarks indicated by number and right bracket *n*) in the right column protocol (from Ingwersen 1982).

A protocol consists of statements of talking (or thinking) aloud by selected actors, transcribed to a text. The stream of logged data simultaneously derived from an IR system during interaction can extend it. Commonly, Fig. 5.8, the protocol is divided into short sense-making 'statements' or utterances representing considerations made between physical activities by the subject(s), like entering commands or moving about.

Fig. 5.8 originates from Ingwersen (1982) and is an example on analyzing and coding protocols. He analyzed 23 protocols representing librarians' search procedures, 7 protocols representing end-users' search procedures in a library and 4 protocols representing end-user–librarian negotiations both at the micro and the macro levels. The macro-level analysis was based on chunks of 'statements' (passages) in order to observe *search activity elements*, e.g., the use of information sources. The microanalysis spotted patterns of the decision-making processes and mental considerations in relation to search tasks, such as intentionality behind actions. In the latter analysis type thinking-aloud protocols as well as search interview recordings were divided up into semantically self-contained 'statements', often separated by pauses.

According to the goals of analysis, such statements and their patterns may be used to generate hypotheses for further analysis. For example, statements can be analyzed for occurrences of terms and concepts applied, their modification through interaction, and from which sources such concepts originate. The observational remarks in the protocols were found to be of significant value, for instance, when subjects moved along the shelf arrangement, looking up documents or pointing to classification indicators on top of shelves, without stating aloud the actual object or location (e.g., a librarian to a client: 'here we are you see and this book should give you some indications ...').

In the case of search dialogue, the protocol consists of three columns: one for the user statements, one for the intermediary's part of the conversation, and one for the observations taken during retrieval.

Qualitative Analysis Methods. During the 1990s Fidel discussed qualitative research designs for IIR (1993), which became increasingly popular. According to Fidel qualitative research is non-manipulative and non-controlling. It focuses on processes, like IS&R processes, interaction, etc. and applies multiple methods. What she meant was that qualitative research does not attempt to determine cause and effect, or to test hypotheses or theories (p. 222). In order to collect data for qualitative analysis a variety of methods can be applied, from observation and logs to interviewing, talking (thinking) aloud and the use of diaries as well as critical incident techniques – see Sect. 3.2. However, the very same methods might indeed be applied to collect data to be analyzed quantitatively. The difference between quantitative and qualitative research lies in what *kind* of *approach*(es) are used during the analysis phase. In this respect the 1990s saw an increased use of analysis methods that support qualitative perspectives like, for instance, time-line interviewing[3] and inductive content analysis as explored by Schamber (2000).

---

[3] See Dervin's time-line interview method (Sect. 3.2.2), which uses open-ended questions.

It was probably typical for qualitative research to emphasize the awareness of the observer-observed (researcher-respondent) rapport (Fidel
1993), also owing to the fact that other variables than strictly cognitive
ones became objects for study, like affective aspects of IS&R (Kuhlthau
1993b). However, this awareness is not necessarily a privilege of qualitative research and can also be found in quantitative studies. Exactly that
dimension of research methodology does rarely exist in experimental laboratory situations.

5.9 Interactive IR Evaluation Methods: Simulated Work Task Situations

Robertson and Hancock-Beaulieu (1992), and later Hancock-Beaulieu,
Fieldhouse and Do (1995) as part of the OKAPI project, pointed strongly
to the problematic methodological issues connected to the three revolutions they saw taking place in IR research from the start of the 1990s, that
is, the interactive, the cognitive, and the relevance revolutions: How to extend the laboratory model into the context of the searcher during experimentation and, at the same time, keep the variables (and research situation)
under control?

In OKAPI this was partly achieved by moving the laboratory setting out
into naturalistic environments with real searchers, and then to try to control
the variables, for instance, by involving many test persons with their own
or assigned information requirements. In the former case the test persons
assessed the relevance corresponding to their own needs, but the experiments were less in control of the researchers. If sets of pre-defined queries
were assigned to test persons, as in interactive TREC, the problem of control was solved to an extent but the research situation became less realistic.
Also, it became an issue who was to assess the retrieved documents, the
test persons or the TREC assessors? This methodological state of affairs
led to the development of the *IIR Evaluation Package* (Borlund 2000a-b;
2003b; Borlund and Ingwersen 1997).

From a holistic cognitive approach, one way of solving the research
problem would be to provide for more realism, i.e., allow for individual interpretations of the search situation and, at the same time, to make control
of the experiment feasible. It would be advantageous also to apply non-
binary relevance assessments in a best match retrieval setting. By employing the evaluation package, one might achieve two research goals at the
same time, if required: studying IS&R behavior, including work task development and search task execution in quite realistic situations; and test-

ing performance of interactive retrieval systems in rather realistic situations. The first goal is basically achieved by applying a necessary number of test persons, since what is measured are behavioral elements. In performance test situations fewer test persons should apply a necessary number of different search situations. The 'necessary' number depends on the involvement of variables to be investigated and the level of statistical significance one wishes to attain. There are various well-known methodological ways of creating the research design so that the outcome is balanced and un-biased, Fig. 5.10. These are not treated here.

The Borlund IIR Evaluation Package (2000a-b; 2003b) was initially designed and tested in a small-scale investigation (Borlund and Ingwersen 1997) involving graded relevance measures and so-called *simulated work task situations* – see Fig. 5.9.

Simulated situation: sim A

Simulated work task situation: After your graduation you will be looking for a job in industry. You want information to help you focus your future job seeking. You know it pays to know the market. You would like to find some information about employment patterns in industry and what kind of qualifications employers will be looking for from future employees.

Indicative request: Find for instance something about future employment trends in industry, i.e. areas of growth an d decline.

Fig. 5.9. Example of a simulated work task situation (Borlund 2000a-b)

In its mature form (Borlund 2000a-b; 2003b) the IIR package has the following three basic components:

- *A set of components* which aim at ensuring a functional, valid, and realistic setting for the evaluation of IIR systems;
- *Empirically based recommendations* for the application of simulated work task situations; and
- *Alternative performance measures* (Sect. 4.10):
  1. *Relative Relevance* (RR)
  2. *Ranked Half-Life* (RHL)
  3. *Cumulated Gain* (CG) and *generalized R/P*

The simulated work task situation – Fig. 5.9 – signifies a short 'cover story' that describes a situation potentially leading to IS&R activities, like the 'job seeking situation'. It serves two main functions. It 1) triggers the simulated information need, and 2) is the platform against which situational relevance (usefulness) is assessed. In more specific terms the simulated work task situation can display degrees of semantic openness, i.e., degrees of freedom for the test person for interpretation, and thus degree of control of the experiment. It describes the *source* or reason for the information need, the *context* of the situation, the *problem* that has to be solved, and serves to make the test person understand the *objective* of the search. By being the same for all the test persons, better experimental control is provided, although each person is free to make his/her own potentially dynamic information need interpretations of the given situation. Note that issues other than cognitive ones – like affective factors and physical activities – may very well be covered by such simulated situations and hence be investigated.

Simulated work tasks have been used previously in IS&R studies (Sect. 3.2.1), but were never tested against real information needs from a methodological point of view, as done by Borlund (2000b; 2003b). It is of central importance whether simulated situations make subjects behave the same way as when employing their own information situations to a search. Borlund's test results demonstrated that the IS&R behaviour was identical regardless whether simulation (with or without indicative request) or real needs were used. In total, the package ensures investigations and experiments both realism and control and contains several methodological *recommendations*:

- To employ both the simulated situation/simulated work task situation *and* real information needs within the same test for comparative reasons;
- To *tailor the simulated work task situations* towards the test persons with reference to:
  1. a situation of the type which the test persons can relate to easily and with which they can identify themselves;
  2. a situation that the test persons find topically interesting; and
  3. a situation that provides enough imaginative context in order for the test persons to be able to apply the situation;
- To *permute the order of search jobs* between the test persons in order to avoid possible bias of the relevance assessments owing to human behaviour when comparing across system features and test persons – Fig. 5.10, and
- To *pilot test* prior to actual testing.

A Latin square-like procedure should be applied – Fig. 5.10 – so that all test persons (say 1-6) search all simulated situations (say A-F), but only once each, against all system features (say X and Y).

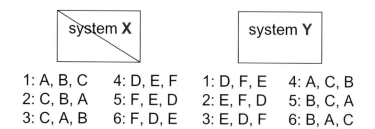

1: A, B, C   4: D, E, F   1: D, F, E   4: A, C, B
2: C, B, A   5: F, E, D   2: E, F, D   5: B, C, A
3: C, A, B   6: F, D, E   3: E, D, F   6: B, A, C

Fig. 5.10. Permutation of six situations A-F across two systems X-Y and six test persons 1-6.

The IIR evaluation package has implications for test collection design. A test collection cannot be historical, as the TREC news collections, since realistically people prefer to seek information on recent events and might be less motivated if information situations are forced upon them owing to collection attributes. Further, the work task (daily-life task) situations, that potentially and realistically appear in the information environment or domain in which IS&R performance is to be measured, determine the characteristics of the test collection to be applied.

5.10 Central Achievements, Limitations and Open Problems

We may regard the years 1977-1982 as the time when the cognitive view was established as a theoretical perspective that moved into a research program. It produced initial research models and empirical investigations carried out in accordance with those models. This is in parallel with the shift into a process view in user-centered research. During the period 1982-1986 we find the next wave of empirical research and theoretical analyses, which achieved the ASK hypothesis (Belkin, Oddy and Brooks 1982a-b), the MONSTRAT Model for knowledge-based intermediary and systems design (Belkin, Seeger and Wersig 1983), and the observation of the Label Effect, information need typologies and online feedback features (Ingwersen 1982; 1984; 1986). The direct user-system interaction was not (yet) a central issue.

From 1986 to 1991 we observe the raise of many interface designs of supportive nature, and the raise and imminent fall of the intelligent (knowledge-based) IR approach (Brooks 1987). But we may also observe the first serious attempts to integrate the variety of investigative models in IR, including laboratory approaches (Belkin et al. 1987). The main reasons for the downfall of intelligent IR are known. Automatic knowledge acquisition in complex IR scenarios thus far is unsolvable and presumes *the same* user and domain analyses carried out as for supportive systems. The latter are easier to design and implement than expert systems (Pejtersen 1989; Ingwersen 1992). Most importantly, according to Sparck Jones (1987) at that time, best match retrieval systems yield better IR results than the expert systems based on question answering.

During the 1990s cognitive and user-oriented research made the following achievements:

- *Comprehensive research models* became generated, fundamentally based on and then applied to empirical investigations, Sect. 5.1. As a novel attribute to the research environment the models became sometimes integrated with one another or did converge over the period. This was in contrast to the ad hoc models (and research) from earlier periods, like the laboratory model.
- More *comprehensive theory constructions* were attempted, Sect. 5.2, in contrast to the earlier periods. Aside from elements of a cognitive theory for IIR leading to hypotheses about polyrepresentation, the period experienced the development of substantial assumptions concerned with work task complexity and work task situations as central for understanding IS&R phenomena. Most developments were based on empirical investigations.
- Novel *evaluation methods* for IR were designed to cope with dynamic information situations in a multi-dimensional relevance landscape, e.g., the cognitively inspired Evaluation Package for IIR – Sect. 5.9.
- *Relevance studies* succeeded in producing a robust but limited range of relevance types and workable taxonomies of relevance criteria and, in searcher-associated best match, to observe and discuss (indirect) relevance feedback and query modification algorithms, involving searchers in realistic environments.
- *Multi-graded relevance* was re-discovered and, most importantly, empirically studied, Sects. 4.3.3 and 5.7. This gave raise to a number of:
- *Novel performance measures* suitable for realistic interactive IR research evaluation, hereby bridging over to the laboratory IR community, Sect. 4.10.
- *Empirical studies* of central IS&R phenomena and objects increased greatly in number during the 1990s and applied quite robust methodologies – see e.g. the rigorous studies by Saracevic and colleagues (1988; 1988a-b). In particular:
- *Longitudinal studies* were carried out, not only in traditional adult information contexts, but also with children as actors and in the novel information context – the Web – Sects. 5.4-5.

5.10.1 Limitations and Open Problems

With the exception of Brookes (1980), the founding of a dominant and holistic cognitive approach to IR based on the notion of information interaction was unfortunately not the case until the mid-1990s. For instance, until 1990 it would have been bold but appropriate to ask which (combinations of) retrieval engines and relevance feedback methods best suit different types of information needs, and *why*. Only the Belkin and Kwasnik work comes to mind as an explicit example of addressing such issues (1986). Although Croft and Thompson's (1987) I³R system did make use of clustering and probabilistic models, and searcher modeling, this was done to advance precision and recall but not founded in any particular (cognitive) theory of, say, searcher relevance.

Instead, the main bulk of user-centered and cognitive researchers focused on the behavior and cognitive structures of users, human intermediaries, their interactions (including interactions with operational Boolean IR systems), and individual information need formation in a range of empirical studies. The goal was to obtain an improved understanding in order to improve IR performance from a stand different from that of the prevailing system-driven laboratory research.

Information needs were commonly taken for granted as context-free. Where such needs actually came from was not a central issue. During the 1980s this attitude changed somewhat with the ideas of problem situations and personal cognitive goals, as triggers for information need formation and development. However, the research views, whether cognitive or pragmatic, tended to see the actors in ad hoc individualistic fashion.

Further, the systems under investigation were mainly Boolean, large-scale online systems, not experimental best-match retrieval engines. Although realistic, the operational systems did not offer much novelty or challenges. They were not seen as variables under investigation. Research hence tended to be driven by the prevailing conditions and became too descriptive. The most interesting and promising exception was the THOMAS retrieval system Oddy (1977a-b). THOMAS represented an approach quite different from traditional online *or* experimental IR to the nature of the direct dialogue-based interaction between a searcher and a database.

Why did researchers rarely move beyond the operational Boolean systems during the period? One reason is that the online systems, intermediaries and users were readily available. Secondly, the existing test collections – the bridge to laboratory IR research – were regarded unrealistically small and artificial to be of use to users. In contrast, the academic online systems were very large. This was seen as a positive sign of robustness, a sound view later to be taken by the system-driven research into IR in TREC.

During the 1990s graded relevance became trendy. However, the notions of the relevance grades became not standardized. In some studies the grades were non-relevant, partially relevant, and relevant; in others they were non-relevant, moderately relevant, highly relevant; or non-relevant, possibly relevant, relevant. There are two problems connected to this issue. First, searchers (or assessors) might not understand 'partially relevant' in the same way, since what does 'partially' mean? Some passage of the document is (highly) relevant, other passages are not – or the entire document is not 'really' relevant? There is also the degree of novelty of the document to one searcher, which may lead to downgrading the relevance in his/her case, but not in the case of another searcher. Secondly, if Lickert scales are used one operates on ordinal scale. One must be very careful when interpreting the outcome of any statistical calculations, since it may not be so that a highly relevant document (say on value 3) is 'three times more relevant' than a marginally relevant document (value 1). In particular, if values are assigned to each category by the researchers after the searchers/assessors have categorized the documents according to relevance, one is into statistical problems. We refer here to the robust four-graded relevance category definitions made by Sormunen and applied to the TREC collection (2002)[4], and to the test and discussions by Järvelin and Kekäläinen (2002).

In relation to best match IIR it is an open issue how to make workable query modification with searcher participation. The problem is that the results of some investigations disagree on the effect of query modification on retrieval outcome. Belkin and colleagues (1996a) maintained that interactive (intellectual) query modification adds to the performance of the total IR system, measured as recall and precision in interactive TREC experiments. In contrast, Hancock-Beaulieu, Fieldhouse and Do (1995) claimed that intellectual query expansion in various forms does not increase overall performance, but rather decreases it. Magennis and van Rijsbergen (1997) have confirmed the latter result. However, their study was based on simulated searchers. The investigations on this central matter are too few and, owing to the diversity of experimental settings, difficult to compare. We have indications that successful use of IR systems with ranking facilities (for relevance feedback) depends heavily on the searchers' mental models of how such systems operate (Belkin et al. 1996b). Hence, the *balance issues* of human vs. automatic query modification with elements of relevance feedback should definitely be explored much more in depth and with rigor.

---

[4] Non-relevant; marginally relevant; fairly relevant; highly relevant.

In Web IIR, digital library, and portal studies there are four central factors to be taken into account: the searcher, the work and search task, the search system, and the search session. Studies have shed light on some, mainly confined factors that influence Web searching. They have, however, often limited explanatory capability because fairly little interplay of factors is taken into account. Significant factors so far not dealt with are the contexts in which the searcher operates, the nature of work tasks related to information needs, and types of information needs (and requests). This can be explained by the fact that these studies either use anonymous transaction log data or use assigned or imposed search tasks – not situations. With few exceptions, one cannot observe, for instance, how the searcher's organizational background affects his/her search task strategies or how the complexity of the search task affects the time spent searching the system. Exceptions are the Bilal studies of children's Web searching behavior (2000 2001 2002), Kim and Allen (2002) observing cognitive task influence on searching behavior, and Pharo (2002; and Järvelin 2004) developing and testing a methodology for analyzing Web IIR behavior at micro level. With the notable exception of Hölscher and Strube (2000), Pharo, and, to an extent, Dennis, Bruza and McArthur (2002) none of the studies on the Web or digital libraries have been concerned with searching from a process perspective.

Nevertheless, around the millennium the human-related Web research seems to accelerate and start providing more insight into complex search situations – like it happened in traditional online IR interaction during the 1990s.

6 The Integrated IS&R Research Framework

In the introductory chapter and Sect. 5.1.2 we stated that interactive IR and information seeking are nested in Information behavior as special cases (Wilson 1999), Fig. 5.2. As information behavior we regard generation, acquisition, management, use and communication of information, and information seeking; typical information seeking behavior is acquisition of information from knowledge sources, for instance, from colleagues, through (in)formal channels, and from an information system; (I)IR is information acquisition via formal channels and in organized knowledge sources, such as, information systems like the Internet. Interaction and information acquisition are thus regarded central phenomena of information behavior, including IS&R. In its most general sense information acquisition is also a process of cognition associated with non-information objects, e.g., objects and phenomena in nature, in accordance with the discussions in Sect. 2.4. Consequently, there exists a range of information acquisition phenomena directly associated with IS&R, of which a research framework must take account. The present chapter seeks to establish such a conceptual framework for research on IS&R phenomena, founded on the holistic cognitive viewpoint, and based on relevant empirical results discussed in Chapts. 3-5.

Cognitive Actors and Structures in Integrated IS&R. In the holistic cognitive framework, Sect. 2.1, cognitive structures are seen as manifestations of human cognition, reflection or ideas. In principle they hold emotional characteristics as well[1] – see Fig. 2.1. In IS&R viewed as instances of information behavior, they take the form of transformations and interpretations made by the variety of human actors that participate in IS&R. We should also bear in mind that, in principle, any communicated and stored message looses its meaning and underlying intentionality during its cognitive free fall, Sect. 2.2.3. It is reduced to fragmented signs that are cognitively and emotionally potential to any recipient – whether concurrently or in future – depending on the perception of the message. The char-

---

[1] In our framework "cognitive" signifies also emotional/affective perceptions and structures.

acteristics and structure of the generated message obviously determine which signs are to be interpreted. But the nature of the *receiving* cognitive structures in *their* context determines the nature of the interpretations that are made.

The variety of human actors of different cognitive origins in time and space communicating during interactive IS&R consists, at least, of:

- Authors of all kinds of information objects, carried by various media;
- Human indexers analyzing selected information objects for improving the access to and informativeness of objects;
- Designers of retrieval and communication interface functionalities, information presentation and visualization software;
- Designers of database structures, retrieval engines and logics, indexing algorithms, filtering mechanisms, navigational tools etc.;
- Selectors deciding the commercial or public availability of objects or their inclusion into collections or carriers, such as journal editors, conference committees, employers, reviewers, database producers, etc.;
- Information seekers searching for information owing to intent, i.e., perceived interests, problems, or work tasks;
- Communities of individuals organized in a social, cultural or organizational context.

Each kind of actor produces cognitive manifestations during their activities: Authors and human indexers as well as thesaurus or ontology/semantic net designers generate all kinds of *information objects*, constituted by all kinds of signs over times, i.e., texts, images, sound, speech, art, etc., in a variety of styles – Fig. 6.1. Human and algorithmic indexing may add value to the original signs, that is, by exhibiting otherwise hidden aspects of an object (the human indexer) and by selecting and exhibiting (weighting) particular sign structures, indexing keys, of the original object (the designer of indexing algorithms), Fig. 2.2. See further Sects. 6.1.1-2.

The selectors are responsible for information availability – Sect. 6.1.4. They create policies of (in)exclusion of objects (and often also database structures and algorithms) in collections. The designers of the organization of objects in database architectures and their way of being manipulated in retrieval engines by means of algorithms produce the *IT component* of information systems. The designers of *interfaces* are associated to the former actors by providing intellectual access to information through presentation of data structures and other functionalities. The division of IT from the interface is deliberately made for the sake of advanced IT configurations in a networked society in which interfaces can be separated from underlying database structures. The more primitive the IT applied, for instance, in the

form of clay, papyrus or paper, or as stand-alone systems, the more indi-
visible the IT and interface components – and the more inseparable from
the information objects proper.

The information seekers are *cognitive actors* acting in a social, organizational and cultural *context* – Sect. 6.2.1. The latter – together with the
systemic context, the left-hand side of Fig. 6.1 – influence the activities,
perceptions, and interpretations of each individual over time, Sect. 2.1.4.

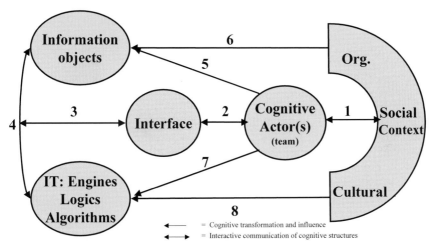

Fig. 6.1. Interactive Information Seeking, Retrieval and Behavioral processes.
Generalized model of any participating cognitive actor(s) in context. Revision of
Ingwersen (1992, p. 55). Numbers are explained in the text.

Numbers on the model basically deal with processes of interaction (1-4),
such as social interaction (1), or refer to different kinds of generation and
transformation of cognition or cognitive influence (5-8). They are explained below in more detail and applied to the ensuing models when appropriate – Sects. 6.1.1-5.

The model emphasizes the information processes that are executed during IS&R in context over time: First, processes of social interaction (1) are
found between the actor(s)[2] and their past and present socio-cultural or organizational context. Social interaction may instigate IS&R activities, but
may also form part of their fulfillment. Secondly, information interaction
also takes place between the cognitive actor(s) and the cognitive manifes-

---

[2] In the text and figures the notion used to depict the role of the actor can be in
   singular, like 'Interface designer' or plural, as in 'Author(s)' or 'Program
   Committee Members', but regardless the notion, individuals as well as groups
   or teams may indeed carry out the role discussed.

tations embedded in the IT and the existing information objects via interfaces (2/3). The latter two components interact vertically (4) and constitute the core of an information system. This interaction only takes place at the lowest linguistic sign level, Sect. 2.2.2. Third, cognitive and emotional transformations and generation of potential information may occur as required by the individual actor (5/7) as well as from the social, cultural or organizational context towards the IT and information object components (6/8) *over time*. This implies a steady influence on the information behavior of other actors – and hence on the cognitive-emotional structures representing them. The impact entails that actors may collaborate in teams – like in collaborative IR (CIR) – and collectively adapt to their surroundings.

Finally, the model, Fig. 6.1, emphasizes that all the participating cognitive structures are in context of all other cognitive components of the model. Hence, there exists a mutual dependency of context and actor or component, including intra-component structures. For instance, images in objects naturally act as context for the surrounding text – and *vice versa* – see Sect. 6.2.2.

Our approach tries to make a reasonable compromise between monologism vs. dialogism, see Sect. 3.3.1. Our model represents monologism in that that there is a certain focus on an individual, i.e., the cognitive actor. However, her/his context is in no way neglected. We see the cognitive actor (or team of actors) in a four-way interaction with information objects, information technology, interfaces, and the organizational-social-cultural context. There is no contradiction in analyzing the relationship of an individual with information objects separately, for instance, in document creation or interpretation and, at the same time, agreeing that this is a sociocultural process too. In fact, the model not only represents the dialogue between individuals in the organizational-social-cultural context, but also the interaction (or dialogue) between individuals and information objects, IT, and interfaces – all unavoidably culturally affected. Therefore, the model is in fact broader than earlier dialogical proposals that neglect human – IT interaction (or at least are not explicit about it).

We may characterize, Sect. 1.5 that our model is not explicitly a process model – no steps in interaction are explicitly modeled. Nevertheless, it makes the process (interaction) analyzable through its categories and their relationships. It is a concrete model in the sense that it points out (albeit in an abstract way) real stakeholders in IS&R processes and analyzes their interaction. The extensions of the categories are tangible entities like document texts, computer programs, and humans rather than abstract entities like task complexity or type of information. The model is analytical since it classifies and analyzes the relationships between the categories, as the discussion below will explicate. However, this remains at quite a high level of conceptualization. The model is a general one since it applies to any cognitive actor in context. Yet it is hospitable to specification to particular situations as shown in the sections below.

According to D.C. Engelbart (1962), developing conceptual models means specifying essential entities and phenomena to be studied and their relationships, analyzing the interaction processes of the entities/relationships and suggesting fruitful goals and methods of research. Chapts. 7-9 will elaborate on these aspects.

This chapter is organized as follows. Based on the understanding of cognitive actors of different origin in time and space, Sect. 6.1 develops the conceptual cognitive model as the framework for IS&R research. The framework is applied to and discusses, at a generalized level, the central cognitive structures and actors taking part in IS&R. Sect. 6.2 analyzes situations and contexts and discusses in more detail the complexity of the IS&R phenomena by developing the central components of the model. Perceived work and daily-life tasks or interests leading to information behavior, problem situations, and search tasks based on information needs, are seen as the central instigators of IS&R, integrating information seeking and (I)IR. The central IS&R phenomenon for study consists of the processes of information interaction and acquisition in a work task context. Sect. 6.3 discusses the appropriateness of the cognitive framework in light of Engelbart (1962) and Bunge's criteria for scientific theories (1967) and summarizes the chapter.

6.1 Building the Conceptual Framework

The model – Fig. 6.1 – originates from Ingwersen (1992, p. 55). In that study it illustrated the processes of interactive IR with the individual searcher at the center, in context of his/her social or organizational environment.

However, we now regard the model also as a *generalized framework* for understanding IS&R: For any cognitive actor (or team) engaged in IS&R we are informed of the possible relationships and contextual properties of that actor (or team). The actor *stands out* from that environment, so to speak, although still influenced by social interaction. This is the reason for the puzzle-like shape of the actor-social context relationship on the model– arrow (1). Any actor may alter its role in the model. The model is intended to demonstrate what happens to the central relationships between cognitive components during such shifts. For instance, the cognitive actor may play the role of an information seeker or searcher to become author or designer at different times, but with short intervals. In such cases the contextual elements influencing the actor change accordingly. The social context may take two forms: (a) that context which signifies the actor's *peer community* influencing the actor historically, for instance, fellow computer scientists for systems designers, domain colleagues for indexers or searchers; (b) that context that denotes the *'utility' community* for which the present design (or indexing or authorship or IS&R) is intended, such as, the (future) searchers or readers in a domain.

The remaining relationships of transformation and influence over time represented in the model (5-8), are only indirectly involved in IS&R. They become directly active in connection to other phenomena of information behavior, for instance, the use, generation and communication of information objects, as shown on the model in Fig. 6.2. The ensuing sections demonstrate the flexibility of the model, depending on actor's role in information behavior. We elaborate Fig. 6.1 into a cognitively more complex model, Fig. 6.8.

6.1.1 Authors of Information Objects

Based on Fig. 6.1 we first analyze an *author* (or group of authors) of (potential) information[3] in context of his/her socio-organizational or cultural environment – illustrated by Fig. 6.2. The author is influenced by this context through social interaction – arrow (1): in the past with colleagues and friends – the peer community – and presently in context of his/her utility community, i.e., the author's perception of potential (future) readers. The two communities may be similar or indeed overlap. But the author is also often – but not always[4] – in contact with a universe of information and information systems through interfaces, gateways or gatekeepers – the left-hand side of Fig. 6.2.

When in the actual situation of generating an information object the author (or co-authors) transforms his/her/their interpretation of the world directly into a message of signs, for instance, a spoken or written one, i.e., he/she/they creates an information object – arrow (5). An actor may also

---

[3] Potential information is understood as the signs in a message at low linguistic levels, however, always with the potential of providing information in a real sense to a recipient (Ingwersen 1992, p. 31-33).

[4] In principle an author of information, for instance in an illiterate society, may merely depend on the social interaction with the socio-cultural environment, i.e. the fellow tribesmen, when generating signs.

interact horizontally with a data entry interface to a system in order to generate information objects.

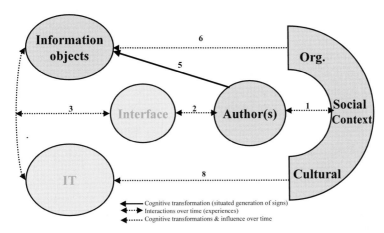

Fig. 6.2. Cognitive model of *authorship* of information objects in relation to IS&R, including the influence over time of contexts. Model components in gray signify indirect involvement; numbers as in Fig. 6.1.

The interpretation is shaped – *not only* by the socio-organizational or cultural context (1) – *but also directly* by the actor's own pre-understanding and assumptions of what already exists of information objects and IT structures. That understanding is obtained in the past by the author in his/her role as an *information seeker* of such knowledge sources via information interaction (2-4). Otherwise, the author has been informed about their properties through learning from secondary sources, such as textbooks.

The *time dimension* is central to the understanding of what occurs during generation of potential information: the already existing information objects were generated by a multitude of authors through time, also in a variety of multi-media forms and versions, each in a particular location, situation and context – arrows (6 and 8) – and structured according to the prevailing level of IT – the interactive connection (4).

In our holistic cognitive view authors may well be part of a paradigm but they are free to interpret existing information objects, as well as the prevailing attitude of the community towards natural objects and phenomena, in a way that is different from that paradigm. This *freedom of interpretation* exists because information transfer is based on the principle of complementary social and cognitive influence, with the individual actor as the determining factor, as discussed earlier in Sect. 2.1.4.

As part of generating information objects the actor may thus *acknowledge* or recognize the intellectual and/or emotional impact of his/her situation at hand, made by other contextual sources – for instance by the peer community. Depending on the available IT the author may be able to *point* to useful sources by means of, for instance, scholarly references, acknowledgements, or navigational Web outlinks. The pointers form part of the generated object, but are also representative of the objects pointed to. They act as document features and are examples of *situational relevance* representations, on the side of the author - see also Fig. 1.3 and Sect. 5.7.2.

6.1.2 Adding Value to Information Objects – the Human Indexer

The *human indexer* presupposes the role of a searcher or seeker (analyzer) of the information objects to be indexed. Authors, Fig. 6.2, may in practice also act as an indexer, making representations of their own objects, for instance, when applying Dublin Core elements for document representations. Authors may add references or outlinks as additional and functional representations of the information object under generation, by pointing to other associated information objects, Sect. 5.2.3.

Like an author, a human indexer is a generator of signs that hold potential information. The typical situation of indexers is that of generating knowledge representations of existing information objects, Fig. 6.2 arrow (5) – according to some explicit rules or standards, already accessible as information objects, or in line with conventions implicitly existing in the peer community of the indexer. Alternatively, the indexer may investigate pragmatically how the 'utility' community understands and uses the objects to be indexed and carry out the indexing accordingly (Hutchins 1978). In addition, rules may perhaps include general or domain-dependent thesauri, designed by other cognitive actors in the past – i.e., arrow (6), Fig. 6.2. At its generation a thesaurus can hence be seen as a result of collective cognitive structures, or socio-cognitive conceptual assessments of domain phenomena and document structures. They are based on retrieval interactions (2-4), Fig. 6.2. However, often a team of few isolated domain experts construct thesauri – arrow (5) – representing the perception by the entire community of the domain also through social interaction (1).

During indexing we are essentially dealing with processes of interpretations of objects in context: one such context, to the right-hand side, Fig. 6.2, belongs to the social environment in terms of, for instance, a scientific or professional domain. Probably some prevailing paradigmatic beliefs, methods, etc. guide the domain, influencing the indexer's judgments and interpretations over time (arrow 1). At the left-hand side, Fig. 6.2 – replacing the author by the indexer – a second kind of context is manifest: the indexer is cognitively influenced by already existing information objects – arrows (2-4) – providing experience. Similarly, the indexer is subjective to his/her perception of the existing kinds of knowledge organization and representation, as well as the actual IT into which new representations will be stored, *and* the perception and interpretation of the information object at hand.

In order to produce adequate representations the indexer must interactively retrieve and/or access the object[5]. This implies that the information object at hand goes through a full circle counterclockwise, Fig. 6.2: starting from its position in Information Objects, via IT, arrow (4), over the Interface (2/3), through the perception, interpretation and information acquisition of the indexing actor, and ending again physically or virtually in the pool of information objects via arrow (5) – with the representations added, e.g., as keyword phrases. On Fig. 6.2 the interactions between objects, IT, interface, and indexer are *in progress* in terms of the object to be represented, and *over time* concerning the experience of the indexer of similar objects, etc.

We may observe that the indexer, like the author, has the *freedom of interpretation* to make new representations, for example in a 'utility context' of (future) searchers – not necessarily in line with the prevailing attitudes of the current social (peer/utility) community. He/she may consequently exhibit hidden semantic aspects or stress facets of contents that might be different from the intentions of the original author. In addition, the indexer may be encouraged by conventions or rules to translate the subject matter *and* other types of object and contents features, such as institutional, personal or journal names, as well as metadata, into standardized vocabularies, representations and name forms. Further, we may observe that knowledge representation may indeed be a mixture of *different cognitive interpretations* or attitudes of the same or alike objects. This happens in particular if identical information objects are analyzed and represented by indexers in different information systems or domain collections. This polyrepresentation at domain, database or system levels can be positively explored during IS&R, also owing to the impact of the Selectors, as outlined in Sects. 5.2.3 and 6.1.4.

The Designer of Automatic Indexing Algorithms. In automatic indexing applied to information objects, any different weighting function or

---

[5] We assume that if the indexer is *given* the object in question he/she does not retrieve it in the real sense of the concept. The indexer must, however, access the object to make interpretations of its meaning.

best match algorithm reflects a transformed cognitive structure of the *designer(s)* of the given function or algorithm: A kind a generalized (human) indexing mechanism.

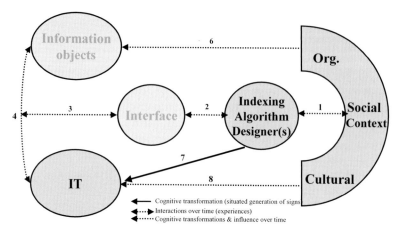

Fig. 6.3. Cognitive model of cognitive actor(s) responsible for *automatic indexing* of information objects in relation to IS&R, including the influence over time of contexts. Model components in gray signify indirect involvement; numbers as in Fig. 6.1.

The designer creates IT-embedded algorithms – arrow (7), Fig. 6.3. However, in contrast to prevailing beliefs automatic indexing is *not* at all *context-free*. Often, the designer's situation is in direct context of the actual IT solution by means of interaction and the body of features embedded in the kind of information objects to be indexed (arrows 2-4). The influencing social context (arrow 1) commonly embodies only peer system developers, but ought also to mirror the potential 'utility' community of the indexing system. The peer computer scientists have imposed their algorithmic solutions on the IT component over time – arrow (8). Without the involvement of the utility aspects, this view of indexing belongs solely to the system-driven laboratory tradition of IR.

Automatic indexing results commonly in representations of low-level linguistic nature, for example, in the form of strings of many independent feature representations, see Sect. 4.4 and Fig. 2.2, added to information objects. On the other hand, human indexing commonly results in *reductionism* and thus heavy semantic openness owing to the relatively few keywords allocated for the entire information object. The most rich knowledge representation seems to be a combination of the two (Lancaster 1972; 1998), i.e., a polyrepresentation consisting of indexing keys derived from one (or more) algorithmic weighting schemes and representations created by humans. This combination is only feasible, for cost reasons, in selected domains or institutions for which information plays a crucial (economic) role.

6.1.3 Cognitive Actors as Designers of Interfaces and IT Algorithms

The conditions for the cognitive actors responsible for *interface design* are similar to those of the variety of other IT designers – if the interface is logically and physically *separated* from an existing IT platform. This is the case for many commercial interface designs, metasearch engines and gateways located outside the IR system proper as shown, e.g., in the central models, Figs. 6.1 and 6.8, and in the design model, Fig. 6.4. Searchers perceive such interfaces as one with the system only during session time.

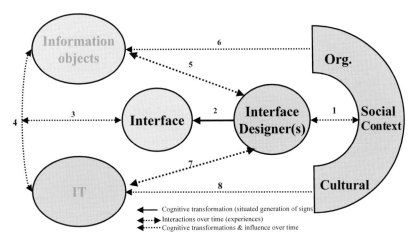

Fig. 6.4. Design situation of an interface as a separate logical-physical entity located *outside* existing information system in context. Model components in gray signify indirect involvement; numbers as in Fig. 6.1.

In Fig. 6.4, the central activity of an interface designer concerns the generation of the interface configuration by transformation of the designer's cognitive structures (2). The arrows between the cognitive actor and the IT and information object components (5/7) are interactive, demonstrating how the designer obtains knowledge concerning these components' impact on interface design. They operate as a 'utility' context. The designer is also situated in social contexts (arrow 1), i.e., the peer and the user communities. They in turn, as well as the retrieval and indexing interactions between objects and IT platform (3-4), are mainly *out of control* of the interface designer. Hence, an isolated interface may fast become obsolete if not capable of learning about novel characteristics of objects, IT, searchers and retrieval modes.

Only in a *stand-alone IIR system* does the interface become an integral part of the IT configuration, Fig. 6.5. In such systems the current IT platform is *also* directly under control of the (interface) designer, as are the interactive processes between objects and IT configuration (3-4). No direct influence occurs between the social context and the IT platform – as was indeed the case in the model Fig. 6.4. Arrow (8) does not exist. Social contextual influence on IT only exists indirectly via social interaction, arrow (1). The 'utility' community may be studied as a prelude to the design, whilst the peers may influence the situation, also historically. In a stand-alone IIR system the (interface) designer will have direct interactive access to the system's information objects (arrow 5), which other cognitive actors have authored over time (arrow 6).

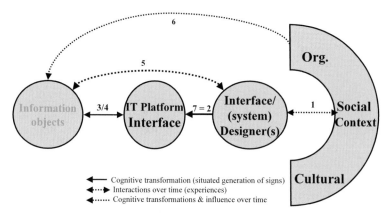

Fig. 6.5. Interface design in a *stand-alone IR* system configuration in context. Model components in gray signify indirect involvement; numbers as in Fig. 6.1.

This distinction of having or not having control of the direct manipulation of information objects by the IT platform (arrow 4) is important. Interface functionalities located outside retrieval systems may only process and present information objects in a form *totally dependent* of the underlying (remote) software platforms.

It is interesting to note that almost all mainstream IR experiments based on the Laboratory model, including the current TREC experiments, fundamentally operate with stand-alone systems that compete with one another.

We bypass the analysis of other IT designer cases since it is quite similar to the interface designer (or automatic indexing) situations as depicted in Figs. 6.3-6.5. The reader may take the analysis of the IT designer case as an exercise.

6.1.4 Selectors – Actors Responsible for Availability and Access of Information Objects

Information Selectors are deciding the commercial or public availability of information objects or their inclusion into collections. They are responsible for the existence, the *isness,* of the information object hand in hand with authors, see polyrepresentation, Sect. 5.2.3, Fig. 5.5. Selectors are, for instance, journal editors and reviewers, conference committee members, employers, database producers, etc. They possess quite a comprehensive control over the entire information system for which they make policy and strategic decisions – Fig. 6.5. Some selectors directly manipulate the objects, e.g., their presentation or contents, like editors. Others are rather acting in the role of advisor; some work as teams. Selectors (and thus 'isness' of objects) are represented by common media-dependent bibliographic data (and metadata) that are non-aboutness-related, such as author employer's corporate source (affiliation), journal names, publication date, document type, publisher, sponsor, etc. – Sect. 4.4.

The collective nature of the actors responsible for *input selection* of objects is different from that of other cognitive actors in charge of information isness, availability and access: they act like a team in context of their peers and domain over time, arrow (1), but do not directly manipulate the information objects. Conference PC members act in the context of the accepted papers and structures of previous similar conferences *and* in the context of the papers submitted to the present conference, arrow (6), and their reviews by domain peers. The committee's function is to accept (5) papers into a constructed conference program (acting as interface), arrow (7) – or to reject them.

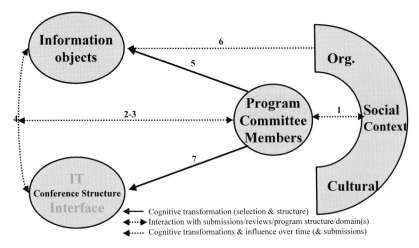

Fig. 6.6. Information selection, exemplified by Program Committee members deciding the contents and structure of a conference within scientific or professional domain(s). Model components in gray signify indirect involvement; numbers as in Fig. 6.1.

The model, Fig. 6.6, may thus depict the reviewers' role as cognitive actors as well: they review the submissions via interaction processes, arrows (2-4), with or without conference software in between. The function of the reviewers and PC members, and their combined relevance assessments, is of *socio-cognitive* nature (Cosijn and Ingwersen 2000). See also Sect. 5.7.3.

Information selections are typical examples of the principle of complementary social and cognitive influence, with the team of individual actors as the determining factor, as discussed earlier in Sect. 2.1.4. By their policy and decisions of acceptance and rejection, and their choice of types and structure of presentations in a selected IT solution – electronic peer review, full-papers and posters, conference themes and session order, key-notes, doctoral forums, video conference transmission, etc. – the selectors clearly influence the future of the domain(s) in a bottom up mode. At the same time, through social interaction – arrow (1) – they themselves are affected by their affiliation to the domain(s) and its/their history, methods and paradigms over time.

Owing to their responsibilities information selectors become often turned into highly *authoritative* (search) keys to information objects, like editor and conference chair names on proceedings, employer (corporate) name, etc. Journal and conference titles obtain reputations for high quality due to the combined degree of respect earned by teams of editors, PC members *and* publications (as well as their authors) over time.

6.1.5 The Information Seeker as Explorer of Sensory Data

In order to act as an author, an indexer, a designer of IT solutions, or as selector – as stated above – an actor first has to function as a person seeking information, and/or he/she analyses by thinking how to generate information objects or IT configurations, see also Fig. 7.3, Sect. 7.2.

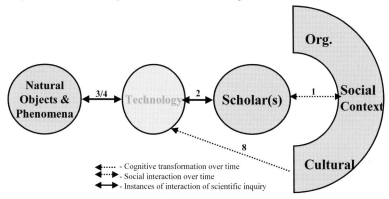

Fig. 6.7. Cognitive framework for scientific information acquisition from nature. Model components in gray signify indirect involvement; numbers as in Fig. 6.1.

The Japanese sign and the Arlanda cases, Sect. 2.4.1 illustrate daily-life information acquisition from man-made, but perhaps unknown signs. The case of the Okawango Pursuit deals with man-made signs in natural settings, Sect. 2.4.2. A particular situation occurs when the information seeker is a *scholar(s)* making scientific inquiry by information acquisition from *natural phenomena* via sensory data. The IS&R framework, modeled on Fig. 6.7, illustrates this case, discussed in Sect. 2.4.3.

In Fig. 6.7 the scholar interacts with and is influenced by his/her own domain context, including recorded knowledge, prevailing research beliefs and traditions of that domain and colleagues over time, arrow (1). To the left the scholar interacts with the natural phenomena under investigation – arrows (2) and (3/4) – following the stages of information acquisition demonstrated in Fig. 2.5. This situation of scientific inquiry increasingly involves complex technological tools produced by other actors – arrow (8). If the technology component does not exist, however, the model becomes even more simplistic with direct interaction between man and nature – arrows (2=3/4). This was indeed the case in Astronomy prior to the invention of the binocular. If Fig. 6.7 is intended to depict information acquisition from man-made signs (like in some instances of the Okawango pursuit), the component 'Natural Objects and Phenomena' becomes replaced by Information Objects. Consequently, some human actors, not nature alone, have generated such signs over time whereby arrow (6) is re-introduced into the model.

6.2 Approaching the complexity of IS&R

The previous sections, and Fig. 6.1 in particular, represent the general cognitive framework for IS&R research, centered on the variety of cognitive actors directly involved in IS&R. The detailed model, Fig. 6.8, demonstrates the complexity of the framework's cognitive structures associated to its five components that play the essential roles for understanding the Field. Many of these structures constitute the prevailing *variables* of IS&R research. The central cognitive actor in our framework is the information seeker.

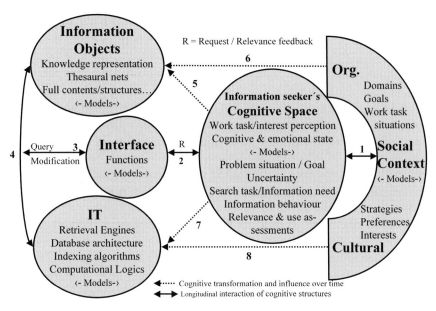

Fig. 6.8. Cognitive framework of (longitudinal) IS&R – including the changing role of the information seeker(s) into generator over time (arrows 5 and 7). Extension of earlier model by Ingwersen (1996, p. 9).

The model, Fig. 6.8, points to the central processes of *interaction* and *perception*, and thus to information acquisition that comprise of the engagement into information seeking behavior and/or interactive IR, also in a longitudinal sense. The conception of daily-life or job-related *work task* situation and human cognitive-emotional interest in context and the concept of *search task* constitute the rationale behind the processes. The *perception* of work task or interest, that is, the intentionality (Searle 1984a) of the seeker, acts as the central factor affecting IS&R.

Other types of the seeker's perceptions are also present, for instance, his/her awareness of self, of the interface presentations, the interpretation of information objects in terms of relevance feedback, and/or the sensitivity towards the IT setting – Fig. 6.9. The work or daily-life task or interest, as perceived by a person, may be physical or purely intellectual. A physical work task or interest may be tuning a car as mechanic or traveling to another city; an intellectual task may be solving a problem, e.g., concerned with the tuning activities or writing a report. The *search task* is understood as defined by Borlund (2000) and Vakkari (2001b; 2003) to be the mental actions and physical activities necessary as *means* during IS&R to an *end*: the work or daily-life task fulfillment.

A work or daily-life task may exist and be observable in an objective sense, Fig. 5.7, because its solution is required by a third party, e.g., by actor(s) in a given situation in context – say in an organization. When perceived, the task becomes subjective – as when it is invented by the seeking actor him/herself. Similar conditions apply to the search task. Commonly, it is intrinsic and subjective. But when given to a searcher it possesses momentarily objective characteristics in the form of a request. In experimental settings an objective search task may take the form of an assigned 'topic' or a simulated work task situation. See also Sects. 5.9 and 6.2.3-5.

By integrating information seeking and interactive IR the model points to how evidence of a searcher's information behavior may be applied to guide or adjust algorithmic information processing in system components through IR *interaction*. Interactive IR takes place, in particular via requests, information acquisition, relevance assessments and feedback, arrow (2). Further, the better we understand such evidence deriving from the context located *outside* IR systems proper, the better support can be provided to the algorithms in order to better serve the searcher, as increasingly demonstrated Sect. 5.6.2 and further discussed in Sect. 6.2.8. This adjustment of information processing in IS&R is common during inter-personal communication, i.e., interaction at the right-hand side of the model - arrow (1). Unlike algorithms, people adjust much better and faster to communicative attitudes and behavior. That is probably a major reason why colleagues and other human experts are so predominant as knowledge sources and information providers – see Sect. 3.1.4.

Each component of the research framework, Fig. 6.8, is represented by a selection of embedded cognitive structures. Each structure may take different form depending on the type of information objects, media and domain. The framework may consequently suggest *empirical variables* that can be combined for research, and from which one may make hypotheses and predictions of potential solutions, for instance, for systems development or evaluation. Chapt. 8 provides suggestions for research designs.

The central component, the information seeker, is analyzed in more detail in Sect. 6.2.1. The notion of 'Models' of contexts is in common to all the five components and is discussed in Sect. 6.2.2.

To the right we find the social, organizational and cultural context or environment of the seeking actor(s). That environment takes the form of layman groupings, scientific, professional, and social/cultural *domains*. It endorses *strategies*, conventions, *goals* and *preferences*, for instance of economic and knowledge management nature, as well as *real tasks* and interests to be fulfilled.

On the left-hand side the framework demonstrates the main structures embedded into the information objects[6]: their *full contents* and structures, the conceivable ways of representing the objects by *knowledge representation*, e.g., via semantic nets or *thesauri*. The representation can be carried out by human indexing – concurrently: arrow (5) and over time: arrow (6). Yet, indexing is commonly done by means of *algorithms* placed in the IT platform together with *database architectures* that frame the information objects, arrow (4). The *retrieval engine* is the central cognitive structure of the IT component. The framework shows the interface in close connection to the IT and information space components, arrows (3-4), and consisting of *interface functions.*

6.2.1 The Information Seeker: The Central Actor in the Framework of IS&R

The individual information seeker – or team of individuals – displays a cognitive space that is assumed to consist of a cognitive model ('← models →' – Fig. 6.8) developed over time from cultural and social experiences (De Mey 1980; Ingwersen 1982).

The research framework operates with the notions of *information behavior* and *relevance assessments* as part of the cognitive space of the information seeker. When that actor turns into a state of uncertainty and eventually engages into search task processes, he/she engages automatically into information behavior activities, guided by his/her current cognitive-

---

[6] A more detailed display of the divergence of cognitive structures in (academic) information objects is shown and discussed in associated with polyrepresentation, Sect. 5.2.3 and Fig. 5.5.

emotional state. Information actors perform relevance assessments, for instance, directly in relation to *relevance feedback* in interactive IR systems.

There is hence a strong emphasis on the *interaction* between the individual information seeker(s) and the environment surrounding that individual, also over time. One should again stress that the left-hand side of the framework: the systemic context, Fig. 6.8, also constitutes that environment. This would typically be the case in enterprises or organizations, but also in scientific communities and daily-life. The actual work task or interest perception may thus originate from: a) the social-organizational context by social interaction, arrow (1); b) be produced by the person him/herself; *and/or* c) derive from interactions with information objects through IT – arrows (2-4).

Fig. 6.9 is designed in accordance with the two-level principle of the cognitive communication system, Fig. 2.1. It illustrates the central components of the cognitive framework for IS&R, as shown in Figs. 6.1 and 6.8, but without the detailed structures of each component. The lower social/physical level of Fig. 6.9 signifies how the components (and their substructures) as well as their interactive phenomena are observable in the social and physical world by means of some investigative method. At the same time, the cognitive (and emotional) level denotes the perception or interpretation by the information seeker of the situation, including his/her perception of information objects, IT, interface, social context, *and* the perception of his/her work and search tasks, information need and potential information sources. By means of different research methods it is possible to obtain (albeit obtrusive) data on such perceptions from the information seeker. Such data collection methods could be discourse analysis, introspection, and thinking or talking aloud, diaries, post-search open-ended interviews, etc. – see Sects. 3.2 and 5.8.2.

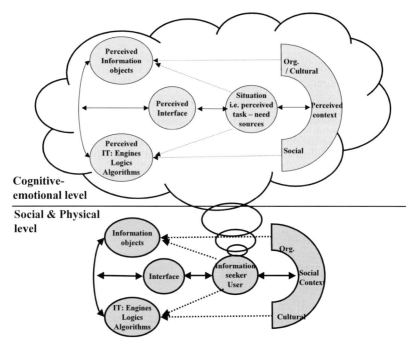

Fig. 6.9. The central components of the cognitive framework for IS&R, centered around the information seeker, as it stands in the physical world and constituting directly observable entities, as well as when perceived by the information seeker at his/her cognitive-emotional level. Arrows correspond to arrows in Fig. 6.8.

Classifications can be applied to the objects at both levels to suggest and test hypotheses either on their perception by actors or on their relationships. Models shaped like Fig. 6.9 could be designed for each of the actor categories discussed previously in Sect. 6.1.

6.2.2 Situation at Hand and Models of Context

As already emphasized by Wilson (1981), the *situation* in the current context plays a central role in information seeking. Our cognitive framework extends this understanding by *also* stressing the role of the *historic context* – both contexts driving the shape of the current situation of the information seeker. In a narrow sense only the five central components of the framework, and their interaction, condition the shape of the situation at hand; but also the societal contexts in a wide sense – like economic and technocultural infrastructures – influence the current situation as perceived by the information seeker or communicator[7].

The Situation at Hand. Fundamentally, the current situation is a personal cognitive construct made in contexts – Sect. 2.1.4. The seeking actor's temporal perception and interpretation of many levels and dimensions of contexts is central to how that situation develops. In this process the perceived work or daily-life task is an important interpretation outlining – but not totally defining – that situation at hand. Also included in the construct are the perceptions and interpretations of:

- Knowledge gap or ASK and relevance;
- Uncertainty and other emotional states;
- The potential sources for the solution (if any) of the work task or interest;
- The intentionality, i.e., goals, purposes, motivation, etc.;
- Information preferences, strategies, pressures (costs, time)
- Self, i.e., of own capabilities, health, experiences, knowledge state – and
- Systemic and interactive features and information objects.

Indeed, present expectations relying on past experiences (the historic context), '←Models→' – Fig. 6.8, may *not* be satisfied by the conditions offered by the current context. For instance, the interface does not present documents in the expected form, the search algorithm seems incomprehensible, or the documents do not immediately satisfy the requirements as well as in previous IS&R situations.

Models of Context. The notion '←Models→' is common to each of the five central components of the research framework. The notion refers back to the first condition of the cognitive information concept, Sect. 2.2. That condition states that the cognitive structures, transformed into a message, have been created as signs with some intention *and models* of other recipients (e.g., other IS&R actors or components) in mind. In this way, the notion reflects *what* any given actor or component in IS&R perceives as its own context in a given situation through implemented design or by learning over time. Fig. 6.9 thus illustrates the model (perception) of the IS&R world as seen from the information seeker's point of view.

---

[7] A typical example of this (economic) influence – also directly on empirical research settings – was the high *cost* of public online searching in the 1970-80s. This lead to many investigations of the so-called "pre-search interview" – a phenomenon not applicable in free-of-charge in-house online systems or realistic to systems design.

Other cognitive actors, like authors, have at least some model of their (future) readers, listeners or spectators in mind. On the Internet authors also have to think about the IT platforms to which they load their objects. Computer scientists may design system architectures and indexing algorithms only with information objects in mind, but increasingly also with people (the utility community) in focus (Oddy et al. 1992). Most commercial interface models in IR search engines, e.g., on the Web or Dialog, have been modernized in order to accommodate (and profit from) both the advanced expert searcher *and* the more novice-like or casual end-searcher. Collectively, social environments or communities themselves in turn carry models of their members and more remote social and systemic constructs, including information infrastructures of potential utility.

Such actor models of IS&R situations in context are scientifically interesting. They can be compared at a given point in time for different IS&R components and actors – or over time – following the framework.

Context is Not only a Searcher Phenomenon. The system itself can (learn to) be context-aware in use, i.e., to possess an extensive model of IS&R. Interacting with searchers means more to the system than simply capturing request input data. Rather, temporal searcher interaction with a system forms a rich network of potential information regarding preferences, style, experience and knowledge as well as interests. This information helps to constitute a *context of interaction* (session), arrow (2), Fig. 6.8 and context dimension (3), Fig. 6.10. This is a rich source of evidence available for the system to interpret current searcher actions. See also Sect. 5.6.2 for recent attempts to apply such evidence algorithmically in interactive best-match IR. From the system's point of view ergonomic behavior, like mouse or eye movements, patterns of relevance feedback or evidence of the immediate perceptions and interpretations by the searcher constitute this interactive session context. The seeking actors and *their* current situations in context act as more remote contextual phenomena – context dimension (4), Fig. 6.10. The latter may be manifestations of cultural conventions, organizational preferences, or domain-specific traditions. For IR systems design it is crucial to uncover patterns of *tangible* evidence of actors' interpretations as well as of influence of the socio-organizational or cultural context. Without evidence the system cannot react properly during session time.

The system in turn has technical characteristics, relating to how information is presented by interfaces, arrows (2-3), Fig. 6.8 that influence the interaction context. They also affect the searcher's perceptions of the system's competence and the quality of information sources. Consequently, models of context represent a *shared process* of interpretation and adaptation on both sides of the interface.

Dimensions of Context in IR. For each component of the cognitive research framework there exist representative objects that are media-dependent. Such objects are, for instance, software entities in the IT component and interface or the documents (information objects) in the information space. Within each object a range of contextual elements exists: the *intra-object* structures, context dimension (1), Fig. 6.10. For instance, in the IT component the lines of programming form such structures as do the variety of cognitive structures in the searcher's mind. Within information objects images are contextual to a surrounding text or other structures attached to them, and *vice versa*. Paragraphs serve as context for their own sentences and words: signs are seen in context of sign structures.

The objects themselves are contextual to one another – forming *inter-object* relationships or networks, context dimension (2), Fig. 6.10. Properties of documents, like references or outlinks to other information objects as well as citations or inlinks, are seen as giving context to, and taking context from, the contents of other objects.

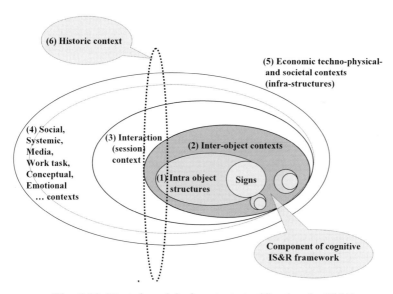

Fig. 6.10. Nested model of context stratification for IS&R.

The kind of component from the cognitive framework for IS&R research that is placed as the core of the nested model, context dimensions (1-2), Fig. 6.10, determines the kind of interaction (session) context (3) and the remaining framework components, which serve as further context dimension (4). In the case of the *searcher*(s) as the core, interaction consists of social interaction as well as interactive IR activities. In turn, these are nested in context of the other framework components (context dimension 4), such as, the socio-organizational and the systemic ones (IT, interface and documents); the former containing real work or daily-life tasks and the latter being media and domain-dependent. However, in the case of the *interface* as the core component of the model, Fig. 6.10, interaction (context dimension 3) signifies the retrieval session. This includes intrasystem interaction like query expansion processes; the IT and information object components of the framework, as well as the searching actors with their conceptual-emotional traits, form the adjacent contextual dimension (4, inner ring). The current but more remote socio-organizational context then constitutes dimension (4, outer ring). All the nested elements are influenced by prevailing societal infrastructures (5). Across this stratification operates an additional dimension, i.e., that of the historic context of *all* participating actors' experiences (6) – Fig. 6.10 – forming their expectations. All IS&R processes and activities are under influence of this temporal form of context.

Consequently, IS&R in context does not only deal with the contexts of searchers or searchers *as* context. IS&R in context also concerns the interaction between documents and IT platform in context of domains and different kinds of work tasks (and situations), i.e., an extension of the laboratory model, not necessarily always involving test persons – see design proposal 8.1.

The idea of demonstrating the nested model of context stratification involved in IS&R is to emphasize that research – following our framework – should focus not only on a specific component or narrow process in its close context, but ought to keep an eye on the temporal dimension and include the adjoining context as well.

6.2.3 Work and Search Tasks

The notion of work task is central to IS&R. In the present discussion the (perceived) level of complexity is of importance, Fig. 3.8, Sect. 3.1.3. This is analyzed further within our framework, Sect. 6.2.5. The conception that the work task serves as the *driving force* underlying IS&R, and indeed information behavior, originates from Järvelin (1986) and was analyzed by Ingwersen (1992) associated with interactive IR.[8] We have extended the

---

[8] Wersig (1973) was a precursor – see Sect. 3.1.3 – in emphasizing the role of work tasks.

notion of work task also to cover non-job-related (daily-life) tasks, including emotional interests like entertainment.

In order to obtain information to fulfill a perceived work task, the information seeker is required to perform some instrumental *search tasks*, i.e., a sequence of IS&R activities, see Fig. 6.11, Sect. 6.2.6. To exemplify: An actual work task may be tuning a car as a mechanic. A daily-life work task or interest may be finding a new flat in another city owing to imposed conditions like increased local taxation. It might be of cultural nature, e.g., leisure: are there some theaters located in the neighborhood of the new location? In all those cases there exists a specific situation at hand in context of available information infrastructure (a car manual and Yellow Pages), and either a social convenience, an economic community (the firm or tax rules), and/or a set of emotional experiences and expectations. An actor may perceive the work task processes (in context) in his/her own way. The strategic and tactical *ways* he/she obtains information on car tuning, flats, or theater locations constitute the search (sub) tasks he/she follows or applies. As stated previously, they are the means to fulfill the work task as perceived.

The framework operates with two kinds of search tasks, *retrieval* and *seeking tasks*, the former embedded in the latter. This is in line with the nested conception of IR into information seeking behavior, Fig. 5.2. A retrieval task is, e.g., first looking up and searching the Web for portals with homes and flats to hire or buy – then to search such portals. Seeking tasks are, e.g., phoning or e-mailing a friend in the other town in order to use his personal network. See also on the consequences of the two kinds of search tasks, Sect. 7.1, and further.

Work and daily-life tasks, as well as their sub-tasks, can lead to physical and intellectual activities. The work tasks can be:

- Natural manifestations;
- Simulated situations;
- Requests for information.

Natural work tasks are carried out in real-life. They may exist objectively as tasks within an organization. They may, for example, be given to employees by employers to be fulfilled as part of their jobs. When received, that employee perceives the task in his/her own context. This creates the situation at hand, which develops as the task progresses. Perceived work tasks are of subjective nature. Natural work tasks may also be non-job-related. They can be constructed or discovered intellectually by actors and are in this case from the start subjective.

Simulated work and daily-life tasks/interest situations are designed for IS&R research settings by involving a specified but invented scenario or cover story of semantic openness. This assigned situation at hand is meant to trigger individual information problems in test persons in a controlled manner, Sect. 5.9. Like natural work tasks, a simulated one is also designed to function as the intellectual platform for relevance assessments (Borlund and Ingwersen 1997; Borlund 2000).

Requests for information are more simplistic ways to assign search 'topics' or requirements meant to represent information needs, typical of TREC-like IR experiments. However, requests may in addition refer to the situations of information professionals in which clients assign perceptions of their own natural work tasks *as search tasks* to be fulfilled as work tasks by the former. To the professional they are perceived as natural manifestations; see also Sect. 6.2.7, Table 6.3.

Hence, the three different kinds of work tasks correspondingly entail natural, simulated or assigned instrumental search tasks and information needs, as discussed by Vakkari (2003), i.e., retrieval and seeking tasks.

Other researchers, like Marchionini (1995), have focused on the instrumental side (retrieval tasks) of interactive IR when analyzing and using the notion of 'tasks'. In addition, the notion 'search task' has a confusing meaning or application in the literature: Search tasks are often understood as equal to *assigned* search *requests* (also named search jobs or topics) – not as a sequence of IS&R sub-tasks to be performed to find information. Hence, in our framework we define search topics (or jobs) as a subcategory of the generic notion 'searches'.

In relation to the models, Figs. 6.8 and 6.9, one *might* intuitively believe – and pointed to above – that work tasks are solely deriving from the right-hand side in the models, that is, from the social, cultural or organizational context. Likewise, one might believe that search tasks are directed only towards the left-hand side, i.e., towards the information and IT spaces. These interpretations are false. Although basically retrieval tasks are directed towards the IT and information space, information seeking search task activities may indeed point towards both the social context by social interaction (arrow 1) *as well as* towards a non-systemic, unstructured or informal information space to the left-hand side of the models. In short, work tasks are directed *towards* the actor – and search tasks *away* from the seeking actor.

6.2.4 Knowledge Types in a Task Framework

As stated in Sect. 2.3.2, our framework operates with two different kinds of knowledge during IS&R: Domain knowledge and IS&R knowledge. Both are in procedural and declarative forms. Table 6.1 demonstrates the latter two forms as well as the task related dimensions of knowledge involved in IS&R on the information seeker's side, Fig. 6.8.

Table 6.1. Matrix of knowledge types and skills, defined from dimensions of task type. Emotional factors are involved in all 6 cases (Kuhlthau 1991; 1993).

Perception ➡ Task type ⬇	.. of *declarative* features of task	.. of *procedural* features of task
Work & daily-life ***task*** *or interest*	Work task (contents) knowledge (1)	Problem & work task solving knowledge (2)
Search task – *interactive IS&R*	Information source & system knowledge (3)	Search task solving knowledge (4)
Search task – *inter personal* *communication*	Person & group knowledge (5)	Social interaction skills (6)

Essentially, six types of cognitive structures are involved, *all* including *emotional states*:

1. *Work task knowledge* deals with task and problem contents. This is domain and context-related knowledge and models (presuppositions and experiences) required to perceive, acquire, and interpret information and its relevance to work tasks contents (Sect. 3.1.3). For instance, it requires the capability of interpreting documents on leisure, taxation, or car tuning. Intentionality, motivation as well as knowledge of what may not be known are included in task knowledge.

2. *Problem and task solving* knowledge, i.e., the perception (or knowledge) of the process of performing the work task (Sect. 3.1.3). For instance, understanding the car tuning process itself, e.g., knowing how to remove the manifold and to carry out tuning. At least *some* task solving knowledge is a prerequisite for understanding information on the process.

3. *Information source and system* knowledge encompasses retrieval and seeking task knowledge. It concerns understanding the declarative structures of information objects, like personal desk-top knowledge sources, web-page organization or informative potentials of video pas-

sages, and of IR systems, i.e., the context of sources (Borgman 1986), like visual interface patterns or icons, and database contents.

4. *Search task solving* knowledge on how to perform seeking and retrieval, i.e., procedural experiences on (in)formal search strategies, tactics and techniques, e.g., invoking retrieval commands, or understanding probabilistic relevance feedback and query modification processes.

5. *Person and group* knowledge signifies acquaintance of and expectations about other people or teams as reliable information sources. It also involves declarative knowledge on communication channels, formal as well as informal.

6. *Social interaction skills* (White 1975) imply knowledge of social communication conventions, behavior, procedure and codes, e.g., in sociocultural, daily-life or organizational environments, and how to operate the communication channels.

The knowledge types 1) and 2) are associated with *domain* and *problem solving knowledge* of Sect. 3.1.3 for work task performance. The types 3) through 6) are instrumental knowledge or skills required to communicate with other persons (the social context) and to search information systems (interface; IT setting), in order to reach into the information space for some useful sources for information needs, that is, all the horizontal interactive processes, Fig. 6.8. Similar cognitive-affective declarative and procedural structures, 3) – 6), are necessary for performing other kinds of information behavior, e.g., document generation or use.

All six types of knowledge are important to IS&R. It is characteristic that all six types may lead to problematic situations, uncertainty and confusion on the human side of the interaction. See for instance Kuhlthau (1993b) for work task as well as (procedural and declarative) IS&R knowledge-related uncertainties and doubt; or Beaulieu (1997) and Beaulieu and Jones (1998) for human uncertainty in understanding query modification (domain knowledge *and* procedural search task knowledge) or interface functionality (both procedural and declarative search task knowledge, Table 6.1). According to many studies of searcher-librarian communication, personal or social interaction uncertainties surface and may limit the negotiation and IS&R outcome (e.g., Belkin 1984; Ingwersen 1982). The matrix may thus be applied as a guide to further empirically study the interaction properties of IS&R, both successes and breakdowns. Levels of expertise and knowledge types are treated in Sect. 7.3, Table 7.1.

A retrieval system, i.e., the IT component, Fig. 6.8, in principle *also* requires elements of all six kinds of knowledge in order to perform adequately. However, the inclusion of levels of inter-personal knowledge and social interactive skills, boxes (5) and (6) have so far not been successful. The influence of seeking knowledge (parts of (3) and (4)) is just under development, Sect. 5.6.

6.2.5 Work and Search Task Complexity in IS&R

Both work task and search task complexity may be divided into five categories of perceived complexity over a complexity continuum (Byström and Järvelin 1995; Byström 1996), see Sects. 3.1.2-3. We discuss the following three categories by collapsing two pairs of complexity categories:

- *Automatic/routine tasks* of information processing;
- *Normal tasks* – of information processing or decision nature;
- *Genuine tasks* – genuine but known decisions, or genuine unknown decisions

Typically, *routine work tasks* are carried out by means of simplistic information processing, fast and commonly without problems. Both procedural and declarative cognitive structures are assumed available. Information acquisition takes place as routine search tasks where information, mostly facts in this case, is gathered for verificative or familiar routine processing and problem solving.

Normal work tasks are tasks, for which the perceived task solving process as well as the domain are largely familiar to the actor, but not necessarily the task contents itself, e.g., tuning the engine of a new car model. Owing to lack of prior knowledge, such work tasks often require information acquisition on task contents *and* input even on broader domain and contextual knowledge, e.g., from colleagues via social interaction. But the requirements do *not typically include* information concerned with the overall problem and task solving procedures and processes. Because of the higher complexity and the involvement of different information types, normal work tasks entail at least normal search task complexity – see below.

Genuine (decision) work tasks constitute the most complex work task type. They can be genuine but somewhat *familiar* to the actor (i.e., the outline of the performance procedure is known from analogous unique decisions made before) – or they can be highly complex, genuine *and* un-preceded to the actor. They require long solving time, task and domain or context information acquisition, *as well as* (situational) *task solving* information. The required information is mainly acquired from expert colleagues via social interaction (Byström 1996).

In genuine cases the information need may only vaguely exist, lack a distinct focus and hence be ill defined – see Table 6.2. Only the knowledge of the task exists as a problematic situation and as a state of uncertainty, simply because no pre-suppositions exist as to the information required to solve the task. Similar characteristics and levels of work task complexity have been demonstrated empirically by Kuhlthau (1999) in her longitudinal investigations of (insurance) information work and IS&R processes and by Kuhlthau and Tama (2001) on lawyers information work. Naturally, what one person perceives as 'genuine' may be 'normal' or 'routine' to another person.

The more complex a work or search task is perceived, the more one needs to acquire task-solving information, Sect. 3.1.4 and box (2), Table 6.1. This coincides with the discovery by Luria (1976) that *situational* problem solving knowledge commonly is easier to learn and remember – and least likely to slip the memory – than categorical hierarchical conceptual structures on contents, which are the first to be forgotten.

In the case of daily-life task or interests, we believe the same kinds of increasing complexity occur. But their manifestations may be different from those of job-related work tasks – and should be further investigated.

Search Task Complexity. We believe that the dimension of *task complexity* also applies to the other rows of Table 6.1, i.e., search tasks and interpersonal communication. To fulfill a perceived *routine search task* one would expect a simplistic information need and the actor to possess deep declarative and procedural IS&R knowledge.

For *normal search tasks* one would expect the actors to be largely familiar with the IS&R process, the available systems and databases or human sources in general. But the exact source or specific content features of potential objects may be unfamiliar to the searcher. We may probably talk here about surface or shallow knowledge to distinguish further between levels of complexity. This degree of search task complexity requires supplementary information on the declarative IS&R knowledge, boxes (3) and (5), Table 6.1. These assumptions are in line with the empirical results obtained by Byström and Järvelin (1995), Vakkari (2000; 2001) and Vakkari and Hakala (2000).

Finally, for highly complex *genuine search tasks* the cognitive framework and Table 6.1 suggest that such tasks fundamentally require information acquisition on both declarative *and* procedural IS&R knowledge. Probably also social interaction knowledge is required – owing to lack of deep knowledge on such IS&R facets; for instance, the seeker first has to find personal details about a potential human source. In such seeking tasks *also* the solution procedures are largely unfamiliar, e.g., attempting retrieval in a totally new source, unfamiliar database *and* in a retrieval system rarely used.

Search task complexity may vary *irrespectively* of the work task complexity. A highly complex work task may entail a routine search task; and a routine or normal work task may lead to a highly complex (genuine-like) search task. In the latter case the information to be acquired on the contents and/or contextual facets of the work task may only momentarily be difficult to locate by IS&R by the same actor possessing the work task *and* performing the IS&R activity. Otherwise the work task would not be perceived as 'routine' or 'normal'.

However, in the case of a *third party* – a professional (online) intermediary – who carries out the search task on behalf of the original work task owner, the latter search situation might be different. One may expect a prolonged and fairly high degree of seeking or retrieval task complexity if in a generalist environment. In that situation the actor commonly possesses deep knowledge of the structural declarative IS&R characteristics – but could be unfamiliar with carrying out parts of the IS&R procedure, say, has forgotten particular retrieval command sequences owing to casual use of the system. The seeking process becomes more complex and may be regarded a normal or perhaps even a *genuine search task*. This is in contrast to the commonly experienced case of increased work task complexity, in which procedural skills is the *last* knowledge to be forgotten (and required).

In the first case of high work task complexity, a third party may indeed be seen to succeed fast and effective by skills and knowledge of similar work tasks from other actors in an organization.

Search task complexity is hence dependent on both the perceived complexity of the work task and the perceived nature of the information need reflecting the work task. The perceived complexity is an emotional and cognitive individual phenomenon. It depends on, and is influenced by, the experiences of a given actor in context, whether being the original work task owner or a third party.

6.2.6 From Work Task to Information Need Formation in Search Tasks

As we have seen in Sects. 3.1.2 and above, task complexity affects the information situation at hand and information needs. This suggests the following typology of such needs.

In the cognitive sense one may assume that in genuine decision-like situations only something shallow or vague is known about the (work) task or problem at hand *and* its solution. The perceived information need is quite ill defined or completely open.

In less complex situations, e.g., in the case of routine or normal information processing work (or daily-life) tasks, the information need would seem potentially more articulated. To IS&R this means that one should then not only ask what the searcher wants. Rather, one should always inquire about *why* he or she wants it and *what* he/she knows about the matter. This implies to inquire about the *task solving* knowledge, Table 6.1, since this information is the last to be lost from memory. It becomes then possible to gather more evidence on the information need situation as a whole, i.e., on the searcher's current state of work task perception or problem state, rather than just on the information gap (or ASK).

As a consequence of the relationships between task complexity and knowledge types on the one hand, and information need formation and development on the other, it is important to explore which features of seekers' knowledge and goals generate which types of information needs. This analysis is central to IS&R because IS&R deals with providing *information* for work task/interest performance – *not* directly with the solving process itself. Hence, if we can establish properties of information needs we are better capable of designing IS&R environments that may act on such properties during interaction with natural work and search tasks.

First, we explore the knowledge types discussed in Sect. 6.2.4 and their impact combined with the kind of information sought after on information need formation. We display and analyze a matrix of eight intrinsic types of information needs. Secondly, we discuss the consequences of such types for search task execution and information interaction.

Table 6.2. Intrinsic information need types defined by three dimensions: 1) the intentionality behind the search task (IS&R); 2) the type of current knowledge concerned with IS&R and the underlying work task; and 3) the quality of what is known.

IS&R goal ➡ Known data type ⬇	Searching for information source *contents* as	Searching for informative *data entity*(ies) as	Quality of current knowledge
Declarative IS&R knowledge (e.g. bibliographic or relational data)	*Known item* (1) *Muddled item* (5)	*Known data element* (2) *Muddled data element* (6)	**Well-defined** vs. **Ill-defined** (exploratory)
Declarative & procedural domain knowledge (e.g. on contents data)	*Known topic or contents* (3) *Muddled topic or contents* (7)	*Factual* (4) *demand* *Muddled factual* (8)	**Well-defined** vs. **Ill-defined** (exploratory)

The following three dimensions are used for classifying information needs: 1) the *intentionality* or goal of the searcher; 2) the *kind of knowledge* currently known by the searcher; and 3) the *quality* of what is known, i.e., how well-defined are the features of the required information objects that are anticipated to solve the underlying perceived work task. Further below, we add a fourth dimension, i.e., that of *specificity* of the knowledge state.

The intentionality dimension is divided into two categories: searching for the *contents* of unstructured information sources; and searching for self-contained and structured *data entities* or elements. Both categories cover the goal of getting to declarative and procedural work task information.

Procedural IS&R knowledge, e.g., online retrieval commands, is necessary for searching but not an obligation for information need formation. In this respect declarative IS&R knowledge of potential information sources signifies one central type of features that may be known *a priori*. Procedural as well as declarative domain knowledge, e.g., on contents, structure or aboutness of information sources, forms another class of features potentially known by the searcher.

The quality of such current knowledge, as a third dimension, may take continuous range of levels between two opposite values: intrinsically well defined (deep knowledge) or ill defined (surface knowledge). 'Shallow knowledge' signifies typically an intermediate quality level.

Table 6.2 displays the following information need types in which a seeking actor may find him/herself at the start of a IS&R session:

1. *Known item searching* for unstructured information object(s) (or passages of contents), like a journal article or book chapter/section, a melody, a video cut, or an artwork, by known features of isness, i.e., by structured bibliographic or non-topical metadata often determined by selectors, Sect. 6.1.4. Such features could be journal or author names, publication date, music performer, video run time, or Web server address.

2. *Known data element searching* for a priori structured (relational) information entities, e.g., the address of clients, by means of other known structured data elements, e.g., such clients that are located in a given town having acquired products in the last three month; looking for related terms in a thesaurus; asking for the original performer of a rock classic; or finding data on experts, e.g., their e-mail, by some known personal properties of such experts, like their names and affiliations.

3. *Known topic or contents searching*, i.e., to clarify, review or pursue unstructured information (subject matter or contents, including potential emotions) by known (commonly unstructured) keys or features, like words, or image color/shape, and/or by knowledge of sequential structures of potential information sources, like section sequences in texts or video. Media-dependent features are at play. For instance, by pursuing music recordings of a particular melody by means of a played tune, we are concerned with seeking contents with affective connotations – not subject matter.

4. *Factual data searching* for informative answers (facts) to conceptual questions by known content-associated or aboutness-related (unstructured) data, as in questioning-answering systems, like: when and where did Napoleon die? What are the names of the tools that are usually used for car tuning? – Who knows something about car tuning?

5. *Muddled item searching* for full information objects (or passages) by insufficient (shallow or surface) knowledge of features of isness, which hampers the search task execution, e.g., owing to ill-defined or wrong bibliographic data.

6. *Muddled data element searching* for (or exploring or mining) relational data entities or structures by vague or ill-defined (structured) data features, which are insufficient to carry out the search task in a straightforward manner. Possible a priori feature relations are unknown.

7. *Muddled topic or contents searching*, i.e., exploring or mining cognitive-emotional contents or subject matter in novel information environments by ill-defined domain/work task solving knowledge or vaguely known or defined emotional contents of potential information sources.

8. *Muddled factual searching* for informative answers to content-related or topical questions by ill-defined (or only vaguely known) unstructured conceptual features as the starting point. For instance: where did this French emperor die – what's his name? … at the beginning of the 19th century?

The first four cases deal fundamentally with searching for specific information sources or data elements whilst the latter four muddled cases are rather exploratory.

It is important to note that the eight cases are sometimes overlapping. Table 6.2 does not display static instances of IS&R; rather it demonstrates that a seeking actor may very well start in one type, say the factual searching instances, boxes (4) or (8), for later to change into a known topical/contents seeking activity owing to the development of the current IS&R situation, information acquisition, and dynamic learning processes.

One may in addition observe information needs, and consequently search task activities, that are mixtures of known structured data (say, bibliographic data), and *also* by known topical and contents features. The searcher may very well seek for known items – avoiding topical searching – feeling the former as easier. In some seeking strategies a Known Item (search) – case (1) – may function as the starting point for finding 'something topically *similar* or content-like', with respect to the found item – a case (3) information need.

Aside from the seeking actor being in a state of uncertainty at instances of a ill-defined (or even shallow) knowledge state concerning the need, also the information systems and other contextual components of the IS&R framework will become smitten with and suffer from uncertainty. As discussed above the level of search task complexity may well be independent of the complexity of the work task – although the same complexity levels exist for both types of tasks – as illustrated in Fig. 6.11.

Knowledge State Specificity. The fourth dimension of the information need formation, its intrinsic degree of *specificity* (Saracevic and Kantor 1988b; Meadow 1992; Qui 1993a), is involved in all the eight kinds of information needs – Table 6.2. Specificity means that the features applied to express (intrinsically or openly) the information gap are found at a certain level of specificity according to, for instance, a domain thesaurus. Hence, the words or concepts used to formulate the information need may be detected (as evidence) to a certain indexing level. They could be very general or less general, tending to be quite specific – according to the vocabulary tool applied.

Obviously, this is a media (and domain) dependent dimension. In textual media many levels of word specificity are possible. One may hence expect up to *eight additional* types of intrinsic information needs – since each type, Table 6.2. – may be of specific or general conceptual property. Naturally, a continuum exists between the two extremes. In other media, e.g., music, the specificity of features is less pronounced, e.g., figuring vs. note, or 'specificity' as concept is simply meaningless.

The three dimensions depicted in Table 6.2 and associated specificity are commonly *subjective*. However, the expressed manifestations can be observed or measured in an *objective* manner, e.g., words used in a request or the features shown in relevance feedback or pointed to on a GUI.

In the four cases of well-defined intrinsic information requirements, there is a substantial chance that the searching actor may express the *intentionality*, i.e., what is expected to be found and why, and what is known *a priori*. Probably, its quality and specificity can be detected, at least to some extent, if the searcher is presented with incentives to do so. For an interface, or relevance feedback and query modification algorithms, this means a chance to detect evidence of the kinds of knowledge available by the actual actor. That evidence concerns both human domain knowledge *as well as* declarative and procedural IS&R knowledge. One may for example assume that a request belonging to a highly specific level in a domain signals rather profound knowledge of the requirement (and probably also of the underlying work task). Thus, a hypothesis could be that, with the use of specific vocabulary or features, the actor employed in that domain may be more certain in relevance assessments, and be quite articulated concerning the context of the requirement. Also, if there are developments during session time towards more specific search keys, then the assessments may be more dependable.

Search Task Dynamics. Fig. 6.11 depicts the explicit causal relationship between the work task/interest complexity levels, as perceived by the seeking actor, the ensuing range of possible information need types that triggers an instance of a search task. The *degree of complexity* of that seeking or retrieval task instance is determined by the degree of declarative and procedural IS&R knowledge possessed by the seeking actor. As discussed above, search tasks may be genuine, normal or routine. The *outcome* of the seeking or retrieval instance implies some type of information that becomes evaluated for usability, quality and relevance – see Sect. 7.1.3. The outcome may (in part) support the work task/interest resolution and/or lead to further developments of the information need, probably altering the type of need.

Information need types are *dependent* on whether the outcome of a search task instance is successful or not. If not successful, the information need may turn into a muddled one or change direction or focus completely. We may argue that the sequence of source or system and search mode applied by an actor *reflects* (elements of) his/her knowledge – and hence may reveal some facets of the current information need type of that actor.

The matrix, Table 6.2, and Fig. 6.11 suggest that in the four muddled cases we are concerned with either normal or genuine decision work tasks. High complexity of the search task is determined by the quality of procedural IS&R knowledge. If ill defined or not existing – as is often the case for lay people – we regard the search task as of *genuine unknown* complexity. This implies lack of knowledge on both procedural *and* declarative IS&R, and human sources are momentarily unknown to the actor.

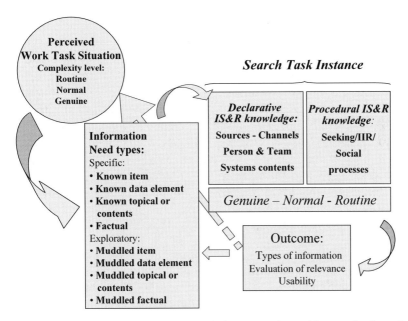

Fig. 6.11. Complexity of the search task in connection with perceived work task situations. The dotted arrow signifies that information has been found (partly) useful to perform the perceived work or daily-life task or interest situation.

On the other hand, the actor may be more knowledgeable by being a casual searcher. The complexity is reduced to a *known genuine decision* search task. Similar but genuine tasks have been solved earlier – and some procedural IS&R knowledge is present. This level of search task complexity (known genuine) may often be the most complex one since the actor, as frequently is the case, may consult a *known* human *source*. In that event, the information need type changes from a muddled one to a 'known item' type, since declarative IS&R knowledge incorporates also social and personal knowledge, Table 6.1. For muddled information need types the seeking behavior is assumed to be highly exploratory for a period – and one might say to have exploratory information needs. This phenomenon is further analyzed below in Sect. 6.2.7 and Table 6.3.

The four well-defined information need types are assumed to be the result of routine or normal processing work tasks for which almost all the solving processes and contextual/domain and most of the work task contents information is known to the actor. The search task, whether of seeking or retrieval nature, is then commonly assumed to be of the routine and normal processing nature – as discussed Sect. 6.2.5 – but sometimes with the exception of a third party acting on behalf of the work task owner.

6.2.7 The Label Effect

If searchers constantly paid more effort to IS&R, more specifically, if they *expressed everything* they know about their perceived work task and information need, IS&R could possibly handle the well-defined information needs quite properly. Besides, the assumption in the system-driven approach to IR, that information needs are stable and requests (queries) exactly mirror the underlying needs, would be much more in line with reality. However, the problems in IS&R are not restricted to muddled need situations alone, whether stable or variable. People tend to act more at random, to be uncertain, and not to express everything they know. Instead they express what they assume is *enough* and/or suitable to the human recipient and/or IR system. They compromise their statements under influence of the current and historic context and situation, Fig. 6.10. This phenomenon is called the *Label Effect* (Ingwersen 1982).

The Label Effect is always present in the case of ill-defined information needs, although aspects of the work task may be known. In addition, the effect means that searchers, even with well-defined knowledge of their information gap, tend to label their initial request for information verbally by means of very few (1-3) words or concepts. The effect implies three obstacles to successful IS&R.

First, retrieval mechanisms have difficulty in reaching out into the proper directions in information space where data relevant to that particular searcher are located. Owing to the *lack of context* in the request, and the ensuing semantic openness, a multitude of directions are indeed possible. This is what was observed in the online age 10-20 years ago, and the same phenomenon is dominant today in web searching. This effect is probably also the underlying intuitive reason for developing GUIs at which searchers may point – without expressing a query.

Secondly, there exist no or few insufficient clues of information objects to work on from the system's point of view. However, if the searcher's need is intrinsically well defined, he or she may aid the system by supplying rich additional data via relevance feedback behavior, Sects. 4.6.1 and 5.6. Knowing about the searcher's current knowledge state becomes hence crucial to search task execution by the system.

Thirdly, interfaces or humans may not directly from the request (or GUI pointing) be capable of distinguishing between searchers with deep, shallow, or surface knowledge about their information requirements. They cannot detect whether the searcher's need is intrinsically well or ill-defined concerning the knowledge gap. Without ensuing instances of *interaction* it becomes hence difficult for a person or a system adequately to support the information seeker in his or her endeavors.

Ingwersen (1996) proposed to view the perceived work task as a rather stable cognitive state during retrieval session time, but not in a longitudinal sense. The nature of the corresponding information need may indeed be expected to change even during session time, from a muddled to a more well-defined type, with input from clarifying information and via learning during search task activities. However, one may also experience that the information need does stay stable – at least for a while. Accordingly, one may view the eight basic cases of information need types in the form of a matrix, defined by two dimensions. One dimension is the *quality* of what is known of the need; see Table 6.2. This concerns how well the information gap, or declarative/procedural knowledge, is defined in the mind of the searcher at a given point in time, Table 6.3.

The other dimension corresponds to the *variability* of the need *over time*, i.e., the actor's motivation and ability for change. It mirrors a *fifth dimension* of the information need typology, shown Table 6.2. Each searcher should have a minimum degree of understanding of the work task – even in complex genuine cases. Otherwise there would not exist any *reason* for engaging in information seeking or IIR, or that would be irrelevant for work task accomplishment.

Depending on the current cognitive-emotional state, the searcher may belong to one of the four instances of human information needs at the initiation of the IS&R session, the four boxes, Table 6.3. During such activities he or she may move to the other instances and hence require different kinds of support. The transition between the four instances is continuous.

Table 6.3. Matrix of four distinct cases of human intrinsic information requirements across the eight types of information needs during an IS&R session, given a perceived work task situation, and the corresponding search (task) behavior (Ingwersen 2001a, p. 164) – altered version of Ingwersen (1996, p. 15). 'Known Contents' is identical to the information need type: Known topic or contents.

Intrinsic information need variables – given a perceived work task type	**Well-defined** (Work task: Routine or Normal)	**Ill-defined**
Stable	*Known Item – Known Data Element* *Known Contents – Factual* *Querying* *Filtering behavior*	Genuine work task *Muddled: Item – Data Element – Contents – Factual* *Search loops*
Variable	*Known Contents - Factual* *Querying – Navigation* *Dynamic interaction*	Genuine/normal work task *Muddled: Item – Data Element – Contents – Factual* *Browsing* *Trial & error behavior*

A closer observation of the matrix, Table 6.3, suggests the following issues of concern for IS&R research. The mainstream IR research is fundamentally associated with the investigation of the well-defined and stable box of the matrix. The underlying work tasks are then assumingly of routine or normal nature[9]. Indeed, we have such kinds of needs, for instance, in connection with patent retrieval and filtering, i.e., selective dissemination of information (SDI). In this case IR may support searchers by means of hierarchical conceptual (thesaurus) structures, querying and/or confined navigation. Searchers may be expected to be less uncertain. Owing to their rich cognitive state they may be assumed capable of relevance feedback, query modification as well as assessing topical relevance and/or pertinence, as well as situational relevance. See also Sect. 5.2.7 on the relevance typology.

In the case associated with *well-defined but variable* information needs people are assumed to be willing (or forced) to learn and shift focus after

---

[9] This assumption is based on the inference that searchers displaying a well-defined information need containing 'many' keys are indeed facing less complex work tasks.

initial engagements. We may expect exploratory navigation, also by consulting several human sources, and stages of *uncertainty* throughout the IS&R session. This behavior is in line with the 'berry-picking' exploration suggested and modeled by Bates (1989). Cognitive-emotional uncertainty has been empirically found to increase during the initial stages of IS&R processes owing to the quality of the cognitive-emotional state, expectations and interpretative problems of the retrieved data (Kuhlthau 1991; 1993), Sect. 3.1.2. Situational relevance assessments and judgments based on topicality and pertinence are possible, as is relevance feedback and human query modification. That assumes that the underlying work task is perceived as routine or normal. The Known Item and Data Element types of information needs are not present since such types are defined as stable during a session exactly because the goal is fixed and all necessary data is available. Obviously, a negative outcome of IS&R may alter the goal and thus the type of information need.

The *ill-defined and variable kind* of information needs assumes means of browsing rather than querying or navigation owing to the inherent Label Effect. Cognitive-emotional uncertainty may be expected to be high and we may observe exploratory trial & error behaviors during searching, since adequate search features may be non-existent or hard to recall from memory. However, the *motivation and curiosity* of the searcher may make the session progress – as demonstrated by Kuhlthau (1991). Wrong or lacking data elements may then be corrected or verified. Judgments of topicality and pertinence, and query modification may be unreliable or vague at initial stages of the engagement with persons or systems (Spink, Greisdorf and Bateman 1998). The cognitive structures assumed to be present are those associated with a work task of perceived normal or genuine complexity, i.e., data in part associated with its domain and solution. Problem knowledge and task definition is lacking.

The final instance of *ill-defined* but *stable* information needs in addition assumes high complexity and a genuine work task with properties and mode of solution that are only vaguely perceived by the actor. Uncertainty is taken for paramount. Assumingly it leads to a vaguely defined, quite complex or scattered and hence confusing search task perception or to multiple small ones on separate aspects as they are identified. But the work task may also be vaguely represented in a cognitive sense for another reason. In the case of human mediators (librarians), Ingwersen found (1982) that they rarely possess a comprehensive and reliable picture of the work task or problem of the end-searcher. What they often only know is 'something' – a few words or concepts – extracted or received from the searcher during personal communication. The Label Effect clearly appears in such cases and the mediator runs into problems of interpretation and search loops. In order to break the deadlock the mediator's cognitive state must rapidly absorb knowledge about the current searcher situation. In generalist circumstances, for instance, in public libraries, this 'getting to know' the underlying situation is often hampered by lack of domain knowledge on the mediator side. This leads to quite complex search tasks or suboptimal results.

On the other hand, in specialized information services of organizations the mediators often know of the current tasks of their end-searchers, owing to collaboration, and the muddled case can be rapidly solved or moved to another case in the matrix by the third part, see above. Nevertheless, when being in the fourth case the actor has severe *difficulty* of all kinds of relevance assessments as well as query modification activity. The reason that public librarians after all often succeed is grounded in their extensive patterns of IS&R knowledge that may guide them to unlock the situation and lead to potentially adequate locations in information space.

The matrix, Table 6.3, demonstrates that only in one or two cases can we hope searchers to act according to plans in rational ways, i.e., in the well-defined cases. This difference also lies in the notions of navigation versus browsing. Navigation is seen as purposeful moves by links or similar activity in networks of information objects. The searcher seeks to reach a goal, either by navigating in a confined space or by a more exploratory behavior – but constantly with the work task or final goal in mind. Browsing signifies an activity of randomness in searching. The searcher is open to novel paths and serendipity effects may occur.

6.2.8 Interaction as the Vital Process in IS&R

Aside from perceived work tasks or interests as one central phenomenon in IS&R, various processes of information interaction constitute the second important issue.

Preferably, information retrieval systems should be designed to cope with and support all different kinds of conceivable uncertainties through IR interaction. This implies to help the searcher help the system to support the searcher, etc. – i.e., *making the searcher more informative* towards the system, which, in turn, then increases its informativeness toward the searcher. Ideally, this is what happens in successful social interaction.

Interaction is exchange between two or more contexts of actors and a two-way communication activity. However, following the communication patterns between the cognitive actors of the framework, the arrows (1-8), Fig. 6.8, many more instances of one-way communication or information transfer take place for each two-way communication act.

Short-Term Interaction. Short-term interaction with information sources, human or artifacts, is here understood as a few iterations including
clarification of information need and probably relevance feedback, briefly
interrupted (ended) by some other line of action or intellectual behavior,
for instance social interaction. Three instances of interaction constitute a
typical Short-Term episode of interactive IR. Fig. 6.12 depicts short-term
interaction. During this period learning processes are assumed marginal
and the current information need can be regarded stable[10]. Between short-
term interactions, however, we assume that learning and change of information need situation may occur. Learning might for instance take place
based on information acquisition from the presented information objects or
other features displayed as well as by social interaction. We regard the
short-term interaction period as a fundamental entity for data analysis of
verbal protocols, talking aloud or other forms of analysis, e.g., discourse
analysis.

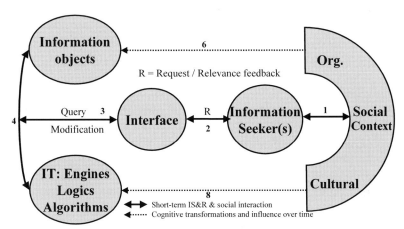

Fig. 6.12. Short-Term Interaction episode in IS&R carried out in a situation in
context. Numbers are as in Fig. 6.1.

The briefest way of performing IR with interactive best match retrieval
algorithms results in *five instances* of communication, as demonstrated on
Fig. 6.12. The request or pointing at a GUI (communication arrow (2)) is
transformed into a query (3) that, by communication between a search engine and the objects (4), entails a retrieval result communicated to the interface (3). The ranked objects are presented to the searcher (2). If the al-

---

[10] Short-term interaction comprises hence also typical one-run IR experiments. A
typical Cranfield or TREC-like test run includes three instances of data transfer
at the extreme left-hand side of Fig. 6.12.

gorithm involves relevance feedback[11], the interactive processes consequently increase to *ten instances* of communication or data transfer. This is the minimum number of one-way communications that allow the searcher influence on the retrieval process.

In the OKAPI investigations the relevance feedback and the query modification processes were further separated from one another (Robertson et al. 1995) producing *five additional instances* of communication: Based on the relevance feedback, Fig. 6.12, arrows (2/3), a best match algorithm would suggest optimal search keys by automatic query modification (4/3) to be presented by the interface (2). The human searcher is *then* allowed to modify the query, arrow (2). This is followed by internal processing of the search engine (3/4). It retrieves (3) a new modified ranked result. By observing the human-computer interaction, three consecutive instances of IIR can be detected. But in reality 15 one-way communications are carried through as a maximum, before an entire retrieval cycle is finalized. This includes re-ranking of results for which the searcher *also* is responsible. In this scenario there exist many *dependent variables*, also of hidden nature. See Sects. 4.6.1 and 5.10.1 for discrepancies of research outcome concerned with relevance feedback issues and query modification.

Social interaction with the community – arrow (1), Fig. 6.12 – is illustrative of the situation where the searcher interacts with a colleague or other persons on the current information situation in context – for example a complex one. Social interaction associated with information seeking entails, as a minimum, a question and a reply or statement. A new statement (clarification/question) from the seeker might follow this exchange, resulting in a second reply. We regard this double exchange, four instances of human one-way communication, as the maximum frame for short-term social interaction, since clarification (searcher influence) has been possible. However as stated earlier, pure information seeking behavior, Fig. 5.2, not involving formal systems, *not only* takes place towards the right-hand side of the model, Figs. 6.8 and 6.12. If the IT is primitive or encourages informal communication with knowledge sources, pure seeking behavior is also pointing towards the left-hand side. In such cases the sources (the information objects) are less or not at all systematically stored or presented. This may be the case in a paper office environment with piles of personally

---

[11] Relevance feedback, query provision and modification are only meaningful processing activities carried out by an interface if that component possesses adequate knowledge of the remaining part of the information system(s), i.e., the IT platform(s) and information objects. Otherwise, the interface only acts as a message channel to an underlying system.

(un)structured files (Kwasnik 1988; 1991). Over time the objects and IT settings surrounding the information seeker are results of generation processes – the arrows (6) and (8). With really advanced digital IT solutions the left-hand side of the model increasingly consists of interactive IR and formal communication behavior. Thus, pure information seeking behavior will increasingly involve the social context only (arrow 1, Figs. 6.8 and 6.12).

Session-Based Interaction. Several short-term interactions make up session-based interactions. The information seeker may indeed change roles during a session, for instance, by a click of the mouse becoming an author, an indexer, a selector, or database designer – again returning as an information seeker, as depicted on the models in Figs. 6.1-6.5. We may observe the behavior in the form of berry-picking (Bates 1989). This integrated role-shift over time is IT and situation-dependent. Figs. 6.1 and 6.8 illustrate such cases by including the two transformation arrows (5) and (7) directed towards the objects and the IT components from the information seeker, in the roles as author, designer, or selector. During session-based interaction we expect to observe the dynamism and variability of the perceived information need and search task owing to interactive processes of learning and cognition. Focus shifts may occur (Belkin 1984; Kuhlthau 1993a; Cole 1999). We regard the perceived work task (the intentionality) as a quite stable phenomenon during a session (Vakkari and Hakkala 2000).

Longitudinal IS&R Interaction. A further prolonged IS&R activity may contain several sessions over a longer period of time, e.g., days, weeks, or months, Fig. 6.8. Clearly, information need situations are then highly dynamic and the underlying intentionality (work task, interest, goal, etc.) is also assumed to undergo alterations. The horizontal transformation and influence (arrows 6 and 8), Fig. 6.8, signify the involvement of the social communities, via social interaction, in the processes of collectively generating information objects and IT settings over time. Fig. 6.9 illustrates the snap-shot perception of the current situation by the searcher.

Interaction as Magnifying Tool. As stated earlier, information seeking increasingly integrates with formal IR through IIR (and HCI) owing to integration of social communication in advanced digital IT settings. Hence, the matrix, Table 6.1, as well as the cognitive framework proposes to further investigate the associations between types of human uncertainty in the interpretation of system data, *and* the different uncertainty connected to the contents and meaning of information objects. As a promising start, Campbell (2000; Campbell and Rijsbergen 1996) and Ruthven (2001) suggested to apply knowledge of the information behavior of the searcher during IIR *to adjust* the algorithmic retrieval process and search task execution by *implicit relevance feedback*.

HCI in IIR is hence an obvious phenomenon to be investigated (Spink and Saracevic 1997; 1998). But human IR interaction also provides *a limitation*. Human searchers become easily bored, tired, and lazy and follow the principle of least effort. For instance, how far down a ranked list of information objects can we expect people to look for relevance before turning into other behavior or quitting?

One might argue that we know a lot about searcher behavior, also as end-searchers, their interaction patterns, knowledge deficiency and information acquisition, information need formation and development, relevance assessments, cognition processes, etc. We even know it from different philosophical viewpoints and epistemological stands. However, a vital problem is how to make that knowledge *operational* in IT settings and retrieval systems. It is vital to show which features and objective characteristics of information objects and sources are linked to which behavioral patterns and features of work tasks and information problems. During IS&R the interaction processes magnify such features and making them central study objects. Further discussions on issues along this line of thought are given briefly below and in the Chapts. 7-8.

6.2.9 Cognitive Use of IS&R Effectiveness Measures

The traditional effectiveness measures in IR, recall and precision, as well as several novel ones discussed in Sect. 4.10, are not really cognitive measures. The recent new measures, e.g., ranked half-life, cumulated gain, etc., are inspired by the cognitive approach and the relevance revolution, mainly in relation to graded relevance and the modern typology of relevance due to the searcher involvement in assessments. Recall, precision and the alternative measures can be used in *novel ways*, better serving the cognitive viewpoint. When traditional topical (and graded) relevance assessments are used these effectiveness measures suit the traditional Laboratory Model evaluation.

The new measures proposed in Sect. 4.10, however, allow for subjective graded relevance assessments and therefore augment traditional recall and precision in evaluation. Like recall and precision, however, the new measures are just measuring devices based on any kind of relevance assessments they are supplied with. They are all immune to the *way* of assessing relevance (whether graded and subjective or not). For example, Borlund (2000) states that the RHL and RR measures may well be used in non-interactive experiments within the Laboratory Model. Järvelin and Kekäläinen's (2000; 2002) measures are directly used within the Laboratory Model.

Borlund (2000) notes that there is a need for a measure bridging between the subjective assessments and objective system performance. She also correctly states that the RR measure does this (save for identified problems with differing scales of evaluation in some cases). However, also traditional PR-curves already do this between any chosen kinds of subjective assessments and the objective system performance, indicated by retrieval scores of documents and their ranking (or algorithmic relevance).

It is therefore appropriate to take heed and think of really new ways of assessing the outcome of IS&R processes from searchers' point of view. Perceived work tasks and search tasks should play a central role – but so far IS&R research has fallen short of such novel evaluation tools.

By applying non-topical, higher-order relevance assessments in IR experiments one may find out to what degree IR algorithms or searcher-system interactions are able to reflect higher-order relevance in matching and ranking documents. This may be measured in terms of the traditional or the novel measures – when higher-order graded relevance assessments are applied. This bridges the information seeking real-life and the laboratory experiments – but requires well-tailored simulated work tasks and sensible collections. In addition, measuring performance or other parameters, like usability, implies to have quite established criteria associated to each relevance type, discussed in Sect. 5.7, according to media and document genre.

6.3 Characteristics of the IS&R model: a summary

First, we summarize the general characteristics and major points of our proposed cognitive holistic framework for IS&R research. Secondly, we discuss the framework in the light of the criteria Engelbart (1962) and Bunge (1967) have presented – see Sect. 1.5.

6.3.1 Major Characteristics of the Cognitive IS&R Framework

Our model depicted in Fig. 6.8, and in the derived preceding and ensuing figures, has a monological flavor, i.e., an individual being in focus – Sect. 3.3.1. Notwithstanding, the *contexts* are in no way neglected in this conceptual framework. The framework depicts concepts necessary for carrying out analyses in the area covered and points to relationships, processes or phenomena to be empirically investigated. The framework ought hence also to pave the way for hypothesis generation and theory building. That dimension of the model is followed up in the ensuing Chapts. 7-8.

First, the IS&R framework is intended as media-independent and operates with five central components, each consisting of data structures representing the cognitive structures of the actors involved in their generation, maintenance, and modifications over time: 1) the IT setting; 2) the information space holding objects of potential information value to 3) information seekers via 4) interface mechanisms – all set in 5) socio-organizational contexts.

Secondly, contexts are seen as a) historical, i.e., constituted by the experiences and knowledge gained over time by the actor(s) dealing with a utility community and his/her peers – or b) contexts nested around and within the components of the framework. Contexts may hence be of social, cultural or organizational nature, associated with objects, systems and domains, searchers' work and daily-life tasks and emotional interests, intentionality and preferences. Together with the immediate interaction (session) context those current circumstances directly influence the involved actors' perception of the situation at hand. Within each framework component divergent intra-component representations are contextual to one another, down to the smallest sign element.

Third, the principle of complementary cognitive and social influence, with the individual actors as the determining factor, forms a central characteristic of the cognitive holistic framework. This principle, in turn, makes the framework operate with the notion that to each component the other components form its context. The individual components' models of the world displayed in Fig. 6.8 signify the perception and/or representation of that context. In other words: such models are experiences gained over time and transformed into expectations – see for instance Fig. 6.9.

Fourth, the conceptual framework, Fig. 6.8, is intended also to cover the cases of *information behavior* that are not information seeking, where the latter is seen as nested within the former. Such activities are, for instance, the use, creation, communication and selection of information objects or human indexing of such objects. By focusing on particular components of the framework, and their immediate relationships and interactivity, the framework demonstrates its strength as modeling tool – also in such behavioral instances.

A fifth central dimension of the framework is its ability to point to the possibility of hitherto largely neglected conceptual relationships between core variables of IS&R. Such relationships are, for instance, between human graded relevance assessment patterns in given work task situations and the corresponding appropriateness of relevance feedback algorithms stored in the IT setting. The framework is thus highly flexible. It opens up for the study of many relationships involving variables from three or more associated components. It incorporates the Laboratory Model, which allows the relationships of any combination of at least 7 central variables to be studied: collection, request set, indexing, query (re)formulation, matching, relevance assessment, effectiveness measures. In the case of three or four variables applied to a research design, 126 or 504 combinations of variables exist, respectively, solely for that part of the framework.

The capability of the framework to explore the detailed relationships between cognitive (and social) elements *within a component* signifies a sixth dimension of the model, Fig. 6.8 and Chapt. 7. For example, the framework enables one to model the kinds of knowledge required for executing IS&R, i.e., IS&R, domain and social knowledge, of declarative as well as procedural nature, e.g., in the form of work or search task solving skills. Another example is the systematic association between work tasks (and cultural-emotional non-job related tasks or interests), their perceived complexity, and information need formation and development during search task execution. This underlying intentionality can be modeled by the framework as deriving from the social context of the actor (the logical intuitive choice), but indeed also from information objects by interaction with information space. The framework thus supports a more structured and detailed way of investigating central issues in IS&R than, for instance, the former models on interactive IR by Ingwersen (1992; 1996), information seeking by Byström and Järvelin (1995) or by Wilson (1999).

6.3.2 The Cognitive IS&R Framework as a Meta Theoretical Model

As a meta-theoretical model the framework emphasizes the core elements that prevail in the contemporary IR research traditions. It incorporates the original simplistic laboratory model applied to mainstream system-driven retrieval research, Fig. 1.1. If we make a vertical cut on the left-hand side of the model, Fig. 6.8, to the right of the notion of 'query', and exclude the interface component as well as the remaining right-hand side of the framework, we observe a limited triangular interactive model consisting of the information objects, the IT, and (a set of) queries discussed in Chapt. 4. A more complex investigative setting integrates the interface and information seeker, moving towards the right-hand side of the framework. That scenario constitutes the searcher-oriented research efforts, discussed in Chapt. 5.

Obviously, one might move further to the extreme right-hand side of the model, Fig. 6.8, and place the focus of investigation on the socio-organizational or cultural environment. This might lead to information or knowledge management research. But it may also signify a social constructionist view of the information seeking processes (Talja 1997 2001; Tuominen and Savolainen 1997; Tuominen, Talja and Savolainen 2002) or reflect a social-realistic domain analytic approach to information and information transfer, as put forward by Hjørland and Albrechtsen (1995) and Hjørland (1997; 1998; 2000a; 2001), and associated with a socio-cognitive view of document representation (Jacob and Shaw 1998). In such views the social context, domain, epistemological or cultural-organizational construct serves as the determining factor in processes of representation and cognition – illustrated by the left-oriented one-way arrows (1), (6) and (8), Fig. 6.8.

The most comprehensive and complex scenario involves information seekers *and* their past and current social contexts, including cognitive-emotional as well as probabilistic uncertainties in objects, IT, and interactive processes. That is the holistic cognitive framework of IS&R as presented in the entire Fig. 6.8, and relying on the principle of complementary social and cognitive influence, as discussed in Sect. 2.1.4.

The model, Fig. 6.8, may similarly serve as a framework in relation to the development of *conceptions of information* over time – Sect. 2.2. Information regarded as thing (Buckland 1991b), that is, equal to data or signs, is explicitly located in information objects (and information systems). In Shannon's mathematical information theory (1949) information equals signals transmitted or processed via a channel, e.g., during the interaction between objects and IT or horizontally via an interface to a human recipient. When information is seen as the process of becoming informed a similar interaction takes place, but this time not at signal or morphological level of communication. In contrast, the communication process takes place at the semantic / cognitive level, albeit suffering from the cognitive free fall. With the conception of reduction of uncertainty at the recipient side (Wersig 1971; 1973; Artandi 1973) we move into the cognitive state of the information seeking actor in a social context, at the center of the framework: information as knowledge. With Talja (2001) we are at the right-hand side of the framework – within the socio-cultural environment and its social formation of knowledge structures. As with the research traditions previously analyzed, the conditional cognitive information understanding – Sect. 2.2 – requires the entire framework as its foundation and is not limited to some parts of the model.

Owing to its cognitive, social and technological complexity we conceive that experimental settings in IS&R are forced *also* to incorporate elaborated social science methodologies – Sects. 3.2 and 5.9.

6.3.3 The Cognitive IS&R Research Framework: An Evaluation

Developing conceptual models means, according to D.C. Engelbart (1962), specifying the following (Sect. 1.5):

- Essential objects or components of the system to be studied.
- The relationships of the objects that are recognized.
- What kinds of changes in the objects or their relationships affect the functioning of the system – and in what ways such changes occur? – i.e., provide predictive power.
- Promising or fruitful goals and methods of research.

The model, Fig. 6.8, can be regarded a conceptual model or framework. It has developed over a decade (Ingwersen 1992; 1996; 2001; Byström and Järvelin 1995). It may, through several studies and empirical tests during recent years of at least parts of the model, be claimed to meet most of the requirements. In Engelbart's terms the framework suggests the five components and their relationships mentioned above as central objects for research in IS&R. Further, it proposes to investigate in detail what happens when the seeking actor(s), or other information actors, modify their state and type of knowledge when engaging with information space or via social interaction in context. The framework may, as demonstrated above throughout the sections, predict certain manifestations in relation to concepts like relevance, relevance feedback, (perceived) work (or daily-life) task complexity, the derived information need type and the ensuing search task performance. Hence, we claim that the framework proposes fruitful goals of research and directly produces promising novel areas for study (Chapts. 7 and 8). However, the conceptual model, Fig. 6.8, only indirectly leads to research methods, such as the use of verbal protocols for data collection or discourse analysis.

Bunge's Functions for Scientific Theories. In relation to Bunge (1967) we believe that his functions also are suitable as means to evaluate conceptual models or frameworks. Scientific theories – hence frameworks – are needed (used) for the following central functions in science:

1. Systematization of knowledge
2. Guiding research
3. Mapping the area of reality

We find the following functions fulfilled or dealt with to some extent as to heading (*i*) by the cognitive conceptual framework for IS&R research – see also Sect. 1.5.

The framework clearly *integrates* hitherto disparate parts of knowledge. It coordinates and combines the mainstream laboratory research environment, foci and methods with various searcher-centered research traditions in IS&R, foremost the empirical information seeking and IIR environment, into a holistic cognitive model. In minor scale it attempts to integrate theory and findings from organizational task complexity research with IS&R studies and findings.

The framework seeks to generalize and explain the perception of work tasks and non-job-based tasks or interests in context, causing information need formation and development as well as relevance assessment capacities, by means of higher level knowledge constructs and types. Procedural and declarative knowledge associated with domain, IS&R, and social awareness constitute such knowledge types.

The cognitive IS&R framework may explain facts hitherto not explained, for instance, by the laboratory model, such as the variability of the information need over time, and hence producing the hypothesis that weighting over time of search keys should be considered in retrieval algorithms. Several other causal relationships have been suggested by the model, of which some have already been tested. For instance, the direct relationship between knowledge levels, information gap and relevance assessment characteristics.

A central virtue of the framework is its capability of expanding knowledge by deducing new propositions. By circumscribing perceptions and interpretations of information objects deriving from very different cognitive actors and origin – also over time – the framework directly leads to a set of propositions that makes evident specific kinds of multi-evidence (or polyrepresentation) of the same objects by different actors. Further, the framework proposes, e.g., the work task perception-information need association. Knowledge of this relationship is useful for retrieval algorithm design, as currently under investigation, Sect. 5.6.

With respect to functions *guiding research* (*ii*) our framework in general is pointing towards the incorporation of socio-organizational, systemic and work task-related contexts. In this respect there is a lack of frameworks in IS&R. Our framework, for instance, sees the socio-organizational context with features, such as, tasks, strategies and preferences, that affect the IS&R processes by (teams of) individuals. Which features, and to what extent, influence the IS&R activity is an issue. Similarly, knowledge state, types and levels, kind of information need, and relevance assessment capacity seem strongly interconnected: What kind of patterns emerge in given (real or simulated) information situations?

The framework seems indeed capable of proposing particular data collection and methods. Obviously, as stated above, data collection is proposed concerning several interactive variables, including the social context, or concerned with particular phenomena, such as work task complexity perception associated with graded relevance judgments. The conception to apply simulated work task situations providing context for a semantically open interpretation by test persons is a direct spin-off of the cognitive model.

Further, the framework proposes new lines of research by pointing to the combination of the following four elements: 1) the involvement of the information seeker in a dynamic situational context in direct relation with a formal IR system; 2) how to carry out such a line of investigation or performance testing – depending on the goals of research; 3) the involvement of best match retrieval algorithms directly in information seeking activities in line with other informal knowledge sources, like people; 4) the way to carry out such studies in a multi-variable environment.

With respect to novel research questions the framework proposes to investigate the distribution of (in)dependent, controlled and, hence, hidden variables associated with and between the framework components – Chapt. 8.

In relation to the *mapping capacity* function by Bunge (1967) (*iii*), the framework seems quite capable of modeling the objects and relationships of the IS&R area, and not simply summarizing the data. This function is identical to Engelbart's points outlined above (1962).

However, as a tool for providing novel data, aside from providing new hypotheses and lines of research, the cognitive IS&R framework does *not* directly produce such data. But the model, Fig. 6.8, points to empty spots or conceptualizations – for instance – in connection with the temporal relationship between the socio-organizational context and the IT settings or information objects, seen with commercial or economic views.

Regarding general scientific principles, we are aware that for comprehensive theories and frameworks to prove their fertility may take some time. However, investigations and direct testing of central phenomena and proposals of the framework are underway. We are confident that our model and theoretical proposals are general in nature and capable of meeting the criteria stipulated in Sect. 1.5.

7 Implications of the Cognitive Framework for IS&R

As our framework in Chap. 6 suggests, we are interested in a cognitive, task-based perspective on information seeking and retrieval (IS&R). This perspective puts new requirements on research in IS&R, that are not traditionally taken into account to a sufficient degree. Based on the preceding Chapters and our framework, there are five broad categories and nine classes of variables that interact in IS&R processes, here called research dimensions:

1. The Organizational Task Dimensions
- The work task dimension: the work task[1], (social) organization of work, collaboration and the system environment.
- The search task dimension, i.e., seeking and retrieval tasks, as understood in the organization.

2. The Actor Dimensions
- The actor dimension: the actor's declarative knowledge and procedural skills.
- The perceived work task dimension: the actor's perception of the work task
- The perceived search task dimension, the actor's perception of the search task including information need types regarding the task and the task performance process; emotions.

3. The Document Dimension
- The document dimension: document genres and collections in various languages and media, which may contain information relevant to the task as perceived by the actor.

4. The Algorithmic Dimensions
- The algorithmic search engine dimension: the representations of documents / information and information needs; tools and support for query formulation; matching methods.

---

[1] As in previous chapters the notion 'work task' implies also non-job-related daily-life tasks and/or interests.

- The algorithmic interface dimension: tools for visualization and presentation.

5. The Access and Interaction Dimension

- The access and interaction dimension: strategies of information access, interaction between the actor and the interface (both in social and in system contexts).

Each of the dimensions is complex, containing multiple variables, as demonstrated in Fig. 6.8. It is obvious that IS&R is performed in very diverse work and leisure situations characterized by diverse values on the variables of the broad dimensions. Consequently, also IS&R becomes quite different. In many situations, if not in the most, the actors are ignorant about IS&R – professionally mediated information retrieval being a notable but no more so frequent an exception to the contrary. Mostly the actors view IS&R instrumentally, not as a goal in itself, and want to get over with it fast. They want just to cope with the tools and practices supplying information usable for augmenting their deficient knowledge. Therefore, they may consider IS&R just a pain in the neck and use various tools for information access in uninformed and ineffective ways – from the tool designer's viewpoint.

With this perspective in mind we do not really know how well current IR systems serve their users in various situations. At least the systems have been evaluated in IR research only for some limited use scenarios, mostly excluding searchers in context with their work tasks. Current information seeking research neither provides much help in this regard. While the information seeking practices of various actor populations have been investigated, much remains still unexplored. Moreover, the majority of information seeking studies does not look at IR systems at all or not at the level of system features, interaction and support for query formulation and searching. This situation, illustrated in Fig. 7.1, sums up the sections on Limitations and Open Problems in Chaps. 3-5.

The real-life issue in IR systems design and evaluation is not whether a proposed method or tool is able to improve recall / precision by an interesting percentage with statistical significance. The real issue is whether it helps the searcher better solving the seeking and retrieval tasks (faster, with less resources, with better result quality). This has to do with learning about the search task, formulation of the request, a variety of tactics. Quite different needs (types and formulations), with corresponding found information, may serve a given work task. One source may indeed not provide all the information required. Recall and precision only become relevant *after* the need formulation. Systems for information access have a job to do *before* the actor commits on a formulation.

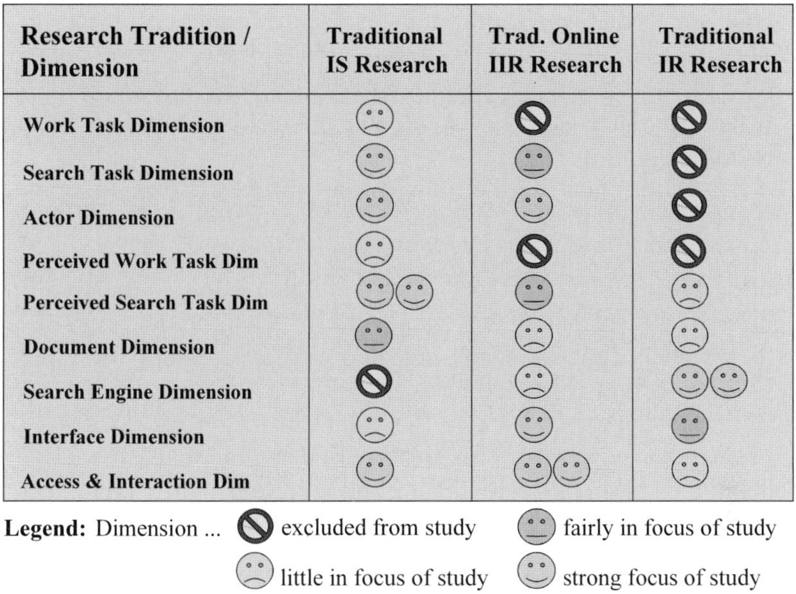

Research Tradition / Dimension	Traditional IS Research	Trad. Online IIR Research	Traditional IR Research
Work Task Dimension	☹	⊘	⊘
Search Task Dimension	☹	☹	⊘
Actor Dimension	☹	☹	⊘
Perceived Work Task Dim	☹	⊘	⊘
Perceived Search Task Dim	☹☺	☹	☹
Document Dimension	☺	☹	☹
Search Engine Dimension	⊘	☹	☹☹
Interface Dimension	☹	☹	☹
Access & Interaction Dim	☹	☹☹	☹

Legend: Dimension ... ⊘ excluded from study   ☹ fairly in focus of study

☹ little in focus of study   ☺ strong focus of study

Fig. 7.1. Foci of traditional IS&R research

Two action lines are therefore needed.

On the one hand, IR research needs to be extended to capture more context but without totally sacrificing the laboratory experimentation approach – the controlled experiments. Only by this line of action one may approach real *IR engineering*. IR engineering allows one to specify necessary IR system features by looking at the description of IR systems use in terms of tasks, users, documents and access requirements. Such features are, for instance, document and request representation, their matching, and various support tools. IR systems (the IT component) are thus seen in context of the other central components of the framework – Sect. 6.2.2.

On the other hand, current information seeking research needs to be extended both toward the task context *and* the technology, that is, towards the right and left hand sides, away from the actor, Figs. 6.1/6.8. We appreciate the efforts so far exploring information seeking in diverse task/actor contexts (see Chap. 3) but also think that the diversity of contexts is far from exhausted. Therefore lots of research is needed exploring IS&R in various task/actor contexts. Moreover, the systems context in information seeking research so far has been limited and often nonexistent. This research should reach toward system and interaction features so that communication with system design is facilitated.

Already studies limited to intra-component contexts, e.g., cognitive and linguistic representations within and between information objects or between actors, are complicated. By further adding interactive session-based features and task context, complexity increases – see Fig. 6.10, Sect. 6.2.2. This extension of variables is unavoidable but can be controlled by applying the framework.

The two action lines are the topic of the present Chapter. Figuratively, they induce a space for IS&R research to be explored and, so far, only a fraction of that space has been investigated. Sect. 7.1 discusses design and evaluation frameworks for IS&R with a starting point in the five broad categories of dimensions of the framework of Chap. 6. The ensuing sections detail each dimension into selected central variables for IS&R research. Each section is headed by an image of our framework, in order to symbolize the category in focus. For each dimension we discuss how it may provide (or capture) more context, first for the extension of IR research and then in order to broaden information seeking research. Sect. 7.7 presents the space for IS&R research and illustrates the elements research so far has covered.

7.1 Design and Evaluation Frameworks for IS&R

In this section we present the design and evaluation framework.

The Organizational Task Dimensions. This category contains two dimensions – the work task and search task dimensions. These two dimensions contain three nested levels of tasks: natural work tasks, seeking tasks and retrieval tasks (search tasks), including the corresponding task processes. The work task subsumes the search task and process and the embedded ones serve the goals of the subsuming ones. Each work task may induce several search tasks and each search task different combinations of seeking and retrieval tasks, with the former directing the latter. They may run in parallel. The complexity of each task may vary and its process (or stages) may be more or less defined in its social / organizational and cultural environment. That environment provides various systems and tools, as well as more or less articulated expectations regarding how each task should be carried out, often in collaboration with other actors.

The Actor Dimensions. The actor's *perception* and *interpretation* of the natural work task at each stage, with varying levels of cooperation with other actors – the perceived work task dimension – greatly affects her search task and information needs – the perceived search task dimension –

as do her third dimension: prior knowledge, skills and experience of procedural and declarative nature, Sect. 6.2.4. The actor's perception of the organizational and systemic environment, and her experience regarding them, together with the information needs, are the main factors in the formation of seeking tasks, the choice and use of systems and tools. The actor's perception and interpretation of various tasks are not independent – they have a history in the actor's life experiences, entire career and the present organization. Also the pressures (e.g., hurry) and emotions affect her situation, perception and interpretation.

The Document Dimension. Various types of documents may be relevant for a given work task. The documents form different genres in different contexts of generation and use, e.g., orders, invoices, applications, plans and designs, guidelines and instructions, research reports, novels and poems, photos, films, musical records – to name just a few. From a task (daily-life) viewpoint, documents in such genres may (not) have been carefully selected and organized in collections with provided access tools. They may also lie unorganized in the actor's vicinity with her personal memory as the only access tool. Documents (genres) may come in many languages and representations, as information objects – some of which being digital. They can all can be exploited for IS&R, Sects. 5.2 and 6.1.1-3.

The Algorithmic Dimensions. The two algorithmic dimensions deal 1) with the representations of documents / information and information needs, methods for matching these representations, tools and support for query formulation, and 2) tools for presentation via an interface. In addition to content, document representations may (or may not) cover explicitly their structure and layout. Likewise, information need representations may (or may not) cover explicitly their structure, content and motivation. A range of best match and exact match matching methods are available. The tools and support for query formulation may cover ontologies, thesauri, relevance feedback, and other QE/QM. Access to documents / information may be through any combination of their metadata, full content, structure and layout, as well as contextual link structures. Document / information presentation may be based on visual abstracts, best matching snippets, extracted facts or structural components – Sects. 4.5 and 6.1.3-5. The alternatives are many. What makes sense depends in a complex way on contexts, i.e., on natural and perceived works tasks, search tasks, other actors, and available information objects, systems and tools.

The Access and Interaction Dimension. Topical well-defined requests on content (only) is just one approach to document retrieval, albeit the most popular in IR research. Requests may be vaguely defined, non-topical (e.g., by journal or genre) and/or non-content-based (e.g., on given substructures). This will probably influence the nature of relevance and relevance assessment. The strategies of information access cover interaction modes like browsing and navigation in addition to retrieval. These may alternate and evolve from instance to instance of short-term interaction over session time and longitudinally due to the searcher's perception, line of progress, and learning – Sects. 6.1.4-6 and 6.2.6-8. The alternatives are many. What makes sense depends in a complex way on works tasks, search tasks, other actors, and other available systems and tools.

We will concentrate on the contextual *manifestations* that are available as evidence from these dimensions. Remote contexts, like the societal and social-organizational environment surrounding the searcher(s), will only be incorporated when its manifestations occur, e.g., in documents, as task evidence, or during interactive processes. Speculative considerations of what *might* direct people's behavior or shape the contents of information objects will not be dealt with unless manifestations can be detected. This sound attitude to research will decrease the number of variables to be dealt with in IS&R.

7.1.1 IR Research in Isolation

With a view on the five broad categories of dimensions presented above, traditional IR research is quite limited. While it has progressed considerably over the years, the context of use of IR systems has not developed sufficiently. Typically, the core of traditional IR is the Algorithmic Search Engine Dimension in close interaction with the Document Dimension. These two dimensions are contextual to one another – both as viewed from our cognitive framework and in a laboratory IR perspective. That is the reason for trying out the same retrieval algorithms on many different types of media. But much more could be done exploring that association alone.

In Sects. 1.2 and 1.3 we discussed the objections against the laboratory evaluation model made by user-centered and cognitive research – as well as the replies and justifications as they could be formulated from within the system-driven IR approach. According to Sect. 1.3 each objection can be met by sound arguments. In view of the framework, however, each of the subsequent major subsections, 7.2 – 7.6 will re-evaluate relevant limitations and assumptions of laboratory IR.

Two general observations of the counterarguments, Sect. 1.3, are quite significant: The standard focus in IR is search tasks of topical nature; and all counterarguments rely on an atomic or monadic view of IR as well as interactive IR. Each instance of retrieval (one run and result presentation) is seen in isolation. The general idea is that if the effectiveness of an IR instance can be maximized, then the entire performance over a range of instances is automatically maximized. Yet, this logic may not hold for retrieval algorithms that rely on relevance feedback, see also Fig. 6.12, Sect. 6.2.8. In laboratory IR automatic or human query modification or enhancement, based on relevance feedback, has in fact only meaning if there exists a *transfer of evidence* from instance to instance of IR. There has to be a temporal precedent from which to improve. Nevertheless, once a query has been modified, there is a new instance of single-shot IR. The system should take the modified query seriously and have as good as possible document representations and matching algorithms available. The laboratory experiments seek to develop the latter.

IR research typically considers only *retrieval tasks.* Moreover, these tasks are most often (a) purely topical, (b) content-only, (c) well-defined, (d) static, and (e) exhaustive retrieval tasks: One should find as many documents as possible matching the well-defined static topical need irrespective of document quality (binary topical relevance) and document overlaps. When designing and evaluating IR systems to serve such tasks one should identify the real-life seeking tasks that give rise to such retrieval tasks and their frequency, Fig. 7.2. One should also identify alternative types of retrieval tasks, e.g., non-topical, non-content or structural, weakly defined, dynamic, and non-exhaustive – and various combinations. These have received much less attention in IR research.

Focus on the standard type of retrieval task is justified if (a) it clearly is the most frequent type in real life, and (b) by solving such tasks well all other types of retrieval tasks become easy to solve. Both points are at least questionable – perhaps incorrect while nobody knows the answers yet. Therefore IR should look into the non-standard retrieval tasks.

Still, one may claim the standard focus justified if the study of the alternatives would not make any difference in the design on IR systems. Several of the objections and responses of Sect. 1.3 culminate at this point – in the defense of the laboratory model. What are IR systems? – Algorithms for the representation and matching of documents and requests? Or tools for solving human information seeking tasks, contributing to work task performance? More fundamentally, what *is* IR as a discipline about? – About the algorithms for the standard retrieval task? Or about solving human information seeking problems through computers, with a focus on information represented in documents, as opposed to knowledge personally possessed by humans, and to data or collections of facts. If IR is about the algorithms only, the responses to objections in Sect. 1.3 may be justified – but with the exception hinted at above. We believe however, based on our cognitive framework, that IR should have a much broader focus than the focus on representation and matching of documents and requests.

7.1.2 Information Seeking Research in Isolation

Information seeking research was over the years often criticized for uselessness, Sect. 3.3. Those working in the area have not been very critical anymore in the nineties but – we believe – the sentiment has been, and still is, shared by many working in information retrieval. One should therefore consider the motivations of the study of information seeking. In principle, the motivations, and benefits, may lie in (a) theoretically understanding information seeking, (b) empirically describing information seeking in various contexts, and (c) providing support to the design of information systems and information management.

Developing *theoretical understanding* of a domain is a necessary task for any discipline – and why this is important may be read in Sect. 1.5. An essential issue is the definition of the domain. It should cover a meaningful system of phenomena that supports explanation and understanding. The theoretical understanding of information seeking clearly has advanced in the 1990's as the models show, discussed in Chap. 3. Taken together they suggest a perspective covering phenomena from information systems and their design, through information access by various processes to work tasks (or other activities). The focus of theoretical analysis, however, has been in the *seeking process*: its stages, actors, access strategies, and sources. Work tasks and information (retrieval) systems have received less theoretical attention.

Developing *empirical understanding* of phenomena within the domain is also necessary for a discipline. Theoretical understanding must be grounded on observables. Otherwise it turns into speculation. Information seeking phenomena in various contexts are understood, explained and predicted by having theoretically justified findings on work and seeking tasks and their context. With a few exceptions, the empirical findings concentrate on the seeking processes, with less attention to work or daily-life tasks and information (retrieval) systems. They are often quite descriptive, Sect. 3.3.2. The process oriented modern approach in Information Seeking has covered several empirical domains in, e.g., Social Science and Engineering, and some work task contexts, e.g., student information seeking for a term paper or research proposal. However, many remain unexplored. This is only healthy for a research area.

Supporting information *management* and information *systems design* may be the weakest contribution of Information Seeking. This may be understood through Fig. 7.1. Studies in Information Seeking rarely include information (retrieval) system design features in their study settings – features that the information (retrieval) system designers find relevant and deal with. In such a situation the research results cannot communicate to systems design. The worlds do not touch[2]. While our understanding of work task requirements and effects on information seeking has advanced, the understanding on how to derive and apply design criteria for information (retrieval) systems has not advanced correspondingly.

These considerations suggest that research in Information Seeking should be extended both toward work tasks and toward information (retrieval) systems (or technology) – see Fig. 7.2. Having its roots in Library Science user studies, Information Seeking has come a long way toward research that is no more revolving around the users of a single institution. However, information seeking as such is the study of *something-in-between* and not a theoretically justified area in isolation. Paying due attention to the goal of augmenting work task performance and alike daily-life phenomena (Fig. 7.3) as well as the available technologies, makes Information Seeking much alike the disciplines of Information Management, Information Systems, Organizational Design, etc. One may loose one's independence but gain a better ability to communicate across disciplinary boundaries.

7.1.3 The IS&R Design and Evaluation Framework

Basically, we approach IS&R design and evaluation as embedded contexts of retrieval, seeking and work tasks/interests – Fig. 7.2 – an extension of Fig. 1.1. IR serves the goals of seeking, and information seeking the goals of the work or daily-life task. The same person symbol in all the three contexts denotes the same or another actor(s) performing the work task, the seeking task and the retrieval task – interpreting the tasks, performing the process and interpreting the outcome – possibly resulting in task reformulation in each context. The person symbol in IR context signifies the possibility of applying human relevance feedback during a traditional two-run IR experiment as well as real interactive IR over several short-term interactions. Possible evaluation criteria in each context are given: A – D. The nine dimensions of variables outlined above are rewrapped in Fig. 7.2.

De-contextualized, IR may be designed and evaluated in its own context – the laboratory IR approach. In this confined context the evaluation meas-

---

[2] In principle, it may also be that IR system designers are busy with wrong variables or features.

measures are the traditional ones, recall and precision, or novel measures discussed in Sect. 4.10. In addition, one may assess the system's efficiency along various dimensions during IR interaction, the quality of information (documents) retrieved, and the quality of the search process like searcher's effort (time), satisfaction, usability measures and various types of moves/tactics employed.

However, IR belongs to the searcher's information seeking context where it is but one means of gaining access to required information. This context provides a variety of information sources/systems and communication tools, all with different properties that may be used based on the seeker's discretion and in a concerted way. The design and evaluation of these sources/systems and tools needs to take their *joint usability*, quality of information and process into account. One may ask what is the contribution of an IR system at the end of a seeking process – over time, over seeking tasks, and over seekers. Since the knowledge sources, systems and tools are *not* used in isolation they should not be designed nor evaluated in isolation. They affect each other's utility in context.

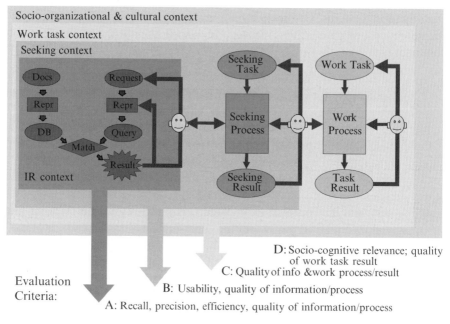

Fig. 7.2. Nested contexts and evaluation criteria for task-based IS&R (extension of Kekäläinen and Järvelin 2002b)

An obvious counterargument is that there are too many seeking contexts with too many possible combinations of systems and tools: The design and evaluation of IR systems becomes unmanageable. Therefore it is best to stick to the tradition of design and evaluation. If one does not know more than one's own unsystematic recollection of personal IR system use, such design and evaluation demands may be of tall order, indeed. However, even limited knowledge on real IS&R may reveal typical uses, strengths and weaknesses of various tools and systems – and how their users perceive them. This provides a better basis for design than de-contextualized standard assumptions and measures. If automobile designers would behave alike, they would focus on the engines (e.g. horsepower, acceleration) no matter whether they design a sports car, pick-up or a truck! A nice parallel may be observed in the critique of Information Seeking research by Dervin and Nilan (1986) – see Sect. 3.1.2 – *mutatis mutandis*.

Finally, information seeking seldom is an end in itself but rather serves a work task (or other interest). The real impact of information seeking and retrieval is its contribution to the work task process (e.g., effort, time) and the quality of the result. Therefore, in the end, IS&R should be designed and evaluated for their utility in the work task context. Again, an obvious counterargument is that there are too many work task contexts that are too weakly related to IR. The design and evaluation of IR systems, one might argue, thus becomes unmanageable and cannot learn from all too remote task requirements. Therefore, the counterargument goes, it is best to close one's eyes and stick to the tradition of design and evaluation. However, even limited knowledge on real work tasks may reveal typical uses, strengths and weaknesses of various tools and systems – and how their real users perceive them. Moreover, many work task requirements are relevant to IR design. For example, by looking at work task situations one may learn about the typical handles actors have available for accessing relevant information/documents.

Modern work is increasingly knowledge work. Access to recorded information or human sources is essential. Task requirements must affect the design of information access. As stated in Sect. 1.1 on motivation for this book, means of access and sources increasingly become electronically networked and formalized in systems. This integration of e-generation, e-access, and e-use makes IR engineering complex – but not unmanageable. The question for IR engineering is: *which* additional *variables* from the immediate contexts does one wish to include in a *controlled* relationship with one another. The use of only one variable, as commonly attempted in laboratory IR, is insufficient and pursues only a limited case of IR.

It is not just retrieval that matters, information systems also need to support reading (watching) as well as document processing and information use.

7.2 Variables of the Organizational Task Dimensions

Work tasks have many variables, some of which were listed in Sect. 3.1.3. There are many work task types relevant for IS&R. They cause different kinds of information requirements and thus seeking and retrieval tasks *by actors*, and because they affect information use. The ultimate goal of IS&R is to augment work task performance and fulfillment.

Fig. 7.3 illustrates means and ends in task performance augmentation. Its upper part is inspired by D.C. Engelbart's (1962) framework for knowledge work augmentation, where a human is augmented by language, artifacts and methods in which (s)he has been trained.[3]

In Fig. 7.3, information seeking is somewhat remote from the work task – with document retrieval even more remote and behind many decisions. In line with Fig. 7.2 this underlines our view that IS&R belongs to a context in real life. The distance however does not make IR independent of work tasks – it needs to contribute to the work task, which sets a number of situational requirements on IR.

The work task type space hardly has been explored in Information Seeking and IR. The following list proposes some central *work task variables* relevant for IS&R (see also Sect. 3.1.3):

- *Work Task Structure:* Unstructured vs. structured tasks; novel vs. repeated tasks; tasks with no vs. many open constraints.
- *Work Task Strategies and Practices:* Tasks with vs. without professionally / organizationally delineated practices (solving methods and procedures).
- *Work Task Granularity, Size and Complexity:* Sheer size in person-months; duration; granularity in a subtask hierarchy; task complexity.

---

[3] Engelbart (1963) proposes his framework for *augmenting human intellect.* This is the ultimate goal of *instrumental* IS&R no matter whether it takes place in professional or leisure contexts. This is a strong legitimization to our *cognitive* viewpoint – IS&R should augment human intellect – in context.

- *Work Task Dependencies:* Dependencies within task and between tasks; dependencies within one actor and between actors; dependencies within and between organizations; all dependences are also of *temporal* contextual nature.
- *Work Task Requirements:* Information intensiveness; information requirements and preferences;
- *Work Task Domain and Context:* Diverse domains, e.g., a scientific discipline or profession; professional level, e.g., research, administrative planning, vocational, lay/hobby contexts, e.g., a given organization and unit, team culture, home or club, etc., and their development over time.

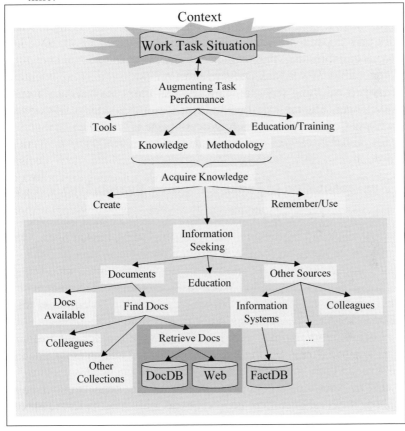

Fig. 7.3. Augmenting work task performance – perhaps by IS&R

In this multidimensional space actually only a few cells and dimensions have been investigated empirically in relation to IS&R. Exploration centers around complexity studies in public administration, Sect. 3.1.4, and specific work task types in selected environments, like information seeking or online/Web IR associated with student term papers and research proposal development, Sects. 3.1.4, 5.4 and 5.5.

(Un)structured work tasks are related to (socio-organizational) practices and strategies. Tasks and solving procedures may be heavily documented (or not at all) owing to legislation or other external or internal constraints – like in the case of local GLP (Good Laboratory Practice) guidelines (see the relationship of work task and documents in Fig. 5.7, Sect. 5.7.3). In such cases we possess objective relevance assessment tools and features of socio-cognitive nature. Obviously such tasks may be of diverse complexity and granularity. Work tasks and their contextual features may hence produce manifestations in information objects to be explored during IS&R.

Work task dependencies, requirements, and practices are highly context dependent variables, i.e., they vary according to organizational and cultural environment: the Work Task Domain and Context.

Methods for dealing with the work task variables are basically from the Social Sciences. The relationships to Information/Knowledge Management research and Cognitive Systems Engineering are evident. See further Sects. 3.1.3, 5.1, and 8.2.

7.2.1 Representation of Tasks for IS&R – Search Task Variables

With reference to Sect. 6.2.3 work tasks, as well as their sub-tasks, can lead to physical and intellectual activities, including search tasks. Work tasks may be represented for IS&R through their *perception by actors* and translated into seeking and/or retrieval tasks, with the information need as the central element – Fig. 6.11. Work tasks therefore affect access strategies that are relevant (Sect. 7.6). Moreover, especially in end-user searching, the work task is permanently present as perceived in the actor's mind during seeking and retrieval processes, under redefinition, and affecting the modification of the seeking and retrieval tasks. Search tasks are represented through their content (the kinds of information need, see below) and in IR also by relevance criteria. But other relevance aspects may be added – people as sources, document genres, collections, substructures, isness attributes, searching exhaustivity, allocated recourses, etc. These deal with non-topical aspects of relevance, for instance pertinence, and the logistics of seeking information.

Search Task Variables/Characteristics. Search tasks have similar variables and characteristics as work tasks above. Information systems and information management tools capture representations of known frequent search tasks and some of their characteristics. When actors engage in search tasks they reflect upon these characteristics and thus construct their perceived search tasks. This is a bridge to the searcher and information need dimensions, Sect. 7.3.

According to Sect. 6.2.3 work tasks and search tasks can be 1) *natural* manifestations carried out in real life by an actor; 2) *simulated* situations designed for IS&R research by involving a specified but invented scenario or cover story; or 3) *assigned* requests for information meant to representing information needs, like 'topics' in TREC-like IR experiments.

In the first case the search tasks are also natural and realistic with real information needs. Evidence from the actor exist but is quite unpredictable and the problem for research is to control the variables involved. However, *known patterns* of search tasks and task execution associated to the natural setting under investigation may ease the research setting. In information seeking studies one of the research goals is to detect such patterns, see Sects. 3.1.4 and 5.3-5.5.

In the second case the cover story acts as a controlled variable of context – but with a (known) semantic openness. The latter may trigger more predictable information needs from the actor and hence evidence in the form of rather naturalistic requests and other task descriptions, see Sect. 5.9. The simulated case is feasible in information seeking studies as well as in interactive IR experiments.

The third case does not operate with a work task at all. But there exists a request manifestation in a highly controlled manner. If assigned in an interactive IS&R investigation such search task representations are rather artificial. As a consequence investigations ought to study a *realistic variety* of such assigned topics in order to observe patterns and characteristics of search task performance. A similar approach would improve the understanding of how search algorithms and engines perform with different request types within the laboratory framework for IR, Sect. 4.11, although the retrieval task undertakings clearly are quite limited.

7.2.2 IR Research Questions: Capturing Task Types and their Representations

When designing and evaluating IR systems to serve retrieval tasks one should identify the real-life seeking tasks that give rise to such tasks and their frequency, Fig. 7.2. One should also look into non-standard retrieval tasks, e.g., of non-topical nature or non-exhaustive. These have received much less attention in IR research, probably owing to the constant changes of task patterns caused by IT development, such as recently the Web.

A broader context for IR is the information seeking context – Figs. 5.2 and 7.2. IR research and engineering would benefit from learning about real IS contexts, because thus one may:

- Learn what kinds of *seeking tasks* occur in real life and what handles for access to information are available in various situations, also over time;
- Learn what kinds of *systems and tools* for information access various actors use, how they use them and how they perceive their strengths and weaknesses; what is the access network, what is the practice of its use;
- Learn about the kinds and strength of the actor's current perceptions and *knowledge states*; IS&R knowledge; work task and domain knowledge; declarative and procedural knowledge;
- Learn about the *actors' learning*, how seeking tasks are redefined (dynamically) and what compromises the actors make when seeking tasks cannot be readily solved;
- Learn what *weaknesses* there are in current practices that might be alleviated by redesign or through new systems and tools.

Research Questions. Systems and tools for information access are not used in isolation and therefore their design and adaptation should be aware of the *collection* of systems and tools. Finally, IR research would benefit from learning about real work and daily-life task contexts, the right hand side, Figs. 6.1, 6.8 and 7.2, because, after all, the whole point of real-life IR is to contribute to the *work task* process – to augment task performance.

Through the task context IR research would in addition become about:

- The kinds of *work processes* and their information requirements that occur in real life and what handles for access and acquisition of information are available in various situations – affected by the structured nature and repetition of work tasks, search tasks and the characteristics of the actors;
- The nature of *complexity* and attributes of routine and normal work tasks vs. more complex genuine cases;
- Which kinds of *information requirements* might be suitable for the IR type of access? Which are more effectively served by which retrieval models, or even better by other approaches? The required adaptation of IR systems to the work task context, the organization and system environments;
- The actors' *learning and cognitive* styles, i.e., how work tasks are dynamically redefined and what compromises the actors make when work tasks or search tasks cannot be readily solved;

- Learn what weaknesses there are in current practices that might be alleviated by *work task redesign* in the organization or through new systems and tools.

Mixing carefully the work and search task lists of variables one might develop typical research questions – with the above research goals in mind. For instance, one might ask: what kind of evidence can be extracted from work task, seeking or retrieval task processes performed by actors in organization X – for the purpose of supporting source selection and query modification? – Or: when during a search task execution are the actors most convinced of source relevance/usefulness to the task? – And: in what way does task complexity and repetition/novelty influence that conviction? – For the purpose of assessment of the certainty of relevance judgments.

When work tasks have been involved in IR test designs they have so far been bound by the test collections (mainly news) and the test persons (often students), Sects. 5.4 and 5.6. Therefore these work tasks simply *do not* represent the variability of real-life work tasks in which IR is or could be used and beneficial.

7.2.3 Information Seeking Research: Capturing Work Task Context

Information seeking has been studied in many contexts (see Chap. 3), but without carefully analyzing specific work tasks. Job level analyses do not go into specifics on how to augment human task performance. They are predominantly descriptive on the application of sources and actor behavior. It is important to investigate the multidimensional space along and across dimensions and their variables, not just phenomena in specific cells.

Fig. 3.9 suggested that work task goals, processes, available information and information seeking, as well as information systems interact strongly. This means that redesigning information access and systems affect work task performance through its actors – both processes and goals – and vice versa.

In the following, and over all the ensuing information seeking sections, we shall discuss two *sample work tasks* in socio-organizational contexts.

Case A is a professional one in public administration. It is a frequent structured task at a city social welfare office, where a social worker makes a decision on social benefits based on a client's application. There is an established practice on how to perform the task. Such decisions are made on a daily basis and typically require 15 to 30 minutes to conclude. The task is information intensive and dependent on earlier decisions regarding other clients, the same client, his/her other current applications and current policies and budget.

Case B is an once-in-a-lifetime project on writing a book on the cognitive viewpoint in IS&R with loose ideas of what to cover, what to contribute, and what the result would be (except for lots of printed pages). To begin with, this task is unstructured, has many open constraints, there is no mapped out process through the task, the process might be a couple of person years in size but is heavily dependent on other tasks by the same actors – tasks which contribute to the book project or vice versa, or just consume the actors' resources. Moreover, one's working on one bit of text has an impact on the other's work on another bit and one's own earlier and later bits. The task is heavily information intensive, a scholarly task in Information Science and takes place at two different universities and various meeting places around the globe. A major part of the task lies within the actors' own discretion.

Aspects of the Case A, and alike information seeking and behavioral phenomena, were originally studied by Wilson (1981) – however not with the notion of work task in mind – Sects. 3.1.2-3.1.4. Case B-type cases are more rarely studied due to their longitudinal and complex nature.

With respect to the seeking tasks, and thus also the embedded retrieval tasks, there is a multidimensional space of combinations of variables according to the work and search task dimensions discussed above. Many locations in that space have been investigated, at least analytically, but not all have been empirically explored. In our two sample cases the seeking tasks are quite different.

In *Case A* the seeking task is to find information on prior benefits paid to the client at the welfare office. This seeking task is well-defined, routine, repeatedly performed, factual, specific, simple, typically stable, guided by an organizational practice, and served by an information system. Prior payment decision documents are retrieved when the client's personal ID is entered into the system. Similarly, all applications by the client with their appendixes have been scanned into the information system and are retrievable by the client ID number – as a 'known item/data element' search. The seeking task is a necessary one – the information *must* be found – at a professional level and has no dependencies with other seeking tasks. Here the information systems and the procedures have been adapted to the work task.

In *Case B* the whole search task consisted of hundreds of smaller semi-independent seeking and retrieval tasks, which were impossible to predict at the outset. The most simple tasks were well-defined, specific 'known item' searches and often repeated, e.g., "find Gary Marchionini's home page" or "find the document by Beaulieu and others (1997), entitled

'Okapi at TREC–5", and sometimes factual, e.g., "how many test topics are there in the INEX 2001 test collection?". However, the higher order information acquisition tasks were often muddled and topical, much more general, complex and dynamic, e.g., "Who in hell has written about clustering and can we relate that to the cognitive viewpoint?" Yet, such tasks were not executed as topical searches. To begin with, one perhaps has a couple of author names, which one might try in the ACM Digital Library – or go to their homepages. Perhaps one had a rough idea of a year when one of the authors might have presented something at the SIGIR Conference (if not every year) – to check the SIGIR Conference CDs or the proceedings on the shelves. Citation chaining tactics came into use, based on reference lists in known items (rarely by means of online retrieval). There was no well-defined practice on how to find the information or when to stop. One had to repeatedly find and evaluate ("Is this relevant? Does it make sense? Can we use it?") whether a reasonable body of literature was covered to make an assessment and synthesis. There were perhaps not many dependencies between the seeking tasks but still one was stumbling on documents on other active but suspended work and seeking tasks when working on one. These seeking tasks were in the scholarly domain (Information/Computer Science). The information (retrieval) systems were *not* designed with these particular seeking tasks in mind, but were generic and flexible enough to be usable.

In relation to both cases, work task-based information seeking research would profit from asking about the variety of such routine tasks, their attributes, etc. in order to be able to specify some system components with the intention to augment the total of task performance in that office.

7.3 Actor and Perceived Task Dimensions of Variables

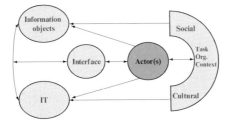

Cognitive actors performing tasks have several dimensions relating their knowledge and experience to the tasks – the historic context – and related to the situation they perceive at a given point in time. The following central variables belong to the Actor Dimension. They are concerned with the seeking actor as an individual or team:

- *Actor's Domain Knowledge:* Deep vs. no declarative knowledge; deep vs. no procedural knowledge;
- *Actor's IS&R Knowledge:* Deep vs. no declarative knowledge; deep vs. no procedural knowledge;
- *Actor's Experience on Work Task:* Experienced vs. inexperienced actor in work task execution and problem solving; temporal aspects: work task history and patterns;
- *Actor's Experience on Search Task:* Experienced vs. inexperienced actor in search task execution; temporal aspects: search task history and patterns;
- *Actor's Stage in Work Task Execution:* The actor's perception of *where* in the process of solving the work task or associated problem(s);
- *Actor's Perception of Socio-Organizational-Cultural Context:* The actor's interpretation of circumstances may (or may not) differ from the common practice or paradigm;
- *Sources of Difficulty:* too many open constraints, insufficient information basis, lack of productive ideas, lack of productive methods;
- *Actor's motivation and emotional state:* passionate vs. ignorant actors; level of uncertainty and confusion; degree of clarification, relief and satisfaction.

Based on the knowledge types of declarative and procedural nature, Sect. 6.2.4, combined with the level of knowledge/experience on work and search tasks we may construct a 16-cell matrix of various actor types – Table 7.1. This matrix extends the more simple one published by Ingwersen (1992, p.142) on identical matters. From the above list we apply the actor's domain and IS&R knowledge variables as well as the experiences on tasks. The remaining variables may further contribute to detailing the matrix if required, e.g., by involving the motivation variable.

The actual number of different cells, Table 7.1, depends on the definitions of the range of experience, from deep to no previous knowledge. One might, for instance, define an *expert* as having all the knowledge types (1-4) currently available; an *IR specialist* would then possess the types (3-4) and a *domain expert* the types (1-2). A *non-expert* then equals types (13-16). Definition problems concern the 'shallow' and 'surface' knowledge levels. According to our discussion in Sect. 6.2.5 on task complexity, shallow knowledge/experience would entail the possession of some procedural experience but only little or none declarative knowledge, since that kind of skills are first to be lost by memory.

Table 7.1. Types of seeking actors according to knowledge types and levels of experience

Knowledge Types/*Levels*	*Deep*	*Shallow*	*Surface*	*None*
Declarative Task Knowledge	1	5	9	13
Procedural Task Knowledge	2	6	10	14
Declarative IS&R Knowledge	3	7	11	15
Procedural IS&R Knowledge	4	8	12	16

This means that an *experienced work task solver* would be equal to a domain expert; a *casual work task solver* would be found in cell (6) with cell (5) quite empty; an *inexperienced work task solver* in cell (9), with cell (10) empty; and a *novice work task solver* equaling a non-expert, cells (13-14). Similarly, for *casual searchers* cell (8) knowledge on general seeking processes is available whilst for *inexperienced searchers* only some source data is left as knowledge and procedural skills are lost (cell 12). *Novice searchers* then occupy the cells (15-16). Naturally, other definitions might be made, but the matrix still holds as such.

Actor's Perceived Work Task. A second dimension of variables consists of the Actor's Perceived Work Task. The variables are the same as for natural work tasks (WT), Sect. 7.2, i.e., perceptions of: WT structure; WT strategies and practices; WT granularity, size and complexity; WT dependencies; WT requirements; and WT domain and context.

The actor's perceived work and search tasks have all the dimensions and variables discussed in the preceding sections. For example, a structured task by organizational practices may be chaotic to a novice actor – an expert may not consciously recognize all aspects of a task, a novice may commit errors by neglecting aspects of a task and by including unnecessary aspects (Kuhlthau 1999; Kuhlthau and Tama 2001). These dimensions form a multidimensional space and several among them have been explored in IS&R. However, it has not been exhausted.

Actor's Perceived Search Task Dimension of Variables. When an actor perceives and performs a work task, its requirements induce information needs. The eight central information need types, their degree of specificity and the Label Effect, discussed Sects. 6.2.6-7, provide potentials for producing contextual *evidence* during interaction that may be applicable in IS&R. These potentials depend on the type and quality of the searcher's current knowledge state and the kind of information sought for (her/his goal). The needs translate into perceived search tasks, i.e., perceived seeking tasks embedding retrieval tasks that may be classified along the following variables:

- *Perceived Information Need Content:* the search task content – the representation of the information desired – with characteristics as in Table 6.2.
- *Perceived Search Task Structure/Type:* Well defined vs. muddled tasks; novel vs. repeated tasks; factual or verificative (known item or data element) search tasks vs. topical tasks.
- *Perceived Search Task Strategies and Practices:* Tasks with professionally / organizationally defined practices vs. tasks without them; searching styles and modes; search tactics.
- *Search Task Specificity and Complexity:* Specific vs. general search tasks; simple vs. complex tasks; granularity in a subtask hierarchy.
- *Search Task Dependencies*: Dependencies within and between search tasks; dependencies within one searching actor and between actors; all dependences are also of *temporal* contextual nature.
- *Search Task Stability:* Stable vs. dynamic tasks.
- *Search Task Domain and Context:* Diverse domains, e.g., a scientific discipline or profession; professional level, e.g., scholarly vs. professional vs. popular information; variety of contexts, e.g., a given organization and unit, team culture, home or club, and their development over time.

Consequently, we may have eight quite distinct search task procedures; each one in accordance with an information need type, e.g., a 'known item search task procedure'. How to perform them would depend on the surrounding contexts.

Further, we may encounter the degree of *articulation capability* of the actor of his/her work task – information need – search task requirements. In line with this variable the *specificity* of the articulated information need, the request, is of importance to IR research, as well as information seeking studies – Sects. 6.2.6-7. To the former, the captured specificity level may indicate the certainty of relevance assessments made by the actor during IR interaction:

- The more specific the request features the more certain the relevance assessments (if the actor works in her professional domain).

From the interaction partner's point-of-view the articulation capability reflects the reliability of the assessments. To information seeking studies the level of articulation is important owing to capability to carry out social interaction with human sources.

7.3.1 Polyrepresentation of the Actor's Cognitive Space

IR research and Information Seeking may profit from capturing a variety of cognitive evidence from the searcher during IR or social interaction. Like for the information space the principle of polyrepresentation may be applied to the cognitive space, Sect. 5.2.3. In accordance with the knowledge and perception variables outlined above for searchers, the following kinds of evidence are *potentially* available at any given point in time:

- Perceived work task description.
- Work task execution stage description – current problem statement.
- Perceived search task/information need – a series of requests.
- Current domain knowledge state.
- Experience on work task execution.
- Current emotional state.
- Relevance assessments – session-based and longitudinal.
- Current IS&R knowledge state and experience.

Work task descriptions, problem statements, request formulations, and relevance assessments are causally related to the perceived work task. During actual IS&R they might be used separately or in combination owing to their relationships. In that way they supply much more evidence concerned with the search tasks than the request formulation alone. Each of the articulations may be used algorithmically to construct polyrepresentative overlaps of information objects, see further Sect. 7.5, and to query modification.

The various cognitive and emotional representations above belong to the Request Model Builder functionality in the Mediator Model (Ingwersen 1992) – Sect. 4.8.1.

7.3.2 IR Research: Capturing Evidence on Searchers and Information Needs

Evidence on Searchers. Most IR research goes without users in the laboratory setting. When searchers have been unavoidable in test settings, they have sometimes been *simulated* – for example in relevance feedback experiments an algorithmically simulated user is expected to recognize top scoring relevant documents in the retrieval result.

Real actors (searchers) are however important for IR research because their context varies: task stage, learning, knowledge, articulation capability, and motivation. Due to their current *stage* and (lack of) *learning* they may be more or less *knowledgeable* regarding the domain of their work or daily-life task, regarding suitable IR processes, and regarding the (collections of) documents and information they wish to access. This affects their capability to *articulate* their information needs as requests, to understand and assess the retrieval results, and their ability to *manage* the retrieval process. They may also be more or less *motivated* in their whole work task (interest) or the retrieval task. This affects the efforts they may invest in searching.[4]

Many types of actors may be formed along these variables. Depending on the type, different types of IR systems or system components may be preferred and different types of support may be helpful. IR-ignorant and unmotivated actors may prefer to use, and benefit from, high degree of automation and may not want to learn about the process, even less guide it.

The actor/searcher categories employed in IR research are far from exhausted. When users have been involved in IIR experiments, they have been of limited types, mainly students that are easily available. Sometimes random sub-sets of library clients are used – like in the OKAPI project, Sect. 5.6.1. In field studies, information specialists and students have been used. Recently, some specific actor groups, like children, have been studied for their information access and system use in their real-life situations – Sect. 7.2.5. This is welcome progress. It is important to involve actors of several types in diverse task-based retrieval situations.

However, in general there is much room in (I)IR research to look into different types of actors as users of IR systems. The response to Objection 1 in Sect. 1.3 says that users are not needed for testing the algorithms for the limited task the algorithms are intended for, i.e., retrieval and ranking of topical documents. Human actors are nevertheless invaluable for designing and evaluating IR systems that contribute to their seeking processes and work tasks; and human actors actually act as *relevance assessors* during laboratory IR experiments. This owes to the invention of the Cranfield model – with all the cognitive-emotional implications that follow.

---

[4] It may be reasonable to use simulated users when investigating in a general common sense domain of news collections using binary topical retrieval. However, in professional domains and with varying searcher knowledge it is questionable to assume that all users would identify a given relevant document as relevant.

Actors and actor types may be modeled and represented for IR systems, as the IR expert systems attempted, Sect. 4.8. However, it is more important to look into different actor types, their *current* task knowledge, and their information behavior in a systematic and controlled way. *Request and task modeling* is more central to IR than general user modeling. From a work task perspective there is no general user model. Even a single person is more or less experienced, depending on the particular task performed.

Evidence on Information Needs. The standard IR test requests are wordy, well-defined topical requests. As in TREC they may contain detailed *guidelines* as to what kinds of documents are relevant and what not. Some of the requests are very *specific*, referring to a particular person and/or event. Others are more *general*. Further, some state a *complex* relationship between several concepts or facets while others remain *simple* in this regard. From these features we may form six dimensions of IR requests: (1) well vs. vaguely defined; (2) generic vs. specific; (3) simple vs. complex; and (4) short vs. wordy requests. Further dimensions are (5) real vs. assigned information needs, and (6) articulated vs. implicit needs (e.g., due to the Label Effect). Because they have not been systematically identified by type, retrieval performance regarding many types has not been sufficiently explored.

7.3.3 The Assumption of Information Need Invariability

With the dimensions and variables of seeking actors, their knowledge and information need types and requests in mind, *ready for capture*, the standard laboratory IR approach must move beyond its own invariability and independency assumptions. There are three such assumptions underlying IR: 1) A searcher's information need is static throughout retrieval – also during short-term and session-based IR interaction; 2) features of information objects are independent of one another; and 3) relevance assessments are done independently of one another. The latter two assumptions are discussed in Sects. 7.5.2 and 7.6.1.

When analyzing these assumptions in the context of IIR and Information Seeking they look quite unrealistic. Already Robertson (1977) pointed to the dimension (and question) of realism of the second and third assumption and Belkin, Oddy and Brooks questioned the first one in the ASK hypothesis discussion (1982a-b). Analyses of some of their problematic aspects were carried out by, for instance, Swanson (1986) on relevance. However, according to Sect. 1.3 each objection against the degree of realism in IR can be met by sound arguments – if one is interested in the design of algorithms only.

Notwithstanding, the three assumptions are intermingled and deeply founded in Salton's (1968) particular conception of information, including to an extent Shannon (and Weaver 1949), namely that information *is* the generated, transmitted, or recorded *signs*, see Sect. 2.2.4. In a system-driven view information is definitely not seen as resulting from a cognitive interpretation. Features in both information objects as well as in information requests are hence objective and tangible, representing meaning or sense (of their authors) and *functionally reflecting* the underlying information need, problem or task situation. Following a Saltonian view, an uncertain, muddled or well-defined information need may indeed exist (as may a perceived work and search task in the mind of a searcher) but only its manifestation counts for IS&R. If seekers are vague, retrieval (or seeking) is vague. Regarding the invariability assumption of information needs this implies that:

- A request formulation does represent the underlying need (or work task) in absolute terms;
- The seeking actor does not learn anything over instances of IR – not even during periods of person-to-person information seeking – because otherwise the information need might change and the original relevance assessments become invalid. Since the actor does learn, the assessments are invalid.
- Whether indeed the information need changes or just its formulation over instances of IIR is all the same to the algorithm in its isolated step-by-step mode, since
- Each instance of IR is independent from other instances – they are context-free.

When is the assumption unrealistic? It is always unrealistic as a description and prescription of what happens in the real life. In other words, the assumption is always unrealistic when human actors are involved directly during IR interaction and information seeking.

It is our view however that the invariability and the independency assumptions are definitively reasonable in an IT and IS&R environment dominated entirely by (artificial, digital) *representations* of perceptions of human actors, as in the original IR laboratory model, Fig. 4.1. Only a human recipient *may* – if capable – counterweight the cognitive 'free fall' of the generated and communicated message and hence reconstruct (parts of) its meaning at high levels of information processing – Sect. 2.2.3. As long as the recipient processing device is only representing (the perception of) a human actor, the algorithmic processing commonly stays at the monadic/structural levels[5]. For the algorithm the explicit representation, however vague it may be, is the only one to act on.

However, in its extended version, Fig. 1.1, the laboratory IR evaluation model directly depicts one human actor forming a part of a feedback loop in order to initiate a second retrieval attempt – probably with an altered request or query. Likewise, a second hidden actor is constituted by the 'relevance assessment' representations providing the recall base for evaluation. In this way the laboratory model involuntarily embraces a cognitive explanation of the interactive retrieval process: *Somebody* has actively to supply evidence as to the relevance of found objects to make the model work – although the processing of the search engine itself stays at monadic/lexical or structural/syntactic levels. Indeed, even the original evaluation model pre-supposes a human (cognitive) assessor, Fig. 4.1.

Consequently, there exist an inherent mismatch within the laboratory IR evaluation model between its context-free independency and invariability assumptions and the way it actually is seen to function by means of an active cognitive actor, at least in its extended IIR version. From a cognitive stand it matters if the searcher changes information need perception during interactive IR: then one cannot assign the *same weights* to features in objects already judged relevant a few instances of interaction ago – e.g., during session-based interaction. Even if the original information need is maintained by the searcher one would expect some development over the sequence of retrieval runs, e.g., particular information objects are seen less relevant since they have already been read or evaluated. Hence, retrieval models maintaining equal weighting over retrieval time seem unrealistic. See also Sect. 5.6.2. If the information need indeed develops over the session and the searchers, at each instance, enter the *full* query instead of relevance feedback then the assumption works.

Thus, the third and fourth implications outlined above are the most unrealistic ones – even in a laboratory setting. The only conceivable cases of stability of information needs are found depicted in Table 6.3, Sect. 6.2.7, depending on work task complexity.

7.3.4 Information Seeking Research: Capturing Evidence from Searchers' Cognitive Space

Capturing evidence from searchers' cognitive space is commonly the central trait of information seeking studies. However, as already mentioned,

---

[5] We may perhaps push processing to a contextual/semantic level under our framework in the future.

the seeking research has rarely dealt with seekers' perceptions of work and daily-life tasks – although many studies are done in various contexts. We outline what the cases A and B might be shown to capture from actor characteristics and information need types.

In *Case A* the actor is a Master in Social Science, majoring in Social Policy Studies, and has 15 years of experience in the welfare office in work with the clients. He may be considered an experienced expert in welfare benefit decisions and in the associated information seeking – see Table 7.1. The current work task and information need are well defined, rather stable and present no difficulties and, while not being passionate after 15 years, he knows how to do the work well.

In *Case B* the poor guys writing their book are experts in some Information Science sub domains, which they do not dare to list. They are experts in scholarly writing (if not book writing in particular) in their area as their several publications might suggest. However, their book project encompasses much more… In part they know the document space they are dealing with quite well. In part they are rather ignorant. However, being experienced in IS&R research they have at least good theoretical knowledge (declarative and procedural) on finding the information they need in their project. Another issue is, how relevant this knowledge is and how it translates into practice. Even if they have a master plan they frequently alter sub-sections of the task owing to changes elsewhere – and their subsequent consequences. They suffer from too many open constraints and insufficient information basis, lost in too many publications of potential interest.

7.4 Document and Source Types: Range of Variables

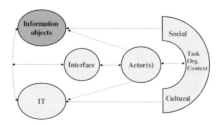

Information objects are documents sought and/or created and may be classified in a multivariable space like (not necessarily distinct):

- *Document Structure:* Explicitly vs. implicitly structured documents; precisely structured vs. semi-structured vs. unstructured documents;

- *Document Types:* Some examples of types are: monographs, journal articles, conference papers, films, recordings, video, images, administrative forms;
- *Document Genres:* Some examples of genres are: horror films, jazz recordings, email and SMS messages, poems and novels, and popular and scholarly journal articles;
- *Document Information Type:* Factual (case-based or generic); methodological; conceptual or theoretical; documentary (descriptive or prescriptive) vs. fictive.
- *Document Communication Function:* Some examples of communication functions are: stating some facts (e.g., in statistics), recording a decision (e.g., in administration), describing an event (e.g., in news), entertainment, and reporting research results;
- *Temporal Aspects of Document Functions.* Patterns of document generation and use, utility of genres and documents types; aging and obsolescence;
- *Document Sign Language:* The natural sign language of information objects, e.g., writing in case of text documents or information objects containing text; form and color, etc. in images; sound frequency, temporal movements, pitch in music;
- *Document Layout and Style:* Movie format; sheet music vs. recordings; academic documents from various domains;
- *Document Isness:* Media-dependent data associated with the production, existence, and mediation of information objects; bibliographic and metadata;
- *Document Contents:* Media and domain-dependent subject matter or expression that can be interpreted intellectually;
- *Contextual Hyperlink Structures:* Anchor texts for outlinking vs. inlinks; linked objects; academic references vs. citations; citing objects.

Document structure, sign language, and content as well as document layout are intra-document features and hyperlink structures are inter-document access keys that often are contextual to one another, for instance, single signs in context of structure, Fig. 6.10; or citations giving context to documents. Many locations of this multidimensional space have not been explored in IR research or Information Studies.

All sources of information are not documents sought. Sometimes information is acquired from *many* documents. Eventually only bits and pieces from several documents, not entire documents, may be useful.

7.4.1 Polyrepresentation of Information Objects

Principally IR research, but also information seeking studies, has been dominated by content (-only) representation of documents. However, recent efforts have enriched the representations by document structure and layout. Further, language technology increasingly simplifies access to all languages through morphological processing of index entries and search keys. While traditional online systems represented documents through their bibliographic metadata and assigned index terms, the proliferation of digital non-text-media calls for derived metadata and assigned annotations for such documents. Access through metadata, i.e., the data associated with document isness, Sect. 6.1.5, may need new and increased attention in IR.

Sect. 5.2.3 outlined the principle of polyrepresentation for information objects, foremost concerned with text-documents of scientific nature. Some passages of academic papers can be seen as more central for IS&R than others, e.g., introductory and concluding sections, table captions or methodological descriptions, and reference lists. In one document they are all by the same author(s) but they have different communication functionalities. One way of applying the principle of polyrepresentation is hence to test whether search keys are found in specific portions of document structure across documents that cite each other. Larsen (2004) carried out one such experiment in the INEX test collection (Fuhr et al. 2002). He found that, at least in Computer Science papers, it did not make any difference in which part of the document content search keys were placed. What made a performance difference was if the keys also were found in papers that were cited by retrieved documents. We observe an explicit use of document structure and content to capture structured data, in particular by incorporating *additional context* from cited and citing documents. Recommender systems – like citation indexes – provide such contexts. However, in order to use the context its underlying conventions must be understood.

One might also apply polyrepresentation principles to *other media* than text. With reference to Fig. 5.5, Sect. 5.2.3, music recording objects would display polyrepresentative structures different from those in text documents. Composer(s) would replace author(s), possible libretto and lyrics would replace thesaurus structures, inlinks (on the Web) might occur, and indexing as well as selector data might be present – but associated to music interpretation and production. The performing actor(s) would form an additional representative structure, typical for the performing arts. They would, with the different producers and other selectors, be responsible for the existence of *different versions* recorded over time. It is thus possible to construct a range of polyrepresentative models for each distinct media type and genre.

7.4.2 IR Research: Capturing Evidence on Documents and Sources

Objection 6 in Sect. 1.3 is about lack of variety in test collections. It states that test collections, albeit nowadays large, are structurally simple (mainly unstructured text) and topically narrow (mainly the news domain). The test documents mostly lack interesting internal structure that some real-life collections do have (e.g., field structure, XML, citations). News documents form a narrow genre, have little structure, are relatively short, and mostly lack links in the form of citations. In addition, news databases are only motivating for test persons in interactive IR experiments if they are up-to-date. Historic requests are less interesting (Borlund 2000a; 2003b). Furthermore, the (English) language of news is particular – dominated by journalistic practices, meant for the general public, non-scholarly, non-technical. One should not hold findings regarding the effectiveness of various methods for query modification, for example, as true for other types of collections until empirically shown valid. Non-text collections have received even less attention.

Recent efforts in IR research have produced the TREC Web collection (Hawking et al. 2000) and the INEX test collection (Fuhr et al. 2002) – Sect. 4.3.1. These are positive developments. IR should continue to look at documents in various media, in various languages, several genres, in organizational contexts, and serving several communication functions. IR research should also be aware of documents/data managed by other technologies (e.g., structured databases; hardcopy archives) – all document types used in real work task settings.

7.4.3 Information Seeking Studies: Capturing Evidence of Documents and Sources

As in the preceding sub-sections also Information Seeking studies should look at documents in various media, in various languages, several genres, in organizational contexts, etc., including human sources, and also be aware of documents/data managed by other technologies (e.g., structured databases; hardcopy archives). Some studies have been done, e.g., on administrative documents, Sect. 3.1.4, but they need to be continued in various environments. In our two seeking sample cases the documents used and produced are quite different.

In *Case A* the documents sought and used are structured records on past decisions regarding benefits paid out to the client, the application forms filled out by the client and some free text appendixes. The sources supplying these documents are task-based in-house information systems and the social worker's folders in his personal working environment. Law books and organizational guidelines are within reach when needed.

In *Case B* the documents sought and used are scholarly publications in Information Science, mainly IR and Information Seeking, as well as in Computer Science, mainly IR and Database Management. The document types and genres are reviews, journal articles, monographs, grey literature reports, web pages, personal communications etc. as the over 700-item reference list suggests. However, *during* the writing *process* even more documents were used – all of them did not make it to the reference list while being relevant for the process. The sources supplying these documents were diverse – home pages, personal communications and student comments, by oral communication or e-mail, directories, indexes, digital libraries, citation databases, and personal hardcopy collections.

7.5 Algorithms and System Components: Dimensions of Variables

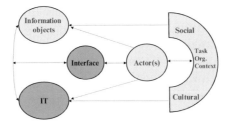

IR systems are based on many diverse types of algorithms – Fig. 4.2 – developed through laboratory experiments over decades. Broadly speaking, they concern a) indexing, representation and matching of information objects and request formulations, e.g., by query modification and other means – the dimension of variables of the IT component, see Figs. 4.2-4.4. In addition, algorithms treat b) modeling, presentation and visualization of retrieval results in *interfaces*. This second dimension of variables consists of the 13 central functions (and 54 sub-functions) of the Mediator Model; see Fig. 4.12 and Sect. 4.8.1.

While such algorithms are at the heart of IT in IR, the cognitive work-task perspective suggests that the steps *preceding* and *following* a retrieval instance or an entire session are also important. If the request the system is able to elicit from the actor, given his/her limitations, is off-target or incomplete, even the best search engines run into difficulties, even with relevance feedback. Serious attention is therefore needed on IR system *inter-*

faces and the tools they provide for the searcher to learn about the domain of the request (e.g., ontologies) and the retrievable documents (e.g., genres and structures). Such tools are required – especially if the searchers are in muddled situations and incapable of articulating their needs properly – and to express non-topical relevance criteria. Such components may affect retrieval effectiveness more than the question of matching models – at least for some task / actor / need / document types.

The way documents are used *after retrieval* needs to be investigated in various work task contexts in order to be able to design retrieval result and document presentation properly. Objection 10, Sect. 1.3, suggests that IR (as simplistic document retrieval) is just a part of document based information access.

7.5.1 IR Research: Capturing Evidence on Algorithms and System Components

In laboratory IR, algorithms are used to represent information needs (requests) as queries, to represent documents, and to perform the matching of the representations – Fig. 7.2, left-hand side. The representations of information needs in IR research are typically explicit topical and textual statements, e.g., TREC topics, and queries (automatically) derived from them. However, the representations could cover non-content attributes (e.g., authors or selectors), structural requirements (like INEX test requests), or be implicit (e.g., find similar to an image). The three latter kinds may reflect non-topical relevance and may be frequent in real life – and available for retrieval tasks.

Bag-of-words (unstructured) queries have dominated request representations. However, there is recent evidence suggesting that more structured representations, reflecting the traditional online Boolean query approach may be effective (Sects. 4.6.1 and 4.6.4). Recent findings also suggest that IR should look more into using document structures and query components – although at INEX 2002 the structurally insensitive best-match queries delivered the best performance.

Matching Methods. In addition to the traditional matching methods – Sect. 4.1 – IR research needs to look into non-content features of documents, like document and citation/link structures, and metadata as well as their combinations, Sects. 4.3.2 and 5.2.3. From the cognitive viewpoint, the non-content features may be better sensitive to other types of relevance (e.g., socio-cognitive relevance) than the purely topical ones.

The proliferation of document collections, and NLP tools as well, in more and more languages suggests continued attention on the application of NLP tools in various languages on IR problems.

7.5.2 Polyrepresentation of Document Components and by Cognitive Space Statements

Matching of the cognitive structures represented by information objects and the searcher's cognitive space is supposed to create overlaps of documents sets, Fig. 5.5, Sects. 5.2.3 and 7.3-4. The principle of polyrepresentation suggests that the more cognitively and functionally different the representations that point to documents, and the more intensively they do it, the higher the probability that those documents are relevant, useful, etc. to a request, an information need or a work task situation.

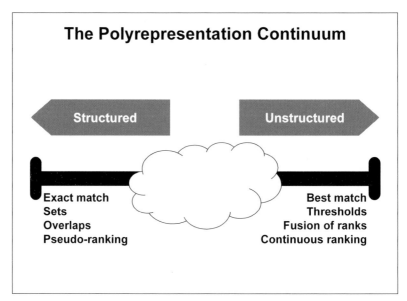

Fig. 7.4. The polyrepresentative continuum (Larsen 2004)

Only few empirical studies have so far looked into *which kinds* of cognitively different representations best lead to good retrieval (and seeking) results, see Sect. 5.2.4. For instance, it is known that retrieval of document by search keys found in titles and abstracts *and* by involving the citations to such documents (made by some other cognitive agents at a later time) produces much higher odds for finding relevant documents in the constructed overlap than in each of the retrieved sets independently. A few other matching combinations have been tried so far. It seems that polyrepresentation best functions in combination with structured queries – Sect. 4.6.4. Also, there seems to exist a continuum of polyrepresentative solutions, Fig. 7.4, from one extreme of hard structured exact match-like formulations to a standard unstructured bag-of-words mode of the principle. Ontology (or thesaurus) support seems to improve the outcome along the continuum.

However, the entire principle of polyrepresentation does not rely on one request formulation from a searcher. It assumes that functionally different representations of the searcher's cognitive structures come into play too, Sect. 7.3.1.

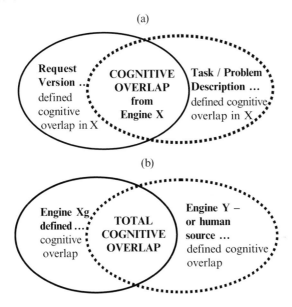

Fig. 7.5. Polyrepresentative IR by two functionally different representations of the same actor's cognitive state (a); the result is merged by sets of documents retrieved in similar polyrepresentative ways by another search algorithm/engine (b)

Fig. 7.5(a) demonstrates how a matching function in search engine X retrieves a set of documents defined by search keys from the actor's request formulation, and how the same engine X retrieves another set defined by search keys found in the same actor's work task description. The combination creates conceivable overlaps (Cognitive overlap X). That overlap might indeed be matched with a similar one from engine Y, Fig. 7.5(b). Since the two retrieval algorithms are cognitively (or functionally) different they are also covered by the polyrepresentative principle.

In practice, many different overlaps would occur during such matching functions, defined by the different representations that actually make overlaps possible. Hence, weighting of the variety of overlaps is achievable and an element of retrieval fusion associated with polyrepresentation exists.

From a cognitive stand, the objects found in the central cognitive overlap should be ranked *prior* to other objects since they are assumed most relevant. With data fusion we encounter the issue of scaling: which of the fused ranking scales to apply. This issue calls for further investigations, for instance, if we assume that the best fusion is obtained by giving the probabilistic ranking scheme priority over, for instance, number of inlinks or citations; or perhaps the opposite order or aggregation of scores might lead to improvement of interactive retrieval performance (Smeaton 1998).

By capturing the variety of representations, IR (and Information Seeking) research adds handles to access to information sources, alternative or supplementary to the more traditional tools. It has to be tested not only which kind of polyrepresentation on the continuum that best suits particular work task and information contexts – but also which combinations of representations – with the least effort – provide reasonable performance results when seeking actors are involved.

7.5.3 The Assumption of Feature (term) Independence

With reference to Sect. 7.3.3 the second assumption underlying best match retrieval was discussed by Robertson (1977) and later heavily criticized by Ellis (1990; 1996). The assumption implies that each term or feature in a document (or request formulation) is independent from any other term or feature – at least what concerns the probabilistic and vector space retrieval models. It is simply a prerequisite determined by the mathematics involved in the models. Of course, intuitively the assumption is unrealistic and indeed an absurd premise for all sequentially generated and perceived objects like text documents, music records or video. But also in connection to non-sequential objects like images, the assumption is unrealistic. The image features exactly coincide and belong together to promote a view, see the Mark Twain Painting Case, Sect. 2.3.1. Why then, does the assumption work?

Behind the statistical IR models lies Zipf's 'law' of individual term frequency and ranking distribution in large text corpora (1932). The distribution follows a highly skewed pattern. Its regularity owes to the idea that text writing is a non-chaotic but stochastic process (Egghe and Rousseau 1990). However, this is only true for so-called 'function words' i.e., non-content bearing words, which are Poisson distributed from document to document (Bookstein and Swanson 1974). 'Specialty words' are content bearing words, i.e., informative or discriminating about document contents. They are not randomly distributed. Such words appear in a text following a pattern organized by the thematic progression (Katz 1996, p. 16). Katz also claims that the number of instances of such words is not directly associated with document length, but rather a function of how much the document is about the concept expressed by that word. The co-occurrence of content-rich words in texts does not happen randomly, but is determined by the preceding chain of signs that commonly follows some rules or conventions, e.g., grammar. Almost all information objects provide some sense or meaning, owing to the intentionality of its author(s). This feature is employed by the recent language model approaches to IR, e.g., Hiemstra (1998) and Ponte and Croft (1998).

Consequently, when a given request made into a query is broken down into features, like single words, and is matched against the objects in information space, and a portion of a text matches (a part of) the query – then the probability is high that the retrieved text (object) is *meaningful*. This is owing to the nature of text generation described above. One may combine search features in random order because hardly anybody generates random text. Another question is whether the retrieved text provides information in a real sense, aside from being meaningful. Obviously, the larger the *context* of the request – and hence the number of keys in the query – the better the odds for finding something meaningful in information space and semantically related to the request. The shorter the request, e.g., in the case of Label Effects as commonly on the web, the lower the likelihood for finding something directly semantically related to the information need (problem or work task/interest) underlying the request. The semantic openness of the statements of need and the semantic variety of the retrieved objects is vast. Such phenomena depend on the type of information need.

The assumption works differently in different media, different contexts and domains, and under influence of different language styles. Also the outcome of the assumption is situation dependent, due to the different work task circumstances of searchers. One might hence expect that frequently occurring work and search tasks entail certain frequent *combinations* and *structure* of independent features that may be explored for the improvement of IS&R performance and quality – see Sects. 4.6 and 5.2.3.

7.5.4 Information Seeking Studies: Capturing Evidence of Algorithms and System Components

The majority of Information Seeking research has looked at exact match systems providing bibliographic data on documents. As such, this work is relevant, but the gap in research regarding best-match retrieval systems supplying full documents (not just metadata) is unfortunate. Best-match systems *may* serve their users' information seeking better for vague / brief requests than exact match systems. They *may* also make the identification of relevant documents easier (through ranking) even when the requests are extensively articulated. However, we do not know whether there is a significant difference in favor of one or other type of systems. The most important problems / possibilities from the searcher's point of view may lie elsewhere. Moreover, excluding the Web and its search engines with ranking facilities, there have not been that many possibilities for investigating real-life IR with best-match systems.

Several studies on search engine log files suggest that Boolean operators are seldom used in Web-IR and, even if sometimes used, they are probably often used incorrectly – Sect. 5.5.1. This suggests that the operators rather belong to the intermediary-based online IR age – that is, to history. Best-match systems perform retrieval with no or minimal explicit operators that searchers would have to apply. The information seekers are not likely to learn them. They simply lack interest.

Researchers of information seeking processes should not be blind for the fact that IIR often is, and increasingly becomes, an *intermediate and necessary* tool for the natural progress in people's information seeking behavior. Hence Information Seeking studies ought to move into and intensify studies of IIR in connection to information seeking, for instance, in local best match environments.

By explicitly studying IR system features and the contribution their components deliver in the overall retrieval effectiveness, Information Seeking research could inform IR research *what to pursue in systems design* – from the broader seeking and work task viewpoint. It might also seek to analyze whether, and how, the goals of current IR research are relevant from the seeking viewpoint in various contexts.

In *Case A* the social worker has at his disposal an information system designed to supply the documents needed in the decision process. Moreover, in the current working environment this system is the only practical means to access this information. The social worker is ignorant about the information system principles. However, the system provides easy access through person names and IDs – to fill in a form – and this matches well what he has available in the situation.

In *Case B* there is no single IR system to use, and no system required to use in the book writing process. A number of systems are available and provide partially overlapping, partly disjoint information in diverse ways. These included the Web, publishers' journal databases, the ACM Digital Library, ResearchIndex, Reference Manager, etc. These systems were flexible enough to serve browsing, navigation, and bibliographic access – e.g., searching for a web page with few but adequate bibliographic keys to find a link to the cited document or its page numbers.

7.6 Access Types: Variables of Interaction

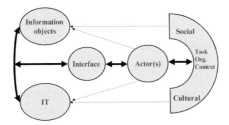

Access strategies connect the actor's information need (the unknown ASK), her available work task and domain knowledge and the ways to use information systems and sources (documents) – all through information interaction. It would be healthy for IS&R research to look into information access and acquisition strategies and practices in real-life work task contexts (rather than at job-level) to learn what the actors' information problems are and to gain insight into how they are currently being served and how they might be – by what kinds of strategies?

Variables of Information Interaction. Interaction comprises all the components of the cognitive framework. It forms a specific session context to the components under study – Fig. 6.10. The following central variables are contained in the interaction and access dimension:

- *Interaction Duration*: The number of instances of interaction under study; short-term, session-based, longitudinal interaction;
- *Interaction Actors or Components*: The focus of interaction; the variables involved from the dimensions of participating framework components;
- *Kind of Interaction and Access:* Social interaction vs. HCI; physical vs. intellectual; patterns of IS&R interaction in a temporal sense;

- *Interaction Strategies and Tactics:* Rhetorics; types of HCI; IIR strategies and search tactics;
- *Purpose of Human Communication:* Request formulation, work task description, problem statement and state description; knowledge state description; search task formulation; relevance assessment; query modification; question vs. answering; data presentation;
- *Purpose of System Communication:* Query production; object indexing; feature on object weighting; automatic query modification; feature or object selection; object retrieval; result presentation of objects and features; presentation of other interface features;
- *Interaction Mode:* Verbal or oral, pointing, iconic, other action;
- *Least Effort Factors:* Tiredness, motivation, emotional state, control.

7.6.1 IR Research: Capturing Evidence on Access and Interaction

IR research sees information access mainly as document access and being either searching (i.e. typical topical requests) or less importantly, browsing or navigation. Objection 3 (Sect. 1.3) suggests that there is lack of tactical variability in IR research, with too narrow focus on topical searching.

Marcia Bates (1990) suggests that searchers use various stratagems (e.g., journal run, citation search) in searching (Sect. 5.4.1). David Ellis identified in real-life contexts a number of "features" (or stratagems) like browsing, chaining, and extracting (Sect. 3.1.2). While these were not really task and situation specific, they are steps toward understanding the actors' interaction behavior, their strategies and available access criteria in real-life settings – how inefficient it may be when viewed through an IR mind set. Clearly, access happens not only through topical-analytical search requests. It also occurs through the use of other socio-cognitive features and poly-representation – like text content, link anchors and citations. Access happens via orchestrated systems, tools and colleagues – not just IR systems, nor just through a single system. After all, we do not know how significant a percentage of information access is covered by topical searching, be that through just one or more search keys.

We believe that it would be healthy for IR research also to look into what kinds of search criteria the actors are able and willing to express and what criteria may be automatically available in their digital environment. In many ways this is the essence of what the session context can be used for in a narrow sense – as previously discussed, e.g., request specificity and relevance assessment reliability, in Sect. 6.2.6.

Online bibliographic search processes were analyzed in much detail for their moves, tactics, effort and effectiveness (Sects. 5.3 and 5.4.1). However, the primary focus was on professional searchers and excluding work-task contexts, with a session focus. Some studies have been longitudinal, Sect. 5.8.2. However, at the moment, too little is known about real-life information retrieval processes in work and daily-life task contexts and how they evolve – and why. Too little is also known about how much automation the actors would prefer having for information access – and how much control they would appreciate. Much has been said on this issue, but mainly connected to Boolean operational system contexts. Situations probably vary heavily in this regard and ought to be tested.

Objection 10 (Sect. 1.3) reminds us that information access (retrieval) is not just document retrieval. The actors may rather want to retrieve pertinent information and answers to questions. If we observe them in a context limited to document retrieval, and take their behavior for granted, we may not identify potentially effective access types and strategies for interaction.

7.6.2 The Assumption of Independent Relevance Assessments

Objection 2 on the 'lack of interaction and dynamic information needs'; Objection 5 on 'lack of user-oriented relevance; and Objection 7 on 'document independence and overlap', Sect. 1.3, coincide with the three more or less unrealistic assumptions underlying algorithmic statistical IR, Sect. 7.3.3. We discussed in particular the problems concerned with the assumption on information need invariability over several instances of short-term interaction and session-based interaction. Much of laboratory IR regards each instance as independent. That assumption is strongly connected to the ideas of document independence *and* the assumption of independence of relevance assessments, also when made by human assessors.

The first argument, that each search iteration is independent, is problematic for two reasons already stated: probabilistic retrieval requires relevance assessments in order to proceed, and those assessments *bridge* the iterations providing synergy. The second reason is based on the fact that the searcher seldom forgets entirely what just has occurred – whether it is an assessment or an instance of search task execution. However, if the whole query is entered anew like in Boolean systems (but modified) then the iterations are less dependent.

It is thus an open question if the TREC assessors are capable of forgetting what they just assessed over several hundred documents or maybe constantly remember, say, the last 5 assessment results and reasons. Obviously, if the criteria for relevance are very lax, like in TREC, the chance of forgetting past assessments increases.

When building a *test collection,* relevance assessments *must* be made as independent as possible. The reason is (but often being overlooked): one never knows which documents are retrieved in which order during tests! When *retrieving* documents, relevance assessments are naturally dependent of one another, hence the 'cognitive' measures – Sect. 4.10.

The volume of entities presented for assessment is one factor influencing the judgments, e.g., via saturation. An additional factor is the size and *kind of information entities* presented to the assessor, see also Figs. 5.3 and 5.4. From this perspective, five classes of relevance can be defined:

- *Bibliographic relevance.* The assessment is based on bibliographic metadata;
- *Extended bibliographic relevance.* The assessment is founded on bibliographic metadata with a table of contents (or web page anchors), a range of descriptors from an authoritative thesaurus and/or abstract added;
- *Document Feature Relevance.* The relevance assessment is based on extracted features of information objects that may have been processed prior to presentation, such as, term maps, text passages, or video stills, etc.
- *Document relevance.* The assessment is based on the full object, e.g., in full text, but with no additional features added;
- *Extended document relevance.* The assessment is based on the full object, with added data on contents, topicality, relationships (referral to inlinking and/or citing objects, no. of links or citations), and alike, most of which are socio-cognitive.

We note that during the Cranfield experiments, and later evaluations based on that model and on the pre-TREC test collections, only (extended) bibliographic relevance was used. Due to the shortness of the records and their condensed nature in those cases, the assumption of independence of assessment seems quite unrealistic. If, however, '(extended) document relevance' is applied, the assumption may seem more likely to be realistic.

An obvious implication is that assessments may vary – depending on the amount and nature of data to which the assessor is exposed. The assumption is that the same document presented in different ways to an actor may thus entail different degrees of relevance.

7.6.3 Information Seeking Studies: Capturing Evidence on Access and Interaction

For example, in *Case A* the social worker has an information system supplying the documents containing the required information, given the client's ID number. The actor's information need (or ASK) here is about past payments to the present client. He may readily explain the *type* of relevant answers (e.g., dates, sums, accounts, justifications) but not their *content*. However, the actor has the client's name and ID available as part of his task knowledge. Luckily, these can be used to effectively match the relevant documents – the ASK aspect need not be articulated at all for successful matching of the relevant documents.

One might claim that *Case A* is too simple an example, because the person ID is a simple handle to relevant documents. However, are more complex seeking situations really different regarding this aspect? In *Case B* the two guys writing their book found most of the time well-defined topical searching useless in their situations because they knew the structure of the document space quite well and each situation into which they were thrown supplied them also with other clues (e.g., authors, forums, known relevant items) than just topical ones. Therefore they found Marcia Bates' (1990) non-topical stratagems quite useful (Sect. 5.4.1). However, they were professionals in the domain and IR – not representative of (seeking-wise) lay people.

Even here it might be claimed that the ASK problem is circumvented via document attributes and the real ASK problem remains. We are not saying it does not exist; we are just convinced that all situations are not like that. If one observes library clients, researchers and students, the likelihood of observing an ASK situation with poor handles to documents is greater than in a professional work place context.

We believe that Information Seeking research does not know in general, whether (or when) the documents that match the available and expressible state of knowledge the actor possesses, tend to be relevant, i.e., discuss the actor's ASK in a usable way. Neither is there knowledge, in general, on what it is in the state of knowledge that provides access to relevant documents – what kind of handles that support the access. In the *Cases A* and *B* the handles were distinct from the answers – but they were metadata document attributes rather than content. Even in strictly topical situations it may often be that the available topical access point (knowledge handle) is distinct from the relevance bearing content of relevant documents. We do not know. If they are the same, then there is a serious ASK problem for the searcher.

The actors successfully carrying further their professions may know well – having learned this in Siberia over the years so to say – which access handles are effective. It is just we in Information Studies who do not know because we never asked this question! In addition to *Cases A* and *B* there is a whole range of work tasks and seeking practices which are more or less structured and provide different kinds of current knowledge to access the documents needed. Therefore, IS&R should study what kind of access handles the actors are able and willing to express and use – in current situations – and how these relate to documents, their relevance and organization / representation for access.

7.7 The Multidimensional Research Design Cube

The nine broad dimensions – see the beginning of this chapter – form a multidimensional research design cube with an assortment of variables for each dimension. Table 7.2 present the design cube in 2D, although there are nine dimensions. In Chap. 8 we propose selected research designs based on illustrative combinations of the variables.

Table 7.2. The research design cube for nine IS&R research variables

Natural Work Tasks (WT) & Org	Natural Search Tasks (ST)	Actor	Perceived Work Tasks	Perceived Search Tasks
WT Structure	ST Structure	Domain Knowledge	Perceived WT Structure	Perceived Information Need Content
WT Strategies & Practices	ST Strategies & Practices	IS&R Knowledge	Perceived WT Strategies & Practices	Perceived ST Structure/Type
WT Granularity, Size & Complexity	ST Granularity, Size & Complexity	Experience on Work Task	Perceived WT Granularity, Size & Complexity	Perceived ST Strategies & Practices
WT Dependencies	ST Dependencies	Experience on Search Task	Perceived WT Dependencies	Perceived ST Specificity & Complexity
WT Requirements	ST Requirements	Stage in Work Task Execution	Perceived WT Requirements	Perceived ST Dependencies
WT Domain & Context	ST Domain & Context	Perception of Socio-Org. Context	Perceived WT Domain & Context	Perceived ST Stability
		Sources of Difficulty		Perceived ST Domain & Context
		Motivation & Emotional State		

Table 7.2. (Cont.)

Document and Source	IR Engines IT Component	IR Inter-faces	Access and Interaction
Document Structure	Exact Match Models	Domain Model Attributes	Interaction Duration
Document Types	Best Match Models	System Model Features	Actors or Components
Document Genres	Degree of Doc. Structure and Content Used	User Model Features	Kind of Interaction and Access
Information Type in Document	Use of NLP to Document Indexing	System Model Adaption	Strategies and Tactics
Communication Function	Doc. Metadata Representation	User Model Building	Purpose of Human Communication
Temporal Aspects	Use of Weights in Doc. indexing	Request Model Builder	Purpose of System Communication
Document Sign Language	Degree of Req. Structure and Content Used	Retrieval Strategy	Interaction Mode
Layout and Style	Use of NLP to Request Indexing	Response Generation	Least effort Factors
Document Isness	Req. Metadata Representation	Feedback Generation	-
Document Content	Use of Weights in Requests	Mapping ST History	
Contextual Hyperlink Structure		Explanation Features	
Human Source (see Actor)		Transformation of Messages	
		Scheduler	

8 Towards a Research Program

In this chapter we discuss elements of a research program for IS&R, based on our framework. Basically, considering all combinations of our 9 major dimensions in Chapt. 7, Table 7.2, research should be directed at cells, by a systematic combination of dimensions, where there has been little or no research so far. One might want to find out how IS&R is explicated in that particular cell or combination with as many variables as possible controlled and a few describing the IS&R processes as pseudo-dependent[1]. Further, we need systematic research on individual dimensions. For example, we need to study how variation within one single dimension, like in the variable work task complexity, affects IS&R as seen through some dependent variables. However, it is even more important to study the interaction of dimensions, and their variables, so that some variables are controlled as far as possible, some are deliberately independent while yet others are the dependent ones. Observing the fact that each major dimension contains multiple variables, there is a nearly endless number of research questions to look at. Clearly, this would be too much to handle with resources that are always limited. Therefore we need a research program, which makes strategic suggestions regarding which variable combinations to look at and how to treat each of them. These suggestions should be chosen so that the two action lines of Chapt. 7 are followed: Information Seeking and IR are extended toward context as economically as possible and the results, when put together, accumulate the understanding of task-based IS&R.

One may use the 9 dimensions as a checklist for what should be taken into account when designing an investigation. One may also use them to suggest possible hidden variables, and to check whether the features of a study design are relevant and sufficient in its intended application domain – e.g., whether or not topical information need types really are representative in the intended domain.

---

[1] By pseudo-dependent we mean observed and reported variables in descriptive study settings, which have no independent variables, either. For conceptions of variables in detail, see Sect. 5.8.1.

This chapter suggests some investigation approaches for IS&R, but the proposed set can easily be extended. It does not go into detail as to research methodology, statistical testing and validity. For that purpose, relevant textbooks are available (Frankfort-Nachmias and Nachmias 2000; Siegel and Castellan 1988). Methodological facets are only discussed when it is evident or highly relevant from the point of view of the research setting.

The Sects. 8.1 – 8.4 attempt to provide a bottom up exercise of combining or comparing variables systematically from a variation of dimensions. First, Sect. 8.1 is concerned with the Laboratory Model and how to extend it towards its work task and organizational context. Secondly, Sects. 8.2 and 8.3 involve the seeking actor in the laboratory model settings. First, Sect. 8.2 compares actor variables to information objects and algorithmic IT, then Sect. 8.3 combines information objects, interface functionality and actor variables. Finally, Sect. 8.4 leaves the laboratory model completely out by taking it as a fixed (controlled) variable. The section discusses the combination of seeking actors interacting with the interface component, in context of a socio-organizational work task environment.

Basically, *three* or more *dimensions* are compared from a strategic point of view. The reason is that when systematic empirical research is carried out in a conscious and careful manner, three independent variables are indeed manageable. We use the image of our framework to point to which research dimensions are in focus in each section. We are not exhaustive regarding possible combinations dimensions; some remain outside of our discussion. However, these may be analyzed by swapping between controlled and independent dimensions. For example, modifying the research design in 8.4, one might turn IT (the engines) into independent variables and the interfaces into controlled ones – same interface(s) to different IR systems.

8.1 Information Objects, IT and Natural Task Contexts

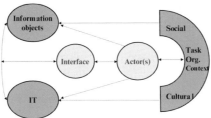

The basic Laboratory Model, Fig. 5.1, revolves around document and request representations and their matching. As stated earlier, research this far within the model has not exhausted the model's possibilities. The test collections may be extended toward diverse contexts and thereby refining the findings achieved so far regarding what works, and what does not, in IR. Possibilities along these lines involve:

- More varied *document collections* in diverse media and domains: traditional document collections may be extended into diverse *domains* (which affects the vocabulary and style of the documents), and *structurally*. For example, collections of scholarly documents in various domains, or documents in public and business administration – and relevant mixtures – should be looked at.
- *Request sets* should be collected from the domains and work task contexts for which the document collections are relevant. The requests should be analyzed and organized by their features (Sect. 7.3.), e.g., simple vs. complex ones or factual vs. topical ones or by the types of handles they have (content features vs. attributes). Further, the requests should be equipped with proper work task descriptions in order to support relevance assessments and to be used as cover stories in simulated work task situations. Finally, the requests should be equipped with descriptions on how many documents actors in the domain would *expect to retrieve* in a collection and how many they want to see. In this way the request sets may be used to serve even other purposes than just as a tool for obtaining performance measures for traditional IR statistics.
- *Graded relevance assessments* should be produced with not just topicality in mind but rather with respect to defined types of work tasks – and by competent people for each work task. Panels of professionals could produce the judgments to increase their reliability and validity. This means that some documents which are relevant for, e.g., a complex work task, may be irrelevant for a simple one in a domain. If economi-

cally possible, relevance assessments should state which parts of each document are relevant, and how, to a search task.

- *User population* characteristics should be described for which the collection is intended, if searchers are to be involved, Sects. 8.2-8.4. In case of application of the collection to other groups of test persons than the intended, one should be aware of this introduction of an additional actor and knowledge-related variable, Sect. 7.3.

In effect, this allows work *without test persons* to be continued within the Laboratory Model – but with consciously designed new kinds of test collections, which also allow pursuing research slightly further than the traditional test collections. There is also a pragmatic consideration at play: existing expertise in research must be *gradually* directed toward novel research questions. Anything else would be impractical.

However, the drive in research here should not be the ability to create some new kinds of test collections. The drive should be novel research questions that motivate the test collections as tools. Below we outline some research questions. Given a work task Domain X:

- What kinds of work tasks are typical in Domain X?
- What kinds of search tasks do these work tasks typically generate?
- What kinds of documents or other knowledge sources tend to be relevant for these search tasks? How many documents would actors in the domain expect to retrieve in a collection and how many do they want to see?
- Which indexing methods are possible and effective for the document collections? What features / structures should be indexed, and how?
- Which search task representation methods are possible and effective for the document collections?
- Which matching methods prove effective?
- Which document *and* request representation methods are possible and effective for selected types of natural search tasks in the domain?

The Domain X may be any professional or lay domain, ranging from lay (hobby) contexts to various professions in society, including administrative and scholarly work. The documents in the collections should be of all natural kinds, with full content, full structure and full attributes and links / references, and in any relevant media. The first three research questions require field studies and are related to creating the test collections. The last four are to be answered by laboratory experiments.

This approach is motivated because it would (1) extend IR research to novel domains and communication contexts and we do not know whether contemporary findings hold in all domains, and (2) provide more realism to laboratory-based experiments through work task-based competent relevance assessments covering all document properties, not just content features. This line of extension of the Laboratory Model follows the responses to Objections 1, 2, 4, and 6 in Sect. 1.3. Regarding Objection 5 (Lack of user-oriented relevance), this approach bypasses users and focuses on task features. Regarding Objection 7 (Assuming document independence and neglecting overlap), this approach allows overlap analysis and need not assume independence.

Table 8.1. Independent (dark shading, framed) and controlled (light shading) variables to look at in extended laboratory experiments

Document and Source types	Natural Work Task	Natural Search Task	Algorithmic IT Component	Assessor Characteristics
Doc. structure	Structure/openness	Structure/type	Doc. metadata rep.	Domain knowledge
Doc. types	Strategy/practice	Strategy/practice	Doc. content rep.	IS&R knowledge
Doc. genres	Granularity/size	Complexity/specific.	Doc. structural rep.	Work task exp.
Information types	Dependences	Dependencies	Req. metadata rep.	Search task exp.
Comm. function.	Requirements	Stability	Req. content rep.	Work task stage
Sign language	Domains/context	Domains/context	Req. structur. rep.	Context perception
Layout & style	…	…	Match methods	Constraints
Doc. isness			…	Motvat./emotion
Link structures				…
Human source				
…				

Table 8.1 lists independent and controlled variables to look at in extended laboratory experiments that attempts to give answer to the last research question above. Columns 1-3 give the dimensions: Document and Source Types, Natural Work Task, and Natural Search Task. They are represented in the test collection as fixed sets. The cells in the columns give their exemplary variables, which should also (at least some of them) be represented in the test collection in the form of classifications. The fourth column contains typical experimental independent variables. The fifth column is the actor typically excluded in laboratory experiments but which *sneaks in* to the experiments in the disguise of an assessor with all actor-related variables present. The dependent variables in the extended laboratory experiments would be typical performance measures.

The shadings in Table 8.1 represent experimental laboratory research designs where search task types, document representation methods and request representation methods are systematically varied – dark framed shading – and document types and work task structure / openness, as well as the chosen domain, are controlled – light shading. The assessor column is fixed as given in the test collection (relevance assessments) and must have been controlled when constructing the test collection. White background in the cells suggests possible hidden variables. Of course, many other designs are possible.

A notable contemporary step toward the proposed direction for laboratory experiments is the INEX campaign as an extension of the TREC approach due to its structured full-text scholarly documents and expert topic creation and graded relevance assessments.

Methodologically these research designs may be handled as in the Laboratory Model tradition. One needs more than 30 search tasks to run an experiment within a given work task / search task type in order to obtain statistically significant results. However, systematic variation of work task / search task type requires many more search tasks representing them – and (graded) relevance assessments for each. This may become an inhibiting factor economically. Therefore the document and source types as well as task contexts, and their precise variables, need to be carefully chosen to represent the kind of variation of contexts that allows analyzing where each representation method is able to contribute.

8.2 Information Objects, IT and Actors

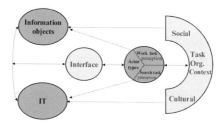

This research setting incorporates the basic laboratory model components, but extends it by including the seeking actor, like in Fig. 1.1, into an interactive (IR) scenario. As the iconic figure of dimensions illustrates, the actor is divided into its three main dimensions of variables – Sects. 7.2-3:

- Actor type variables
- Perceived work task variables
- Perceived search task variables

According to some specific research questions, the researcher has to select an independent variable from *one* of these three dimensions. The research question (RQ1) could be:

- Given a specific organizational context X with known work task types, which IR method performs best considering different searcher work task experiences and knowledge and a variation of document types?

The context might, for instance, be a selected medical domain and organizational environment. Typical work task types are clinical diagnosis, treatment, clinical testing, chirurgical procedures and execution, medical prescriptions, etc. The matching techniques undergoing performance evaluation are, e.g., a probabilistic model versus a browsing based access tool. The searching actors are either experienced doctors vs. 1st year medical students. The documents used as knowledge sources are either academic full-text journal articles, or academic web sites. The searches to be done during experimentation are instigated by a set of realistic simulated work task situations given to the test persons. The set is chosen to be of the semantically closed kind, but could also consist of naturalistic work task assignments lacking cover stories. Preferably, such cover stories / assignments should lead to search tasks adhering to the factual Information Need Type. Cover stories or assignments might consist of Roentgen photos or video shots by micro cameras of specific cases – largely replacing written statements. The actors may execute their IS&R as they would like in realistic terms, but cannot make use of human information sources.

Table 8.2. Independent variables (dark shading, framed) and controlled variables (light shading) combined in an IIR experiment

Document and Source types	Algorithmic IT Component	Actor Characteristics	Perceived Work Task	Perceived Search Task
Doc. Structure	Doc. Metadata rep.	Domain Knowledge	Struture/Openness	Inform. Need Types
Doc. Types	Doc. Content rep.	IS&R Knowledge	Strategy/Practice	Structure/Type
Doc. Genres	Doc. Structural rep.	Work Task Exp.	Granularity/Size	Strategy/Practice
Information Types	Req. Metadata rep.	Search Task Exp.	Dependencies	Complexity/Specific.
Comm. Function.	Req. Content rep.	Work Task Stage	Requirements	Dependencies
Sign Language	Req. Structural rep.	Context Perception	Domains/Context	Stability
Layout & Style	Match Methods	Constraints	...	Domains/Context
Doc. Isness	...	Motivat./Emotion		...
Link Structures		...		
Human Source				
...				

The motivation for the research is the assumption that the traditional academic documents are better information sources for solving the work tasks by the experienced doctors than web-based material. Secondly, it is interesting to find out which access technique, the browsing based technique or the probabilistic engine is more effective.

Table 8.2 demonstrates which variables (dark shaded framed cells) from the three central research dimensions that are involved in answering the research question. Each variable in question may take a range of values. For instance, in general the Document Dimension variable Document Type contains values ranging from newspapers over monographs to journal articles, conference papers, music recordings, Web-based data, etc. In the specific case the range has been limited to a few selected types, as stated above. In this research question the Work Task Structure/Openness, the Domain/Context as well as the Information Need Type and Human Source variables are all controlled (light shaded cells) – since all the simulated work task situations are of the factual type and from a selected domain. By being the same throughout the investigations the Interface Component as well as the Socio-Organizational Context dimensions are also controlled. The dependent variable is performance. It is measured using the performance measures of Sect. 4.10. All other variables (white background) suggest potential hidden variables.

The proposed research design operates with combining the selected variables from three dimensions in such a way that, e.g., 32 test persons (16 doctors and 16 medical students), 8 simulated work tasks / assignments (Q1-Q8), the two retrieval methods (a and b), and the two document types (D1 and D2) are systematically and symmetrically combined during the investigation. The design implies that 8 test persons (doctors) as well as 8 test students each search two assignments (Q1-2) for method (a) + document type (D1) *and* (Q3-4) for method (a) + D2. The same test person groups then search (Q5-6) and (Q7-8) via the method (b) + D1/D2 configurations respectively. Eight new test doctors and eight new medical students then repeat the design symmetrically, so that the assignments (Q1-4) are tested on the two configurations: method (b) + D1/D2 and (Q5-8) are tested on method (a) + D1/D2. The operations can be done by means of contingency tables – see also Fig. 5.10, Sect. 5.9.

The proposed research design thus operates with eight assignments per test person, a doable set of search tasks, and 32 search events defined by the four assignments dealing with each model/document type combination – in total 64 search events over all eight assignments for each combination. Hence, for each searcher type there are generated 32 search events per combination. In total 256 searches (32 persons x 8 assignments) are conducted. The design makes it possible also to study the searcher behavior of the different groups. Obviously, if it is not feasible to reach the necessary number of test persons, each participant is then required do more than eight searches. Then the behavioral aspects of the investigation become less statistically reliable. The assignments do not have to be carried out during one day, but can be distributed over several days.

8.2.1 Alternative Research Question

An alternative research question (RQ2) might be the original one, except that the investigation operates with uniform (controlled) searcher experience, e.g., 1st year medical students alone. As before the Matching Methods and Document Type variables are independent, but the third independent variable shifts into the Perceived Search Task dimension, i.e., values of the Information Need Type variable – Table 8.2. They might take two forms, e.g., short and vague (semantically open) simulated topical work task situations vs. factual assignments. The former may reflect complex work tasks and lead to different information needs and search task executions – yet in a controlled manner – Sect. 5.9. As in the original research question the dependent variable in RQ2 is performance, but could be extended into measures of task fulfillment and satisfaction.

Essentially, the simulated work task situations assigned to the test persons, the medical 1st year students, are of realistic complex nature that entail different information needs and search task executions – yet in a controlled manner, like above concerning RQ2.

The research design proposed above with respect to the number of participants and assignments holds also for RQ2. For both the stipulated research questions involving the seeking actor(s) non-topical, higher-order and graded relevance assessments can be applied. This is a way to bridge the information seeking real-life and the laboratory experiments – but requires realistic simulated work tasks or assigned search tasks as well as sensible collections – Sect. 6.2.9. In addition, measuring performance or other parameters by means of the relevance types, discussed in Sect. 5.7, implies to have quite established criteria associated to each type, according to context, media and document genre. In the RQ1-2 cases above, the medical context should provide such criteria for relevance of information in connection to the realistic work tasks applied to the investigation.

8.3 Information Objects, Interface and Actors

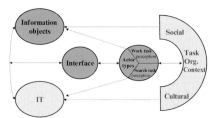

This combination reflects research designs in which the controlled dimensions are the work task domain and socio-organizational/cultural as well as the IT-based contexts. The search engine and indexing algorithms are fixed, as is the community environment. The design also reflects an extended simultaneous involvement of characteristics of documents, source collections and interface functionalities in contrast to what traditionally forms part of IIR research.

Such extensions concerned with the information object space, and correspondingly with the interface, could be:

• Documents with or without structure, specific structural properties or a variety of document types, genres and information types. The communication functionality could be looked at, and multi-media or selected media-specific documents might form a suit of interesting as well as highly relevant characteristics to investigate;

- Interfaces with (or without) different supportive conceptual tools, like ontologies or thesauri, with a range of presentation and visualization features represented by a response generator, including inference and request modeling characteristics, with mapping functions for recommender features or with (or without) manipulative feedback facilities, like for supporting query modification.

A strategic research question suggested by this research design could be:

- Given a specific organizational context X with known work task types and a given IT configuration, which features make a multi-media document appear relevant at different time constraints – with two different interface configurations?

Essentially, one wishes to find out: How do people assess the relevance of multimedia objects under varying time constraints? What parts do they look at? The multi-media information objects could be documents incorporating images and associated text, presented in two different presentation layouts by two different interface modes: Bibliographic image record (metadata without the image) or image with text caption. The interfaces might be a detail-whole GUI vs. a menu-based interface. Table 8.3 displays the relevant Document and Source Type variables to be tuned: Layout and Style combined with Document Isness (metadata).

Finally, the test persons are put under different time constraints with respect to their relevance assessments.

The motivation behind the research questions could be hypotheses on issues of bibliographic relevance vs. document relevance, Sect. 7.6.2, with respect to the variation of document presentation. In particular, hypotheses might be established concerning portions of documents (images) that are applied for relevance assessments under four different conditions: two kinds of time constraints (very short vs. longer assessment time) combined with the two different interface display forms.

The dependent variables could be relevance behavioral traits, like number of interdependent assessments remembered, emotional and cognitive evidence displayed and the extent to which particular document features are used.

This approach is additionally motivated because it deals with the independency objections stated in Sects. 1.3 and 7.6.1.

Methodologically speaking, a similar operation as demonstrated in Sect. 8.2 with number of test persons etc., can be applied to this research design.

Table 8.3. Independent (dark shading, framed) and controlled variables (light shading) combined in an IIR experiment.

Document and Source types	IT Interface Component	Perceived Work Task	Perceived Search Task	Actor Characteristics
Doc. Structure	Domain Model	Struct/Openness	Inform. Need Types	Domain Knowledg
Doc. Types	System Model	Strategy/Practice	Structure/Type	IS&R Knowledge
Doc. Genres	User Model	Granularity/Size	Strategy/Practice	Work Task Exp.
Information Types	Syst. Model Adap.	Dependences	Complexity/Spec ific.	Search Task Exp.
Comm. Function	User Model Build.	Requirements	Dependencies	Work Task Stage
Sign Language	Retrieval Strategy	Domains/Context	Stability	Context Percept.
Layout & Style	Response Generator	...	Domains/Context	Constraints
Doc. Isness	Feedback Generator		...	Motivat./Emotion
Link Structures	Request Model Build			...
Human Source	...			
...				

Alternative research question versions could be to observe the relevance assessments, involving the same documents, carried out with time intervals – replacing the time constraint on the searchers. That constraint might also be fixed as one value (i.e., controlled). In both cases the simulated work task situations (and the entailed perceived search tasks/information needs) should be designed to allow for the time prolongation of fulfilling the task. In the original research question, the assignments could refer to Known Item searches.

8.4 Interfaces, Actors and Socio-organizational Contexts

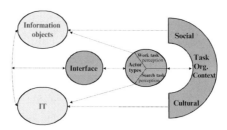

In this combination of dimensions one investigates the interaction of actors and information system interfaces in diverse socio-organizational contexts.

Contemporary research may be extended in each dimension. Possibilities along these lines involve:

- More varied socio-organizational (or leisure) contexts: so far IS&R has looked into some domains, but above the work task level; into the student term paper task; into task complexity in public administration; and into sense making in the personal health domain. IS&R could look at task types (e.g., by complexity and frequency) in different kind of information access environments (e.g., by availability of access tools).
- More varied actor groups: actor groups in various domains have been explored but not from an integrated point of view. Research may be diversified by looking at how different kinds of actors (e.g., by expertise) perceive their work or daily-life tasks and at which kinds of search tasks (e.g., how often, which kinds of access handles) they arrive, or how much tutoring or collaboration they employ with human sources.
- Interfaces to information (retrieval) systems: Interface functionalities have not been a hot topic in IR since the era of intermediary systems (Sect. 4.8) – the most popular kind of interface being a plain text window for entering search keys and another for listing the matching links. In order for the actor to be able to effectively interact with information / documents various functionalities of interfaces could be considered, Table 8.4 – also in other information systems than pure IR systems of the organizational environment.

Investigations should be conducted in a variety of socio-organizational (or leisure) contexts, which differ in the kinds of information-intensive work or daily-life tasks they contain. Given Domain X, some relevant research questions are:

- How are work tasks perceived in X? Are organizational work tasks perceived differently depending on task type or actor type? How are search tasks perceived in X? Are search tasks perceived differently depending on work task type or actor type?
- What are search task characteristics in X – depending on work tasks? What are their properties regarding handles to needed information, amount and type of information, and socio-cognitive relevance criteria? Do search task characteristics differ by actor types?
- How do actors behave in their information (system) environments when performing the search tasks? What kinds of needs are directed at which types of sources? Are there stable patterns in the order? How do actors collaborate in information access?

- How do actors use each particular source or system? How does each source or system match the access handles to desired information the actors have? How are such sources or systems applied in concert to solve tasks? How do they adapt to the actors' situations? How do they aid the actors in the formulation of their requests?
- Is a given interface functionality ever used? If so, how is it used and does it make a difference?
- Do actors find the desired information in the available natural environments? What obstacles do they encounter? Which are the strengths and weaknesses of each access attempt? How do actors assess them?

The first two research questions are about the formation of the actor's search tasks in context. The middle three are about the interaction between actors and sources or systems, and the last one about the results. These research questions are about a natural socio-organizational (or leisure) context. One may also ask similar questions about a controlled laboratory context specifically set up for the investigation of, e.g., specific interface features.

This approach is motivated by Objections 1 – 6 in Sect. 1.3 because it employs real actors and tasks, observes real interaction and dynamic requests as well as tactical variability. It also captures actors' uncertainty and personal relevance assessments. Finally, the natural variety of collections is part of the study settings.

Table 8.4 Independent (dark framed shading) and controlled (light shading) variables to look at in investigations on interfaces and actors in socio-organizational contexts.

Natural Work & Search Task	Actor Characteristics	Perceived Work Task	Perceived Search Task	IT Interface Component
Structure/openness-/type	Domain knowledge	Struture/openness-/type	Information need types	Domain model
Strategy/practice	IS&R knowledge	Strategy/practice	Structure/type	System model
Granularity/size/-complexity/specific.	Work task exp.	Granularity/size-complexity/specific.	Strategy/practice	User model
Dependences	Search task exp.	Dependences	Complexity/specific.	System model adaptor
Requirem./Stability	Work task stage	Requirem./Stability	Dependencies	User model builder
Domains/context	Context percept.	Domains/context	Stability	Retrieval strategy
...	Constraints	...	Domains/context	Response generator
	Motivation/emotion		...	Feedback generator
	...			Request model builder
				...

Table 8.4 lists independent and controlled variables to look at in investigations on interfaces and actors in socio-organizational contexts. Columns 1, 3 and 4 give the dimensions Natural Work / Search Task, and Perceived Work / Search Task. Often the natural work and search tasks leave room for interpretation, and if actors vary, then the perceived tasks may vary considerably. The second column presents actor characteristics through a number of variables often used as experimental independent variables. The fifth column details interface variables, which may be independent variables in experimental settings and pseudo-dependent in others. The dependent variables in the extended laboratory experiments would be typical performance measures.

The dark and framed shadings in Table 8.4 represent a *field experiment* research design in a given socio-organizational context where certain types of natural work tasks are focused on. The actors in the context are selected to represent a variation in domain knowledge and work task experience. The overall perceived work task strategy is assumed stable while the search tasks vary and are observed. The interface component is fixed and the use and contribution of its functionalities is observed. The dependent variable is not IR performance, at least not predominantly, but rather related to work/search task completion and actor experiences. Of course, many other designs are possible. This study approach goes beyond traditional online IIR studies because of rigorous application of the work task – search task – actor dimensions.

Methodologically these research designs may be handled as field studies (e.g., how do people use information systems in natural settings?), field experiments (e.g., what kind of handles to desired information do novices or experts have in diverse task contexts), or laboratory experiments (e.g., by using a collection of assigned simulated work tasks, how do various kinds of actors find the information they need or use the functionalities available). The IT engine components may be as they are in the actors' natural environments – possibly creating hidden variables – or they may be controlled. The field studies may be of qualitative nature – to reveal the variety in information access – but not aiming at statistical generalizations. In this latter case one should collect data on 30 to 50 work task processes, depending on the tediousness of data collection, for the selected combination of work task and actor characteristics. In experimental settings one uses set-ups similar to those described in Sects. 8.2-3.

8.5 Methodological Caveats and Summary

Essentially, IS&R research deals with the following central IS&R phenomena – all observed in a variety of contexts according to the research framework, Chapts. 6-7:

- *IS&R processes*: interactions of various kinds between and within the components of the framework;
- *IS&R behavior*: behavior of all actors in play during IS&R, such as, searchers, generators, designers, selectors, members of peer or utility communities, etc.;
- *IR system functionality*: the algorithmic and inference facilities situated in and between the triangular set of components of the framework: IT settings, interface and information objects;
- *IS&R performance*: the effectiveness, efficiency, and usability of the outcome of IS&R processes, behavior and system functionality, seen in association with the information retrieval tasks, seeking tasks and work or daily-life tasks, situated in some given context – see Fig. 7.2.

It is important to stress that by forcing the number of independent variables up from the usual one or two into three, combined in systematic ways by well-planned research designs, one achieves much more than simply capturing more data that provides more results: The researcher(s) becomes increasingly aware of which variables that are crucial in the IS&R contexts which they investigate. Further, they become attentive to the kinds of central characteristics, properties and values of such variables. This fruitful achievement holds regardless whether we talk about laboratory-like experiments, field experiments applying test persons or field studies in natural settings.

Caveats to be Avoided. No research is context-free, and no research object can be made context-free. There have been many occasions in the history of laboratory IR research, where the research design has been regarded as isolated in the sense of a classic experiment in physics. As we have demonstrated above, even in the laboratory model the hidden assessor 'sneaks in' as the ghost in the machine. When hard core IR thinks to play with one independent variable, two algorithms fighting one another, the field actually embraces more.

By being aware of the nature of an increased number of variables, (in)dependent, controlled and hidden, IS&R research attempts to move beyond ad-hoc solutions, towards an increase in hypothesis generation and possibilities of generalization. This means to follow one or several research programs. TREC and INEX are such programs. What seems completely irrational and immature of a scientific field that involves a high amount of empirical research is when it does not allow experimental repetition – that is confirmation of findings – to be published. In most scope notes, editorial statements and reviewing forms of central IS&R journals and conferences it is explicitly stated that research, if to be published, must be original, involve novel methods and algorithms, provide new insights, etc. This policy, having implicitly been hovering over the IS&R communities for decades, makes generalization almost impossible and falsification improbable. A counter argument is that one might apply identical methods to novel phenomena, that is, old methods in new settings. For instance, one could argue, employing well-known methods of data collection and analysis, even including identical hypotheses, as used during the old online age to novel web investigations. However, we are not questioning this kind of research, which actually does not repeat anything. We point to the unfortunate fact that it is not 'in' to repeat and get published, say, an experiment by Salton, Croft, van Rijsbergen or TREC in detail. Simply for the benefit of verifying that they work(ed) – or actually did not – or only did work out as stated providing unknown factor X.

An additional caveat is to observe the way the laboratory approach is pushed to its limit within any symbol system available – be that text, music, chemical formulae – but without paying attention to how people in that symbol system actually act; what they regard as 'relevant', useful' etc. in that system. As we have argued in Sect. 5.7, topical relevance is not applicable in symbol systems like music performance. We have not, albeit, attempted to produce a range of relevance criteria for such non-textual media – but we have hopefully provided the means for future development via the research framework.

Lastly, some IS&R researchers may argue that not only the 'immediate' context, such as the socio-cultural or organizational context with its domains, tasks and preferences should be present in the research agenda. They would prefer also to include more remote 'societal' politico-economic and technical infrastructures and contexts, Fig. 6.10. Our answer to that issue is two-fold:

If the objective of IS&R is to enhance and support people's work and daily-life task performance systematically via information systems and knowledge sources, then one can only take such 'remote' contexts into account when their manifestations can be recorded. If there are no ways of capturing features of context – then such contexts do not matter for that goal of IS&R – although they indeed may influence the activities. The key is to be able to *capture analyzable evidence.*

If the goal of IS&R research alone is to describe and analyze, phenomena and activities concerned with information (seeking) behavior, analytic as well as empirical studies of all kinds of variables and contexts, for instance as provided by our framework, are valid and justified. They may indeed provide an understanding of variables very valuable to research following the objective above. Notwithstanding, in isolation, without reaching out towards the reality of systems, the studies may only with difficulty contribute to the improvement of seeking, retrieval and access of information.

9 Conclusion

Our starting point in this book was that at their present state, both Information Seeking and Information Retrieval fall short regarding the goals of (a) theoretically understanding the phenomena of information access, (b) empirically describing and explaining (predicting) these phenomena, and (c) supporting the development of technology – in the broad sense, covering both tools, systems and social practices. We then set forth to integrate research in IS&R from the cognitive viewpoint. In addition, we wanted to develop the cognitive viewpoint, meeting the criticism leveled at it – the claimed individualism and non-sociality of the early cognitive approach – by extending it to cover both technological, human behavioral and cooperative aspects in a coherent way.

The present book offers the following:

- Analytical tools for treating research frameworks (models) applied on IS&R – introduced in Chap. 1 and applied through the book. This Chapter also presents a discussion between adherers of system-driven laboratory IR and their critics from the user-driven spectrum of IS&R research on central issues and phenomena of IR.
- An analytical discussion of the conception of information for Information Science, leading to the cognitive conception of information: on the one hand as being something which is the result of a transformation of a generator's knowledge structures and on the other hand being something which, when perceived, affects and transforms the recipient's state of knowledge. Its implications are discussed for other conceptions of information, meaning and information acquisition, including sensory data – Chap. 2.
- Selection, organization and analysis of the development of IS&R research with emphasis on system-driven laboratory IR research *and* the cognitive and user-oriented IR and information seeking approaches – in terms of models, concepts, and empirical findings, as well as methods. The time period ranges from the 1960s to present, culminating in each case, in a summary of central achievements and a discussion of limitations and open problems – Chaps. 3-5. The selections are deliberately not made comprehensive for the fields but rather covering ana-

lytic studies, empirical field investigations and experiments that are central for developing an integrated research framework for IS&R.

- Extension of the cognitive viewpoint toward socio-organizational context and the development of a comprehensive and integrated cognitive framework for the study of IS&R. The framework is intended as media-independent and operates with five central components, each consisting of data structures representing the cognitive structures of the actors involved in their generation, maintenance, and modifications over time. The central elements of the framework are the conceptions of work, daily-life and search tasks and the processes of information interaction taking place in a variety of context types – Chap. 6.
- Proposal of two action lines of research development in IS&R – one extending IR research to capture more context, but without sacrificing the laboratory experimentation approach. The other extending information seeking research both toward the task context *and* the technology. The construction and application of nine major dimensions of variables to be applied to the two action lines – Chap. 7.
- Demonstration of how the integrated framework of Chap. 6 and the dimensions of variables, Chap. 7, are turned into illustrative study designs within integrated IS&R – Chap. 8.

In more specific terms we have focused on the following questions throughout the monograph:

- What is the representative conceptual *framework* of the approach under scrutiny? Which phenomena are suggested as important to study? Which not?
- What is the *model* of the approach? How does it represent and relate the phenomena to be studied? Where is the focus, what are fringe areas, what is excluded?
- What kind of *hypotheses* and *theories* may one test within each approach?
- What kind of *research designs* and *contributions* are offered?

We have attempted to create some future archetypical study designs for cognitive IS&R. Field studies, field experiments as well as laboratory experiments are possible. Field studies need not be explanatory – they may be exploratory – and thus lead to more rigorous field and laboratory experiments. The research framework is not geared only toward explaining the variation of retrieval effectiveness. There is no single way of selecting the independent, controlled or dependent variables. Several dependent, controlled and independent variables lack standard operationalization crossing from the field into the laboratory. Cooperation across studies is thus more difficult. Cognitive IR needs to be convincing about the generalizability of findings, in particular derived from of user-oriented studies.

In theoretical study designs the backgrounds differ – formal sciences in the case of laboratory IR vs. Social Sciences in the other case. In methodological studies there also is a difference, since the cognitive IR approach needs to control for human variation and thus the designs become quite different from standard IR experiments.

The contributions of the laboratory IR approach are novel IR techniques and an understanding on how they affect retrieval effectiveness. The contributions of cognitive IR are findings on information access processes and effectiveness in different situations deter-mined by actor / searcher, task and need characteristics. These may lead to the development of interface functionalities or retrieval techniques. Shared interest in developing information access and explaining IR effectiveness is the connection between the approaches. Therefore the two communities seem to need to learn from each other.

Even if laboratory IR would choose to be a science / technology about IR techniques and their effectiveness, it should react to the challenge on its generalizability. If one suspects the generalizability of the findings to *all* conceivable contexts of IR systems application, one might acknowledge that, contrary to the beliefs so far, 80% of the IR terrain remains unmapped and thus more funding and research is needed. On the other hand, IR may be seen as a science / technology about augmenting human task performance through improved access to information in documents in a variety of media. The laboratory approach forms a most central contribution to that goal. In this case however much more remains to be explored – and cognitive IR is a step in that direction.

We feel that this book opens up an intriguing avenue for research into IS&R. At the same time we hope that many among out readers find the avenue equally intriguing, and those who do not, at least find ingredients for the development their own, possibly conflicting approaches to Information Science. There obviously is much to do in the area of IS&R and many approaches are welcome and possible. Progress may be achieved also through disagreement.

Finally, the practical fruits for society that the IS&R research provides are improved tools, systems and social practices for information access, acquisition and use. These are needed in accomplishing work tasks, solving everyday problems of life, or fulfilling cultural or other leisure interests. Managing such tools requires communication between people. Work tasks, other interests and communication are therefore there to stay in all human societies. Whatever tools, systems and social practices are developed to serve them, are transient, bound to change. Therefore the work task, other interest and communication contexts must be observed when understanding, explaining and/or developing IS&R.

Definitions

The central concepts used in this monograph, including the ones displayed in Sect. 1.7, are defined below.

Aboutness. Fundamentally, the concept refers to 'what' an *information object*, text, image, etc. is about (i.e. the topic it discusses), and the 'who' deciding the 'what'. Several definitions exist. In this book, aboutness is not an inherent feature of a document, but dependent on the *cognitive actor(s)* who determines the 'what' during the acts of interpretation and representation in a time-space continuum.

Actor, see *Cognitive Actor*

Affective Relevance. A assessment of emotional nature of *information objects* made by a seeking *cognitive actor* in strong association with subjective relevance types, such as, *topicality, pertinence, situational relevance* and, to an extend, *socio-cognitive* relevance.

Algorithmic Relevance. An objective assessment made by a retrieval algorithm, resulting in a calculated retrieval status value (RSV) for ranked output of the search engine. It refers to the degree of match between the *query* and a retrieved object as determined by the *retrieval model.*

Author Aboutness. The *aboutness* determined by the author(s) of *information objects* through natural language and other means of representation. For instance, the full document as well as author-generated abstract reflects author aboutness. See also *indexer aboutness*.

Bibliographic Relevance. That kind of *relevance* for which the relevance assessment is based on representations of metadata (catalogue records) of information objects, i.e., title and subtitle, author, publisher, year, small contents description (note), class code(s), a few descriptors, and alike restricted metadata.

Categorial Classification. The categorization of objects of any kind in a hierarchical and abstract manner, e.g., by means of generic or part-whole relationships. For example, a *cognitive actor* chooses 'tools' to cover hammer and saw. Related to *situational classification*.

Cognitive Actor. A person responsible for the interpretation or provision of *potential information* or signs represented as *information objects, IT, interface* functionalities and during communication. Central actor categories in IS&R are: searchers or seekers; authors; indexers; algorithmic system designers; interface designers; selectors, such as publishers, editors, employers.

Cognitive and Emotional Work Task Knowledge. See *Work Task Knowledge*.

Cognitive IS&R Framework. The research framework (or model) for studying IS&R phenomena based on the holistic *cognitive viewpoint*. It consists of five central components: *information seeker*(s); *interface*; social-organizational *context*; *IT*; *information objects* –connected by *information interaction*.

Cognitive Model. A model possessed by a *cognitive actor* itself representing its *state of knowledge*, such as cognition, expectations, emotions, intentionality, experiences, imagination, intuition, values, and its environment, and consisting of *declarative* and *procedural knowledge* in the form of *cognitive structures*. Cognitive models can be implemented into information processing devices. See also *knowledge.*

Cognitive Structures. The system of categories and concepts that, for an information-processing device –whether human or machine –constitute his/its model of the world, i.e., the *knowledge* and *emotional state* of the *cognitive actor* or device. Used for knowledge structures. At any given point in time, the current cognitive structures, including emotions, are determined by the actor and its/his/her socio-organizational experiences, education, etc., in context. See also *Principle of complementary social and cognitive influence in IS&R* and *cognitive model.*

Cognitive Viewpoint. An epistemological holistic view whose central point is that any processing of *information*, whether perceptual or symbolic, is mediated by a system of categories or concepts which, for the information processing device, are a model of his/its world –whether the device is a human or a machine. According to this view, the 'world model' consists of *cognitive structures* (or knowledge structures) including emotions, which are determined by the individual and its social/collective experiences, education, etc. in social/organizational/cultural and systemic *contexts*. The cognitive viewpoint is born out of investigations of human mental behavior; computers (and their behavior) are seen as non-semantic manifestations or simulations of certain human mental processes, but not all.

Cognitivism. The epistemological view that the brain is (regarded as similar to) a digital computer and that the human mind is (regarded as similar to) a computer program. According to this view, and in contrast to the *cognitive viewpoint*, the thinking process is information processing, that is, symbol manipulation only, and human mental activities are carried out as if they are processed in computers. Cognitivism does not claim, unlike the related position of 'strong AI', that computers have feelings and thoughts.

Complementarity Principle, see *Principle of complementary social and cognitive influence in IS&R*.

Concept. Perceived regularities in events or objects as designated by a sign or symbol.

Conceptual Domain Knowledge. See *Domain Knowledge*.

Context. In IS&R *actors* and objects associated with each component of the *cognitive IS&R framework* function as context for their own elementary *cognitive structures* (intra-object context), as context to one another (inter-object context), and in context of the interaction processes between framework components, which themselves are contextual to each other. In the latter case one may talk about social/organizational/cultural as well as systemic contexts. The context of *interactive IR* processes ranges from algorithmic IR processes in context of interactive IR as well as information seeking processes to information behavior. All IS&R components and activities are in context of common social, physical and technological infrastructures as well as their history over time.

Daily-life Tasks or Interests. All kinds of *work tasks* and interests that are not job-related activities or *search tasks*. Such tasks may be of social and cultural nature, including leisure and entertainment.

Declarative Knowledge. In IS&R signifying *cognitive structures* of actors concerned with (passive) content properties of *IT, interface, information sources*, including persons and groups, in socio-organizational or cultural *contexts*. Declarative *domain knowledge*, including *work task* (content) *knowledge, domain* and *concept* perceptions belong to this kind of knowledge, as does declarative *IS&R* (search task) *knowledge*, including *information source & system knowledge*. It contrasts *procedural knowledge*.

Document. See *Information Objects*

Document Feature Relevance. That kind of *relevance* for which the relevance assessment is based on extracted features of information objects that may have been processed prior to presentation, such as, term maps, sentences, passages, leit motifs, web page anchors, video stills, picture fragments, etc.

Document Relevance. That kind of *relevance* for which the relevance assessment is based on the full *information object*, e.g., in full text, natural language; no additional features have been added.

Domain. A scientific or professional field of activity, or a socio-organizational-cultural field of activity.

Domain Knowledge. Declarative and procedural knowledge concerned with cognitive actors' perception of work task (content-related) issues, concepts and domains, including problem and work task solving knowledge. In IS&R it contrasts IS&R knowledge.

Emotional State. The state of emotions of a cognitive actor at a given point in time. Emotions may be uncertainty, doubt, clarity, (dis)satisfaction, etc., and are closely associated and intermingled with *cognitive structures.*

Episodic Memory. Those parts of the human memory (long term memory), which refer to *knowledge* of (or *information* about) particular events experienced by the individual. The concept is related to *semantic memory*, and is eventually intermingled with *situational* and *categorial classification.*

Extended Bibliographic Relevance. That kind of *relevance* for which the relevance assessment is based on representations of bibliographic data with a table of contents (or web page anchors), a range of descriptors from an authoritative thesaurus and/or abstract added.

Extended Document Relevance. That kind of *relevance* for which the relevance assessment is based on the full object, with added data on contents, topicality, relationships (referral to inlinking and/or citing objects, no. of links or citations), and alike, most of which are of socio-cognitive nature.

Indexer Aboutness. The *aboutness* determined by an indexer or algorithmic indexing device, implying an analysis of an *information object,* which results in the addition to or/and a transformation of original features and concepts into those accepted by the indexer or indexing device. The use of controlled vocabularies or a thesaurus typically results in indexer aboutness.

Information. The concept of information, from a perspective of information science, has to satisfy dual requirements:

On the one hand information being the result of a transformation of a generator's *cognitive structures*
(by intentionality, model of recipients' states of knowledge, and in the form of signs).

On the other hand being something which, when perceived, affects and transforms the recipient's *state of knowledge*.

Information is seen as supplementary or complementary to a conceptual system that represents the information processing system's *knowledge* of its world. If only the first condition is met, we are talking about *potential information*, i.e., data or similar entities stored in *information sources*, that is of potential value to recipients (whether humans or machines). If only the second condition is met, we are talking about perceived sensory data or signals from nature –not information.

Information Behavior. Human behavior dealing with generation, communication, use and other activities concerned with *information*, such as, *information seeking* behavior and *interactive IR*.

Information Need. Signifies a consciously identified gap in the *knowledge* available to an actor. Information needs may lead to *information seeking* and formulation of *requests* for information. Information needs may also be of collective cognitive nature, e.g., as experienced in organizational contexts.

Information Interaction. Signifies the exchange between two or more *cognitive actors* in contexts of IS&R. Interaction is a two-way communication activity, and information interaction signifies the central contextual bridge between the five components of the *cognitive IS&R framework*. In IS&R three kinds of interaction exist:short-term; session-based; and longitudinal IS&R interaction.

Information Objects. Physical (digital) entities in a variety of media belonging to the *information space* of IR systems, providing *potential information*, data or signs. Information objects are used interchangeably with the term documents, and are in line with people and other *information sources*.

Information Retrieval. The processes involved in representation, storage, searching, finding, filtering and presentation of *potential information* perceived *relevant* to a requirement of information desired by a human user in context. Information retrieval (IR) is commonly divided into algorithmic IR and *interactive IR*.

Information Searcher. See *Information Seeker*.

Information Seeker. The *cognitive actor*(s) seeking (or searching) for *information* in *information sources* by means of IR and *social interaction*. Equivalent to the term Information Searcher.

Information Seeking. Human information behavior dealing with searching or seeking information by means of *information sources* and (interactive) *information retrieval* systems; also called IS&R behavior.

Information Source & System Knowledge. Declarative *IS&R* (or search task) *knowledge,* associated with understanding the declarative (passive) structures of document representation means and types, database structures, and algorithmic contents of *IT* and interfaces as well as humans as *information sources*.

Information Sources. Physical (digital) entities in a variety of media providing *potential information*, data or signs that, when perceived, may affect and transform a recipient's *state of knowledge*, thus turning into *information*. Information sources are divided into entities belonging to *information space* and human information sources.

Information Space. That component of the cognitive IS&R framework that is represented by *information objects* consisting of *potential information* and commonly structured according to *IT* settings of information systems.

Information technology, see *IT*

Intentionality. The underlying cognitive/emotional reasons for engaging into physical and mental activities, such as, information and IS&R behavior. Regarded the generic conception of terms like:purpose, aim, goal, objective, etc.

Interactive IR. The interactive communication processes that occur during retrieval of *information* by involving all major participants in IS&R, i.e., the *searcher*, the *socio-organizational context,* the *IT* setting, *interface* and *information space*.

Interface. A mechanism located as the go-between two electronic or human components of an information system. In IS&R commonly referred to as the (user) interface between the *IT* and *information space* components of an IR system and the seeking actor(s). The interface may be placed locally as a front-end to one or several IR systems, or it may be in full control of (being part of) the underlying IR system's IT components and information space, as a stand-alone system.

Intermediary. A person located in the communication channel between an IR system and current searcher(s) with the purpose interactively to transform *requests* for information into *query* formulations that suit the *IT* system component's retrieval algorithms, logic and commands.

IR System. An information system which is constituted by interactive processes between its *information space, IT* setting, *interface* functionalities and its environment, and capable of searching and finding *information* of potential value to seeker(s) of information.

IS&R Behavior, see *Information seeking*.

IS&R Knowledge. *Declarative* and *procedural IS&R knowledge* concerned with *cognitive actors'* perception of *search task* (content-related) issues, such as, perceived information need and *information source and system knowledge,* as well as *search task solving knowledge* and communication and *social interaction* skills. Contrasting *domain knowledge*.

IT. The component of the *cognitive IS&R framework* concerned with the *IR system*'s information technology architecture, i.e., primarily the algorithmic structures, *retrieval model,* computational logic and database design.

Knowledge. An individual's total understanding of itself and the world around it at any given point in time, incorporating thinking and cognition as well as emotional, intuitive properties and (sub)conscious memory (tacit knowledge).

Knowledge is structured in a variety of ways and displays semantic as well as pragmatic characteristics. In contrast to computers and other man-made mechanisms storing data, human knowledge and *cognitive structures* are capable of self-regulation and acute, non-predetermined transformations, based on self-generated expectations. The former devices contain only manifestations of actors' cognitive structures.

In *IS&R* one may operate with *declarative* and *procedural knowledge* as one dimension and, as another dimension, *domain knowledge*, that is, knowledge of work task contents, *domains, concepts,* topics, persons, *problem and work task solving* processes, etc., and *IS&R knowledge* concerned with *IT setting, information space* and *information sources, interface* and *search task solving* activities and *social interaction.*

Knowledge Representation. The representation of the *aboutness* (and other content-related features) of *information objects* in the form of signs (metadata) made by a *cognitive actor* in order to ease the intellectual access to such objects by *information seekers*.

Knowledge Structures, see *Cognitive Structures.*

Label Effect. The phenomenon that *request* formulations may often consist of one or few concepts, which are of a more general nature or out of the context that constitutes the perceived information need.

Longitudinal IS&R Interaction. A prolonged IS&R activity containing several sessions over a longer period of time, e.g., days, weeks, or months.

Person and Group Knowledge. The acquaintance of and expectations about other people or teams as *information sources*. It involves *declarative knowledge* on formal as well as informal communication channels.

Pertinence. The relationship between the nature of retrieved and viewed *information objects* and the *information need* as perceived by the searcher at a given point in time. Important features are:document currency, novelty of information, interpreted cognitive authority of authors, publishers, institutions and carriers (e.g., journals), etc.

Potential Information. The data or sign structures that are the result of a transformation of a generator's *cognitive structures* (by intentionality, model of recipients' states of knowledge, and in the form of signs). *IR systems* contain potential information, or *information* metaphorically speaking, that is, information of potential value to recipients.

Principle of Complementary Social and Cognitive Influence in IS&R. This combined bottom-up and top-down view of cognition reflects the holistic cognitive view of Information Science and IS&R that mutual connections and influences exist between the individual *cognitive actor(s)* and socio-organizational, cultural and systemic *contexts*, including *domains*, as well as between individual and collective *intentionality,* knowledge, preferences and emotions, expectations and experiences and behavior. Through the actor's interpretations of the latter, via interactive communication processes, the former is the determining factor for change.

Problem Space. A situation-specific state of mind in which the individual *cognitive actor* recognizes lack of *knowledge*, e.g., in order to choose between possibilities of action, of solution to problems, or in relation to the fulfillment of factual or emotional goals and tasks. The problem space forms part of the actual *state of knowledge* and the *cognitive model* of the individual at any given point in time and may change properties through time.

Problem and Work Task Solving Knowledge. *Procedural knowledge* concerned with the execution process and procedures of fulfilling a *work task* or non-job related *daily-life task* or interest.

Procedural Knowledge. *Cognitive structures* concerned with procedural *IS&R knowledge,* such as *search task solving* processes as well as *social interaction* skills, and procedural *domain knowledge,* i.e., activities and processes associated with *problem and work task solving.*

Query. A transformation of a *request* formulation made by an *intermediary* or an *interface* in order to interrogate an *IR system*'s *information space,* in concordance with the system's indexing and retrieval algorithms.

Relevance. The assessment of the perceived topicality, pertinence, usefulness or utility, etc., of *information sources,* made by *cognitive actor*(s) or algorithmic devices, with reference to an information situation, it being a perceived *work task* situation, *problem state* or *information need* formulation, at a given point in time. It can change dynamically over time for the same actor. Relevance can be of a low order objective nature or of higher order, i.e., of subjective multidimensional nature. It's measurement can be binary or graded.

Relevance Types. Aside from the forms of objects assessed, i.e., *bibliographic relevance* or *document relevance,* this monograph operates with the following five types of relevance:algorithmic relevance; topical relevance (or (intellectual) topicality); pertinence; situational relevance; and socio-cognitive relevance. The latter four relevance types are of higher order, due to their subjectivity, and the dimension of *affective relevance* is involved in those types.

Request. The formulation of the information need or the underlying states of *intentionality,* as perceived, and provided at a given point in time by the actual searcher to an *IR system* or other *information sources.* Requests are causally associated to the same cognitive actor(s)' formulations of intentionality in the forms of problem statements and work task descriptions.

Retrieval Model. A retrieval model comprises of a specification (and method) for document representation, a specification (and method) for request representation as a query, and a specification (and method) for matching these representations. Major retrieval models include the Boolean Model within exact match models and the Vector Space and Probabilistic Models within the best match models.

Search Task. The task to be carried out by a cognitive seeking actor(s) as a means to obtain information associated with fulfilling the *work task.* Search tasks are either seeking tasks or retrieval tasks, depending on the involvement of *IR systems*, and include information need generation, information interaction and search task solving. Search task situation are natural in real-life settings and simulated or assigned (as plain requests) in IR experiments.

Search Task Knowledge. Declarative and procedural *IS&R knowledge* concerned with *information sources and systems,* perceived information need and *search task solving.*

Search Task Solving Knowledge. The procedural *IS&R* (or search task) *knowledge* on how to perform information seeking and retrieval, i.e., experiences on (in)formal search activities, strategies, tactics and techniques.

Semantic Memory. Those parts of the human memory (long term memory) that refer to the class of *knowledge* characterized by the definitions of concepts that people have acquired during their experiences of the world. Semantic memory is dependent on the individual's socio-cultural experiences, education, etc., and may demonstrate conceptual relations and definitions shared by many individuals (collective *cognitive structures*), e.g., within particular social groups. The concept is related to *episodic memory*, and is eventually intermingled with *situational* and *categorial classification.*

Semantic Values. Linguistic interpretations of a sentence in a text. Through (morpho)-syntactic analysis, one or several possible 'explicit' interpretations can be made out of a sentence. For example, the sentence 'Time flies like an arrow' may contain at least four different explicit semantic values. For each explicit value a set of 'implicit' semantic values may exist, as actor-generated associative interpretations made by adding own context, not present in the explicit value.

Session-Based Interaction. Several *short-term interactions* make up session-based interactions.

Short-Term Interaction. Short-term interaction with *information sources*, human or *information objects*, is here understood as a few iterations including clarification of information need and (probably) relevance feedback, briefly interrupted (ended) by some other line of action or intellectual behavior, for instance *social interaction.*

Simulated Work Task. *Work tasks*/interest situations designed for IS&R research by involving a specified but artificial scenario or cover story of semantic openness. The situation at hand is meant to trigger individual information needs in test persons in a controlled manner –functioning like natural work tasks.

Situational Classification. The categorization of objects of any kind in a process or event-related structure of concepts. Individuals performing situational classification involve the objects encountered in concrete situations, thereby grouping them together, e.g., 'during house construction hammers are used to hit nails driving them into wood'. 'Related terms' in a thesaurus consist mainly of situational relations. Related to *categorial classification*.

Situational Relevance. The relation between the retrieved and viewed information sources, including human ones via social interaction, and the work task situation as perceived by an individual searcher.

Social Interaction Skills. Implies *procedural knowledge* of social communication conventions, behavior, procedure and codes. Is incorporated into procedural *IS&R knowledge*.

Socio-Cognitive Relevance. It signifies *situational relevance* assessments and interpretations made by *cognitive actors*, either simultaneously (like in a team) and/or over time. Citations (or inlinks) given to objects or collective selections during editorial work, are exemplary manifestations of socio-cognitive relevance judgments made by actors over time. Socio-cognitive relevance is commonly tangible and measurable.

State of Knowledge. The state of the individual's cognitive-emotional structures which, at a given moment, holds what is known and emotionally experienced by the individual, including its attention, actual *intentionality*, as well as its perceived *work task, problem space* and *state of uncertainty*.

State of Uncertainty. An emotional state of conscious doubt in which the cognitive actor's own *state of* (domain) *knowledge* cannot fill the *problem space* by thinking, causing interaction with the world around it to obtain supplementary *information*, e.g., by *information interaction* or *social interaction*.

Topical Relevance. Signifies the relation between the *aboutness* of *information objects* and the *aboutness* of *requests* as perceived by an actor (whether task performer, searcher or judge in IR experiments). Owing to the human assessment (interpretation) this type of relevance is of subjective emotional and intellectual nature.

User Aboutness. 1) The *aboutness* of information object(s) determined by the seeking actor(s) when confronted with such objects. See also *relevance types*. 2) The kind of *indexer aboutness* that attempts to tailor *knowledge representations* of *information objects* to known presuppositions of the searchers in *domain*(s).

User Interface. See *Interface*

Work Task. A job-related task or non-job associated daily-life task or interest to be fulfilled by *cognitive actor*(s). Work tasks can be natural, real-life tasks or be assigned as *simulated work task* situations or assigned *requests*. If perceived and not immediately solvable by actor(s), a work task may lead to *state of uncertainty* and to *search task* situations.

Work Task Knowledge. Declarative as well procedural *domain knowledge* dealing with cognitive and emotional *work task* contents, *state of uncertainty, problem space* as well as *problem and work task solving.*

Work Task Execution. See Problem and Work Task Solving.

References

Abu-Salem, H., Al-Omari, M. & Evens, M.W. (1999). Stemming methodologies over individual query words for an Arabic IR system. *Journal of the American Society for Information Science, 50*: 524-529.

Agosti, M. & Smeaton, A. (1996), Eds. *Information Retrieval and Hypertext.* Boston, MA: Kluwer.

Akmajian, A., Demers, R., Farmer, A. & Harnish, R. (1990). *Linguistics: An introduction to language and communication.* Cambridge, MA: The MIT Press.

Alkula, R. (2001). From plain character strings to meaningful words: Producing better full text databases for inflectional and compounding languages with morphological analysis software. *Information Retrieval, 4*: 195-208.

Allen, B.L. (1991). Cognitive research in information science: Implications for design. In: Williams, M.E. (Ed.) [ARIST 26]: 3-37.

Allen, T.J. (1966a). *Managing the Flow of Scientific and Technological Information.* Cambridge, MA: MIT, Sloan School of Management, PhD. Thesis.

Allen, T.J. (1966b). Studies of the problem-solving process in engineering design. *IEEE Transactions on Engineering Management EM-13*(2): 72-83.

Allen, T.J. (1969). Information needs and uses. In: Cuadra, C.A. (Ed.) [ARIST 26]: 1-29.

Allen, T.J. (1977). *Managing the Flow of Technology: Technology Transfer and Dissemination of Technological Information within the R&D Organization.* Cambridge, MA: MIT Press.

Allen, T.J., Lee, D.M. & Tushman M.L. (1980). R&D performance as a function of internal communication, project management, and the nature of work. *IEEE Transactions on Engineering Management EM-27*(1): 2-12.

Almind, T. and Ingwersen, P. Informetric analyses on the World Wide Web: Methodological approaches to "webometrics". *Journal of Documentation,* 53(4), 1997, 404-426.

Anon. (1974). *Tietosysteemin rakentaminen* [Information system design]. Helsinki, Finland: Tietojenkäsittelyliitto, Publ. 25. [In Finnish.]

Aparac, T., Saracevic, T., Ingwersen, P. & Vakkari, P. (1999), Eds. *Digital Libraries. Interdisciplinary Concepts, Challenges and Opportunities, Proceedings of the CoLIS 3 Conference,* Dubrovnik, Croatia. Zagreb. Lokve, Croatia: Naklada Benja.

Arampatzis, A., van der Weide, Th.P., Koster, C.H.A. & van Bommel, P. (2000). Linguistically-motivated information retrieval. *Encyclopedia of Library and Information Science, Vol. 69.* New York, NY: Marcel Dekker: 201-222.

Artandi, S. (1973). Information concepts and their utility. *Journal of the American Society for Information Science, 24*: 242-245.

Baeza-Yates, R. & Ribeiro, R. (1999), Eds. *Modern Information Retrieval.* Wokingham, UK: Addison-Wesley.

Ballesteros, L. & Croft, W.B. (1997). Phrasal translation and query expansion techniques for cross-language information retrieval. In: Belkin, N.J., Narasimhalu, A.D. & Willett, P. (Eds.) [ACM SIGIR 20]: 84-91. [Available at http:// www.ee.umd.edu/medlab/filter/sss/papers/. Cited Dec. 12, 2003]

Ballesteros, L. & Croft, W.B. (1998). Resolving ambiguity for cross-language retrieval. In: Croft, W.B. et al. (Eds.) [ACM SIGIR 21]: 64-71.

Bar-Ilan, J. (1999). Search engine results over time: A case study on search engine stability. *Cybermetrics, 2/3*(1): paper1. [Online journal; available: http:// www.cindoc.csic.es/cybermetrics/articles/v2i1p1.html]

Bar-Ilan, J. (2000). Evaluating the stability of the search tools Hotbot and Snap: A case study. *Online Information Review, 24*(6): 430-450.

Barr, A. & Feigenbaum, E. (1981), Eds. *Handbook of artificial intelligence: Volume I.* London, UK: Pitman.

Barry, C.L. (1994). User-defined relevance criteria: An exploratory study. *Journal of the American Society for Information Science, 45*(3): 149-159.

Barry, C.L. & Schamber, L. (1998). Users' criteria for relevance evaluation: A cross-situational comparison. *Information Processing & Management, 31*(2/3): 219-236.

Bateman, J. (1998). Changes in relevance criteria: A longitudinal study. In: Preston, C. (Ed.) [ASIS 61]: 23-32.

Bates, M.J. (1972). *Factors Affecting Subject Catalog Search Success.* Berkeley, CA: University of California, Ph.D. Thesis.

Bates, M.J. (1979a). Information search tactics. *Journal of the American Society for Information Science, 30*(4): 205-214.

Bates, M.J. (1979b). Idea tactics. *Journal of the American Society for Information Science, 30*(5): 280-289.

Bates, M.J. (1981). Search Tactics. In: Williams, M.E. (Ed.) [ASIS 16]: 139-169.

Bates, M.J. (1986a). Subject access in online catalogs: A design model. *Journal of the American Society for Information Science, 37*(6): 357-376.

Bates, M.J. (1986b). An exploratory paradigm for online information retrieval. In: Brookes, B.C. (Ed.) [IRFIS 6]: 91-99.

Bates, M.J. (1989). The design of browsing and berrypicking techniques for the online search interface. *Online Review, 13*(5): 407-424.

Bates, M.J. (1990). Where should the person stop and the information search interface start? *Information Processing & Management, 26*(5): 575-591.

Bates, M.J. (2002). The cascade of interactions in the digital library interface. *Information Processing & Management, 38*(3): 381-400.

Bates, M.J., Wilde, D.N. & Siegfried, S. (1993). An analysis of search terminology used by human scholars: The Getty Online Searching Project report no. 1. *Library Quarterly, 63*(1): 1-39.

Bateson, G. (1973). *Steps to an Ecology of Mind.* Frogmore, St. Albans, Herts, UK: Paladin, 1973.

Beaulieu, M. (1997). Experiments with interfaces to support query expansion. *Journal of Documentation, 53*(1): 8-19.

Beaulieu, M. (2000). Interaction in information searching and retrieval. *Journal of Documentation, 56*(4): 431-439.

Beaulieu, M. & Baeza-Yates, R. & Myaeng, S.H. & Järvelin, K. (2002), Eds. *Proceedings of the 25th Annual International ACM SIGIR Conference on Research and Development in Information Retrieval (ACM SIGIR 25),* Tampere, Finland, August 11-15, 2002. New York, NY: ACM Press.

Beaulieu, M., Gatford, M., Huang, X., Robertson, S.E., Walker, S. & Williams, P. (1997). Okapi at TREC-5. In: Voorhees, E.M. & Harman, D.K. (Eds.) [TREC 5]: 143-166. [Available at http://trec.nist.gov/pubs/trec5/ t5_proceedings.html. Cited Dec. 16, 2003.]

Beaulieu, M. & Jones, S. (1998). Interactive searching and interface issues in the Okapi best match probabilistic retrieval system. *Interacting with Computers, 10*(3): 237-248.

Beaulieu, M., Robertson, S. & Rasmussen, E. (1996). Evaluating interactive systems in TREC. *Journal of the American Society for Information Science, 47*(1): 85-94.

Beghtol, C. (1986). Bibliographic classification theory and text linguistics: Aboutness analysis, intertextuality and the cognitive act of classifying documents. *Journal of Documentation, 42*(2): 84-113.

Belew, R.K. (2000). *Finding Out About: A Cognitive Perspective on Search Engine Technology and the WWW.* Cambridge, UK: Cambridge University Press.

Belkin, N.J. (1978). Information concepts for information science. *Journal of Documentation, 34*: 55-85.

Belkin, N.J. (1984). Cognitive models and information transfer. *Social Science Information Studies, 4*(2/3): 111-129.

Belkin, N.J. (1990). The cognitive viewpoint in information science. *Journal of Information Science: Principles and Practice, 16*(1): 11-15.

Belkin, N.J. (1993). Interaction with texts: Information retrieval as information seeking behavior. In: *Information Retrieval '93.* Konstanz: Universitetsverlag Konstanz: 55-66.

Belkin, N.J., Borgman, C.L., Brooks, H.M., Bylander, T., Croft, W.B., Daniels, P.J., Deerwester, S., Fox, E.A., Ingwersen, P., Rada, R. Sparck Jones, K., Thompson, R. & Walker, D. (1987). Distributed expert-based information systems: An interdisciplinary approach. *Information Processing & Management, 23*(5): 395-409.

Belkin, N.J., Brooks, H.M., & Daniels, P. (1987). Knowledge elicitation using doscourse analysis. *International Journal of Man-Machine Studies, 27*: 127-144.

Belkin, N.J., Cool, C., Croft, W.B. & Callan, J.P. (1993). The effect of multiple query representations on information retrieval performance. In: Korfhage, R., Rasmussen, E. & Willet, P. (Eds.) [ACM SIGIR 16]: 339-346.

Belkin, N.J., Cool, C., Koenemann, J., Ng, W.B. & Park, S. (1996a). Using relevance feedback and ranking in interactive searching. In: Harman, D. (Ed.) [TREC 4]: 181-210.

Belkin, N.J., Cool, C., Koenemann, J., Park, S. & Ng, W.B. (1996b). Information seeking behaviour in new searching environments. In: Ingwersen, P. & Pors, N.O. (Eds.) [CoLIS 2]: 403-416.

Belkin, N.J., Cool, C., Stein, A. & Thiel, U. (1995a). Cases, scripts, and information seeking strategies: On the design of interactive information retrieval systems. *Expert Systems with Applications, 9*(3): 379-395.

Belkin, N.J. & Croft, W.B. (1987). Retrieval techniques. In: Williams, M.E. (Ed.) [ARIST 22]: 37-61.

Belkin, N.J., Ingwersen, P. & Pejtersen, A.M. (1992), Eds. *Proceedings of the 15th ACM SIGIR Conference on Research and Development in Information Retrieval (ACM SIGIR 15).* New York, NY: ACM Press.

Belkin, N.J., Ingwersen, P. and Leong, Mun-Kew (2000), Eds. *SIGIR '2000: Proceedings of the 23rd Annual Conference on Research and Development in Information Retrieval (ACM SIGIR 23),* July 24-28, 2000, Athens, Greece. New York, NY: ACM Press.

Belkin, N.J., Kantor, P., Fox, E. & Shaw, J.A. (1995b). Combining the evidence of multiple query representations for information retrieval. *Information Processing & Management, 31*: 431-448.

Belkin, N.J. & Kwasnik, B. (1986). Using structural representations of anomaleous state of knowledge for choosing documentretrieval strategies. In: Rabitti, F. (Ed.) [ACM SIGIR 9]: 11-22.

Belkin, N.J. & Marchetti, P. & Cool, C. (1993). BRAQUE: Design an interface to support user interaction in information retrieval. *Information Processing & Management, 29*(3): 325-344.

Belkin, N.J., Narasimhalu, A.D. & Willett, P. (1997), Eds. *Proceedings of the 20th ACM SIGIR Conference on Research and Development in Information Retrieval (ACM SIGIR 20).* New York, NY: ACM Press.

Belkin, N.J., Oddy, R.N &.Brooks, H.M., (1982a). Ask for information retrieval: Part 1. *Journal of Documentation, 38*(2): 61-71.

Belkin, N.J., Oddy, R.N. & Brooks, H. (1982b). ASK for information retrieval: Part 2. *Journal of Documentation, 38*(3): 145-164.

Belkin, N.J., Seeger, T. & Wersig, G. (1983). Distributed expert problem treatment as a model for information systems analysis and design. *Journal of Information Science: Principles and Practice, 5*: 153-167.

Belkin, N.J. & van Rijsbergen, C.J. (1989), Eds. *Proceedings of the 12th ACM SIGIR Conference on Research and Development in Information Retrieval (ACM SIGIR 12).* New York, NY: ACM Press.

Belkin, N.J. & Vickery, A. (1985). *Interaction in Information Systems.* London, UK: British Library.

Bellardo, T. (1981). Scientific research in online retrieval: A critical review. *Library Research, 2*: 231-237

Bellardo, T. (1985a). An investigation of online searher traits and their relationship to search outcome. *Journal of the American Society for Information Science, 36*(4): 241-250.

Bellardo, T. (1985b). What do we really know about online searchers? *Online Review, 9*(3): 223-239.

Berger, A. & Lafferty, J. (1999). Information retrieval as statistical translation. In: Gey, F., Hearst, M. & Tong, R. (Eds.) [ACM SIGIR 22]: 222-229.

Bilal, D. (2000). Children's use of the Yahooligans! Web search engine: I. Cognitive, physical and affective behaviors on fact-based search tasks. *Journal of the American Society for Information Science, 51*(7): 646-665.

Bilal, D. (2001). Children's use of the Yahooligans! Web search engine: II. Cognitive and physical behaviors on research tasks. *Journal of the American Society for Information Science and Technology, 52*(2): 118-136.

Bilal, D. (2002). Children's use of the Yahooligans! Web search engine: III. Cognitive and physical behaviors on fully self-generated search tasks. *Journal of the American Society for Information Science and Technology, 53*(13): 1170-1183.

Bilal, D. & Kirby, J. (2002). Differences and similarities in information seeking: Children and adults as Web users. *Information Processing & Management, 38*(5): 649-670.

Bishop, A.P., Neumann, L.J., Star, S.L., Merkel, C., Ignacio, E. & Sandusky, R.J. (2000). Digital libraries: Situating use in changing information infrastructure. *Journal of the American Society of Information Science, 51*(4): 394-403.

Björneborn, L. & Ingwersen, P. (2004). Towards a basic framework for webometrics. *Journal of American Society for Information Science & Technology, 55*(14): 1216-1227.

Blair, D.C. (1986). Full text retrieval: Evaluation and implications. *International Classification, 13*(1): 18-23.

Blair, D.C. (1990). *Language and Representation in Information Retrieval.* Oxford, UK: Elsevier.

Blair, D.C. (1996). STAIRS redux: Thoughts on the STAIRS evaluation, Ten years after. *Journal of the American Society of Information Science, 47*(1): 4-22.

Blair, D.C. (2002a). Information Retrieval and the Philosophy of Language. In: Cronin, B. (Ed.) [ARIST 37]: 3-50.

Blair, D.C. (2002b). Some thoughts on the reported results of TREC. *Information Processing & Management, 38*: 445-451.

Blair, D.C. & Maron, M.E. (1985). An Evaluation of retrieval effectiveness for a full-text document retrieval system. *Communications of the ACM, 28*(3): 289-299.

Blair, D.C. & Maron, M.E. (1990). Full-text information retrieval: Further analysis and clarification. *Information Processing & Management, 26*(3): 437-447.

Boguraev, B.K. & Sparck Jones, K. (1982). A natural language analyzer for database access. *Information Technology, 1*(1): 23-39.

Bonnevie, E. (2001). Dretske's semantic information theory and meta-theories in library and information science. *Journal of Documentation, 57*(4): 519-534.

Bonzi, S., & Liddy, E. (1989). The use of anaphoric resolution for document description in information retrieval. *Information Processing & Management, 25*(4): 429-441.

Bookstein, A. et al. (1991), Eds. *Proceedings of the 14th Annual International ACM/SIGIR Conference on Research and Development in Information Re-*

trieval Retrieval (ACM SIGIR 14), Chicago, IL, Oct. 13-16, 1991. New York, NY: ACM Press.

Bookstein, A. & Swanson, D. (1974). Probabilistic models for automatic indexing. *Journal of the American Society for Information Science, 25(5):* 312-318.

Borgman, C.L. (1986a). Why are online catalogs hard to use? Lessons learned from information-retrieval studies. *Journal of the American Society for Information Science, 37*(6): 387-400.

Borgman, C.L. (1986b). The user's mental model of an information retrieval system: An experiment on a prototype online catalogue. *International Journal of Man-Machine Studies, 24*(1): 47-64.

Borgman, C.L. (1989). All users of information retrieval systems are not created equal: An exploration into individual differences. *Information Processing & Management, 25*(3): 237-252.

Borgman, C.L. (1996). Why are online catalogs still hard to use? *Journal of the American Society for Information Science, 47*(7): 493-503.

Borgman, C.L. (2000). *From Gutenberg to the Global Information Infrastructure: Access to Information in the Networked World.* Cambridge, MA: MIT Press.

Borgman, C.L. et al. (1995). Children's searching behavior on browsing and keyword searching online catalogs: The Science Library Catalog Project. *Journal of the American Society for Information Science, 46*(9): 663-684.

Borlund, P. (2000a). Experimental components for the evaluation of interactive information retrieval systems. *Journal of Documentation, 56*(1): 71-90.

Borlund, P. (2000b). *Evaluation of interactive information retrieval systems.* Åbo, Finland: Åbo Akademi University Press, Ph.D. Thesis.

Borlund, P. (2003a). The concept of relevance in IR. *Journal of the American Society for Information Science and Technology, 54*(10): 913-925.

Borlund, P. (2003b). The IIR evaluation model: A framework for evaluation of interactive information retrieval systems. *Information Research, 8*(3), paper no. 152 [Available at: http://informationr.net/ir/8-3/paper152.html. Cited May 13, 2003.]

Borlund, P. & Ingwersen, P. (1997). The development of a method for the evaluation of interactive information retrieval systems. *Journal of Documentation, 53*(3): 225-250.

Borlund, P. & Ingwersen, P. (1998). Measures of relative relevance and ranked half-life: Performance indicators for interactive IR. In: Croft, W.B. et al. (Eds.) [ACM SIGIR 21]: 324-331.

Brier, S. (1996). Cybersemiotics: A new interdisciplinary development applied to the problems of knowledge organisation and document retrieval in information science. *Journal of Documentation, 52*(3): 296-344.

Brin, S. & Page, L. (1998). The anatomy of a large-scale hypertextual web search engine. *Computer Networks and ISDN Systems, 30*(1-7): 107-117.

Brittain, M.J. (1975). Information needs and the application of the results of user studies. In: Debons, A. & Cameron, W. (Ed.), [Perspectives]: 425-447.

Brittain, M.J. (1982). Pitfalls of user oriented research, and some neglected areas. In: Friberg, I. (Ed.), [IRFIS 4]: 213-227.

Brookes, B.C. (1975). The fundamental problem of information science. In: Horsnell, V. (Ed.) [Informatics 2]: 42-49.

Brookes, B.C. (1977). The developing cognitive viewpoint in information science. In: de Mey, M. et al. (Eds.) [CC77]: 195-203.

Brookes, B.C. (1980). The foundation of information science: Part 1: Philosophical aspects. *Journal of Information Science: Principles and Practice, 2*: 125-133.

Brookes, B.C. (1986), Ed. *Intelligent Information Systems for the Information Society Proceedings of the IRFIS 6 Conference (IRFIS 6),* Frascati, Italy, 1985. Amsterdam, NL: North-Holland.

Brooks, H. (1986). Developing and representing problem descriptions. In: Brookes, B.C. (Ed.) [IRFIS 6]: 141-161.

Brooks, H. (1987). Expert systems and intelligent information retrieval. *Information Processing & Management, 23*(4): 367-382.

Brooks, H. & Belkin, N.J. (1983). Using discourse analysis for the design of information retrieval interaction mechanism. In: McGill, M.J. & Koll, M. (Eds.) [ACM SIGIR 5]: 31-47.

Bruce, H.W. (1994). A cognitive view of the situational dynamism of user-centered relevance estimation. *Journal of the American Society for Information Science, 45*: 142-148.

Bruce, H., Fidel, R., Ingwersen, P. & Vakkari, P. (2002), Eds. *Emerging Frameworks and Methods. Proceedings of the 4th International Conference on Conceptions of Library and Information Science (CoLIS 4),* July 21-25, 2002, Seattle, USA. Greenwood Village, CO: Libraries Unlimited.

Buckland, M. (1991a). *Information and Information Systems.* New York, NY: Greenwood Press.

Buckland, M. (1991b). Information as thing. *Journal of the American Society for Information Science, 42*(5): 351-360.

Buckley, C., Singhal, A., Mandar, M. & (Salton, G.) (1995). *New Retrieval Approaches Using SMART: TREC 4.* In: Harman, D. (1996) (Ed.) [TREC 4]: 25-48. [Available at http://trec.nist.gov/pubs/trec4/t4_proceedings.html. Cited Dec. 16, 2003]

Buckley, C. & Voorhees, E.M. (2000). Evaluating evaluation measure stability. In: Belkin, N.J. et al. [ACM SIGIR 23]: 33-40.

Bunge, M. (1967). *Scientific research.* Heidelberg: Springer-Verlag.

Burgin, R. (1992). Variations in relevance judgements and the evaluation of retrieval performance. *Information Processing & Management, 28*(5): 619-627.

Byström, K. (1996). The use of external and internal information sources in relation to task complexity in a journalistic setting. In: Ingwersen, P. & Pors, N.O. (Eds.) [CoLIS 2]: 325-342.

Byström, K. (1999). *Task complexity, information types and information sources. Examination of relationships.* Tampere, Finland: University of Tampere, Department of Information Studies, Ph.D. Thesis. Acta Universitatis Tamperensis 688.

Byström, K. & Järvelin K. (1995). Task complexity affects information seeking and use. *Information Processing & Management, 31*(2): 191-213.

Bødker, S., Kyng, K. & Schmidt, K. (1999), Eds. *ECSCW'99: Proceedings of the Sixth European Conference on Computer Supported Cooperative work,* Copenhagen, DK, Sept. 12-16, 1999. Dortrecht: Kluwer.

Callan, J.P. (1994). Passage-level evidence in document retrieval. Croft, W.B. & van Rijsbergen, C.J. (Eds.) [ACM SIGIR 17]: 302-310.

Callan, J.P., Croft, W.B. & Broglio, J. (1995). TREC and TIPSTER experiments with INQUERY. *Information Processing & Management, 31*(3):327-343.

Callan, J.P., Hawking, D., Smeaton, A., Clarke, C. (2003), Eds. *Proceedings of the 26th Annual International ACM SIGIR Conference on Research and Development in Information Retrieval (ACM SIGIR 26),* Toronto, Canada, July 28 - August 1, 2003. New York, NY: ACM Press.

Campbell, D.J. (1988). Task complexity: A review and analysis. *Academy of Management Review, 13*(1): 40-52.

Campbell, I. (2000). Interactive evaluation of the ostensive model using a new test collection of images with multiple relevance assessments. *Information Retrieval, 2*(1): 87-114.

Campbell, I. & van Rijsbergen, C.J. (1996). The ostensive model of developing information needs. In: Ingwersen, P. and Pors, N.O. (Eds.) [CoLIS 2]: 251-268.

Caplan, N., Morrison, A. & Stambaugh, R.J. (1975). *The Use of Social Science Knowledge in Policy Decisions at the National Level: A Report to the Respondents.* Ann Arbor, MI: University of Michigan, Institute for Social Research.

Capurro, R. (1992). What is Information Science for? A philosophical reflection. In: Vakkari, P. & Cronin, B. (Eds.) [CoLIS 1]: 83-96.

Case, D.O. (2002). *Looking for information: A survey of research on information seeking, needs and behavior.* Amsterdam, NL: Academic Press.

Catledge, L.D. & Pitkow, J.E. (1995). Characterizing browsing strategies in the World-Wide Web. *Computer Networks and ISDN Systems, 27* (6): 1065-1073.

Chen, H. (2000), Ed. Special topic issue: Digital libraries: Part 2. *Journal of the American Society of Information Science, 51*(4): 311-403.

Cherry, C. (1957). *On Human Communication: A Review, a Survey, and a Criticism.* Cambridge, MA: MIT Press. [2nd ed. 1966].

Chiaramella, Y. (1988), Ed. *Proceedings of the 11th Annual International ACM-SIGIR Conference on Research and Development in Information Retrieval (ACM SIGIR 11).* Grenoble, France: Press Universitaire de Grenoble.

Chinenyanga, T.T. & Kushmerick, N. (2001). Expressive retrieval from XML documents. In: Croft, W.B. et al. (Eds.) [ACM SIGIR 24]: 163-171.

Chowdhury, G.G. (2002). *Natural Language Processing.* In: Cronin, B. (Ed.) [ARIST 37]: 51-89.

Christoffersen, M. (2004). Identifying core documents with a multiple evidence relevance filter. *Scientometrics, 61*(3): 385-394.

Cleverdon, C.W. (1967). The Cranfield tests on index language devices. *Aslib Proceedings, 19*: 173-194.

Cleverdon, C.W. (1984). Optimizing convenient online access to bibliographic databases. *Information Services and Use, 4*: 37-47.

Cleverdon, C.W., Mills, J. & Keen, M. (1966). *Factors Determining the Perform-ance of Indexing Systems. vol. 1: Design; vol. 2: Test Results.* Cranfield, UK: College of Aeronautics, 1966.

Cole, C. (1999). Activity of understanding a problem during interaction with an 'enabling' information retrieval system: Modeling information flow. *Journal of the American Society for Information Science, 50*(6): 544-552.

Cole, C., Cantero, P. & Ungar, A. (2000). The development of a diagnostic-prescriptive tool for undergraduates seeking information for a social sci-ence/humanities assignment. *Information Processing & Management, 36*: 481-500.

Cool, C. & Spink, A. (2002) (Eds.). Issues of context in information retrieval: Special issue. *Information Processing & Management, 38*(5): 605-742.

Cooper, W.S: (1968). Expected search length: a single measure of search effec-tiveness based on the weak ordering action of retrieval systems. *American Documentation, 19*(1): 30-41.

Cooper, W.S. (1971). A definition of relevance for information retrieval. *Informa-tion Storage and Retrieval, 7*(1): 19-37.

Cormack, G.V., Palmer, C.R. & Clarke, C.L.A. (1998). Efficient construction of large test collections. In: In: Croft, W.B. et al. (Eds.), [ACM SIGIR 21]: 282-289.

Cosijn, E. (2003). Relevance Judgements in Information Retrieval. Pretoria, RSA: University of Pretoria, Dept. of Information Science, Ph.D. Thesis.

Cosijn, E. & Ingwersen, P. (2000). Dimensions of relevance. *Information Process-ing & Management, 36*: 533-550.

Cosijn, E., Pirkola, A., Bothma, T. & Järvelin, K. (2002). Information access in indigenous languages: a case study in Zulu. In: Bruce, H. et al. (Eds.) [CoLIS 4]: 221-238.

Cothey, V. (2002). A longitudinal study of World Wide Web users' information-searching behavior. *Journal of the American Society for Information Science and Technology, 53*(2): 67-78.

Crane, D. (1971). Information needs and uses. In: Cuadra, C.A. & Luke, A.W. (Eds.) [ARIST 6]: 3-39.

Crawford, S. (1978). Information needs and uses. In: Williams, M.E. (Ed.), [ARIST 13]: 61-81.

Croft, W.B. (1986). User-Specified Domain Knowledge for Document Retrieval. In: Rabitti, F. (Ed.) [ACM SIGIR 9]: 201-206.

Croft, W.B. & Das, R. (1990). Experiments with query acquisition and use in document retrieval systems. In: Vidick, J.L. (Ed.) [ACM SIGIR 13]: 349-368.

Croft, W.B., Harper, D.J., Kraft, D.H. & Zobel, J. (2001), Eds. *Proceedings of the 24th ACM SIGIR Conference on Research and Development in Information Retrieval (ACM SIGIR 24).* New York, NY: ACM.

Croft, W.B., Krovetz, R. & Turtle, H. (1990). Interactive retrieval of complex documents. *Information Processing & Management, 26*(5): 593-613.

Croft, W.B., Moffat, A., van Rijsbergen, C.J., Wilkinson, R. & Zobel, J. (1998), Eds. *Proceedings of the 21st Annual International ACM SIGIR Conference on*

Research and Development in Information Retrieval (ACM SIGIR 21), Melbourne, Australia. New York, NY: ACM Press.

Croft, W.B. & Thomson, R.H. (1987). I3R: A new approach to the design of document retrieval systems. *Journal of the American Society for Information Science, 38*(6): 389-404.

Croft, W.B, Turtle, H.R. & Lewis, D. (1991). The use of phrases and structured queries in information retrieval. In: Bookstein, A. et al. (Eds.) [ACM SIGIR 14]: 32-45.

Croft, W.B. & van Rijsbergen, C.J. (1994), Eds. *Proceedings of the 17th Annual International ACM SIGIR Conference on Research and Development in Information Retrieval (ACM SIGIR 17).* New York, NY: ACM Press.

Cronin, B. (2002a), Ed. *Annual Review of Information Science and Technology: vol. 36 (ARIST 36).* Medford, NJ: Information Today.

Cronin, B. (2002b), Ed. *Annual Review of Information Science and Technology: Volume 37 (ARIST 37).* Medford, NJ: Information Today.

Cuadra, C.A. (1966), Ed. *Annual Review of Information Science and Technology, vol. 4 (ARIST 4).* Chicago, IL: William Benton.S

Cuadra, C.A. (1967), Ed. *Annual Review of Information Science and Technology: Volume 2 (ARIST 2).* New York, NY: Wiley.

Cuadra, C.A. (1968), Ed. *Annual Review of Information Science and Technology, vol. 3(ARIST 3).* Chicago, IL: William Benton.

Cuadra, C.A. (1969), Ed. *Annual Review of Information Science and Technology: Vol. 4 (ARIST 4).* Chicago, IL: William Benton.

Cuadra, C.A. & Katter, R.V. (1967). *Experimental Studies of Relevance Judgments: Final Report. Vol. I: Project summary.* Santa Monica, CA: System Development Corporation.

Cuadra, C.A. & Luke, A.W. (1970), Eds. *Annual review of Information Science and technology, vol. 5 (ARIST 5).* Chicago, IL: Encyclopaedia Britannica.

Cuadra, C.A. & Luke, A.W. (1971), Eds. *Annual Review of Information Science and Technology: vol. 6 (ARIST 6).* Chicago, IL: William Benton.

Cuadra, C.A. & Luke, A.W. (1972), Eds. *Annual Review of Information Science and Technology, vol. 7 (ARIST 7).* Washington, DC: ASIS.

Cuadra, C.A., Luke, A.W. & Harris, J.L. (1974), Eds. *Annual Review of Information Science and Technology,* vol. 9 (ARIST 9). Washington, DC: ASIS.

Daniels, P. (1986). *Cognitive Models in Information Retrieval: An Evaluative Review.* London, UK: City University.

Davis, M. & Wilson, C.S. (2001), Eds. *Proceedings of the 8th International Conference on Scientometrics & Informetrics (ISSI2001),* Sydney, July 16-20, 2001, vol. 1. Sydney, Australia: The University of New South Wales.

De Mey, M. (1977). The Cognitive viewpoint: Its development and its scope. In: De Mey, M. et al. (Eds.), *CC77: International Workshop on the Cognitive Viewpoint,* March 24-26, 1977. Ghent, Belgium. Ghent, Belgium: University of Ghent: xvi-xxxi.

De Mey, M. (1980). The relevance of the cognitive paradigm for information science. In: Harbo, O. & Kajberg, L. (Eds.), [IRFIS 2]: 48-61.

De Mey, M. (1982). *The Cognitive Paradigm: An Integrated Understanding Of Scientific Development.* Dordrecht, Holland: Reidel.

De Mey, M. (1984). Cognitive science and science dynamics: Philosophical and epistemological issues for information science. *Social Science Information Studies, 4*(2-3): 97-110.

Debons, A. & Cameron, W. (1975), Eds. *Perspectives in Information Science (Perspectives).* Leyden, NL: Noordhoff.

Dennis, S., Bruza, P. & McArthur, R. (2001). Web searching: A progress-oriented experimental study of three interactive search paradigms. *Journal of the American Society for Information Science and Technology, 53*(2): 120-133.

Dervin, B. (1983). An overview of sense-making research: concepts, methods and results to date. In: *International Communications Association Annual Meeting.* Dallas, Texas.

Dervin, B. (1992). From the mind's eye of the user: The sense-making qualitative-quantitative methodology. In: Glazier, R.R. (Ed.): 61-84.

Dervin, B. (1997). Given a context by any other name: Methodological tools for taming the unruly beast. In: Vakkari, P., Savolainen, S. & Dervin, B. (Eds.) [ISIC 1]: 13-38.

Dervin, B. (1999). On studying information seeking methodologically: The implications of connecting metatheory to method. *Information Processing & Management, 35*: 727-750.

Dervin, B. (2002). *Empirical findings based on the Sense-Making Methodology.* Personal communication to Kal Järvelin, July 30, 2002.

Dervin, B. & Dewdney, P. (1986). Neutral questioning: a new approach to the reference interview. *RQ, 1986*(Summer): 506-513.

Dervin, B. & Frenette, M. (2001). Sense-Making Methodology: Communicating communicatively with campaign audiences. In: Rice, R. & Atkin, C.K., (Eds.), *Public Communications Campaigns* (3rd ed). Thousand Oaks, CA: Sage: 69-87. [Available at http://communication.sbs.ohio-state.edu/ sensemaking/zennez/zennezderv&frencamp00.html. Cited Sept. 23, 2002]

Dervin, B. & Nilan, M. (1986). Information needs and uses. In: Williams, M.E. (Ed.) [ARIST 21]: 3-33.

Ding, Y., Chowdhury, G. & Foo, C. (1999). Mapping the intellectual structure of information retrieval studies: An author-co-citation analysis, 1987-1997. *Journal of Information Science, 25*(1): 67-78.

Doyle, L.B. (1962). *Indexing and abstracting by association, Part I.* Santa Monica, CA: System Development Corporation.

Drabenstott, K.M. (2003). Do nondomain experts enlist the strategies of domain experts? *Journal of the American Society for Information Science and Technology, 54*(9): 836-854.

Drabenstott, K.M. & Weller, M.S. (1996). Failure analysis of subject searches in a test of a new design for subject access to online catalogs. *Journal of the American Society for Information Science, 47*: 519-537.

Dretske, F.I. (1981). *Knowledge and the Flow of Information.* Oxford, UK: Basil Blackwell.

Efthimiadis, E.N. (1992). *Interactive Query Expansion and Relevance Feedback for Document Retrieval Systems.* London, UK: City University, Ph.D. Thesis.

Efthimiadis, E.N. (1993). A user-centered evaluation of ranking algorithms for interactive query expansion. In: Korfhage, R., Rasmussen, E. & Willet, P. (Eds.), [ACM SIGIR 16]: 146-156.

Efthimiadis, E.N. (1996). Query expansion. In: Williams, M.E. (Ed.) [ARIST 31]: 121-187.

Egghe, L. & Rousseau, R. (1990). *Introduction to Informetrics: Quantitative Methods in Library, Documentation and Information Science.* Amsterdam, NL: Elsevier.

Eisenberg, M. (1988). Measuring relevance judgments. *Information Processing & Management, 24*(4), 373-389.

Elbaek, M. & Skovvang, M. (2003). *Kortlaegning & visualisering af kompetencenetvaerk i udviklingsprojekter: et casestudie af Oticon A/S.* Copenhagen, DK: Royal School of Librarianship and Information Science, Master's Thesis.

Ellis, D. (1989). A behavioural approach to information retrieval design. *Journal of Documentation, 45*(3): 171-212.

Ellis, D. (1990). *New Horizons in Information Retrieval.* London: Library Association.

Ellis, D. (1992). The physical and cognitive paradigms in information retrieval research. *Journal of Documentation, 48*(1): 45-64.

Ellis, D. (1996). *Progress and Problems in Information Retrieval.* London, UK: Library Association Publishing.

Ellis, D., Cox, D. & Hall, K. (1993). A comparison of the information seeking patterns of researchers in the physical and social sciences. *Journal of Documentation, 49*: 356-369.

Ellis, D., Furner-Hines, J. & Willett, P. (1994). On the creation of hypertext links in full-text documents: measurement of inter-linker consistency. *Journal of Documentation, 50*(2): 67-98.

Ellis, D. & Haugan, M. (1997), Modeling the information seeking patterns of engineers and research scientists in an industrial environment. *Journal of Documentation, 53*(4): 384-403.

Ellis, D., Wilson, T.D., Ford, N., Foster, A. Lam, H.M., Burton, R. & Spink, A. (2002). Information seeking and mediated searching: Part 5 : User-intermediary interaction. *Journal of the American Society for Information Science and Technology, 53*: 883-893.

Eloranta, K. (1974). *Heuristiikat ja heuristisuus.* [Heuristics and Heuristicity] Tampere, Finland: University of Tampere, Dept. of Administrative Sciences, Ph.D. Thesis.

Engelbart, D. (1962). *Augmenting Human Intellect: A conceptual Framework.* Menlo Park, CA: Stanford Research Institute.

Ericsson, K.A. and Simon, H.A. (1984). *Protocol Analysis: Verbal Reports as Data.* Cambridge, MA: MIT Press. [Rev. ed. 1996.]

Erman, L. D., Hayes-Roth, F., Lesser, V. R., & Reddy, R. (1980). The hearsay-ii speech-understanding system: Integrating knowledge to resolve uncertainty. *ACM Computing Surveys, 12*(2): 213-253.

Fawyer, S. & Eschenfelder, K. (2002). Social informatics: perspectives, examples, and trends. In: In: Cronin, B. (Ed.) [ARIST 36]: 427-466.

Feinman, S. et al. (1976). A conceptual framework for information flow studies. In: Martin, S. (Ed.) [ASIS 38]: 106-116.

Fellbaum, C. (1998), Ed. *WordNet: An Electronic Lexical Database.* Cambridge, MA: MIT Press.

Fenichel, C.H. (1980). An examination of the relationship between searching behaviour and searcher background. *Online Review, 4*(4): 341-347.

Fenichel, C.H. (1981). Online searching: measures that discriminate among users with different types of experiences. *Journal of the American Society for Information Science, 32*(1): 24-32.

Fidel, R. (1984a). Online searching styles: A case-study-based model of searching behavior. *Journal of the American Society for Information Science, 35*(4): 211-221.

Fidel, R. (1984b). The Case Study Method: A case study. *Library and Information Science Research, 6*(3): 273-288.

Fidel, R. (1985). Moves in online searching. *Online Review, 9*(1): 61-74.

Fidel, R. (1986). Writing abstracts for free-text searching. *Journal of Documentation, 42*(1): 11-21.

Fidel, R. (1991a). Searchers' selection of search keys, I: The selection routine. *Journal of the American Society for Information Science, 42*(7): 490-500.

Fidel, R. (1991b). Searchers' selection of search keys, II: Controlled vocabulary or free-text searching. *Journal of the American Society for Information Science, 42*(7): 501-514.

Fidel, R. (1991c). Searchers' selection of search keys, III: Searching styles. *Journal of the American Society for Information Science, 42*(7): 515-527.

Fidel, R. (1993). Qualitative methods in information retrieval research. *Library and Information Science Research, 15*(3): 219-247.

Fidel, R. et al. (1999). A visit to the information mall: Web searching behavior of high school students. *Journal of the American Society for Information Science, 50*(1): 24-37.

Fidel, R., Bruce, H., Pejtersen, A. M., Dumais, S., Grudin, J. & Poltrock, S. (2000). Collaborative information retrieval (CIR). *The New Review of Information Behaviour Research: Studies of Information Seeking in Context, 1*(1), 235-247.

Fidel, R. & Soergel, D. (1983). Factors affecting online bibliographic retrieval: A conceptual framework for research. *Journal of the American Society for Information Science, 34*(3): 163-180.

Ford, N. (2000). Improving the darkness to light ratio in information retrieval research. *Journal of Documentation, 56*(6): 624-643.

Ford, N., Miller, D. & Moss, N. (2002). Web search strategies and retrieval effectiveness: An empirical study. *Journal of Documentation, 58*(1): 30-48.

Ford, N., Miller, D. & Moss, N. (2003). Web search strategies and approaches to study. *Journal of American Society for Information Science and Technology, 54*(6): 473-489.

Ford, N., Wood, F. & Walsh, C. (1994). Cognitive styles and searching. *Online & CD-ROM Review, 18*(2): 79-86.

Foskett, A.C. (1996). *The Subject Approach to Information.* 5th ed. London, UK: Library Association Publishing.

Foucault, M. (1972). *The Archaeology of Knowledge.* London: Routledge.

Fox, E.A. (1987). The Development of the CODER System: A Testbed for Artificial Intelligence Methods in IR. *Information Processing & Management, 23*(4): 341-366.

Fox, E.A. & Ingwersen, P. & Fidel, R. (1995), Eds. *Proceedings of the 18th International Conference on Research and Development in Information Retrieval (ACM SIGIR 18),* Seattle, July 9-12, 1995. New York, NY: ACM Press.

Frankfort-Nachmias, C. & Nachmias, D. (2000). *Research Methods in the Social Sciences.* 6th ed. New York: Worth Publishers. xxi, 550 p.

Frei H-P., Harman D.K., Schäuble P. & Wilkinson R. (1996), Eds. *Proceedings of the 19th Annual International ACM SIGIR Conference on Research and Development in Information Retrieval (ACM SIGIR 19).* New York, NY: ACM Press.

Friberg, I. (1981), Ed. *Proceedings of the 4th International Research Forum in Information Science (IRFIS 4),* Borås, September 14-16, 1981. Borås, Sweden: Högskolan i Borås.

Frohmann, B. (1990). Rules of indexing: A critique of mentalism in information retrieval theory. *Journal of Documentation, 46*(2): 81-101.

Frohmann, B. (1992). The power of images: a discourse analysis of the Cognitive viewpoint. *Journal of Documentation, 48*(4): 365-386.

Fugmann, R. (1990), Ed. *Tools for Knowledge Organisation and the Human Interface. Proceedings of the 1st International ISKO Conference,* Darmstadt, August 14-17, 1990. Part 1. Indeks Verlag, Frankfurt/Main.

Fuhr, N. (1992). Integration of Probabilistic Fact and Text Retrieval. In: Belkin, N.J., Ingwersen, P. & Pejtersen, A.M. (Eds.) [ACM SIGIR 15]: 211-222.

Fuhr, N. & Großjohann, K. (2001). XIRQL: A Query Language for Information Retrieval in XML Documents. In: Croft, W.B. et al. (Eds.) [ACM SIGIR 24]: 172-180.

Fuhr, N., Gövert, N., Kazai, G., and Lalmas, M. (2002), Eds. *Proceedings of the First Workshop of the INitiative for the Evaluation of XML Retrieval (INEX 2002).* Schloss Dagstuhl, Germany, 26-32. [Available at: http://qmir.dcs.qmul.ac.uk/inex/]

Fuhr, N. & Rölleke, T. (1997). A probabilistic relational algebra for the integration of information retrieval and database systems. *ACM Transactions on Information Systems, 14*(1): 32-66.

Gaizauskas, R. & Wilks, Y. (1998). Information extraction: Beyond document retrieval. *Journal of Documentation, 54*(1): 70-105.

Garfield, E. (1979). *Citation Indexing: Its Theory and Application in Science, Technology and Humanities.* New York, NY: Wiley. [Reprinted by ISI Press, 1983.]

Garofolo, J.S., Auzanne, C.G.P. & Voorhees, E.M. (2000). The TREC spoken document retrieval track: A success story. In: [RIAO 2000]: 1-20.

Gey, F., Hearst, M. & Tong, R. (1999), Eds. *Proceedings of the 22nd ACM SIGIR Conference on Research and Development in Information Retrieval (ACM SIGIR 22).* New York, NY: ACM Press.

Glazier, R.R. (1992), Ed. *Qualitative Research in Information Management.* Englewood, CO: Libraries Unlimited.

Glaser, B. G. & Strauss, A. L. (1967). *The Discovery of Grounded Theory.* New York, NY: Aldine de Gruyter.

Goldfarb, C.F. (1990). *The SGML handbook.* New York, NY: Oxford University Press.

Golovchinsky, G., Price, M.N. & Schilit, B.N. (1999). From Reading to Retrieval: Freeform Ink Annotations as Queries. In: Gey, F., Hearst, M. & Tong, R. (Eds.) [ACM SIGIR 22]: 19-25.

Greene, S., Marchionini, G., Plaisant, C. & Shneiderman, B. (2000). Previews and overviews in digital libraries: Designing surrogates to support visual information seeking. *Journal of the American Society of Information Science, 51*(4): 380-394.

Guarino, N. (1995). Formal ontology, conceptual analysis and knowledge representation. *International Journal of human and Computer Studies, 43*(5/6): 625–640.

Guarino, N. (1997). Semantic matching: Formal ontological distinctions for information organization, extraction, and integration. In: Pazienza, M.T. (Ed.), [Information extraction]: 139-170.

Guarino, N., Masolo, C. & Vetere, G. (1998). *OntoSeek: Using large linguistic ontologies for gathering information resources from the Web.* Padova, IT: National Research Council, LADSEB-CNR, Technical Report 01/98.

GVU's WWW User Surveys (2001). [Available at: http://www.cc.gatech.edu/gvu/user_surveys/. Cited May 28, 2003.]

Gövert, N. & Kazai, G. (2002). Overview of the INitiative for the Evaluation of XML retrieval (INEX) 2002. In: Fuhr, N. et al. (Eds.) [INEX 2002]: 1-17.

Haas, S. (1996). Natural Language Processing: Toward Large-Scale, Robust Systems. In: Williams, M.E. (Ed.) [ARIST 31]: 83-119.

Hahn, U. (1990). Topic parsing: accounting for text macro structures in full-text analysis. *Information Processing & Management, 26*(l), 135-170.

Hancock-Beaulieu, M., Fieldhouse, M. & Do, T. (1995). An evaluation of interactive query expansion in an online library catalogue with a graphical user interface. *Journal of Documentation, 51*(3): 225-243.

Hansen, P. (1999). User interface design for IR interaction. A task-oriented approach. In: Aparac, T. et al. (Eds.) [CoLIS 3]: 191-205.

Hansen, P. & Järvelin, K. (2004). Collaborative information searching in an information-intensive work domain: Preliminary results. *Journal of Digital Information Management, 2*(1), 26-29.

Hansen, P. & Järvelin, K. (2005). Collaborative information retrieval in an information-intensive domain. *Information Processing & Management, 41*(5), 1101-1119.

Harbo, O. & Kajberg, L. (1980), Eds. Theory and Application of Information Research: *Proceedings of the 2nd International Research Forum on Information Science, (IRFIS 2)* 1977, August 3-6; Copenhagen, Denmark, Royal School of Librarianship. London, UK: Mansell.

Harman, D.K. (1991). How effective is suffixing? *Journal of the American Society for Information Science, 42*(1): 7-15.

Harman, D.K. (1992). Relevance feedback revisited. In N. Belkin, P. Ingwersen & A. Mark Pejtersen (eds.) [ACM SIGIR 15]: 1-10.

Harman, D.K. (1993), Ed. *The first text retrieval conference (TREC 1).* Washington DC: National Institute of Standards and Technology, NIST Special Publication 500-207. [Available at http://trec.nist.gov/pubs/trec1/ t1_proceedings.html. Cited April 12, 2005.]

Harman, D.K. (1993). Overview of the first text retrieval conference (TREC 1). In: Harman, D.K. (Ed.) [TREC 1]: 1-20.

Harman, D.K. (1995a), Ed. *The Third Text REtrieval Conference (TREC 3).* Gaithersburg, MD: National Institute of Standards and Technology, NIST Special Publication 500-226. [Available at http://trec.nist.gov/pubs/trec3/ t3_proceedings.html. Cited Apr. 12, 2005.]

Harman, D.K. (1995b). *Overview of the fourth text retrieval conference (TREC-4)* In: Harman, D. (1996), (Ed.) [TREC 4]: 1-24. [Available at http://trec.nist.gov/pubs/trec4/papers/overview.ps. Cited Nov. 5, 2003]

Harman, D.K. (1996), Ed. *TREC 4: Proceedings of the Fourth Text Retrieval Conference.* Washington DC: Government Printing Office.

Harter, S.P. (1992). Psychological relevance and information science. *Journal of the American Society for Information Science, 43*: 602-615.

Harter, S.P. & Hert, C.A. (1997). Evaluation of information retrieval systems: Approaches, issues, and methods. Williams, M.E. (Ed.) [ARIST 32]: 3-94.

Hawking, D., (2001). Overview of TREC-9 Web Track. In: Voorhees, E.M. & Harman, D.K. (Eds.) [TREC 9]: 87-92. [Available at: http://trec.nist.gov/ pubs/trec9/papers/web9.pdf. Cited Nov. 4, 2003.]

Hawking, D., Thistlewaite, P. & Craswell, P. (1997). ANU/ACSys TREC-6 experiments. In: Voorhees, E.M. & Harman, D.K. (Eds.) [TREC 6]: 275-290. [Available at http://trec.nist.gov/pubs/trec6/papers/anu.ps.gz. Cited March 9, 2004.]

Hawking, D., Voorhees, E., Craswell, N. & Bailey, P. (2000). Overview of TREC-8 Web Track. In: Voorhees, E.M. & Harman, D.K. (Eds.) [TREC 8]: 131-150.

Hearst, M. (1995). Tilebars: Visualization of term distribution information in full text information access. In: Katz, I.R., et al. (Eds.) [ACM SIGCHI 95]: 59-66.

Hearst, M. (1999). User interfaces and visualization. In: Baeza-Yates, R. & Riberio-Neto, B. (Eds.) [1999]: 257-323.

Hearst, M.A. & Plaunt, C. (1993). Subtopic structuring for full-length document access. In: Korfhage, R., Rasmussen, E.M. & Willett, P. (Eds.) [ACM SIGIR 16]: 59-68.

Henderson, D. (1990), Ed. *ASIS '90: proceedings of the 53rd ASIS Annual Meeting (ASIS 53).* Medford, NJ: Learned Information.

Henriksen, T. (1979) (Ed.). *IRFIS 3, Proceedings of the 3rd International Research Forum in Information Science,* Vols I and II, August 1-3, 1979; Oslo, Norway. Oslo, Norway: Norwegian School of Librarianship, 1979.

Henry, W.M. et al. (1980). *Online searching: An introduction.* London, UK: Butterworth.

Herner, S. & Herner, M. (1967). Information needs and use studies in science and technology. In: Cuadra, C.A. (Ed.) [ARIST 2]: 1-34.

Hersh, W. & Over, P. (2000). TREC-8 Interactive Track Report. In: Voorhees, E.M. & Harman, D.K. (Eds.) [TREC 8]: 57-64.

Hersh, W. & Over, P. (2001). TREC-2001 Interactive Track Report. In: Voorhees, E.M. & Harman, D.K. (Eds.) [TREC 10]: 38-41. [Available at http://trec.nist.gov/pubs/trec10/papers/t10ireport.pdf.]

Hersh, W., Pentecost, J. & Hickam, D. (1996). A task oriented approach to information retrieval evaluation. *Journal of the American Society for Information Science, 47*(1): 50-56.

Hertzum, M. & Pejtersen, A.M., (2000). The information seeking practises of engineers: searching for documents as well as for people. *Information Processing & Management, 36*: 761-778.

Hewins, E.T. (1990). Information needs and use studies. In: Williams, M.E. (Ed.), [ARIST 25]: 147-172.

Hiemstra, D. (1998a). A Linguistically Motivated Probabilistic Model of Information Retrieval. In: Nicolaou, C. & Stephanidis, C. (Eds.), *Research and Advanced Technology for Digital Libraries.* Heidelberg: Springer, Lecture Notes in Computer Science, vol. 513: 569-584.

Hiemstra, D. (1998b). Multilingual domain modeling in Twenty-One: Automatic creation of a bi-directional translation lexicon from a parallel corpus. In: Coppen, P-A., van Halteren, H. & Teunissen, L. (Eds.), *Computational linguistics in the Netherlands 1997, Proceedings of the eighth CLIN meeting.* Amsterdam-Atlanta, GA: Rodopi : 41-58.

Hirsh, S.G. (1999). Children's relevance criteria and information-seeking on electronic resources. *Journal of the American Society for Information Science, 50*(14): 1265-1283.

Hjørland, B. (1992). The concept of ʿsubjectʹ in information science. *Journal of Documentation, 48*(2): 172-200.

Hjørland, B. (1997). *Information Seeking and Subject Representation: An Activity-Theoretical Approach to Information Science.* Westport, London: Greenwood.

Hjørland, B. (1998). Information retrieval, text composition, and semantics. *Knowledge Organization, 25*(1/2): 16-31.

Hjørland, B. (2000a). Documents, memory institutions and information science. *Journal of Documentation, 56*(1): 27-41.

Hjørland, B. (2000b). Relevance research: The missing perspective(s): 'Non-relevance' and 'epistemological relevance'. Letter to the Editor. *Journal of the American Society for Information Science, 51*(2): 209-211.

Hjørland, B. (2001). Towards a theory of aboutness, subject, topicality, theme, domain, field, content and relevance. *Journal of the American Society for Information Science and Technology, 52*(9): 774-778.

Hjørland, B. & Albrechtsen, H. (1995). Toward a new horizon in information science: Domain analysis. *Journal of the American Society for Information Science, 46*(6): 400-425.

Hjørland, B. & Nielsen, L.K. (2001). Subject access points in electronic retrieval. In: Williams, M.E. (Ed.) [ARIST 31]: 249-298.

Honkela, T. (1997). *Self-Organizing Maps in Natural Language Processing.* Helsinki, Finland: Helsinki University of Technology, Department of Computer Science and Engineering, Ph.D. Thesis.

Horsnell, V. (1975), Ed. *Informatics 2.* London, UK: Aslib.

Hsieh-Yee, I. (1998). Search tactics of Web users in searching for texts, graphics, known items and subjects: a search simulation study. *Reference Librarian, 60*: 61-85.

Huang X., Peng F., Schuurmans D., Cercone, N. & Robertson, S.E. (2003). Applying Machine Learning to Text Segmentation for Information Retrieval. *Information Retrieval, 6*(3-4): 333-362.

Hull, D. (1993). Using statistical testing in the evaluation of retrieval experiments. In:Korfhage, R., Rasmussen, E.M. & Willett, P. (Eds.), *Proceedings of the 16th International Conference on Research and Development in Information Retrieval.* New York, NY: ACM, 349-338.

Hull, D. (1996). Stemming Algorithms: a case study for detailed evaluation. *Journal of the American Society for Information Science, 47*: 70-84.

Hull, D. & Grefenstette, G. (1996). Querying across languages: A dictionary-based approach to multilingual information retrieval. In: Frei, H-P- et al. (Eds.) [ACM SIGIR 19]: 49-57.

Humphrey, Susanne M. (1991). Evolution Toward Knowledge-Based Indexing for Information Retrieval. In: *Proceedings of the Workshop on Future Directions in Text Analysis, Retrieval and Understanding*, Oct. 10-11, 1991, Chicago, IL: 132-139.

Hutchins, W.J. (1975). *Languages of Indexing and Classification: A Linguistic Study of Structures and Functions.* Stevenage, UK: Southgate House.

Hutchins, W.J. (1978). The concept of 'aboutness' in subject indexing. *Aslib Proceedings, 30*(5): 172-181.

Hyldegaard, J. (2005). Collaborative information seeking behaviour: Exploring Kuhlthau's information search process model in a longitudinal group-based setting of students. *Information processing & Management, 41* (forthcoming).

Hölscher, C. & Strube, G. (2000). Web search behavior of Internet experts and newbies. *Computer Networks, 33*(1-6): 337-346.

Iivonen, M. (1995). Consistency in the selection of search concepts and search terms. *Information Processing & Management, 31*(2): 173-190.

INEX 2003 Workshop Proceedings. Schloss Dagstuhl, Germany. [Available at: http://inex.is.informatik.uni-duisburg.de:2003/ . Cited Apr. 12, 2005.]

Informatics 8 (1985). *Informatics 8: Advances in intelligent retrieval: Proceedings of a Conference Jointly Sponsored by ASLIB and Information Retrieval Specialist Group of BCS;* April 16-17, 1985, Oxford, England. London, UK: ASLIB.

Ingwersen, P. (1982). Search procedures in the library analyzed from the cognitive point of view. *Journal of Documentation, 38*(3): 165-191.

Ingwersen, P. (1984). A cognitive view of three selected online search facilities. *Online and CD-ROM Review, 8*(5): 465-492.

Ingwersen, P. (1986). Cognitive analysis and the role of the intermediary in information retrieval. In: Davies, R., (Ed.), *Intelligent Information Systems.* Chichester, West Sussex, England: Horwood: 206-237.

Ingwersen, P. (1992). *Information Retrieval Interaction.* London: Taylor Graham.

Ingwersen, P. (1994). Polyrepresentation of information needs and semantic entities: Elements of a cognitive theory for information retrieval interaction. In: Croft, W.B. & van Rijsbergen, C.J. (Eds.) [ACM-SIGIR, 17]: 101-111.

Ingwersen, P. (1995). Information and information science. In: Kent, A. (Ed.), *Encyclopedia of Library and Information Science,* 56, Suppl. 19. New York, NY: Marcel Dekker: 137-174.

Ingwersen, P. (1996). Cognitive perspectives of information retrieval interaction: Elements of a cognitive IR theory. *Journal of Documentation, 52*(1): 3-50.

Ingwersen, P. (2001). Cognitive information retrieval. In: Williams, M. (Ed.), *Annual Review of Information Science and Technology, 34*: 3-51.

Ingwersen, P. (2002). Cognitive perspectives of document representation. In: Bruce, H. et al. (Eds.) [CoLIS4]: 285-300.

Ingwersen, P. & Björneborn, L. (2004). Methodological issues of webometric studies. In: Moed, H.F., Glänzel, W. & Schmoch, U. (Eds.) *Handbook of Quantitative Science and Technology Research: The Use of Publication and Patent Statistics in Studies of S&T Systems.* Boston, MA: Kluwer: 339-370.

Ingwersen, P. & Borlund, P. (1996). Information transfer viewed as interactive cognitive processes. In: Ingwersen, P. & Pors, N.O. (Eds.) [CoLIS2]: 219-232.

Ingwersen, P., Kajberg, L. & Pejtersen, A.M. (1986), Eds. *Information Technology and Information Use.* London, UK: Taylor Graham.

Ingwersen, P. & Pejtersen, A.M. (1986). User requirements: Empirical research and information systems design. In: Ingwersen, P., Kajberg, L. & Pejtersen, A.M. (Eds.): 111-124.

Ingwersen, P. & Pors, N.O. (1996), Eds. *Information Science: Integration in Perspective: Proceedings of the 2nd International Conference on Conceptions of Library and Information Science (CoLIS 2),* October 13-16, 1996, Copenhagen, Denmark. Copenhagen, Denmark: Royal School of Librarianship.

Ingwersen, P. & Willett, P. (1995). An introduction to algorithmic and cognitive approaches for information retrieval. *Libri, 45*: 160-177.

Ingwersen, P. & Wormell, I. (1988). Means to improved subject access and representation in modern information retrieval. *Libri: International Library Review, 38*(2): 94-119.

Ingwersen, P. & Wormell, I. (1989). Modern indexing and retrieval techniques matching different types of information needs. In: Koskiala, S. & Launo, R. (Eds.) *Information, Knowledge , Evolution.* London, UK: North-Holland: 79-90.

Isenberg, D.J. (1986). Thinking and managing: A verbal protocol analysis of managerial problem solving. *Academy of Management Journal, 29*(4): 775-788.

Jacob, E. & Shaw, D. (1998). Sociocognitive perspectives on representation. In: Williams, M.E., (Ed.) [ARIST 33]: 131-186.

Jacob, E.K. (2001). The everyday world of work: Putting classification in context. *Journal of Documentation, 57*(1): 76-99.

Jansen, B.J. & Pooch, U. (2001). A review of Web searching studies and a framework for future research. *Journal of the American Society for Information Science, 52*(3), 235-246.

Jansen, B.J., Spink, A., Bateman, J. & Saracevic, T. (1998). Real life information retrieval: A study of user queries on the Web. *SIGIR Forum, 32*(1): 5-17.

Jansen, B.J., Spink, A. & Saracevic, T. (2000). Real life, real users, and real needs: a study and analysis of user queries on the web. *Information Processing & Management, 36*(2): 207-227.

Jepsen, E.T., Seiden, P., Ingwersen, P., Björneborn, L. & Borlund, P. (2004). Characteristics of scientific web publications: Preliminary data gathering and analysis. *Journal of American Society for Information Science & Technology, 55*(14): 1239-1249.

Jing, Y. & Croft, W.B. (1994). *An association thesaurus for information retrieval* Amhesrt, MA: University of Massachusetts, Dept. of Computer Science, Technical Report TR-1994-17.

Jones, S., Gatford M, Robertson S, Hancock Beaulieu M, Secker J & Walker S. (1995). Interactive thesaurus navigation: intelligence rules ok. *Journal of American Society for Information Science & Technology, 46*(1): 52-59.

Järvelin, K. (1986). On information, information technology and the development of society: An information science perspective. In: Ingwersen, P., Kajberg, L. & Pejtersen, A.M. (Eds.): 35-55.

Järvelin, K. & Kekäläinen, J. (2000). IR evaluation methods for highly relevant documents. In: Belkin, N.J., Ingwersen, P. & Leong, M.-K. (Eds.) [ACM SIGIR 23]: 41-48.

Järvelin, K. & Kekäläinen, J. (2002). Cumulated gain-based evaluation of IR techniques. *ACM Transactions on Information Systems (ACM TOIS), 20*(4): 422-446.

Järvelin, K., Kekäläinen, J. & Niemi, T. (2001). ExpansionTool: Concept-based query expansion and construction. *Information Retrieval, 4*(3/4): 231-255.

Järvelin K, Kristensen J, Niemi T, Sormunen E and Keskustalo H (1996) A deductive data model for query expansion. In: Frei H-P. et al. (Eds.) [ACM SIGIR 19]: 235-249.

Järvelin, K. & Niemi, T. (1995). An NF2 relational interface for document retrieval, restructuring and aggregation. In: Fox, E. A. & Ingwersen, P. & Fidel, R. (Eds.) [ACM SIGIR 18]: 102-110.

Järvelin, K. & Niemi, T. (1999). Integration of complex objects and transitive relationships for information retrieval. *Information Processing & Management, 35*(5): 655-678.

Järvelin, K. & Vakkari, P. (1990). Content analysis of library and information science research articles. *Library and Information Science Research, 12*(4): 395-421.

Järvelin, K. & Vakkari, P. (1993). The evolution of library and information science 1965-85: A content analysis of journal articles. *Information Processing & Management, 29*(1): 129-144.

Kalamboukis, T. Z. (1995). Suffix stripping with Modern Greek. *Program, 29*: 313-321.

Kantor, P.B. (1994). Information retrieval techniques. In: Williams, M.E. (Ed.) [ARIST 29]: 53-90.

Karlsson, F. (1994). *Yleinen kielitiede* [General linguistics]. Hki: Yliopistopaino.

Katter, R.V. (1968). The influence of scale form on relevance judgments. *Information Storage and Retrieval, 4*(1), 1-11.

Katz, I.R., Mack, R., Marks, M, Rosson M.B. & Nielsen, J. (1995), Eds. *Proceedings of the ACM SIGCHI Conference on Human Factors in Computing Systems (ACM SIGCHI 95).* Denver, CO: ACM Press.

Katz, S. (1996). Distribution of content words and phrases in text and language modelling. *Natural Language Engineering, 2*(1), 15-60

Katzer, J., Mcgill, M.J., Tessier, J.A., Frakes, W. & Das Gupta, P. (1982). A study of the overlap among document representations. *Information Technology: Research and Development, 2*: 261-274.

Kekäläinen, J. (1999). *The effects of query complexity, expansion and structure on retrieval performance in probabilistic text retrieval.* Tampere, Finland: University of Tampere, Department of Information Studies, Ph.D. Thesis, Acta Universitatis Tamperensis 678. [Available at: http://www.info.uta.fi/tutkimus/fire/archive/QCES.pdf . Cited Dec. 16 2003.]

Kekäläinen, J. (2005). Binary and graded relevance in IR evaluations - Comparison of the effects on ranking of IR systems. *Information Processing & Management, 41*(5), 1019-1033.

Kekäläinen, J. & Järvelin, K. (1998). The impact of query structure and query expansion on retrieval performance. In:Croft, W.B. et al. (Eds.) [ACM SIGIR 21]: 130-137.

Kekäläinen, J. & Järvelin, K. (2000). The co-effects of query structure and expansion on retrieval performance in probabilistic text retrieval. *Information Retrieval, 1*(4), 329-344.

Kekäläinen, J. & Järvelin, K. (2002). Using graded relevance assessments in IR evaluation. *Journal of the American Society for Information Science and Technology, 53*(13): 1120-1129.

Kekäläinen, J. & Järvelin, K. (2002a). User-oriented evaluation methods for information retrieval: A case study based on conceptual models for query expansion. In: Lakemeyer, G. & Nebel, B. (Eds.) *Exploring Artificial Intelligence in the New Millennium.* San Francisco: Morgan Kaufmann Publishers: 355-379.

Kekäläinen, J. & Järvelin, K. (2002b). Evaluating information retrieval systems under the challenges of interaction and multi-dimensional dynamic relevance. In: Bruce, H. et al. (Eds.) [CoLIS4]: 253-270.

Keskustalo, H. & Pirkola, A. & Visala, K. & Leppänen, Erkka & Järvelin, K. (2003). Non-adjacent Digrams Improve Matching of Cross-Lingual Spelling Variants. In: Nascimento, M.A., de Moura, E.S., Oliveira, A.L, (Eds.) [SPIRE 2003]: 252-265.

Kilpeläinen, P. & Mannila, H. (1993). Retrieval from hierarchical texts by partial patterns. In: Korfhage, R., Rasmussen, E. & Willett, P. (Eds.) [ACM SIGIR 16]: 214-222.

Kim, K-S. & Allen, B. (2002). Cognitive and task influences on web searching behavior. *Journal of the American Society for Information Science and Technology, 53*(2): 109-119.

King, D.W. & Tenopir, C. (2001). Using and reading scholarly literature. In: Williams, M.E. (Ed.) [ARIST 34]: 423-477.

Kleinberg, J.M. (1999). Authoritative sources in a hyperlinked environment. *Journal of the ACM, 46*(5), 604-632.

Korfhage, R.R. (1997). *Information Storage and Retrieval.* New York, NY: Wiley.

Korfhage, R., Rasmussen, E. & Willet, P. (1993), Eds. *Proceedings of the 16th Annual International Conference on Research and Development in Information Retrieval (ACM SIGIR 16).* New York, NY: ACM Press.

Koskenniemi, K. (1983). *Two-Level Morphology: A General Computational Model for Word-Form Recognition and Production.* Helsinki, Finland: University of Helsinki, Department of General Linguistics, Publications 11.

Koskenniemi, K. (1985). An application of the two-level model to Finnish. In: Karlson, F. (Ed.) *Computational Morphosyntax: Report on Research 1981-84.* Helsinki: University of Helsinki, Department of General Linguistics, Publications No. 13.

Kristensen, J. (1993). Expanding end-users' query statements for free text searching with a search-aid thesaurus. *Information Processing & Management, 29*(6): 733-744.

Krovetz, R. (1993). Viewing morphology as an inference process. In: Korfhage, R., Rasmussen, E. & Willett, P. (Eds.) [ACM SIGIR 16]: 191-202.

Krovetz, R. & Croft, W.B. 1992. Lexical ambiguity and information retrieval. *ACM Transactions on Information Systems, 10*(2): 115-141.

Kuhlthau, C. C. (1991). Inside the search process: Information seeking from the user's perspective. *Journal of the American Society for Information Science, 42*(5): 361-371.

Kuhlthau, C. C. (1993a). *Seeking Meaning.* Norwood, NJ: Ablex.

Kuhlthau, C.C. (1993b). A principle of uncertainty for information seeking. *Journal of Documentation, 49*(4): 339-355.

Kuhlthau, C.C. (1997). The influence of uncertainty on the information seeking behaviour of a securities analyst. In: Vakkari, P., Savolainen, S. & Dervin, B. (eds) [ISIC 1]: 268-274 .

Kuhlthau, C.C. (1999). The role of experience in the information search process of an early career information worker: Perceptions of uncertainty, complexity, construction, and sources. *Journal of the American Society for Information Science, 50*(5): 399-412.

Kuhlthau, C.C. & Tama, S.L. (2001). Information search process of lawyers: A call for "just for me" information services. *Journal of Documentation, 57*(1): 25-43.

Kuhn, T.S. (1970). *The Structure of Scientific Revolution.* 2. ed. Chicago: University of Chicago Press.

Kuikka, E. & Salminen, A. (1997). Two-dimensional filters for structured text. *Information Processing & Management, 33*(1): 37-54.

Kunttu, T. (2003). *Perus- ja taivutusmuotohakemiston tuloksellisuus todennäköisyyksiin perustuvassa tiedonhakujärjestelmässä* [The effectiveness of inflectional word form index and basic word form index in a probabilistic IR system]. Tampere, Finland: University of Tampere, Dept. of Information Studies, M.Sc. Thesis. [In Finnish]

Kunz, W. & Rittel, H.W.J. (1977a). *A Systems Analysis of the Logic of Research and Information Processes.* München: Verlag Dokumentation.

Kunz, W., Rittel, H.W.J. & Schwuchow, W. (1977b). *Methods of Analysis and Evaluation of Information Needs: A Critical View.* München: Verlag Dokumentation.

Kwasnik, B.H. (1988). Factors affecting the naming of documents in an office. In: Borgman, C.L. & Pai, E.Y.H. (Eds.) [ASIS 51]: 100-106.

Kwasnik, B.H. (1991). The importance of factors that are not document attributes in the organization of personal documents. *Journal of Documentation, 47*(4): 389-398.

Lalmas, M. (1997). Dempster-Shafer's theory of evidence applied to structured documents: Modelling uncertainty. In: Belkin, N.J., Narasimhalu, A.D. & Willett, P. (Eds.) [ACM SIGIR 20]: 110-118.

Lalmas, M. (1998). Logical models in information retrieval: introduction and overview. *Information Processing & Management, 34*(1): 19-33.

Lancaster, F.W. (1968a). *Information Retrieval Systems: Characteristics, Testing, and Evaluation.* New York, NY: Wiley.

Lancaster, F.W. (1968b). *Evaluation of the Medlars Demand Search Service.* Bethesda, MD: National Library of Medicine.

Lancaster, F.W. (1969). Medlars: Report on the evaluation of its operating efficiency. *American Documentation, April 1969*: 119-142.

Lancaster, F.W. (1972). *Vocabulary Control for Information Retrieval.* Washington: Information Resources Press.

Lancaster, F.W. (1998). *Indexing and Abstracting in Theory and Practice.* London: UK, Library Association Publishing.

Lancaster, F.W. et al. (1996). Evaluation of interactive knowledge-based systems. *Journal of the American Society for Information Science, 47*(1): 57-69.

Lancaster, F.W. & Warner, A.J. (1993). *Information Retrieval Today.* Arlington, VA: Information Resources Press.

Lappin, S. & Leass, H.J. (1994). An algorithm for pronominal anaphora resolution. *Computational Linguistics, 20*(4): 535-561.

Large, A., Beheshti, J. & Moukdad, H. (1999). Information seeking on the Web: navigational skills of grade-six primary school students. In: Woods, L. (Ed.) [ASIS 62]: 84-97.

Large, A., Beheshti, J. & Rahmin, T. (2002). Design criteria for children's Web portals: The users speak out. *Journal of the American Society for Information Science and Technology, 53*(2): 79-94.

Larsen, B. (2002). Exploiting citation overlaps for information retrieval: Generating a boomerang effect from the network of scientific papers. *Scientometrics, 54*(2): 155-178.

Larsen, B. (2004). References and Citations in Automatic Indexing and Retrieval Systems: Experiments with the Boomerang Effect. Copenhagen, DK: The Royal School of Library and Information Science, Ph.D. Thesis. [Available at: http://www.db.dk/blar/dissertation . Cited Feb. 11, 2004.]

Larsen, B. & Ingwersen, P. (2002). The Boomerang Effect: Retrieving Scientific Documents via the Network of References and Citations. In: Beaulieu, M. et al. (Eds.) [ACM SIGIR 25]: 397-398.

Larsen, B., Lund, H., Andreasen, J.K. & Ingwersen, P. (2003) . Using value-added document representations in INEX. In: *INEX 2003 Workshop Proceedings*: 67-72.

Lawrence, S. & Giles, C. L. (1999). Accessibility and distribution of information on the Web. *Nature, 400*: 107-110.

Leckie, G.J., Pettigrew, K.E. & Sylvain, C. (1996). Modelling the information seeking of professionals: A general model derived from research on engineers, health care professionals and lawyers. *Library Quarterly, 66*(2): 161-193.

Liddy, E. (1990). Anaphora in natural language processing and information retrieval. *Information Processing & Management, 26*(1): 39-52.

Liddy, E., Bonzi, S., Katzer, J., & Oddy, E. (1987). A study of discourse anaphora in scientific abstracts. *Journal of the American Society for Information Science, 38*(4), 255-261.

Lin, C-Y. (1997). *Robust Automated Topic Identification.* University of Southern California, Ph.D. Thesis. [Availabe at: http://www.isi.edu/%7Ecyl/papers/thesis97.pdf . Cited July 14, 2004.]

Lin, N. & Garvey, W.D. (1972). Information needs and uses. In: Cuadra, C.A. & Luke, A.W. (Eds.) [ARIST 7]: 5-37.

Lin, X. (1997). Map displays for information retrieval. *Journal of the American Society for Information Science, 48*(1): 40-54

Lin, X., White, M.D. & Buzydlowski, J. (2003). Real-time author co-citation mapping for online searching. *Information Processing & Management, 39*(5): 689-706.

Line, M.B. /1974). Draft definitions. *Aslib Proceedings, 26*(2): 87.

Lipetz, Ben-Ami (1970). Information needs and uses. In: Cuadra, C.A. & Luke, A.W. (Eds.) [ARIST 5]: 3-32.

Losee, R.M. (1997). A discipline independent definition of information. *Journal of the American Society for Information Science, 48*: 254-269.

Losee, R.M. (1998). Text Retrieval and Filtering: Analytic Models of Performance, Boston, MA: Kluwer.

Lu, X.A. & Keefer, R.B. (1995). Query expansion/reduction and its impact on retrieval effectiveness. In: Harman, D.K. (Ed.), [TREC 3]: 231-239.

Lucarella, D. & Zanzi, A. (1993). Information retrieval from hypertext: an approach using plausible inference. *Information Processing & Management, 29* (3): 299-312.

Lunin, L. & Rorvig, M.E. (1999). (Ed.) Perspecctives on visual information retrieval interfaces. *Journal of the American Society for Information Science, 50:* 790-834.

Luria, A.R. (1976). *Cognitive Development: Its Cultural and Social Foundations.* London: Harvard University Press.

Lyons, J. (1994). *Language and Linguistics: An Introduction.* Cambridge University Press.

Machlup, F. (1983). Semantic quirks in the studies of information. In: Machlup, F. & Mansfield, U. (Eds.). *The Study of Information.* New York, NY: Wiley: 641-672.

Macleod, I.A. (1991). A query language for retrieving information from hierarchic text structures. *The Computer Journal, 34*(2): 197-208.

Magennis, M. & van Rijsbergen, C.J. (1997). The potential and actual effectiveness of interactive query expansion. In: Belkin, N. J., Narasimhalu, A. D. & Willett, P. (Eds.) [ACM SIGIR 20]: 324-332.

Maglaughlin, K.L. & Sonnenwald, D.H. (2002). User perspectives on relevance criteria: A comparison among relevant, partially relevant, and not-relevant judgments. *Journal of the American Society for Information Science and Technology, 53*(5): 327-342.

Marchionini, G. (1989). Information seeking strategies of novices using a full-text electronic encyclopedia. *Journal of the American Society for Information Science, 40*(1): 54-66.

Marchionini, G. (1995). *Information Seeking in Electronic Environments.* Cambridge, MA: Cambridge University Press.

Marchionini, G., Dwiggins, S., Katz, A. & Lin, X (1993). Information seeking in full-text end-user-oriented search-systems: the roles of domain and search expertise. *Library & Information Science Research, 15*(1): 35-69.

Marchionini, G. & Komlodi, A. (1998). Design of interfaces for information seeking. In: Williams, M.E. (Ed.) [ARIST 33]: 89-130.

Marchionini, G., Lin, X. & Dwiggins, S. (1990). Effects of search and subject expertise on information seeking in a hypertext environment. In: Henderson, D. (Ed.) [ASIS 53]: 129-141.

Marcus, R. (1982). User assistance in bibliographic retrieval networks through a computer intermediary. *IEEE Transactions on Systems, Man, and Cybernetics, SCM-12*(2): 116-133.

Marcus, R. & al. (1971). The user interface for the INTREX retrieval system. In: Walker, D. (Ed.) *Interactive Bibliographic Search.* Montvale, NJ: AFIPS Press: 159-202.

Markkula, M. & Sormunen, E., (1998). Searching for photos - journalistic practices in pictorial IR. In: Eakins, J.P., et al. (Eds), *The Challenge of Image Retrieval: A Workshop and Symposium on Image Retrieval.* University of Northumbria at Newcastle, Newcastle upon Tyne, 5-6 Feb, 1998. [Available at http://www.ewic.org.uk/ewic/workshop/view.cfm/CIR-98 . Cited Apr. 15, 2004.]

Martin, S. (1976), Ed. *Information & Politics: Proceedings of 38th Annual Meeting of the American Society for Information Science, vol. 13(1) (ASIS 38).* Washington DC: American Society for Information Science.

Martyn, J. (1974). Information needs and uses. In: Cuadra, C.A., Luke, A.W. & Harris, J.L. (Eds.) [ARIST 9]: 3-23.

Martyn, J. & Lancaster F.W. (1981). *Investigative Methods in Library and Information Science: An Introduction.* Arlington, VA: Information Resources Press.

Matthews, P.H. (1997). *The concise Oxford Dictionary of Linguistics.* Oxford - New York: Oxford University Press.

McCain, K.W. (1989). Descriptor and citation retrieval in the medicine behavioral sciences literature: Retrieval overlaps and novelty distribution. *Journal of the American Society for Information Science, 40*: 110-114.

McCray, A.T. & Nelson, S.J. (1995). The representation of meaning in the UMLS. *Methods of Information in Medicine, 34*: 193-201.

McGill, M.J. & Koll, M. (1983), Eds. *Proceedings of the 5th ACM-SIGIR International Conference on Research and Development in Information Retrieval, (ACM SIGIR 5).* New York, NY: ACM Press.

McKinin, E. J., Sievert, M.-E., Johnson, E.D. & Mitchell, J.A. (1991). The Medline/Full-Text Research Project. *Journal of the American Society for Information Science, 42*(4): 297-307.

Meadow, C.T. (1992). *Text Information Retrieval Systems.* San Diego, CA: Academic Press.

Meadow, C.T. & al. (1982). A computer interace for interactive database searching. I: Design; II: Evaluation. *Journal of the American Society for Information Science, 33*: 325-332; 357-364.

Menzel, H. (1966). Information needs and uses. In: Cuadra, C.A. (Ed.) [ARIST 4]: 1-29.

Mick, C.K., Lindsey, G.N., & Callahan, D. (1980). Toward usable user studies. *Journal of the American Society for Information Science, 31*(5): 347-365.

Mitra, M., Buckley, C., Singhal, A. & Cardie, C. 1997. An analysis of statistical and syntactic phrases. In: Devroye, L. & Chrisment, C. (Eds.) *Proceedings of RIAO'97, Computer Assisted Information Searching on the Internet,* Montreal, Canadal: 200-214.

Mitra, M., Singhal, A. & Buckley, C. (1998). Improving automatic query expansion. In: Croft, W.B. et al. (Eds.) [ACM SIGIR 21]: 206–214.

Mizzaro, S. (1996). A cognitive analysis of information retrieval. In: Ingwersen, P. & Pors, N.O. (Eds.) [CoLIS 2]: 233-250.

Mizzaro, S. (1997). Relevance: The Whole History. *Journal of the American Society for Information Science, 48*(9): 810-832.

Moens M-F. (2000). *Automatic Indexing and Abstracting of Document Texts.* Boston, MA: Kluwer.

Murtonen, K. (1994). *Ammatilliset tiedontarpeet ja tiedonhankinta tutkimuskohteena : Tutkimus tehtävän kompleksisuuden vaikutuksista tiedontarpeisiin ja tiedonhankintaan* [Professional information needs and information seeking as study objects : A study on the effects of task complexity on information needs and information seeking]. Tampere, Finland: University of Tampere, Department of Information Studies. Lic.Soc.Sci. Thesis. [in Finnish]

Nascimento, M.A., de Moura, E.S., Oliveira, A.L, (2003), Eds. *Proceedings of the 10th International Symposium, SPIRE 2003.* Manaus, Brazil, October 2003. Berlin: Springer, Lecture Notes in Computer Science 2857.

Nielsen netratings (2003) [Available at http://www.nielsen-netratings.com/ . Cited May 28, 2003.]

Nielsen, M.L (2000). Domain analysis, an important part of thesaurus construction. Methodologies and approaches. In: Soergel, D, Srinivasan, P, Kwasnik, B, (Eds.), *Proceedings of the 11ᵗʰ ASIS&T SIG/CR Classification Research Workshop,* November 12, 2000: 9-50. [Available at http://uma.info-science.uiowa.edu/sigcr/papers/sigcr00lykke.doc. Cited May 8, 2001.]

Nielsen, M.L. (2001). A framework for work task based thesaurus design. *Journal of Documentation, 57*(6): 774-797.

Nielsen, M.L. (2002). *The Word Association Method: A Gateway to Work-Task Based Retrieval.* Åbo, Finland: Åbo Akademi University Press. Ph.D. Thesis.

NIST: National Institute of Standards and Technology (2001). USA. [The TREC Web site http://trec.nist.gov/pubs.html. Cited Nov. 18, 2001.]

Nordlie, R. (1999). User revealment: A comparison of initial queries and ensuing question development in online searching and in human reference interactions. In: Gey, F., Hearst, M. & Tong, R. (Eds.) [ACM SIGIR 22]: 11-18.

Norman, D. (1988). *The Psychology of Everyday Things.* New York, NY: Basic Books.

Nowell, L.T., France, R.K., Hix, D., Heath, L.S., & Fox, E.A. (1996). Visualizing search results: some alternatives to query-document similarity. In: Frei, H.P., Harman, D., Schaüble, P. & Wilkinson, R. (Eds.) [ACM SIGIR 19]: 67-75.

Noyons, E., van Raan, A.F.J. & Anthony, F.J. (1998). Monitoring scientific developments from a dynamic perspective: Self-organized structuring to map neural network research. *Journal of the American Society for Information Science, 49*(1): 68-81.

Nurminen, Riitta (1986). *Suomen kielen sanamuotoja tulkitsevien ohjelmien hyödyntäminen tiedonhakujärjestelmissä* [The application of Finnish word form interpretation programs in informtaion retreival systems]. Espoo, Finland: Technical Research Centre of Finland, Research reports 386. [in Finnish]

Oddy, R.N. (1977a). Information retrieval through man-machine dialogue. *Journal of Documentation, 33*: 1-14.

Oddy, R.N. (1977b). Retrieving references by dialogue rather than by query formulation. *Journal of Information Science: Principles and Practice, 1*: 37-53.

Oddy, R.N., Liddy, E.D., Balakrishnan, B., Bishop, A. Elewononi, J. & Martin, E. (1992). Towards the use of situational information in information retrieval. *Journal of Documentation, 48*: 123-171.

Olsen, K. A., Korfhage, R. R., Sochats, K. M., Spring, M. B, & Williams, J. G. (1993). Visualization of a document collection: The VIBE system. *Information Processing & Management, 29*(1):69-81.

Over, P. (1997). TREC-5 Interactive Track Report. In: Voorhees, E. & Harman, D. (Eds.) [TREC 5]: 29-56.

Over, P. (1999). TREC-7 Interactive Track Report. In: Voorhees, E. & Harman, D. (Eds.) [TREC 8]: 65-72.

Page, L. et al. (1998). *The PageRank citation ranking: Bringing order to the Web.* [Available at http://dbpubs.stanford.edu:8090/pub/1999-66. Cited Aug. 12, 2003.]

Paice, C.D. (1991a). A thesaural model of information retrieval. *Information Processing & Management, 27*: 433-447.

Paice, C.D. (1991b). The rhetorical structure of expository texts. In: Jones, K.P. (Ed.), *Proceedings of the Informatics 11 Conference,* York, March 20-22, 1991. London: Aslib: 1-26.

Paice, C.D. & Jones, P.A. (1993). The identification of important concepts in highly structured technical papers. In: Korfhage, R. Rasmussen, E. & Willett, P. (Eds), [ACM SIGIR 16]: 69-78.

Paisley, W. (1968). Information needs and uses. In: Cuadra, C.A. (Ed.) [ARIST 3]: 1-30.

Palmquist, R.A. & Kim, K.S. (2000). The effect of cognitive style and online search experience on Web search performance. *Journal of the American Society for Information Science, 51*: 558-567.

Pao, M. (1993). Term and citation searching: A filed study. *Information Processing & Management, 29*(1): 95-112.

Pao, M. (1994). Relevance odds of retrieval overlaps from seven search fields. *Information Processing & Management, 30*(3): 305-314.

Park, S. (2000). Usability, user preferences, effectiveness, and user behaviors when searching individual and integrated full-text databases: implications for digital libraries. *Journal of the American Society for Information Science, 51*(5): 456-468.

Park, T.K. (1993). The nature of relevance in information retrieval: An empirical study. *Library Quarterly, 63*(3): 318-351.

Partridge, D. & Hussain K. (1995). *Knowledge Based Information-Systems.* London: McGraw-Hill.

Pazienza, M.T. (1997), Ed. *Information extraction: A multidisciplinary approach to an emerging information technology.* Berlin: Springer, Lecture notes in computer science, vol. 1299.

Pejtersen, A.M. (1980). Design of a classification scheme for fiction. In: Harbo, O. & Kajberg, L. (Eds.): 146-159.

Pejtersen, A.M. (1989). A library system for information retrieval based on a cognitive task analysis and supported by an icon-based interface. *ACM Sigir Forum,* June 1989: 40-47.

Pejtersen, A.M. (1991). *Interfaces Based on Associative Semantics for Browsing in Information Retrieval.* Roskilde, Denmark: Risø National Laboratory, Report Risø-M-2883.

Pejtersen, A.M. (1999). Icons for representation of domain knowledge in interfaces. In: Fugmann, R. (Ed.): (no pages).

Pejtersen, A.M. & Fidel, R. (1999). *A Framework for Work-Centred Evaluation and Design: A Case Study of IR on the Web.* Glasgow, UK: University of Glasgow, Department of Computing Science, Working paper for MIRA Workshop TR-1999-35.

Pejtersen, A.M. & Rasmussen, J. (1997). Ecological information systems and support of learning: Coupling work domain information to user characteristics. In: Helander, M.G., Landauer, T.K. & Prabhu, P.V. (Eds.), *Handbook of Human-Computer Interaction.* Amsterdam, Netherlands: Elsevier: 315-345.

Peters, H.P.F., Braam, R.R. & Van Raan, A.F.J. (1995). Cognitive resemblance and citation relations in chemical-engineering publications. *Journal of American Society for Information Science, 46*(1): 9-21.

Pharo, N. (1999). Web information search strategies: A model for classifying web interaction. In: Aparac, T. et al. (Eds.) [CoLIS 3]: 207-218.

Pharo, N. (2002). *The SST method schema: a tool for analysing Web information search processes.* Tampere: University of Tampere, Ph.D. Thesis. [Available at http://acta.uta.fi/english/teos.phtml?6719. Cited Apr. 15, 2004.]

Pharo, N. & Järvelin, K. (2004). The SST method: a tool for analyzing Web information search processes. *Information Processing & Management, 40*: 633-654.

Pirkola, A. (1998). The effects of query structure and dictionary setups in dictionary-based cross-language information retrieval. In: Croft, W. B. et al. (Eds.) [ACM SIGIR 21]: 55-63.

Pirkola, A. (1999). *Studies on Linguistic Problems and Methods in Text Retrieval.* Tampere, Finland: University of Tampere, Ph.D. Thesis.

Pirkola, A. (2001). Morphological Typology of Languages for Information Retrieval. *Journal of Documentation, 57*(3): 330-348.

Pirkola, A. & Järvelin, K. (1996a). The effect of anaphor and ellipsis resolution on proximity searching in a text database. *Information Processing & Management, 32*(2): 199-216.

Pirkola, A. & Järvelin, K. (1996b). Recall and precision effects of anaphor and ellipsis resolution in proximity searching in a text database. In: Ingwersen, P. & Pors, N.O. (Eds.) [CoLIS 2]: 459-475.

Pirkola, A. & Järvelin, K. (2001). Employing the resolution power of search keys. *Journal of the American Society for Information Science and Technology, 52*(7): 575-583.

Pirkola, A. & Toivonen, J. & Keskustalo, H. & Visala, K. & Järvelin, K. (2003). Fuzzy Translation of Cross-Lingual Spelling Variants. In: Callan, J. et al. (Eds.) [ACM SIGIR 26]: 345-352.

Piternick, A.B. (1984). Searching vocabularies: a developing category of online search tools. *Online Review, 8*(5):441-449.

Ponte, J. & Croft, W. B. (1998). A language modeling approach to information retrieval. In: Croft, W. B. et al. (Eds.) [ACM SIGIR 21]: 275-281.

Popovič, M. & Willett, P. (1992). The effectiveness of stemming for natural-language access to Slovene textual data. *Journal of the American Society for Information Science, 43*: 384-390.

Popper, K. (1973). *Objective Knowledge: An Evolutionary Approach.* Oxford, UK: Clarendon Press.

Pors, N.O. (2000). Information retrieval, experimental models and statistical analysis. *Journal of Documentation, 56*(1): 55-70.

Preece et al., (1994). *Human-computer Interaction.* Wokingham, UK: Addison-Wesley.

Preston, C. (1998), Ed. *Proceedings of the 61st ASIS Annual Meeting (ASIS 61).* Medford, NJ: Information Today.

Qiu, L. (1993a). Analytical searching vs. browsing in hypertext information retrieval systems. *The Canadian Journal of Information and Library Science, 18*(4): 1-13.

Qiu, L. (1993b). Markov models of search state patterns in a hypertext information retrieval system. *Journal of the American Society for Information Science, 44*(7): 413-427.

Rabitti, F. (1986), Ed. *Proceedings of the Annual International ACM SIGIR Conference on Research and Development in Information Retrieval (ACM SIGIR 9).* Pisa, IT: University of Pisa.

Rada, R. & Murphy, C. (1992). Searching versus browsing in hypertext. *Hypermedia, 4*(1): 1-30.

Rajashekar, T.B. & Croft, W.B. (1995). Combining automatic and manual index representations in probabilistic retrieval. *Journal of the American Society for Information Science, 56*(4): 272-283.

Rasmussen E.M. (1997). Indexing images. In: Williams M.E. (Ed.) [ARIST 32]: 169-196.

Rasmussen, E.M. (2002). Indexing and Retrieval for the Web. In: Cronin, B. (Ed.) [ARIST 37]: 91-124.

Rasmussen, J. (1990). Models for the design of computer integrated manufacturing systems: the human perspective. *International Journal of Industrial Ergonomics, 5*(1): 5-16.

Rasmussen, J., Pejtersen, A.M. & Goodstein, L.P. (1992). *Cognitive Engineering: Concepts and Applications.* New York, NY: Wiley.

Rasmussen, J., Pejtersen, A.M. & Goodstein, L.P. (1994). *Cognitive Systems Engineering.* New York, NY: Wiley.

Rau, L. F., Jacobs, P.S. & Zemik, U. (1989). Information extraction and text summarization using linguistic knowledge acquisition. *Information Processing & Management, 25*(4), 419-428.

Rees, A.M. & Schultz, D.G. (1967). *A field experimental approach to the study of relevance assessments in relation to document searching.* Cleveland: Case Western Reserve University.

RIAO 2000. *RIAO'2000 Conference proceedings: Content-based multimedia information access.* Paris: C.I.D.

RIAO 2004. *Coupling Approaches, Coupling Media aAnd Coupling Languages for Information Retrieval, Proceedings of RIAO 2004 conference.* Paris: C.I.D.

Rich, R.F. (1983). Management and problem solving styles: An assessment on information system designs. In: Debons, A. & Larson, A.G. (Eds.), *Information Science in Action: System Design.* Boston, MA: Nijhoff: 240-264.

Rieh, S.Y. (2002). Judgment of information quality and cognitive authority in the Web. *Journal of the American Society for Information Science and Technology, 53*(2): 145-161.

Robertson, A.M. & Willett, P. (1998). Applications of n-grams in textual information systems. *Journal of Documentation, 54*(1): 48-69.

Robertson, S.E. (1977). The probability ranking principle in IR. *Journal of Documentation, 33*(4): 294-304.

Robertson, S.E. (1997a), (Ed.). Special issue on the OKAPI projects. *Journal of Documentation,* 53(1).

Robertson, S.E. (1997b). Overview of the OKAPI projects. In: Robertson, S.E. (1997a), (Ed.): 3-7.

Robertson, S.E. (2000). Salton Award lecture: On theoretical argument in information retrieval. *SIGIR Forum, 34*(1), Fall 2000 [Available at http://www.acm.org/sigir/forum/F2000-TOC.html . Cited Jan. 29, 2001).

Robertson, S.E. & Hancock-Beaulieu, M. (1992). On the evaluation of IR systems. *Information Processing & Management, 28*(4): 219-236.

Robertson, S.E., Walker, S. & Hancock-Beaulieu, M. (1995). Large test collection experiments on an operational, interactive system: OKAPI at TREC. *Information Processing & Management, 31*(3): 345-360.

Robins, D. (2000). Shifts of focus on various aspects of user information problems during interactive information retrieval. *Journal of the American Society for Information Science, 51*(10): 913-928.

Rocchio, J.J. Jr. (1971). Relevance feedback in information retrieval. In: Salton, G. (Ed.), *The Smart System - Experiments in Automatic Document Processing.* Englewood Cliffs, NJ: Prentice-Hall: 313-323.

Rowley, J.E. (1988). *Abstracting and Indexing.* 2nd Ed. London, UK: Bingley.

Ruthven, I. (2001). *Abduction, Explanation and Relevance Feedback.* Glasgow, UK: Department of Computing Science, University of Glasgow, 2001. Ph.D. Thesis.

Ruthven, I., Lalmas, M. & van Rijsbergen, K. (2001a). Empirical investigations on query modification using abductive explanations. In: Croft, W.B. et al. (Eds.) [ACM SIGIR 24]: 181-189.

Ruthven, I., Lalmas, M. & van Rijsbergen, K. (2001b). Combining and selecting charactersitics of information use. *Journal of the American Society for Information Science and Technology, 53*(5): 378-396.

Ruthven, I., Lalmas, M. & van Rijsbergen, K. (2002). Ranking expansion terms with partial and ostensive evidence. In: Bruce, H. et al. (Eds.) [CoLIS4]: 199-220.

Ruthven, I., Lalmas, M. & van Rijsbergen, K. (2003). Incorporating user search behaviour into relevance feedback. *Journal of the American Society for Information Science and Technology, 54*(6): 529-549.

Salminen, A., Tague-Sutcliffe, J. & McClellan, C. (1995). From text to hypertext by indexing. *ACM Transactions on Information Systems (ACM TOIS), 13*(1): 69-99.

Salton, G. (1968a). *Automatic Information Organization and Retrieval.* New York, NY: McGraw-Hill.

Salton, G. (1968b). A comparison between manual and automatic indexing methods. *American Documentation, 20*(1): 61-71.

Salton, G. (1989). *Automatic Text Processing: The Transformation, Analysis And Retrieval of Information by Computer.* Reading, MA: Addison-Wesley.

Salton, G., Allan, J. & Buckley, C. (1993). Approaches to passage retrieval in full text information systems. In: Korfhage, R. et al. (Eds.) [ACM SIGIR 16]: 49-58.

Salton, G., Allan, J., Buckley, C. & Singhal, A. (1994). Automatic analysis, theme generation, and summarization of machine-readable texts. *Science, 264*: 1421-1426.

Salton, G. & McGill, J.M. (1983). *Introduction to Modern Information Retrieval.* New York, NY: McGraw-Hill.

Sampson, E. (1993). *Celebrating the Other: a Dialogic Account of Human Nature.* Boulder, CO: Westview Press.

Sanderson, M. (1994). Word sense disambiguation and information retrieval. In: Croft, W.B. & van Rijsbergen, C.J. (Eds.) [ACM SIGIR 17]: 142-151.

Saracevic, T. (1975). Relevance: A review of and framework for the thinking on the notion in information science. *Journal of the American Society for Information Science, 26*(6): 321-343.

Saracevic, T. (1990). *Information Science Revisited: Contemporary Reflection on its Origin, Evolution and Relations.* New Brunswick, NJ: Rutgers University, School of Communication, Information and Library Studies, Res. Rep. Ser. No. 90-24.

Saracevic, T. (1992). Information Science: Origin, Evolution and Relations. In: Vakkari, P. & Cronin, B. (Eds.) [CoLIS 1]: 5-27.

Saracevic, T. (1996). Relevance reconsidered '96. In: Ingwersen, P. & Pors, N.O. (Eds.) [CoLIS 2]: 201-218.

Saracevic, T. & Kantor, P. (1988a). A study of information seeking and retrieving. II. Users, questions, and effectiveness. *Journal of the American Society for Information Science, 39*(3): 177-196.

Saracevic, T. & Kantor, P. (1988b). A study of information seeking and retrieving. III. searchers, searches, and overlaps. *Journal of the American Society for Information Science, 39*(3): 197-216.

Saracevic, T., Kantor, P., Chamis, A. & Trivison, D. (1988). A study of information seeking and retrieving. I. Background and methodology. *Journal of the American Society for Information Science, 39*(3): 161-176.

Saracevic, T., Mokros, H. & Su, L. (1990). Nature of interaction between users and intermediaries in online searching: A qualitative analysis. In: Henderson, D. (Ed.) [ASIS 27]: 47-54.

Saracevic, T., Mokros, H., Su, L., & Spink, A. (1991). Nature of interaction between users and intermediaries in online searching. In: Williams, M.E., (Ed.),

Proceedings of the 12th National Online Meeting May 7-9, 1991 New York. Medford, NJ: Learned Information: 329-341.

Saracevic, T. & Su, L. (1989). Modeling and measuring user-intermediary-computer interaction in online searching: Design of a study. In: *Proceedings of the 52nd Annual Meeting of the American Society for Information Science* 26: 75-80.

Saunders, C. & Jones, J.W. (1990). Temporal sequences in information acquisition for decision making: A focus on source and medium. *Academy of Management Review, 15*(1): 29-46.

Savage-Knepshield, P. & Belkin, N.J. (1999). Interaction in information retrieval: trends over time. *Journal of the American Society for Information Science, 50*(12): 1067-1082.

Savolainen, R. (1992). The sense-making theory: An alternative to intermediary-centered approaches in library and information science? In: Vakkari, P. & Cronin, B. (Eds.) [CoLIS 1]: 149-164.

Savolainen, R. (1993). The sense-making theory: Reviewing the interests of a user-centered approach to information seeking and use. *Information Processing & Management, 29*(1): 13-28.

Savoy, J. (1999). A stemming procedure and stopword list for general French corpora. *Journal of the American Society for Information Science, 50*: 944-952.

Schamber, L. (1991). Users' criteria for evaluation in a multimedia environment. In: Griffiths, J.-M. (Ed.), *ASIS '91: Proceedings of the American Society for Information Science (ASIS) 54th Annual Meeting.* Medford, NJ, Learned Information: 126-133.

Schamber, L. (1994). Relevance and information behavior. In: Williams, M. (Ed.) [ARIST 29]: 3-48.

Schamber, L. (2000). Time-line interviews and inductive content analysis: Their effectiveness for exploring cognitive behaviors. *Journal of the American Society for Information Science, 51*(8), 734-744.

Schamber, L., Eisenberg, M.B. & Nilan, M.S. (1990). A re-examination of relevance: toward a dynamic, situational definition. *Information Processing & Management, 26*(6): 755-776.

Schneider, J.W. (2004). *Verification of Bibliometric Methods' Applicability for Thesaurus Contruction.* Copenhagen, DK: Royal School of Library and Information Science Ph.D. Thesis. [Available at: http://biblis.db.dk/uhtbin/hyperion.exe/db.jessch04 . Cited Apr. 15, 2005.]

Schön, D.A. (1990). *Educating the Reflective Practitioner.* San Francisco, CA: Jossey-Bass Publishers.

Searle, J.R. (1984a). Intentionality and its place in nature. *Synthese, 61*: 3-16.

Searle, J.R. (1984b). *Minds, Brains and Science.* Cambridge, MA: Harvard University Press.

Shannon, C.E. & Weaver, W. (1949). *The Mathematical Theory of Communication.* Urbana, IL: University of Illinois Press.

Shaw, W.M., Wood, J.B. & Tibbo, H.R. (1991). The cystic fibrosis database: content and research opportunities. *Library & Information Science Research, 13*:

347-366.   [Test   collection   available   at
http://www.dcc.ufmg.br/irbook/cfc.html]

Sheridan, P. & Smeaton, A.F. (1992). The application of morpho-syntactic language processing to effective phrase matching. *Information Processing & Management, 28*(3): 349-369.

Shneidermann, B. (1998). *Designing the User Interface: Strategies for Effective Human-Computer Interaction:* Third Edition. Reading, MA: Addison-Wesley.

Shneiderman, B., Byrd, D. & Croft, W.B. (1997). Clarifying search: A user-interface framework for text searches. *D-Lib Magazine*, 1: 1-18. [http://www.dlib.org/dlib/january97/retrieval/01shneiderman.html . Cited Apr. 15, 2005.]

Siegel, S. & Castellan, N.J. (1988). Non-parametric Statistics for the Behavioral Sciences. Singapore: McGraw-Hill.

Sihvonen, A. & Vakkari, P. (2004). Subject knowledge, thesaurus-assisted query expansion and search success. In: RIAO 2004: 393-404.

Silverstein, C., Henzinger, M., Marais, H. & Moricz, M. (1999). Analysis of a Very Large Web Search Engine Query Log. *SIGIR Forum, 33*(1): 6-12.

Skov, M., Pedersen, H., Larsen, B. & Ingwersen, P. (2004). Testing the principle of polyrepresentation. In: Larsen, B. (Ed.) Information Retrieval in Context, Proceedings of the SIGIR 2004 IRiX Workshop, Sheffield UK, July 2004: 47-49.   [Available   at   http://ir.dcs.gla.ac.uk/context/   IRinContext_WorkshopNotes_SIGIR2004.pdf . Cited Apr. 15, 2004.]

Sloane, D. (2000). Encounters with the OPAC: online searching in public libraries. *Journal of the American Society for Information Science*, 8: 757-773.

Sloane, D. (2003). The influence of mental models and goals on search patterns during Web interaction. *Journal of the American Society for Information Science and Technology, 53*(13): 1152-1169.

Smeaton, A. (1992). Progress in the application of natural language processing to information retrieval tasks. *Computer Journal, 35*:268-278.

Smeaton, A. (1998). Independence of contributing retrieval strategies in data fusion for effective information retrieval. In: *Proceedings of the 20th BCS_IRSG Colloquium,* Autrans, France, 1998. Bonn: Springer-Verlag, Electronic Workshops in Computing: 268-278.

Sormunen, E. (2000a). *A Method for Measuring Wide Range Performance of Boolean Queries in Full-Text Databases.* Tampere: University of Tampere, Doctoral Thesis. Acta Electronica Universitatis Tamperensis, [Available at http://acta.uta.fi/pdf/951-44-4732-8.pdf . Cited Apr. 15, 2005.]

Sormunen, E. (2000b). A novel method for the evaluation of Boolean query effectiveness across a wide operational range. In: Belkin, N.J., Ingwersen, P. & Leong, M.-K. (Eds.) [ACM SIGIR 23]: 25-32.

Sormunen, E. (2002). Liberal relevance criteria of TREC – Counting on negligible documents? In: Beaulieu, M. et al (Eds.) [ACM SIGIR 25]: 320-330.

Sormunen, E., Kekäläinen, J., Koivisto, J. & Järvelin, K. (2001). Document text characteristics affect the ranking of the most relevant documents by expanded structured queries. *Journal of Documentation, 57*: 358-376.

Sormunen, E., Markkula, M. & Järvelin, K. (1999). The perceived similarity of photos - Seeking a solid basis for the evaluation of content-based retrieval algorithms. In: Draper, S.W Dunlop, M.D Ruthven, I. &Van Rijsbergen, C.J. (Eds.), *Proceedings of Mira 99: Evaluating Interactive Information Retrieval (Glasgow April 1999)*, published in *Electronic Workshops in Computing*, April 1999. [available at http://ewic.bcs.org/conferences/1999/mira99/ . Cited Apr. 15, 2005.]

Sowizral, H.A. (1985). Expert systems. In: Williams, M.E. (Ed.) [ARIST 20]: 179-199.

Sparck Jones, K. (Ed.) (1981). *Information Retrieval Experiment.* London, UK: Butterworths.

Sparck Jones, K. (1987). Architecture problems in the construction of expert systems for document retrieval. In: Wormell, I. (Ed.) *Knowledge Engineering.* London, UK: Taylor Graham: 34-52.

Sparck Jones, K. (1995). Reflection on TREC. *Information Processing & Management, 31*(3): 291–314.

Sparck Jones, K. (2001). *Natural Language Processing: A Historical Review.* [Available at http://www.cl.cam.ac.uk/users/ksj/histdw4.pdf . Cited Nov. 19, 2003.]

Sparck Jones, K. & Kay, M. (1973). *Linguistics and information science.* New York, NY: Academic Press.

Spark Jones, K. & van Rijsbergen, C.J. (1976). Information retrieval test collections. *Journal of Documentation, 32*(1): 59-75.

Sparck Jones, K. & Willett, P. (1997), Eds. *Readings in Information Retrieval.* San Francisco, CA: Morgan Kaufman.

Spink, A. (1996). Multiple search sessions model of end-user behavior: An exploratory study. *Journal of the American Society for Information Science, 47*: 603-609.

Spink, A. (1997a). Study of interactive feedback during mediated information retrieval. *Journal of the American Society for Information Science, 48*(5): 382-394.

Spink, A. (1997b). Information science: A third feedback framework. *Journal of the American Society for Information Science, 48*(8): 728-740.

Spink, A. (2002). A user-centeret approach to evaluating human interaction with Web search engines: An exploratory study. *Information Processing & Management, 38*: 401-426.

Spink, A. & Cool, C., (2002), Eds. IR in Context. (special issue). *Information Processing & Management, 38*(5): 605-742.

Spink, A., Goodrum, A. & Robins, D. (1998). Elicitation behavior during mediated information retrieval. *Information Processing & Management, 34*: 257-273.

Spink, A., Goodrum, A., Robins, D. & Wu, M-M. (1996). Elicitations during information retrieval: Implications for IR system design. In: Frei, H.P. et al. (Eds.) [ACM SIGIR 19]: 120-127.

Spink, A., Greisdorf, H. & Bateman, J. (1998). From highly relevant to not relevant: Examining different regions of relevance. *Information Processing & Management, 34*(5): 599-621.

Spink, A. & Losee, R.M. (1996). Feedback in information retrieval. In: Williams, M.E. (Ed.) [ARIST 31]: 33-78.

Spink, A. & Saracevic, T. (1997). Interaction in information retrieval: selection and effectiveness of search terms. *Journal of the American Society for Information Science, 48*(8): 741-761.

Spink, A. & Saracevic, T. (1998). Human-computer interaction in information retrieval: Nature and manifestations of feedback. *Interacting with Computers, 10*: 249-267.

Spink, A., Wilson, T., Ellis, D. & Ford, N. (1998). Modelling users' successive searches in digital environments. *D-lib Magazine, 4*(4). [Available at http://www.dlib.org/dlib/april98/04spink.html . Cited Nov. 15, 2001.]

Spink, A, Wolfram, D, Jansen, B. J. & Saracevic, T. (2001). Searching the Web: the public and their queries. *Journal of the American Society for Information Science & Technology, 52*(3): 226-234.

Stegmüller, W. (1976). *The Structure and Dynamics of Theories.* New York: Springer.

Steier, A. M. & Belew, R.K. (1993). Exporting phrases: a statistical analysis of topical language. In: Casey, R. & Croft, B. (Eds.) *Proceedings of the 2nd Symposium on Document Analysis and Information Retrieval.* Las Vegas, NV: 179-190.

Strzalkowski, T. (1995). Natural language information retrieval. *Information Processing & Management, 31*(3): 397-417.

Strzalkowski, T. (1999), Ed. *Natural Language Information Retrieval.* Boston, MA: Kluwer.

Strauss, A. & Corbin. J. (1990). *Basics of Qualitative Research: Grounded Theory Procedures and Techniques.* Newbury Park, CA: Sage.

Strong, G.W. & Drott, M.C. (1986). A thesaurus for end-user indexing and retrieval. *Information Processing & Management, 22*(6):487-492.

Su, L. (1994). The relevance of recall and precision in user evaluation. *Journal of the American Society for Information Science, 45*: 207-217.

Su, L. (2003). A comprehensive and systematic model of user evaluation of web search engines: I. Theory and background. *Journal of the American Society for Information Science and Technology, 54*(13): 1175-1192.

Suchman. L.A. (1987). *Plans and Situated Actions: The Problem of Human-Machine Communication.* Cambridge, UK: Cambridge University Press.

Sugar, W. (1995). User-centered perspective of information retrieval research and analysis methods. In: Williams, M.E. (Ed.) [ARIST 30]: 77-109.

Suominen, V. (1998). *Filling Empty Space: A Treatise on Semiotic Structures in Information Retrieval, in Documentation, and in Related Research.* Oulu, Finland: University of Oulu, Acta Universitatis Ouluensis: Humaniora B 27.

Sutcliffe, A.G. & Ennis, M. (1998). Towards a cognitive theory of IR. *Interacting with Computers, 10*: 321-351.

Sutcliffe, A.G., Ennis, M. & Watkinson, S.J. (2000). Empirical studies of end-user information searching. *Journal of the American Society for Information Science, 51*(13): 1211-1231.

Sutton, S. (1994). The role of attorney mental models of law in case relevance determinations: An exploratory analysis. *Journal of the American Society for Information Science, 45*: 186-200.

Swanson, D.R. (1986). Subjective versus objective relevance in bibliographic retrieval systems. *Library Quarterly, 56*: 389-398.

Tague-Sutcliffe, J. (1992), Ed. Special topic issue: Evaluation of information retrieval systems. *Journal of the American Society for Information Science, 38*(1): 1-105.

Tague-Sutcliffe, J. (1992). The pragmatics of information retrieval experimentation, revisited. *Information Processing & Management, 28*: 467-490.

Talja, S. (1997). Constituting "information" and "user" as research objects: A theory of knowledge formations as an alternative to the information man-theory. In: Vakkari, P., Savolainen, R. & Dervin, B. (Eds.) [ISIC 1]: 67-80.

Talja, S. (1998). *Musiikki, kulttuuri, kirjasto: Diskurssien analyysi* [Music, Culture, Library: An Analysis of Discourses]. Tampere, Finland: University of Tampere, Ph.D. Thesis. [In Finnish]

Talja, S. (1999). Analyzing qualitative interview data: The discourse analytic methods. *Library & Information Science Research, 21*(4): 459-477.

Talja, S. (2001). *Music, Culture and the Library: An Analysis of Discourses.* Lanham, MD: Scarecrow Press.

Talja, S. (2004). Users' library discourses. In: Kajberg, L. & Johannsen (Eds.), *New frontiers in public library research.* Lanham, MD: Scarecrow, forthcoming.

Talja, S., Heinisuo, R., Kasesniemi, E-L., Pispa, K., Kemppainen, H., Luukkainen, S., Järvelin, K. (1998). Discourse analysis of user requests. *Communications of the ACM, 41*(4): 93-94.

Talja, S., Heinisuo, R., Pispa, K., Luukkainen, S. & Järvelin, K. (1997). Discourse Analysis in the Development of a Regional Information Service. In: Beaulieu, M. & Davenport, E. & Pors, N.O. (Eds.) *Library and Information Studies: Research and professional practice. Proceedings of the 2nd British-Nordic Conference on Library and Information Studies,* Edinburg, 1997. London: Taylor Graham: 109-128.

Talja, S., Keso, H. & Pietikäinen,T. (1999). The production of context in information seeking research: A meta-theoretical view. *Information Processing & Management, 35*(6): 751-763.

Tang, R., Shaw, W.M. & Vevea, J.L. (1999). Towards the identification of the optimal number of relevance categories. *Journal of the American Society for Information Science, 50*(3), 254-264.

Tang, R. & Solomon, P. (1998). Toward an understanding of the dynamics of relevance judgment: An analysis of one person's search behavior. *Information Processing & Management, 34*: 237-256.

Taylor, R.S. (1968). Question negotiation and information seeking in libraries. *College and Research Libraries, 29*: 178-194.

Tenopir, C. (1985). Full text database retrieval performance. *Online Review, 9*(2): 149-164.

Tenopir, C. (1989). *Issues in online database searching.* Englewood, CO: Libraries Unlimited.

Thelwall, M. & Harrier, G. (2004). Do the web sites of higher rated scholars have significantly more online impact? *Journal of the American Society for Information Science and Technology,* 55(2): 149-159.

TREC homepage (2001). *Data - English relevance judgements.* [Available at http://trec.nist.gov/data/reljudge_eng.html. Cited July 14, 2004.]

Tuominen, K. (1997). User-centered discourse: An analysis of the subject positions of the user and the librarian. *Library Quarterly, 67*: 350-371.

Tuominen, K. (2001). *Tiedon muodostus ja virtuaalikirjaston rakentaminen: konstruktionistinen analyysi.* [The formation of knowledge anf the building of virtual library: a constructionistic analysis] Espoo, Finland: CSC Research Report R01/01. [English summary].

Tuominen, K. & Savolainen, R. (1997). A social constructionist approach to the study of information use as discursive action. In: In: Vakkari, P., Savolainen, R. & Dervin, B. (Eds.) [ISIC 1]: 81-96.

Tuominen, K., Talja, S. & Savolainen, R. (2002). Discourse, cognition and reality: Toward a social constructionist metatheory for library and information science. In: Bruce, H. et al. (Eds.) [CoLIS 4]: 271-284.

Tuominen, K., Talja, S. & Savolainen, R. (2003). Multiperspective digital libraries: The implications of social constructionism for the development of digital libraries. *Journal of the American Society for Information Science, 54*(6): 561-569.

Turtle, H. & Croft, W.B. (1990). Inference methods for document retrieval. *ACM-SIGIR Forum,* June 1990: 1-24.

Twain, M. (1965). *Life on the Mississipi.* New York, NY: Airmont Press.

UMLS-KS (1995). *UMLS Knowledge Sources.* 6th Edition. Bethesda MD: National Library of Medicine.

Uschold. M. & Gruninger, M. (1996). Ontologies: principles, methods and applications. *The Knowledge Engineering Review, 11*(2): 93-136.

Vakkari, P. (1997). Information seeking in context; a challenging metatheory. In: Vakkari, P. & Savolainen, S. & Dervin, B. (Eds.) [ISIC 1]: 451-464.

Vakkari, P. (1998). Growth of theories on information seeking: An analysis of growth of a theoretical research program on the relation between task complexity and information seeking. *Information Processing & Management, 34*: 361-382.

Vakkari, P. (1999). Task complexity, problem structure and information actions: integrating studies on information seeking and retrieval. *Information Processing & Management, 35*(6): 819-837.

Vakkari, P. (2000). Relevance and contributing information types of searched documents in task performance. In: Belkin, N.J. et al. (Eds.) [ACM SIGIR 23]: 2-9.

Vakkari, P. (2001a). A theory of the task-based information retrieval process: a summary and generalization of a longitudinal study. *Journal of Documentation, 57*(1): 44-60.

Vakkari, P. (2001b). Changes in search tactics and relevance judgments in preparing a research proposal: A summary of findings of a longitudinal study. *Information Retrieval, 4*(3/4): 295-310.

Vakkari, P. (2003). Task based information searching. In: Cronin, B. (Ed.) [ARIST 37]: 413-464.

Vakkari, P. & Cronin, B. (1991), Eds. *Conceptions of library and Information Science: Historical, Empirical and Theoretical Perspectives (CoLIS 1).* London: Taylor Graham.

Vakkari, P. & Hakala, N. (2000). Changes in relevance criteria and problem stages in task performance. *Journal of Documentation, 56*(5): 540-562.

Vakkari, P. & Kuokkanen, M. (1997). Theory growth in information science: applications of the theory of science to a theory of information seeking. *Journal of Documentation, 53*(5): 497-519.

Vakkari, P., Savolainen, S. & Dervin, B. (1997), Eds. *Information Seeking in Context. Proceedings of an International Conference on Research on Information Needs, Seeking and Use in Different Contexts (ISIC 1),* 14-16 August 1996, Tampere, Finland. London: Taylor Graham.

Van Rijsbergen, C.J. (1979). *Information Retrieval.* 2nd ed. London, UK: Butterworths.

Van Rijsbergen, C.J. (1986). A new theoretical framework for information retrieval. In: Rabitti, F. (Ed.) [ACM SIGIR 9]: 194-200.

Van Rijsbergen, C.J. (1989). Towards an Information Logic. In: Belkin, N.J. & van Rijsbergen, C.J. (Eds.) [ACM SIGIR 12]: 77-86.

Van Rijsbergen, C.J. (1990). The science of information retrieval: Its methodology and logic. In: *Conf. Informatienvetenschap in Nederland.* Haag: Rabin: 20-38.

Van Rijsbergen, C.J. (1996). Information, logic, and uncertainty in information science. In: Ingwersen, P. & Pors, N.O. (Eds.) [CoLIS 2]: 1-10.

Vickery, B.C., Robertson, S. E. & Belkin, N. J. (1975), Eds. *Final Report on International Research Forum on Information Science: The Theoretical Basis of Information Science,* 1975, July 29 - August 2. London, UK: British Library, Research & Development Department, Report No. 5233.

Vickery, B.C. & Vickery, A. (1993). Online search interface design. *Journal of Documentation, 49*(2): 103-187.

Vidick, J.L. (1990), Ed. *Proceedings of the 13th International Conference on Research and Development in Information Retrieval (ACM SIGIR 13),* Brussels, Belgium, Sept 5-7, 1990. Bruxelles: ACM Press.

Voorhees, E.M. (1993). Using WordNet to disambiguate word senses for text retrieval. In: Korfhage, R., Rasmussen, E. & Willett, P. (Eds.) [ACM SIGIR 16]: 171-180.

Voorhees, E.M. (1994). Query expansion using lexical-semantic relations. In:Croft, W. B. & van Rijsbergen, C. J. (Eds.) [ACM SIGIR 17]: 61-69.

Voorhees, E.M. (1998). Variations in relevance judgments and the measurement of retrieval effectiveness. In: Croft, W.B. et al. (Eds.) [ACM SIGIR 21]: 315-323.

Voorhees, E.M. (2001a). Report on TREC-9. *SIGIR Forum, 34*(2):1-8.

Voorhees, E.M. (2001b). Evaluation by Highly Relevant Documents. In: Croft, W.B. et al. (Eds.) [ACM SIGIR 24]: 74-82.

Voorhees E.M. & Harman, D.K. (2000), Eds. *Proceedings of the ninth Text REtrieval Conference (TREC 9).* Gaithersburg, MD: National Institute of Standards and Technology, NIST Special Publication 500-249.

Voorhees E.M. & Harman, D.K. (2001), Eds. *Proceedings of the Tenth Text REtrieval Conference (TREC 10).* NIST Special Publication 500-250.

Voorhees, E.M. & Harman, D. (1997). Overview of the Fifth Text REtrieval conference (TREC-5). In: Voorhees, E.M. & Harman, D.K (Eds.) [TREC 5]: 1-28.

Voorhees, E.M. & Harman, D.K. (1997), Eds. *Information technology: The Fifth Text Retrieval Conference (TREC 5).* Gaithersburg, MD: National Institute of Standards and Technology, NIST Special Publication 500-238. [Available at: http://trec.nist.gov/pubs/trec5/t5_proceedings.html. Cited Nov. 4, 2003.]

Voorhees, E.M. & Harman, D.K. (1998), Eds. *Proceedings of the Sixth Text REtrieval Conference (TREC 6).* Gaithersburg, MD: National Institute of Standards and Technology, NIST Special Publication 500-240. [Available at: http://trec.nist.gov/pubs/trec6/t6_proceedings.html. Cited Nov. 4, 2003.]

Voorhees, E.M. & Harman, D.K. (1999). Overview of the eighth text retrieval conference (TREC-8). In: Voorhees, E.M. & Harman, D.K. (Eds.) [TREC 8]: 1-24.

Voorhees, E.M. & Harman, D.K. (1999b), Eds. *Proceedings of the Eight Text REtrieval Conference (TREC 8).* Gaithersburg, MD: National Institute of Standards and Technology, NIST Special Publication 500-246. [Online, available at: http://trec.nist.gov/pubs/trec7/t5_proceedings.html. Cited July 14, 2004.]

Voorhees, E.M. & Tice, D.M (1999). The TREC-8 question answering track evaluation. In: Voorhees, E.M. & Harman, D.K. (Eds.) [TREC 8]: 83-106.

Wagner, D. & Berger, J. (1985). Do sociological theories grow? *American Journal of Sociology, 90*: 697-728.

Wagner, D., Berger, J. & Zeldith, M. (1992), A working strategy for constructing theories. In: Ritzer, G. (Ed.), *Metatheorizing.* London: Sage: 107-123.

Wang, P. (1997). Users' information needs at different stages of a research project: A cognitive view. In: Vakkari, P. et al. (Ed.) [ISIC 1]: 307-318.

Wang, P. (2001). Methodologies and methods for user behavioral research. In: Williams, M.E. (Ed.) [ARIST 34]: 53-106.

Wang, P., Berry, M.W. & Yang, Y. (2003). Mining longitudinal web queries: trends and patterns. *Journal of the American Society for Information Science and Technology, 54*(89): 743-758.

Wang, P., Hawk, W.B. & Tenopir, C. (2000). Users' interaction with World Wide Web resources: an exploratory study using a holistic approach. *Information Processing & Management, 36*(2): 229-251.

Wang, P. & Soergel, D. (1993). Beyond topical relevance: Document selection behavior of real users of IR systems. In: Bonzi, S. (Ed.), *ASIS '93: Proceedings of the American Society for Information Science 56th Annual Meeting: Volume 30,* October 24-28. Medford, NJ: Learned Information: 87-92.

Wang, P. & Soergel, D. (1998). A cognitive model of document use during a research project: Study I: Document selection. *Journal of the American Society for Information Science, 49*(2): 115-133.

Wang, P. & Tenopir, C. (1998). An exploratory study of users' interaction with World Wide Web resources: information skills, cognitive styles, affective states, and searching behaviors. In: M. E. Williams (Ed.), *Proceedings of the 19th National Online Meeting.* Medford, NJ: Information Today: 445-454.

Wang, P. & White, M.D. (1999). A cognitive model of document use during a research project: Study II: Decisions at the reading and citing stages. *Journal of the American Society for Information Science, 50*(2): 98-114.

Waterman, D. A. (1986). *A Guide to Expert Systems.* Reading, MA: Addison-Wesley.

Wathen, C.N. & Burkell, J. (2002). Believe it or not: Factors influencing credibility on the Web. *Journal of the American Society for Information Science and Technology, 53*(2): 134-144.

Wersig, G. (1971). *Information, Kommunikation, Dokumentation.* Pullach bei München, Germany: Verlag Dokumentation, 1971.

Wersig, G. (1973a). *Informationssoziologie: Hinweise zu einem informationswissenschaftlichen Teilbereich.* Frankfurt, Germany: Athenäum Fischer.

Wersig, G. (1973b). Zur Systematik der Benutzerforschung. *Nachrichten für Dokumentation, 24*(1): 10-14.

Wetherell, M. & Potter, J. (1988). Discourse analysis and the identification of interpretive repertoires. In: Antaki, C. (Ed.) *Analysing Everyday Experience: A Casebook of Methods.* London: Sage: 168-183.

White, H.D. & McCain, K.W. (1998). Visualizing a discipline: An author co-citation analysis of information science, 1972-1995. *Journal of the American Society for Information Science, 49*(4): 327-355.

White, M.D. (1975). The communication behavior of academic economists in research phases. *Library Quarterly, 45*: 337-354.

White, M.D. (1998). Questions in reference interviews. *Journal of Documentation, 54*: 443-465.

Willett, P. (1988). Recent trends in hierarchic document clustering: A critic review. *Information Processing & Management, 24*(5): 577-597.

Williams, M.E. (1978), Ed. *Annual Review of Information Science and Technology, vol. 13 (ARIST 13).* White Plains, NY: Knowledge Industry Publications.

Williams, M.E. (1981), Ed. *Annual Review of Information Science and Technology, vol. 16 (ARIST 16).* Medford, NJ: Learned Information.

Williams, M.E. (1985), Ed. *Annual Review of Information Science and Technology, vol. 20 (ARIST 20).* White Plains, NY: Knowledge Industry Publications.

Williams, M.E. (1986), Ed.), *Annual Review of Information Science and Technology, vol. 21 (ARIST 21).* White Plains, NY: Knowledge Industry Publications.

Williams, M.E. (1987), Ed. *Annual Review of Information Science and Technology, vol. 22 (ARIST 22)*. Amsterdam, NL: Elsevier.

Williams, M.E. (1990), Ed. *Annual Review of Information Science and Technology, vol. 25, (ARIST 25)*. Medford, NJ: Learned Information for the American Society for Information Science and Technology.

Williams, M.E. (1991), Ed. *Annual Review of Information Science and Technology: Vol. 26 (ARIST 26)*. Medford, NJ: Learned Information.

Williams, M.E. (1993), Ed. *Annual Review of Information Science and Technology, vol. 28 (ARIST 28)*. White Plains, NY: Knowledge Publications.

Williams, M.E. (1994), Ed. *Annual Review of Information Science and Technology, vol. 29 (ARIST 29)*. Medford, NJ: Learned Information for the American Society for Information Science.

Williams, M.E. (1995), Ed. *Annual Review of Information Science and Technology, vol. 30 (ARIST 30)*. Medford, NJ: Learned Information.

Williams, M.E. (1996), Ed. *Annual Review of Information Science and Technology, vol. 31 (ARIST 31)*. Medford, NJ: Learned Information for the American Society for Information Science.

Williams, M.E. (1997), Ed. *Annual Review of Information Science and Technology, vol. 32 (ARIST 32)*. Medford, NJ: Information Today.

Williams, M.E., (1998), Ed. *Annual Review of Information Science and Technology, vol. 33 (ARIST 33)*. Medford, NJ: Learned Information.

Williams, M.E., (2001), Ed. *Annual Review of Information Science and Technology, vol. 34. (ARIST 34)*. Medford, NJ: Learned Information for the American Society for Information Science.

Williams, M.E., (2001b), Ed. *Annual Review of Information Science and Technology, vol. 35. (ARIST 35)*. Medford, NJ: Learned Information for the American Society for Information Science and Technology.

Wilson, P. (1973). Situational relevance. *Information Storage & Retrieval, 9*(8): 457-471.

Wilson, T.D. (1981). On user studies and information needs. *Journal of Documentation, 37*(1): 3-15.

Wilson, T.D. (1997). Information behaviour: an interdisciplinary perspective. *Information Processing & Management, 33*(4): 551-572.

Wilson, T.D. (1999). Models in information behavior research. *Journal of Documentation, 55*(3): 249-270.

Wilson, T.D. & Streatfield, D.R. (1977). Information needs in local authority social services departments : An interim report on project INISS. *Journal of Documentation, 33*(4): 277-293.

Wilson, T.D. & Streatfield, D.R. (1981a). Structured observation in the investigation of information needs. *Social Science Information Studies, 1*(3): 173-184.

Wilson, T.D. & Streatfield, D.R.. (1981b). Action research and user's needs. In: Friberg, I. (Ed.) [IRFIS 4]: 51-70.

Wilson, T.D. & Walsh, C. (1996). *Information behaviour: an interdisciplinary perspective.* Sheffield, UK: University of Sheffield, Department of Information Studies.

Winograd, T. & Flores, C.F. (1986). *Understanding Computers and Cognition: A New Foundation for Design.* Norwood, NJ: Addison-Wesley.

Wolfram, D, Spink, A, Jansen, B. J. & Saracevic, T (2001). Vox populi: the public searching of the Web. *Journal of the American Society for Information Science & Technology, 52*(12): 1073-1074.

Woods, L. (1999), Ed. *ASIS '99: Proceedings of the 62nd ASIS Annual Meeting (ASIS 62).* Medford, NJ: Information Today.

Wormell, I. (1981b). *Interim Report to the Online Search Division of the European Space Agency.* Frascati, Italy.

Wu, M.-M. & Liu, Y.-H. (2003). Intermediary's information seeking, inquiring minds, and elicitation styles. *Journal of the American Society for Information Science and Technology, 54*(12): 1117-1133.

Xie, H. (2000). Shifts in interactive intentions and information seeking strategies in interactive retrieval. *Journal of the American Society for Information Science, 51*: 841-857.

Xie, H. & Cool, C. (2000). Ease-of-use versus user control: An evaluation of web and non-web interfaces of online databases. *Online Information Review, 24*(2): 102-115.

XQuery (2003). *XQuery: A query language for XML.* [Available at http://www.w3.org/TR/xquery/. Cited July 30, 2002.]

Xu, J. & Croft, W.B. (1996). Query expansion using local and global document analysis. In: Frei, H.-P. et al. (Eds.) [ACM SIGIR 19]: 4–11.

Yang, S. (1997). Information seeking as problem-solving using a qualitative approach to uncover the novice learners' information-seeking process in a Perseus hypertext system. *Library & Information Science Research, 19*: 71-92.

Zhai, C., Tong, X., Milic-Frayling, N. & Evans, D.A. (1997). Evaluation of syntactic phrase indexing - CLARIT NLP track report. In: Voorhees, E.M. & Harman, D.K (Eds.) [TREC 5]: 347-358.

Zipf, G.K. (1932). *Selected Studies of the Principle of Relative Frequencies of Language.* Cambridge, MA: Harvard University Press, 1932.

Zobel, J. (1998). How reliable are the results of large scale information retrieval experiments? In: Croft, W.B. et al. (Eds.) [ACM SIGIR 21]: 307-314.

Zobel, J. & Dart, P. (1996) Phonetic String Matching: Lessons from Information Retrieval. In: Frei, H.P. et al. (Eds.) [ACM SIGIR 19]: 166-173.

Ørom, A. (2000). Information science, historical changes and social aspects: A Nordic outlook. *Journal of Documentation, 56*(1), 12-26.

Index